THE NONRELIGIOUS

The Nonreligious

UNDERSTANDING SECULAR PEOPLE AND SOCIETIES

Phil Zuckerman, Luke W. Galen, Frank L. Pasquale

OXFORD
UNIVERSITY PRESS

OXFORD

UNIVERSITY PRESS

Oxford University Press is a department of the University of Oxford. It furthers
the University's objective of excellence in research, scholarship, and education
by publishing worldwide. Oxford is a registered trade mark of Oxford University
Press in the UK and certain other countries.

Published in the United States of America by Oxford University Press
198 Madison Avenue, New York, NY 10016, United States of America.

© Oxford University Press 2016

Library of Congress Cataloging-in-Publication Data
Zuckerman, Phil.
The nonreligious : understanding secular people and societies / Phil Zuckerman,
Luke W. Galen, Frank L. Pasquale.
pages cm
Includes bibliographical references and index.
ISBN 978-0-19-992494-3 (pbk. : alk. paper) — ISBN 978-0-19-992495-0 (cloth : alk. paper)
1. Secularism.   I. Title.
BL2747.8.Z827 2016
211'.6—dc23
2015025432

9 8 7 6 5 4 3 2
Printed by Sheridan, USA

Contents

THE NONRELIGIOUS

INTRODUCTION

MIKE AND HEATHER are married, have two kids, and live in a small town in eastern Oregon.[1] They own a comfortable house on a pleasant street, with a neatly trimmed front lawn and a hearty vegetable garden in the back.

But Mike and Heather are different from most of their neighbors. There is something that causes them to stand out a bit in their small community: Mike and Heather are not religious. They don't go to church, they don't pray, they don't study the Bible, and as for God—well, Mike doesn't think too much about such matters. He's basically indifferent. If pushed, he'll say that he doesn't really believe in God but also thinks that maybe there is "something out there." Basically, when it comes to religious, cosmic, or existential concerns like life after death, how the universe came about, or the existence of God, he takes a noncommittal "who knows?" position and leaves it at that. In short, he is uninterested in or unconcerned with religious matters. Heather, however, is a committed atheist. She is certain that there is no God, and she finds it baffling that so many people believe there is. And she is fairly concerned that religion has too much influence in society these days. While Mike might best be described as "areligious," Heather is closer to "antireligious."[2]

As a child, Mike regularly went to the local Methodist church that his parents belonged to, but it always seemed more of a social habit rather than a deeply spiritual practice. He enjoyed the church youth group, but he never took seriously the teachings he heard there, and he never "bought" the Christian beliefs he was exposed to. Heather's father was Jewish, and her mother was Catholic, and they decided to raise Heather and her siblings without any religious instruction or involvement. Mike and Heather's irreligiosity wasn't a big deal for most of their lives. They both grew up in large, West Coast cities, where nearly all of the people they knew and hung out with were either nonreligious or else religious in a very understated, marginal, or liberal way. They both went to college in Seattle—where they met and fell in love—and most of their college friends were interested in things like hiking, river rafting, academics, skiing, art, music, and brewing beer. Religion just wasn't part of their college life. After graduating, they traveled for a while in Asia. Then Mike got a construction job in Sacramento, while Heather worked on a master's degree. And then, when Mike was offered a better job as a manager for his uncle's construction company in eastern Oregon, he accepted, and they moved.

Suddenly, and for the first time in their lives, their irreligiosity became an issue. On the day of their arrival at their new home, neighbors came to help them unload boxes out of the back of their truck. "What church do you go to?" was the first question they were asked. When they said that they didn't go to church, they were met with confused looks and mild disapproval. During their first six months in town, they were constantly being invited to various churches by neighbors, colleagues, and acquaintances—and their continued reluctance to attend created a tangible degree of disappointment in the people of their new community, as well as a minor amount of alienation.

Then their older daughter's fifth-grade teacher told her that reading *Harry Potter* books was a bad idea, and that reading such books might invite the Devil into her heart. Both of their daughters were regularly taunted on the school playground about their lack of religious faith, constantly being told by other kids that they would end up in hell. When Mike and Heather complained to the school principal about these matters, he listened politely to their concerns but recommended that they start attending church as a family. It would be the best solution for everyone—and would be really good for their children. Then some of Mike's coworkers urged him to place a "Jesus fish" symbol on their ads in the local paper, which he didn't want to do, causing some consternation.

The fact that Mike and Heather stick out a bit in their small community doesn't bother them too much, but at times it can certainly be uncomfortable. Heather complains that her social life is compromised because almost all of the other mothers she knows are heavily involved in their church communities, and most social events revolve around church life. Mike says that it annoys him when his daughters go to other people's houses and are witnessed to. But he tries to not let it get to him too much. He worries more about other concerns, like his work, the mortgage, and his aging mother, who has Alzheimer's disease. Heather, however, has been a bit more disturbed and troubled by the alienation she feels as a nonreligious person in a very religious community. In the past few years, she has become more active in her atheism. She now regularly partakes in online chat groups for nonbelievers, finding support from secular people all over the country who find themselves in similar situations. She has also read books by the so-called New Atheists—Sam Harris, Christopher Hitchens, Richard Dawkins, and others—and has found comfort in their rhetoric. And she has driven over to Portland a few times to attend meetings of a small secular humanist group there.

* * *

Michael and Heather are not alone. They may be a distinct minority in their eastern Oregon town, but there are many people like them throughout the country and in the wider world: secular people, of varying shades and stripes.[3]

What do we know about people like Mike and Heather? What do social scientists actually know about nonreligious men and women? This book has been written to provide as thorough and empirically grounded an answer as possible to that question. Our goal is simple: to present, in one volume, a comprehensive summation and analytical discussion of existing research on nonreligious people. But we will not only present a critical overview of existing research. We additionally sharpen and improve upon existing conceptual frameworks, theoretical typologies, and empirical trajectories currently in place so as to better advance the newly emerging enterprise of secular studies. Additionally, throughout the book we will present and draw upon results from our own ongoing, original research on secular men and women—people like Mike and Heather.

Of course, one of the primary and most easily observable things that we know about such people is that in many places their numbers have been on the rise in recent years. For example, as sociologists Barry Kosmin and Ariela Keysar note, an increasing number of Americans eschewing religion "has been one of the most important trends on the American religious scene."[4] And as sociologist Darren Sherkat has recently observed, "the most substantial trend in religious identification is the rejection of religious identity...[which] is an indication of growing secularism in the United States."[5] And in 2012, *Time* magazine cited the dramatic increase of people claiming "none" as their religion as one of the ten most significant changes occurring in American society.

GROWTH OF THE NONRELIGIOUS

Secular people constitute a steadily growing proportion of the American population. Their numbers have been increasing for more than half a century in many
other countries as well, particularly in Europe. But let's start with the United States.
Recent survey research reports the following:

- The percentage of Americans who claim "none" when asked about their religion has grown from 8 percent in 1990 all the way up to between 23 percent
  and 30 percent today.[6]
- Approximately 56 million American adults are religiously unaffiliated today,
  up 19 million since 2007.[7]
- Rates of secularity are markedly stronger among younger Americans: more
  than 33 percent of Americans under age thirty are religiously unaffiliated.[8]
- Somewhere between 12 percent and 21 percent of Americans are now atheist
  or agnostic—the highest rates of nonbelief ever recorded.[9]
- 30 percent of Americans consider religion to be largely old-fashioned and
  out of date.[10]
- More and more Americans are being raised without religion; of Americans
  born between the years 1925 and 1943, less than 4 percent were raised with
  no religion; of those born between the years 1956 and 1970, 7 percent were
  raised with no religion; and of those Americans born between 1971 and
  1992, almost 11 percent were raised that way.[11]

Increasing rates of secularity are also evident in many other countries around
the world. For example, neighboring Canada has experienced a pronounced surge
in secularity in recent decades. Today, almost 30 percent of Canadians are secular,
and approximately one in five Canadians does not believe in God.[12] In the city of
Vancouver, 35 percent report having no religion, which is an almost 40 percent
increase in the number of nonreligious residents there since the early 1990s.[13] The
total number of Canadians reporting no religious affiliation is now almost 5 million
people—a dramatic increase from the 1950s, when fewer than 1 percent of Canadians
reported having no religious affiliation.[14]

In Australia, in the 1960s, less than 1 percent of adults in national surveys claimed
to have no religion. But that has risen to nearly 20 percent today, and it is estimated
that now nearly one third of Australian adults does not believe in God.[15]

Over the course of the last half-century, Europe has experienced widespread secularization.[16] In the United Kingdom, rates of church membership, church attendance,

Sunday school attendance, and religious belief—especially belief in God—have plummeted, leading some to speculate that the Christian religion will hardly exist there at all several generations from now.[17] Similar patterns have occurred in the Netherlands, one of the most irreligious countries in the world.[18] In Germany, church attendance rates and rates of belief in God, Jesus, and various other points of Christian doctrine have also been in steady and consistent decline for half a century.[19] We have seen the same pattern of secularization in Scandinavia.[20] In France, 40 percent of the citizenry are now atheists, claiming not to believe in God or any sort of "spirit" or "life force," while in the Czech Republic, the percentage who don't believe in God or any sort of spirit/life force is 37 percent, in Norway and Estonia it is 29 percent, in Germany and Belgium it is 27 percent, and in Spain it is 19 percent.[21]

Beyond Europe and the anglophone world, societies characterized by fairly secular cultures or containing large pockets of secular populations are abundant. Indeed, there are significant percentages of nonreligious people in numerous countries and various regions around the globe, including Uruguay, Japan, South Korea, Israel, and Azerbaijan—to name several disparate examples. Secularity has even been found among indigenous, tribal people deep in the Amazon jungle.[22]

Back here in the United States, not only are more men and women opting out of religion, but the nonreligious are becoming more vocal and public about their secularity, as well as more organized.[23] The increased visibility of affirmatively irreligious Americans is definitely on the rise. For example, there has been significant growth recently among atheist/secular groups in America, such as the Freedom From Religion Foundation and the American Humanist Association. Many secular organizations, such as the Center for Inquiry and American Atheists, have embarked on public ad campaigns in cities across the United States, sponsoring billboards and bus signs with messages such as "Imagine No Religion" and "Are You Good without God? Millions Are." The Secular Student Alliance—a college campus group for nonbelievers—now claims more than 395 chapters nationwide, up from 42 in 2003.[24] Secular families are also becoming more active. Camp Quest, founded in 1996, is the first residential summer camp designed specifically for the children of nonbelievers, with locations all over North America. And the emergence of Sunday Assembly congregations is also novel; sometimes referred to as "atheist churches," Sunday Assembly congregations have sprouted up in major cities all over the the United States in recent years—as well as in many other countries throughout the world—with the explicit intention of creating religious-like congregational experiences, but without belief in God or anything supernatural.

Even in America's military, generally seen as a bastion of traditional Christianity, secular men and women are organizing and speaking out. Soldiers have recently formed an organization called the Military Association for Atheists and Freethinkers

(MAAF), with the goal of providing community, outreach, and support to nonreligious military personnel.

Given the growth in numbers and the increasing public presence of nonreligious people in America, it makes perfect sense that in his inaugural speech, delivered on January 20, 2009, newly elected President Barack Obama described the United States as a nation of "Christians and Muslims, Jews and Hindus—and nonbelievers." This was the first time that an American president had ever acknowledged the existence of nonbelievers in such a public forum. The move was not only politically savvy—it was sociologically astute. For as leading sociologist Darren Sherkat has recently noted, "the rejection of religious identity is an indication of growing secularism in the United States."[25]

Of course, there have always been nonreligious men and women. There exists evidence of skepticism, naturalism, secularism, and anticlericalism from thousands of years ago in ancient India, China, Rome, and Greece.[26] And there were clearly doubters and nonbelievers in medieval Europe as well, even when the power of the Catholic Church was at its apex.[27] However, the actual study of nonreligious people is a relatively new enterprise. Indeed, irreligion and secularity have been sorely neglected by the social sciences for some time.

A NEGLECTED AREA OF STUDY

While there have been countless conceptual, theoretical, historical, and empirical studies of religious people, both qualitative and quantitative, the same cannot be said about the portion of humanity that eschews religious belief and practice.[28] In 1968, Glenn Vernon described nonreligious people as a "neglected category."[29] A few years later, in 1971, Rocco Caporale and Antonio Grumelli characterized unbelief as a "neglected phenomenon," noting an "appalling lack of empirical data" on the subject.[30] That same year, Colin Campbell complained that the sociological study of irreligion was nonexistent and that secular men and women, and even secular movements, have been "entirely ignored."[31] Fast-forward some thirty-five years, and William Sims Bainbridge continues the lament, noting in 2005 that we still know "surprisingly little" about nonbelievers, and that systematic sociological or psychological studies . . . have been rare."[32]

While acknowledging the general validity of these sentiments, it is nonetheless important to recognize two main exceptions. Secularity has not been as totally unstudied or completely ignored as some would assert. First, there has been an extended sociological and historical focus on secularization, the process whereby religious beliefs and practices weaken, diminish, or disappear over time in a given society.[33] This topic has generated significant attention, discussion, and debate for many decades.[34] Second, there is the fact that countless surveys of religion over the years, in numerous fields and disciplines, have included a "nonreligious" category among given variables, generally for the purpose of comparison or contrast—or merely to net a full 100 percent on a certain measurement. That is, when social scientists have wanted to study certain aspects of religiosity in relation to other social or psychological phenomena, there has usually been a residual category included among the survey questions that indicates some degree of irreligiosity. So, for example, in a study seeking to measure church attendance in relation to levels of life satisfaction, or depression, or political preference, or frequency of intercourse, or income, or employment status, a survey would usually include a question about how often one attends church. The options would be more than once a week, once a week, several times a month, once a month, every other month, a few times a year, once a year, every few years, or never. This last option would probably indicate, or at least could be interpreted to indicate, some degree of secularity—but only in a vague and undifferentiated sense. The history of the social scientific study of religion is replete with such studies, which provide at least some minimal, rough information on secular men and women, if only by default.

We certainly have our complaints about this scholarship. While clearly important in its own right, the corpus of extant scholarship on secularization is largely theoretical or broadly historical in nature and doesn't actually examine lived aspects of secular life. That is, scholarship on secularization does not entail a direct focus on the social, anthropological, and/or psychological particulars of how secularity manifests itself or "plays itself out" in the contemporary world, in the real lives of men and women. Nor does it explore the myriad ways in which lived secularity intersects with other aspects of life and culture.

Our main critique of extant scholarship is that secularity in such scholarship remains undifferentiated. The various forms, types, and shades of secularity are overlooked or ignored, and all manifestations of irreligion are lumped together. Yet secularity comes in many shapes and sizes, and this diversity needs to be better understood and better investigated. Previous research often resulted in misleading conclusions because strongly religious individuals (who often are members of socially organized groups or communities) were compared with a mixed group of "nones" with varying levels of disbelief or disengagement. On this shaky basis, lack of religious belief was believed to place nonbelievers at a disadvantage regarding optimal social functioning, mental health, or engagement with the community. Lumping people together waters down or obfuscates important differences between types of nonbelief regarding things like the confidence with which individuals may hold worldviews, their relative interest or apathy regarding existential and metaphysical matters, and their engagement with other individuals or organizations. For example, a weakly religious individual who cannot be bothered to attend church is likely to be quite different from a strongly convinced or committed atheist, yet the majority of studies have treated them as members of the same group.

Fortunately, the scholarship on irreligion has begun to improve. More and more researchers have begun taking secularity seriously as a subject of study in its own right, and conceptual as well as empirical research on the nonreligious within sociology, psychology, and anthropology has been rapidly increasing and diversifying in recent years.[35] This book, obviously, seeks to analyze and synthesize this burgeoning body of research while simultaneously stimulating even more. And it is important to stress that our underlying purpose is not to offer some sort of data-laden advocacy of secularism. Nor do we offer a polemical or even scholarly critique of religiosity. Rather, we seek to offer as unbiased as possible an introduction, summation, and analytical discussion of all relevant data that bear on the nature of lived secularity and irreligion. We envision such work to be a necessary step in the advancing development of secular studies.

SECULAR STUDIES

As the number of secular men and women continues to grow, so too will the number of people interested in studying them. Indeed, this is already happening. This scholarly community has now grown to the point that it can be said to constitute an academic field: secular studies.

In the broadest sense, secular studies is the interdisciplinary study of secular people, groups, thought, and cultural expression in societies and cultures, past and present. Several varieties of secularism fall under that umbrella: political/constitutional secularism, philosophical skepticism, and personal and public secularity. The social scientific study of secularism, which is our focus, aims to understand people and/or groups that affirm or maintain a naturalistic view of the world without any reference to otherworldly, spiritual, or supernatural places, forces, or beings. We are interested in studying and understanding people who live their lives outside of religious communities, and without recourse to, or the need for, supernatural assumptions or beliefs. And while studying those who are comparatively less religious than others is certainly an important endeavor, our primary focus is on the substantially or affirmatively nonreligious. People like Mike and Heather.

OUTLINE OF THE BOOK

This book is divided into two main parts. Chapters 1 through 4 are broadly socio-logical in scope. They take a "macro" or "big picture" view of secularity. Chapters 5 through 10 take a "micro" or psychological view, looking at secularity "on the ground" as it manifests itself at the personal, individual level.

In chapter 1—our most theoretical and broadly conceptual chapter—we explore the very nature of the study of secularity, outlining our vision of what secular studies entails as an academic enterprise. In this discussion, we critically scrutinize relevant terminology, descriptions, and definitions and go on to construct some of our own, before further developing various typologies, dimensions, and continua that are use-ful for advancing the social scientific analysis of secular people and culture.

In order to offer a global assessment of secularity, chapter 2 presents and evalu-ates existing estimates of the number of secular people worldwide, and we further explore and analyze the very different ways in which secularity manifests itself across regions and cultural contexts.

No discussion of what it means to be secular in the modern world would be sat-isfactory if it did not address one of the most widely discussed and widely debated phenomena of the last century: secularization. Thus, in chapter 3, we offer a thor-ough presentation and analysis of secularization, covering relevant theories and untangling the complexities of this process.

In chapter 4, we look specifically at societies today that are "organically" (rather than coercively) the most secular, comparing these with religious societies on mea-sures of societal well-being.

Chapter 5 shifts to the micro-level question of why certain individuals are secular. How did they get to be that way? Drawing extensively from both quantitative and qualitative data, this chapter explores the dynamics of secular socialization and the reasons that might account for apostasy—the relinquishing or rejection of one's reli-gious beliefs and identity.

In chapter 6, we delve head-on into the psychology of secular people, detailing what various studies reveal about their personalities or cognitive strategies and the ways in which secular people tend to be different from religious people, including marriage, family formation, and childrearing.

The next chapter examines the mental and physical well-being of secular individu-als and critically evaluates the often-touted correlation of religiosity with positive mental health.

What about morality and ethics? If there is one stereotype about the nonreligous, it is that they are somehow morally deficient. Chapter 8 looks at morality among the secular, particularly in comparison with and contrast to the religious.

In chapter 9, we look at the social views and political attitudes most prevalent among nonreligious Americans, including such specific questions as party affiliation, the death penalty, abortion, and gay rights.

In chapter 10, we look at the social and institutional behaviors of secular people. We discuss the relationship between secularity and individualism, the types of associations and groups that secular people do tend to join, the types of social networks they tend to establish, and the general reluctance of most secular people to join groups specifically focused on secularity.

The systematic study of secularity is, in a very real sense, a new adventure in human understanding. We conclude with a brief summary of what we do and do not know in the hope and expectation that the adventure will continue!

1

THE STUDY OF SECULARITY AND THE NONRELIGIOUS

IN THE INTRODUCTION, we met Mike and Heather—two people who can reasonably be characterized as nonreligious or secular. But Mike and Heather are secular in different ways. Even though he was raised in a religious household, Mike is basically indifferent to religion and uninterested in ultimate or existential issues like the existence of God. Heather, however, is a committed atheist and pointed critic of religion. The difference is important. And there are many other, distinguishable kinds of people who can meaningfully be called secular or nonreligious. Psychologist Paul Pruyser has spoken of the "complexity of unbelief" or irreligion, suggesting that this "is at least as diversified as religious belief. . . . Irreligion, like religion, can be zealous, militant, declarative, dogmatic, or [persuasive]."[1] Let's look at some examples:

Ruth was raised by parents with no interest in religion whatsoever, so she grew up knowing virtually nothing about it. While she showed an interest in religion during college—more as an intellectual curiosity than anything—she has been religion-less throughout her 70 years of life. When asked to describe her feelings about religion, she says: "Nothing! Too busy to think about it!" Hers has been, instead, a life devoted to art: studying it, making it, and teaching about it.

Bob, by contrast, has turned being nonreligious into a "way of life." Now retired, he's an active member of atheist, freethought, skeptic, and secular humanist organizations. Between trips to conferences with his wife, he writes a local freethought newsletter and organizes meetings. His wife says that he's "ardent but not mean or angry about it all."

Mai, who is in her forties and of Asian descent, dismisses the notion of such things as spirits. Nonetheless, she feels that it is important to carry on family ancestral traditions, so she occasionally goes to a local temple and does what she learned to do as a child with her grandmother. The existence or nonexistence of spirits is "immaterial." Doing the rituals for their own sake just "feels right." It makes her feel peaceful and connected with family—now and through the generations.

Ted, also in his forties, was raised in a virtual Christian cocoon, but he had a crisis of faith as a young adult that propelled him into angry atheism and organized secularism, for a time. Realizing that his anger at being "duped by dogma was eating him alive," he then turned to yoga and Buddhist meditation groups "as therapy . . . to find composure." But he remains antireligious—"an atheist in the ashram," he likes to say.

Finally, consider Alice, aged sixty-five, who was raised in a nominally Protestant family but viewed religion much as she did the Greek or Nordic myths and fairy tales she read as a child. Well-educated and thoughtful, she is an articulate skeptic and philosophical naturalist. She doesn't assent to anything that cannot be scientifically proven. Yet a lifelong love of religious ritual led her down a path through liberal Judaism and finally to Humanistic Judaism. She enjoys the richness of Jewish history and ritual, but without any reference to God or spirits or other supernatural ideas.

Each of these people can be meaningfully designated as secular or nonreligious, in various ways, and to varying degrees. But each is distinctive. They differ in their degree of unbelief: Mai is not as sure as the others. They differ in attitude: Ted is angrily antireligious, while the others aren't angry at all. They differ in behavior: Alice, Mai, and Ted each engage in practices typically considered religious even though they don't interpret these supernaturally. They differ in identity or self-description: Ruth is "nothing," Ted is "an atheist," Alice is a "Jewish humanist," and Bob seems to be a general "secularist." They also differ in organizational behavior or affiliation: Ted is nominally involved in religious groups, Bob and Alice are affiliated with secularist groups, but Ruth and Mai are unaffiliated with either.

These individuals prompt many questions. Notice, for example, how many different terms such people, or others, use to describe them. What do these all mean? What are the actual characteristics that distinguish various types of secular people? And which of these differences, if any, make a difference regarding things like life purpose, well-being, or mental health? Why do some of these people use such terms to describe or identify themselves (privately or publicly), while others do not? Why do some deliberately affiliate with one another—or participate in organizations that espouse such identities—while others do not? How and why do such people become the way they are? And given their apparent diversity, how do we "draw the line" between them and religious people?

The idea of an academic field devoted to answering such questions—and better understanding people like these—is fairly new in the social sciences. While philosophical, theological, and historical considerations of atheism and related topics have a long history, it was only with the attempt to focus research attention on "cultures of unbelief" or a "sociology of irreligion" late in the twentieth century that the notion of a social scientific field of study was considered seriously or systematically.[2] In the early 1970s, Colin Campbell began his groundbreaking contribution, *Toward a Sociology of Irreligion*, with the observation that "no tradition for the sociological study of irreligion as yet exists and this book has been written in the hope that it will help to stimulate the development of just such a tradition."[3] It is only now, more than forty years later, that this has begun to happen in earnest.

As Campbell also suggested, it is difficult to pursue such "an important and viable sphere of study" until the "subject of investigation has been outlined," at least in some preliminary way. It must be "identified, delineated and defined and its various forms described." The purpose of this chapter is to do just that: to take up the challenge of delineating such a field of study—its central focus, its contents, its scope or boundaries, and how best to talk about all of this clearly and consistently.[4]

WHAT IS THE SUBJECT?

In the broadest sense, we are interested in the ways people make sense of their lives and of existence—or their meaning systems. We do this through ideas or by thinking, especially as patterned or organized in what are often called worldviews. We also find meaningfulness in life through our actions or behavior, especially as patterned in routines, rituals, and the social collectives in which we participate—or lifestyles.[5]

Religions have been the dominant focus in the study of meaning systems. A fundamental question in the sociology of religion from Emile Durkheim and Max Weber to the present has been "whether or not religion is the preferred means of making life worth living."[6] Much the same is true in psychology. Gordon Allport, for example, asserted that "from the psychological point of view . . . the ground covered by any secular interest, however vital, falls short of the range that characterizes a mature religious sentiment which seems never satisfied unless it is dealing with matters central to all existence."[7]

The conflation of meaning systems *with* religion has tended to tilt the playing field, as it were, toward very ancient and deeply held views that religious, supernatural, transcendental, spiritual, or "ultimate" beliefs and related behavior are essential for human well-being and a fully satisfying, stable, and resilient sense of meaningfulness. But merely because religions have been dominant means of creating meaningfulness in life in the past does not mean that they are *necessary* ones. Whether supernatural thinking and many of the behaviors and institutions constructed around it are essential or superior paths to satisfactory, healthy, and meaningful living is an empirical question (which we will address in chapter 7). A noticeable tendency to *assume* this is so—and to construct conceptual, theoretical, and methodological means of proving this—has arguably been fostered by approaching such matters *as* the study of religion(s).

It would, perhaps, have been preferable to have framed the field all along as the study of meaning systems, with the presence or absence of transcendental or supernatural thinking just one of many distinguishing factors. The value of broadening the scope of inquiry from the study of religion to that of meaning systems has been recognized from time to time. This is particularly true as the variety and complexity of approaches to finding meaning have become more diverse in today's world. A religion scholar named Ninian Smart, for example, framed at least some of his work as the study of worldviews or world philosophies. This enabled him to even-handedly encompass secular humanism and various forms of nationalism and Marxism, for example, together with commonly recognized religious worldviews. But this approach has made limited inroads into the social sciences. As a result, it is worthwhile to balance the ledger and broaden the scope of inquiry by looking more closely at the other end of the spectrum.[8]

The particular kinds of meaning systems that interest us have been called many things: atheism and atheist(ic); nontheism and nontheist(ic); agnostic(ism); skeptical and skepticism; irreligion and irreligious; nonreligion and nonreligious; areligious; nonbelief and unbelief; infidel and infidelity; freethought; philosophical naturalism; nonspiritual or nonsupernaturalistic; this-worldly; secularity, secularist, and secularism; (secular) humanism and humanist(ic), among others.

Several other concepts have been used by scholars in relevant lines of research with names that are not generally heard in everyday discourse. These include, for example, "apostasy" (or religious "defection," "disaffiliation," "deconversion," or "dropouts"), "nones" or nonaffiliates (those who indicate no specific religious identity or affiliation, particularly in survey responses), the "unchurched," and religious indifference.[9] The focus of much or most of this work has been on why religious belief, identity, or affiliation is "lost" or weakens in certain circumstances. Much of it has come at the issue of secular or nonreligious people "from the side"—as a residual or subordinate aspect of the study of religiosity—rather than having a direct focus on learning what nonreligious people, institutions, and societies are all about. This has influenced the kinds of questions that have been asked, the terms and concepts used to frame them, the research methods used to pursue them, and how the findings are interpreted. As a result, the relevance and validity of a great deal of existing data vary widely. Prior research findings need to be carefully evaluated for what they do and do not tell us about "truly" nonreligious people.[10] Many of these topics are undoubtedly pertinent to our subject. But the question remains: what *is* the subject? What do we call it and how do we define it? By answering these questions, even if only provisionally, we should have a better understanding of what is, and is not, relevant.

We could say that we are interested in nonreligious phenomena or meaning systems, but this begs the question, "What is religious?" This is a tougher question than it may seem. Religion is a well-established subject or field of study in many disciplines, from anthropology to theology. And no doubt everyone who reads this book has some idea of what "it" is. But this said, there is no universally agreed-upon definition—even within the social sciences. In fact, the question of whether "religion" *can* be clearly and consistently defined, and whether it should be used at all, has long been debated.[11]

Part of the problem is that even though each of us has a pretty good idea of what religion is, these ideas—and our definitions of the term—are not all the same. The range of phenomena covered by "religion" is incredibly broad and diverse. One person may have certain examples in mind (like Roman Catholicism), while another may think of something quite different (like tribal shamanism). Moreover, the concept of "religion" does not have the same meaning or relevance from place to place, or even over time. It is arguably more meaningfully applied to various forms of Christianity than to Buddhism or Wicca or Scientology, but it is used to describe all of these.

One way of grappling with the many meanings of "religion," at least in the social sciences, is to distinguish among three general approaches that have been taken: "functional" or "inclusive," "substantive" or "exclusive," and "constructionist" or "relational." Arthur Greil and David Bromley helpfully summarize the first two of these:

> The academic debate over the proper definition of religion has traditionally pitted "exclusivists" against "inclusivists." Exclusivists wish to limit the subject matter of the social scientific study of religion to beliefs, institutions, and practices traditionally thought of as religious. Exclusivists frequently espouse substantive definitions that posit the defining characteristic of religion to be its reference to the supernatural or "superempirical" realm. Inclusivists argue for the expansion of religious definitions to embrace activities, ideologies, and structures that seem to share features in common with religion although they are not always designated as such. Inclusivists often argue for functional definitions of religion, which hold that the essential feature of religion is, not its

reference to the supernatural, but its ability to provide an overarching structure of meaning or grounding for self.[12]

Functional or inclusive definitions aim to render "religion" universally applicable. It is an aspect of human experience that focuses on "ultimate" concerns, "the permanent problems" of existence, or whatever is "most valued" among human beings, for example.[13] From this perspective, "religion" is "intrinsically human." As such, however, "if we are referring to religion in its widest sense . . . then, indeed, every human being is religious."[14] This clearly won't do for our purposes, for it "overlooks the phenomenon of irreligion [or nonreligiosity or secularity] altogether, either by pretending that it doesn't exist, or by defining it out of existence."[15]

Meaningful distinctions can, of course, be made between religious and nonreligious approaches to grappling with permanent or ultimate concerns or values in human existence. Substantive or exclusive definitions of religion allow for this by suggesting religious phenomena contain elements that nonreligious ones do not, such as "supernatural," "transcendent," "superempirical," or "spiritual" ideas, experiences, entities, and realms. While this "makes room" for meaning systems that can be reasonably called nonreligious, this approach brings with it a challenge of a different sort: it is difficult to consistently define what is (and is not) "supernatural." In many cultures or intellectual traditions, distinctions between "natural" and "supernatural" realms or phenomena are blurry or nonexistent. Who, then, is to be the arbiter of *what* is natural or supernatural, physical or metaphysical, this-worldly or transcendently "otherworldly"? Typically, in practice, it is the intellectual perspective or tradition (or bias!) of the investigator that is the arbiter. Most inquiry into such matters has been pursued within and from the Western intellectual tradition. But, as some have pointed out, this is hardly a universally valid or culturally neutral frame of reference.[16]

The third general approach to understanding "religion" seeks to avoid the limitations of functional or substantive approaches. It does so by not defining "religion" at all—at least from the investigator's perspective. It is left to "social actors" to do the defining for us. In social constructivist or relational approaches, we (investigators) simply observe and report how people in various social, cultural, or institutional contexts *use* (or construct) terms and concepts like "religious" or "nonreligious," "believer" or "infidel," "sacred" or "secular," "theist" or "atheist," and so on.

A benefit of the constructivist approach is that we don't need to predefine terms like "religious" or "nonreligious" at all. A problem with this approach, however, is that markers or labels for "religious" or "nonreligious" are no more universal than distinctions between natural and supernatural. In fact, the term or concept of "religion"—even as many of us conceive of it in the anglophone West—does not have precise equivalents in many cultural contexts.

It will come as no surprise that in order to do an online search of relevant research, it is necessary to enter multiple terms, like atheism/atheist, secular/secularist/secularism, nonreligion/nonreligious/not religious/no religion, nonbelief/unbelief, apostasy/apostates, secular/secularism/secularist/secularization, deconversion, and (religious) "nones," among others. If only to streamline this process, it would be helpful to identify a suitable name for the subject area. But there is more to the issue than that. Consideration of what the field should be called is not merely about terminology but about where we should focus our attention, which phenomena are or are not pertinent, how we should think about them, and how they are (or are not) related.

THE ARGUMENT FOR NONRELIGION STUDIES

The name of the largest network of scholars engaged in relevant research indicates two of the principal terms under consideration: the Nonreligion and Secularity Research Network. One of the founders of this network, Lois Lee, has argued on behalf of "nonreligion" as "the master or defining concept for the field." While the term has appeared in occasional political science or theological discussions (typically in scare quotes), it is not currently in general usage. As Lee notes, it does not (yet) appear in the *Oxford English Dictionary*. This means that it is available to be defined and used in whatever way will meaningfully reflect the phenomena of interest.[17]

Lee defines "nonreligion" (or "non-religion") as "anything which is *primarily* defined by a relationship of difference to religion" or "any position, perspective or practice which is *primarily* defined by or in relation to religion, but which is nevertheless considered to be other than religious." Nonreligion "takes 'religion' as its reference point." As such, it is defined "only as a general form of response" or as a "characteristic set of responses" to religion, as Colin Campbell said of "irreligion." As Paul Pruyser has observed, "Irreligion is not merely the absence of something, and certainly not simply the missing of something good, desirable, or pleasant. It is much closer to adopting an active stance or posture, involving the act of excluding another posture which, despite its popularity or naturalness, is deemed to be a poor fit."[18] Irreligion, however, tends to convey hostility or neglect of religion. Lee seeks a slightly broader and more neutral concept that involves a "less oppositional notion of *difference*" rather than rejection or dismissal. This also avoids the connotation of an "outgroup or nonconformist position" such as "infidel" or "heretic" suggested by "irreligion."[19] According to Lee, "Irreligion is the rejection of religion ... and nonreligion is a related, more inclusive concept indicating anything that is identified by how it differs from religion, regardless of whether this sense of difference involves hostility, dismissiveness, curiosity or even veneration."[20]

In more concrete terms, as Lee defines it, nonreligion encompasses atheism, agnosticism, (secular) humanism, antireligious action, irreligious experiences, anti-supernaturalism, anticlericalism, blasphemy, and "indifference towards religion—a stance which requires at least some awareness of religion and therefore taking some position." It does not, however, include "rationalism," which Lee views as "ontologically autonomous from religion" rather than defined or differentiated with reference to "religion."[21]

Lee also considers, but dismisses, variants of "atheism" and "secular" as possible labels for the field of study she has in mind. While "atheism" and to a lesser extent "non-theism" appear in ongoing research with some regularity, Lee points out that—at least semantically, if not always as used—this refers only to the absence or rejection of beliefs in God or gods. As such, this represents "just one aspect of nonreligion studies." She positions "nonreligion" between "atheism" and "secularity" with regard to their breadth of meaning or the range of phenomena they encompass. The former is too narrow, while the latter (together with its many cognates) is too broad and ambiguous.

Lee sees in "the secular" (as well as "secularity," "secularism," and "secularization") a sense of "otherness" or separateness, rather than overt differentiation, from religion. Quoting the *Oxford English Dictionary*, this signifies "attitudes, activities and other things that have no religious or spiritual basis." For Lee "the secular is something for which religion is not the primary reference point."[22] In later work, Lee has argued that "secularisation involves the marginalisation of religion" and "secularity is when religion is relatively, though not necessarily absolutely, marginal." "Therefore," she explains, "marginalisation and marginality are the best and most useful ways to understand secularisation and secularity."[23]

Lee's objections to "(the) secular" as a workable descriptor for a meaningful and manageable field of study are several: its scope, its many variants and referent phenomena, and so, its ambiguity. With regard to scope, it can "incorporate anything from supporting a football team … to subscribing to a humanist value system." With regard to its variants and referents, "secularity" (or "secular-ness") can be applied to individual, institutional, or societal levels of analysis. "Secularism" is often used to signify an ideology or policy rather than a condition or characteristic. Moreover, this may refer to a political policy of neutrality toward religion(s) or criticism, exclusion, or suppression. Some forms of secularism may, thus, be antireligious, while others are not. The particular meaning of each of these terms must therefore be clarified from context to context.

To summarize, Lee defines nonreligion as worldviews and lifestyles that actors overtly perceive or designate as different from religion. Irreligion is contained within nonreligion, but it denotes active (or hostile) criticism, rejection, or dismissal of religion, whereas nonreligion is a more neutral designation. Secularity denotes conditions or circumstances in which religion is marginalized or supplanted by something (sources of authority or "points of reference") wholly apart from or other than religion.

Johannes Quack has joined Lee in promulgating "nonreligion" as a preferred "master concept." He argues that "secularity" is disadvantaged by association with "the secular" and "secularization," both of which have garnered extensive attention both within and outside the social sciences. Based on this association, "secularity" has a "problematic genealogy [of] outdated evolutionistic and modernistic ideas," such as the conviction that religion will inevitably be supplanted by more "rational" ways of thinking and acting as humanity "modernizes." A second, related, objection is that "the secular-religious opposition" is often associated with contrasts between "modern-backward, rational-irrational, liberal-dogmatic, and democratic-theocratic. While one side associates secularity and secularism with freedom, democracy, enlightenment, and rationality, the other side considers it Western imperialism and mental colonialism." Quack's third objection is an association between secular and secularity with the "either-or logic" of secularization. This "often simplistic debate between those who see religion as a vanishing or at least a declining entity in contrast to those who consider it to be merely transforming, re-emerging, or growing" has prevented a more "nuanced" view. Lastly, like Lois Lee, Quack feels that "there are so many different and partly contradictory understandings of terms like secular or secularity that debates often talk past one another."[24]

We agree with Lee's position concerning the narrowness and negative connotations of "atheism" as a suitable identifier for the field we have in mind, even though a considerable amount of contemporary research—particularly in the United States and Europe—uses this term. In light of such forceful argumentation against "secular" and its cognates, it may be foolhardy to argue on their behalf. Nonetheless, things may not be quite so bleak for "secular" and related terms as Lee and Quack argue. We think that there is (or should be) a bit more to the field we have in mind than overt differentiation from something-called-religion. While it is true that "secular" and its cognates, if not appropriately qualified or modified, can be ambiguous or unmanageably broad in scope, this is not necessarily the case if they are carefully distinguished and defined. Moreover, the very diversity of these terms ("secular," "secularity," "secularism," and "secularization") may aptly reflect the real complexity of the range of phenomena we think are relevant and want to understand.

The concept of "nonreligion" as Lee defines it does not avoid all the problems she associates with "secular(ity)." She gives as "examples of nonreligion . . . popular cultures like the New Atheism or rituals and practices developed in contradistinction from prior religious ones like many civil ceremonies and seasonal festivals." One might have thought that the latter reflect something wholly other than religion, lacking a religious "reference point," and so, examples of religious marginalization, particularly (but not necessarily) when ordained by a state—and so, by her definitions, examples of secularity rather than nonreligion.

From Lee's perspective, "secularity is a negative category whilst nonreligion and irreligion are positive ones." On the face of things this seems semantically contrary, but it reflects the view that "nonreligious identities such as 'atheist' and 'humanist' . . . require respondents to affirm a position in relation to religion."

> Non-religion is primarily defined here in reference to religion, whereas the secular is primarily defined by something other than religion. Non-religion is a relational concept; the secular is purely relative. Non-religion is 'stuff'; the secular means only the demotion or absence of some other 'stuff'—the relevance of religion as a variable.[25]

It is possible, however, to turn this around. As Lee suggests, forms of nonreligion like atheism are, in a sense, "positive" in that those who identify themselves as atheists—like Heather, Bob, or Ted in our opening sketches—are deliberately asserting or affirming a position. Yet they are "negative" in the sense that defining features of their worldviews depend upon and deny or dismiss something else called religion. Moreover, recall Ruth, whose life is a decidedly this-worldly absorption in the world of art. Is it reasonable to say that Ruth's "areligious" or this-worldly affirmation of a life in art is any less "positive" or substantive than those whose identities depend upon criticism, rejection, or deliberate dismissal or neglect of something called religion? We don't think so. In one (rather narrow) sense, Ruth's way of thinking and living evinces the thoroughgoing absence of something—religiosity—in belief, behavior, and identity. In another sense, her approach to life can be considered positive, substantive, or affirmative in that it does not depend—partially, primarily, or solely—on differentiation from something else. The same can be said for Heather's husband, Mike, who wishes to live as though something called religion doesn't exist at all.

The field of inquiry that we have in mind is interested in both differentiation from, and marginalization of, religion. It is interested in overt antipathy toward religion, as well as thoroughgoing indifference or ignorance about it. The way we name, define, and circumscribe our subject must make room for the Ruths and Mikes, as well as the Heathers, Bobs, and Teds. And even though they may be at the perimeter of the field rather than at the center, we also think that this must make room for people like Mai and Alice, who enjoy religion-*like* rituals without accepting religious (read: supernatural or transcendentally spiritual) ideas. There are benefits, we think, to "casting a wide net" rather than homing in too finely or narrowly as we begin our exploration.

THE ARGUMENT FOR SECULAR STUDIES

As Lois Lee noted, "the secular" can, at its broadest or most inclusive, refer to every aspect of human thought, behavior, social life, and experience that has no direct or explicit reference to religion. This would admittedly be much too broad for a manageable and coherent field of study. And the several cognates and their meanings can potentially give rise to confusion. But the situation may not be as confusing as some critics suggest, and some of the distinctions suggested by these terms may point to important distinctions among the diverse phenomena we wish to study, as well as lend a degree of order to them.

One source defines "secular" as:

1. concerned with the affairs of this world. . . .
2. not concerned with religion nor religious belief.
3. not ecclesiastical or monastic.[26]

An apt summary term for the first two of these definitions—and for "secular" as we will use it—is "this-worldly."

It is probably best to set "the secular" aside entirely. This noun phrase does carry a good deal of historical baggage, as Lee and Quack suggest. The adjective "secular," however, is more manageable. Admittedly, it is applicable to a very wide range of phenomena that are this-worldly or lacking a religious (or supernatural) reference or significance, such as playing baseball, shopping, joining a club, or working in a corporation. But when it is applied to an individual or a way of life, it is generally understood to be a summary term for relatively enduring ways of thinking and behaving. It suggests an enduring attribute or particular *kind* of individual, behavior pattern, meaning system, or institution. A secular person will typically be taken to mean someone who, over a period of time, exhibits thinking and behavior with no reference to religious ideas, action, or affiliation. A secular worldview is one that makes little or no reference to supernatural ideas. This does not tell us whether the posture toward religion(s) or supernaturalism is substantially ignorant, studiously indifferent, indecisive, critical, or hostile. But it even-handedly encompasses all these postures without privileging some over others.

It is helpful to make a clear distinction between "secularism" and "secularity." The former is typically restricted to political, institutional, or legal concern with the relationship between religion and government, or church and state. This is broadened here to refer to ideologies, principled positions, or attitudes about "the way things should or ought to be" with respect to governments, institutions, societies, or individuals. By contrast, "secularity" denotes an attribute, a characteristic, or a reflection of "the way things actually are"—the degree to which individuals and societies, for example, can meaningfully be characterized as secular or nonreligious.[27]

This said, if we are to keep the field of secular studies manageably focused, not all secular phenomena are equally relevant. For example, participation in "purely secular" institutions, like clubs or corporations, is too inclusive a subject and would move us well beyond a reasonable scope for the field. But people who *restrict* their attention and activities to social institutions (like clubs, corporations, charitable activities, family, and sports organizations) without any recourse to supernatural ideas are at the heart of the subject. Moreover, when a club happens to be the local chapter of Americans United for Separation of Church and State, it is quite pertinent to the study of political secularism and may be relevant to secularity (when, for example, members are also a-, non-, or antireligious). When it is a local chapter of American Atheists, it is clearly pertinent. And when shopping or club participation occurs on Sundays, the Sabbath, or holy days in a society in which such periods are customarily devoted to religious activity, this is pertinent to the study of both secularization and secularity.[28]

With the addition of several modifiers (each pertaining to a different level or aspect of human experience), the distinction between secularism and secularity furnishes a useful partitioning of our subject matter (table 1.1). The pertinent levels are as follows:

- political, or the structure and conduct of governance and the distribution of authority or power in society
- public, or practices, expression, and behavior open or accessible to the observation and reaction of a community or society at large
- popular, or pertaining to defined populations, and
- personal, or the thought and behavior of individuals

"Political secularism" refers to ideological positions or principles concerning the role of religion in political affairs and the process of governance. This involves

TABLE I.I

Forms of secularism and secularity

	Secularism (ideology or principled position; "the way things should be")	Secularity (attribute or characteristic; "the way things are")
Political	Political secularism	Political secularity
Public	Public secularism	Public secularity
Popular	Cultural secularism	Popular secularity
Personal/individual		Personal secularity

the restriction, limitation, or absence of religious institutions or of beliefs, discourse, and rationales in civic government administration, discourse, and decision-making—what is commonly referred to as church-state separation. As such, it also involves the constitutional, legal, judicial, or political principles and structures whose aim is to effect and maintain such a separation (between religion and government) or limitation (of religious institutional involvement or religious expression in civil governance).

While "political secularism" refers to an ideology or principled position that promotes "church-state separation," "political secularity" is the degree to which this is actually the case in a given society. In other words, "political secularity" refers to the degree to which religious influence or references do not play any significant or authoritative role in governmental or political processes.

Similarly, "public secularism" refers to an ideological position or principle concerning the absence, limitation, or suppression of religious expression, practices, or symbolism in public discourse or behavior. "Public secularity" refers to the degree to which this is true in a society.

"Cultural secularism" refers to an ideological position or principle that argues for the absence or elimination of religious beliefs and behaviors among all members and institutions within a society. "Popular secularity" refers to the degree to which this is true of a majority, or all, of the members of a society. "Cultural secularism" is used instead of "popular secularism," since the latter could be misconstrued as an ideological position held by most or all members of a population rather than, as intended, a principled position that this should be the case.

"Personal secularity" refers to the absence, neglect, or rejection of supernatural or substantively religious ideas (and related practices) or nonidentification, nonaffiliation, or nonparticipation in religious institutions at the individual level. (Personal secularism is subsumed by cultural secularism—or the position that all individuals in a society should be philosophically naturalistic, this-worldly, or nonreligious.)

"Secularization" refers to the degree to which, or ways in which, political, public, or cultural secularism and (actual) public or popular secularity increase over time in a population, a particular society, or humanity in general. Conversely, this is the degree to which religions or religiosity, substantively defined, declines.

All these forms of secularism and secularity, as well as secularization, are of interest in the field of inquiry that we envision. All will be touched upon in the pages that follow. But our interest lies primarily with psychology (which focuses on personal and popular secularity) and sociology (which focuses on public and cultural secularism and popular secularity). Secularization has been the subject of extensive theoretical and empirical work in the past several decades—to the virtual exclusion of the nature, details, and dynamics of secularity—and so, will receive somewhat less attention. Similarly, even though political secularism and secularity properly fall within the field of secular studies as we envision the field, because these fall outside our areas of expertise and have been amply treated in legal studies and political science, they will receive limited attention here.

The usefulness of the distinctions outlined here becomes clear when applied to contemporary societies. The United States, for example, is characterized by strong political secularism, in principle, that is nonetheless continually challenged due to comparatively weak cultural secularism, as well as relatively weak popular and public secularity (or comparatively strong cultural, popular, and public religiosity). It could be argued, of course, that the First Amendment's two religion clauses are in tension—that is, that the free exercise of religion presents a continual challenge to the separation of church and state. The result is a weaker form of political secularism, overall, than a strict principle of church-state separation would suggest. Given these tensions, it is not surprising that forms of nonreligion and irreligion are active and vocal, as well.

By contrast, France's implementation of *laïcité* has produced a society characterized by comparatively strong political, public, and cultural secularism, as well as public and popular secularity.[29] The political and cultural strength of secularism and secularity trigger religious advocacy, but comparatively little in the way of organized irreligion.

Despite comparatively weak political secularism in the United Kingdom or Norway—where selected religious institutions enjoy privileged status and governmental largesse—this privilege is rendered rather weak by the progressive secularization of their populations, and so, what we find today are comparatively strong levels of public and popular secularity. The absence of conflict over religion results in the comparatively weak presence of irreligious advocates and organizations.

These distinctions also help to clarify distinctions made by other scholars, like Charles Taylor's multiple uses of "secularity" in his often-cited exploration of the subject. His "type 1" is political secularity ("churches are now separate from political structures"; "you can engage fully in politics without ever encountering God"). "Type 2" is public secularity ("public spaces . . . have allegedly been emptied of God, or of any reference to ultimate reality"), and "type 3" is popular secularity ("a society where belief in God . . . is understood to be one option among others, and frequently not the easiest to embrace"; "belief in God is no longer axiomatic. There are alternatives"; as a result, "it may be hard to sustain one's faith").[30]

It is possible, then, to view secularity and nonreligion (as defined by Lee and Quack) as distinct domains, or to view secularity as a broader category that encompasses areligious (with no reference to religious ideas, activities, or identities) or nonreligious phenomena.

THE SECULAR-RELIGIOUS CONTINUUM

Earlier, we met several people who are fairly clearly secular or nonreligious. The closer we look at such people, however, the more complex the picture becomes. Consider just a few more cases.

Raj is a research scientist who describes himself as nonreligious and a skeptic or agnostic. Based on his reading of major religious texts, however, he finds it "useful to metaphorically embrace selected religious ideas, like samsara and karma." These are not ontologically real, but ethical reminders that what you do (and don't do) has ripple effects in the world far beyond your immediate sphere of influence and experience.

Gunther is "as thoroughly nonreligious as you can get"—no churchgoing, no praying, no belief in gods or spirits or miracles. This said, he is absolutely convinced by personal experience and "intriguing evidence" of the reality of "selected paranormal forces" and the existence of Bigfoot or Sasquatch.

Pat, doesn't "buy" any theistic, religious, or supernatural ideas either. But just the same, he attends Catholic church regularly with his family because he values the ritual, the community, the culture, and even the pastor and his sermons—they're useful moral reminders, and all of this is good for his kids. He says he's an "atheist in the pew."

Carol was raised Protestant but is currently uninvolved and noncommittal. She doesn't go to church or pray or think of herself as religious. She doesn't say she believes in anything religious or spiritual but won't say definitively that she doesn't.

She's "just not sure . . . doubtful but open . . . perched squarely on the fence . . . agnostic, kind of."

Then there is Jill, a self-described "un-Catholic" who abandoned organized religion in her teens and never looked back. She sometimes uses "atheist" or "nonreligious" to describe herself to others even though she "hates these terms—they tell you what I'm *not*, but *not* what I *am*!" She doesn't believe in God or an afterlife or heaven, but she is convinced of the existence of a "spiritual" force or energy in nature that connects everything in the universe.

All these people describe themselves as nonreligious! Their diversity raises questions about how and where we draw lines between secularity and religiosity, "strong" and "weak." This underscores the need for care about how such individuals are categorized and assessed, for some of these variations in worldviews and lifestyles are likely associated with significant differences in other variables, like personality styles and attitudes or even a sense of well-being and mental health. This also raises questions about the language such people use to describe themselves and how social scientists describe and distinguish them—or should. And it makes clear that resorting to relational or constructionist approaches to defining religion or nonreligion does not necessarily eliminate all confusion.

The boundary between religious and secular or nonreligious is unavoidably fuzzy. These are not discrete, dichotomous variables, and each represents incredibly varied, multidimensional categories of human experience and activity. In order to make this complexity manageable, secularity and religiosity are often thought of as a continuum (as in figure 1.1). As such, people in midcontinuum (C to E in ways of thinking and 3 to 5 in behavior) are in a border zone and can rightly be claimed as subjects of research in both secular and religion studies.[31]

People from E to G and 5 to 7 are clearly subjects for religion research. Our primary focus is obviously on those from A to C and 1 to 3. A-1s are thoroughly or affirmatively secular, B-2s substantially so, and C-3s "weakly" so. As we will see, there is

Ways of thinking or believing about existence (worldview) or oneself (identity)	A	B	C	D	E	F	G
	Non-supernatural "This"-worldly					Supernatural "Other"-worldly	
Ways of acting oneself (behavior) or with others (belonging) and how this is interpreted	1	2	3	4	5	6	7

SECULARITY ---------------------------- RELIGIOSITY

FIGURE 1.1 Secular-religious continuum

growing evidence of curvilinear relationships along the continuum, such that those with strong secular or religious convictions (of particular kinds) are similar to one another but both different from those in midcontinuum on a host of variables, from authoritarianism to xenophobia. Worldview conviction may be as important as, or more important than, content.

As the examples just presented also indicate, matters are even more complex, for ways of thinking (including beliefs and identity) and behaving (including practices and institutional participation) are not always neatly parallel or perfectly "consistent" with one another—at least when viewed with certain expectations from "outside." Moreover, the premium placed on the consistency or internal logic of meaning systems likely varies from person to person. Some individuals with strong secular and nonreligious convictions are, as we saw, engaged in religious behaviors or communities in various ways.[32]

The notion of a linear continuum from religiosity to secularity is, at best, a simplification and a heuristic means of grappling with an incredible range of human experience and phenomena. It is far from an accurate or "thick" representation of reality. As Dirk Hutsebaut has said, "Disbelief . . . has its own psychology" (and sociology and political science), just as belief does. "They are not just the two extremes of a continuum."[33]

THE VALUE OF MULTIPLE APPROACHES

We are hardly the only people to grapple with the question of how our subject should be defined or named, and so, which phenomena are or are not relevant. Christopher Silver and his colleagues, for example, found it necessary to broaden the scope of inquiry beyond atheism and nonreligion in an effort to identify distinct types of "nonbelief," by which they meant "the absence of belief in any and all gods." Based on interviews with a range of individuals, they too conclude that relevant types are not always "based off, defined by, and in comparison with, a culturally dominating category . . . such as religion or belief." It is quite possible to "situate 'secularity' or 'nonbelief' as a cultural fact that needs no juxtaposition with other constructs." They therefore "advocate for the investigation of secular and nonbelieving peoples as a cultural fact needing little, if any, juxtaposition or explanation that involves reference to, or distance from religion . . . . Being secular or holding a nonbelief cannot always be considered to be 'in relation to' religion." We, of course, agree, although we would expand nonbelief (or unbelief) to include supernatural ideas or phenomena other than "gods."[34]

Silver and his colleagues have distinguished six types of secularity or unbelief. Non-Theists are "simply not concerned with religion." They may be substantially ignorant of or disinterested in religious ideas, behaviors, traditions, or institutions. They are equally disinterested in nonreligious, irreligious, or antireligious ones. We would say that such individuals are thoroughly secular or this-worldly in their world-views. They "simply do not care" about or pay attention to a religious-irreligious construction of human experience.[35]

All five remaining types pay attention to matters relevant to religion or irreligion, but in different ways. Anti-Theists are explicitly critical of religious ideas, identities, and institutions. (As such, they might be more aptly called antireligionists.) They "view religion as ignorance" and are willing to actively assert their views and engage in activities aiming to contain or diminish religion.

Activist Atheist/Agnostics are also public advocates, but rather than focusing on the criticism or rejection of religion, they focus on "current issues in the atheist/agnostic socio-political sphere." These include, for example, "humanism, feminism, lesbian, gay, bisexual, and transgendered issues, social or political concerns, human rights themes, environmental concerns, animal rights, and . . . the separation of church and state."[36]

Academic or Intellectual Atheist/Agnostics are more concerned with under-standing rather than criticism of religion. They seek to educate themselves about matters ontological (what is the nature of what exists?), epistemological (what do we know?), and empirical (how can our understanding of nature be verified?). They may share such pursuits with others in skeptic, rationalist, or freethought networks.

Seeker Agnostics also pursue understanding but tend to be less definitively or comprehensively skeptical in their approach. They recognize the philosophical and empirical difficulties in making any definitive statements about metaphysics or the ultimate nature of reality. They therefore tend to "keep an open mind" about some religious or spiritual claims. While they hold substantially scientific worldviews, they are aware of the limits to science concerning ultimate questions.

While Ritual Atheist/Agnostics may hold skeptical, agnostic, or substantially nontheistic or nonsupernatural views, they nonetheless find utility or enjoyment in selected religious teachings or practices.

One of the values of distinguishing kinds of secularity, much as has been done extensively for religiosity, is that such differences in worldview and attitude are related to psychological, behavioral, social, and other characteristics. Silver and his colleagues, for example, assessed the six types on measures of autonomy, narcissism, dogmatism, anger, openness, and agreeableness. Anti-Theists were a breed apart, having scored significantly higher than most or all other types on autonomy, nar-cissism, and dogmatism, and significantly lower on agreeableness. They also scored significantly higher on an anger inventory than Intellectual Atheist/Agnostics. Seeker-Agnostics scored significantly lower than all other types on autonomy.

The typology offered by Silver and his colleagues further illustrates the diversity of secularity on many dimensions, but it reflects only the American cultural and religious/nonreligious scene. The degree to which these types are applicable to the rest of world likely varies a great deal. It is to the subject of the varying relevance, meaning, forms, and prevalence of secularity around the world that we now turn.

CONCLUSION

While the study of religion has had a long, multidisciplinary history, the idea of a coherent field of study in the social sciences that focuses on nonreligious individuals and institutions is fairly new. Attempts were made in the late twentieth century to mount studies of "unbelief" and "irreligion," but these did not become enduring fields of inquiry. More recent social and cultural changes have led to a resumption of interest in such a subject, but given its complexity, the focus, scope, and name for such a subject has prompted a variety of views. While "atheism" is often the subject of research, as a master concept to define a field of study, it is arguably too narrow in scope and laden with negative connotations. More broadly defined studies of "nonreligion" and "secularity" have been proposed. There are benefits and drawbacks associated with each approach.

In the final (or working!) analysis, multiple approaches are both unavoidable and potentially beneficial. As Christopher Silver and his colleagues observed, "There is no essential way . . . one *must* explore secular and nonbelieving peoples. A plurality of approaches serves our object of investigation best."[37] This should produce different insights into a subject that is at least as complex as that of religion.

2

SECULARITY AROUND THE WORLD

RAJIV, AGE FORTY-FIVE, is a member of several rationalist, skeptic, and secular humanist organizations in India. He volunteers with the Organization for the Eradication of Superstition, visiting villages and schools to present programs that debunk the magical or supernatural claims of priests and healers. He and his colleagues actually demonstrate techniques and "tricks" used by healers to perform "miracles." The aim is to promote a scientific understanding of the world and to combat beliefs, folk practices, and "healing" methods that are demonstrably incorrect, ineffective, or injurious. Rajiv says his worldview is rooted both in the materialist Carvaka school of classical Indian thought and in Western rationalism and empirical science.[1]

Michiko, a Japanese woman in her sixties, describes herself as nonreligious (*shūkyō wa nai* or *mushūkyō*). Nevertheless, she often makes ritual offerings at both a Shinto shrine and an ancestral Buddhist altar in her home. A visitor once pointed out that what she was doing seemed religious. Michiko thought for a moment and then said, "I guess I'm Buddhist." This confused her visitor even more, so he asked why she made offerings to the Shinto shrine at all. She laughed, saying, "I don't believe in the *kami* (Shintō spirits, deities), but I'm scared that if I don't make these offerings they will punish me."[2]

Erik, now in his thirties, chose to participate in a humanist coming-of-age ceremony more than two decades ago. He maintains membership in the Norwegian Humanist Association (Human Etisk Forbund) through an annual contribution. Even so, he has never elected not to be a member of the established national Lutheran Church—which is automatic at birth. As such, he allows part of his taxes to be used to support the church, since it renders some useful social services, such as hospitals. Although he does not consider himself religious and he does not believe in a Christian God, he and his wife were married in a church, and their son was baptized. But it is likely that their son will follow in Erik's footsteps and choose to have a humanist rather than a Lutheran confirmation.

* * *

As we indicated in chapter 1, secularity is not a simple phenomenon. The individuals just described illustrate that this is all the more true when we look around the world. Forms of secularity always reflect the societal, historical, cultural, and religious contexts in which they emerge.

A sharp distinction—and often antagonism—between "religious" and "secular" is one of the defining hallmarks of Western civilization.[3] But this is culturally and historically unique. Throughout much of human history, and in many cultures today, little conceptual or practical distinction is made between "natural" and "supernatural" phenomena.

In much of East Asia, for instance, "religious" and "secular" are not defined or distinguished as in the West. Ritual behavior often holds greater salience than belief. As a result, the thinking and behavior of people like Michiko appear inconsistent to Western observers.[4] The very terms and concepts that are used to describe the world or human experience do not always correspond with one another across cultures. This is an ever-present challenge for social scientists in the study of "religions" or "secularity" worldwide.

Even cultures characterized by profound neglect, ignorance, or indifference to religion may present apparent inconsistencies, as in the case of Erik in Norway. In places where religion just isn't a "big deal" anymore, personalized admixtures of religious and secular thinking may not be either. The very definition of what is religious or nonreligious tends to erode or dissolve into unimportance. It is usually in dominantly religious contexts that the distinction between secular and religious is most sharply drawn and the "purity" of one's worldview (one way or the other) is a matter of explicit concern.

In India, a multi-cultural country that remains pervasively religious, the meaning of "secularism" has taken on a distinctive nuance. Beyond the "mere" avoidance of religious preference or control by government, it signifies very broad tolerance for religious beliefs and practices by both government and individual citizens. But the breadth of this tolerant "secularism" worries people like Rajiv, who react skeptically and critically to beliefs and practices that are manifestly magical, pseudoscientific, and medically ineffective or, at worst, injurious. Rajiv's "secularism" is something quite apart from, and opposed to, "secularism" as commonly understood throughout much of India.

Some of the Enlightenment philosophers predicted an inevitable progression toward a species marked by pure reason, sans supernaturalism and superstition. En route, some of their intellectual descendants spoke of the achievement of the "pure separation" of church and state. But more recently it has become apparent that human beings—and the world(s) they create—are a great deal messier and more complicated than the philosophers expected or social scientists would like. This said, amid astounding human diversity, there are at least *some* very broad—possibly universal or near-universal—patterns and trends.

In this chapter we will critically tease out some of the apparent patterns in the distribution of secularity (and religiosity) around the world—without unduly minimizing the world's complexity.

SECULARITY WORLDWIDE

Anyone who attempts to chart a global geography of secularity is immediately confronted with daunting challenges. Simply "determining what percentage of a given society believes in God—or doesn't—is fraught with methodological hurdles."[5] Among these are the following:

- inadequate or nonrandom sampling due to a prevalent research focus on religion and small nonreligious populations
- political or social stigma associated with nonreligion that may prevent research participation or discourage honest responses
- a "social desirability" bias that prompts people (whether religious or nonreligious) to give answers that make their group look good
- conceptual and language differences, such that the words "atheist," "nonreligious," "secular," or even "God" or "supernatural" (and their linguistic parallels) do not have the same meanings, relevance, or salience across cultures

Moreover, even if we measure the rejection or lack of belief in God, this does not, as we noted in chapter 1, preclude other supernatural, spiritual, or metaphysical beliefs or religious behavior (congregational affiliation or participation, private or public rituals) whose connection with beliefs is variable or not entirely clear, especially to outside observers. Additionally, where research has been conducted at all, the methodological focus has been on assessing forms and prevalence of religiosity. This means that, at best, indices of secularity have been indirect, inferential, or residual. That is, the absence of reported religiosity has been assumed to indicate secularity, but without more detailed assessment methods, the degrees or kinds of secularity remain unclear.

Despite these challenges, we must press on, doing the best we can with the evidence currently at hand. How many substantially or affirmatively nonreligious people are there in the world? The answer is that estimates vary greatly, so we do not know with any great confidence. We can only suggest orders of magnitude.

Drawing from many sources—most of them studies undertaken between 1990 and 2007—Phil Zuckerman estimated that between 500 million and 750 million humans do not believe in God, or 7.5 to 11.5 percent of the total world population in 2007.[6]

Subsequently, Ariela Keysar and Juhem Navarro-Rivera concluded that there are "approximately 450 to 500 million nonbelievers worldwide, including both positive and negative atheists, or roughly 7% of the global population."[7] "Positive atheism" refers to explicit rejection of the existence of "God"; "negative atheism" refers to the absence of belief in "God" (including agnostics, who do not think that this can be known). Keysar and Navarro-Rivera's estimate was based primarily on survey data from the International Social Survey Program in 2008 for forty countries, with a strong emphasis on Western and Eastern Europe. This was supplemented with World Values Survey estimates (2005–2008) for China, India, Indonesia, and Brazil. But as they themselves note, findings for China are not reliable, and given the size of the population, this has an inordinate influence on regional and world estimates.

The Pew Forum on Religion and Public Life provided worldwide estimates of religiously unaffiliated people (or those who do not report any specific religious identity or affiliation, essentially equivalent to what others have called religious "nones").[8] This does not mean, as they note, that all nonaffiliates, or nonidentifiers, are substantially secular, atheistic/nontheistic, aspiritual, or behaviorally nonreligious. Even though they may not identify or affiliate with particular religious traditions, many hold supernatural, metaphysical, or spiritual beliefs, and many engage in religious behaviors. Overall, The Pew Forum estimated that as of 2010, some 1.1 billion people worldwide (or 16.3 percent) were not religious affiliates.

A WIN-Gallup International survey of 50,000 individuals in 2012 concluded that 23 percent (or an estimated 1.6 billion people) were not religious; additionally, 13 percent (or an estimated 923 million) reported that they were "convinced atheists." An additional 5 percent (or 350 million) didn't respond or said that they don't know. There are, however, reasons to doubt the reliability of these estimates, particularly on the basis of this survey's estimates for China.[9]

The best we can say with any degree of confidence is that there are most likely several hundred million nontheists worldwide, but they are not necessarily comprehensively nonreligious with respect to belief, identity, belonging, and behavior. We really don't know how many substantially or comprehensively secular people there are in the world, or what kinds, but at least in absolute numbers, there are likely quite a few—certainly enough to support the conclusion that the sheer number of secular humans alive today flies in the face of assertions that theism is universal or hard-wired.[10]

REGIONAL AND CULTURAL DIFFERENCES IN SECULARITY

There are significant geographical differences in the prevalence and character of secularity. Available data sources categorize secularity and world geography differently, as indicated in table 2.1. Nonetheless, broad patterns are apparent. Rates of secularity—from the broadest (religious nonaffiliates or nonidentifiers) to the narrowest (atheists)—are comparatively high in East/North Asia, Europe, and North America and low in Africa, the Middle East, and Latin America. This said, purely geographical distinctions such as these tend to obscure significant cultural and country differences. They also fail to fully reflect or elucidate qualitative differences in secularity (and religiosity) around the world. The designation "Africa" in the Pew data, for example, obscures significant differences between the Islamic north and the non-Islamic south; "Asia" and "Asia-Pacific" obscure considerable differences between China and India; "Europe" obscures differences among France, Poland, or the Czech Republic, and so on.

A better framework, perhaps, for understanding such regional differences is to imagine a cultural map, such as Samuel Huntington's delineation of "civilizations." A civilization is "culture writ large"—"the broadest cultural entity" that human beings recognize and with which they identify. Moreover, "of all the objective elements which define civilizations . . . the most important usually is religion." As such, differences in forms or manifestations of secularity are best assessed as they occur among cultural and religious regions.[11]

Huntington identified nine civilizations: Western, Orthodox, Latin American, African, Islamic, Hindu, Sinic, Buddhist, and Japanese.[12] "Western" civilization includes Western (Christian) Europe and its cultural descendants—most notably, North America, Australia, and New Zealand. "Orthodox" encompasses Russia, Ukraine, and non-Islamic Central Asian countries. "Latin American" spans Mexico, Central America, and South America. "Islamic" encompasses North Africa, the Middle East (excluding Israel), Indonesia, and Central Asia. "African" encompasses the parts of the continent that are not dominantly Islamic. "Sinic" includes China, the Korean Peninsula, Vietnam, and Taiwan. "Buddhist" spans the remaining Southeast

TABLE 2.1

Secularity across geographical regions

	Markham and Lohr (2009)			Pew Forum (2010)	WIN-Gallup International (2012)	
	Atheists	Nonreligious	Total	Religious non-affiliates	Not a religious person	Convinced atheist
Africa	.067	.68	.75		7	2
Sub-Saharan Africa				3.2		
Middle East/North Africa				.6		
Arab world					18	2
Latin America	.49	2.90	3.39	7.7	13	2
North America	.63	9.83	10.46	17.1	33	6
Europe	3.00	14.94	17.95	18.2		
Western Europe					32	14
Eastern Europe					21	5
Asia-Pacific				21.2		
Oceania	1.25	12.06	13.31			
Asia	3.22	15.62	18.83			
North Asia					30	42
East Asia					57	0
West Asia					30	3
South Asia					11	3

Asian countries, Tibet, and Mongolia. Japan is deemed sufficiently distinctive from "Buddhist" and "Sinic" to warrant its own civilizational status. Huntington considers the possibility of a "Jewish" civilization, but given Jews' comparatively small numbers, geographical dispersion, and variable identification with Judaism, Israel, or Jewish heritage, he opts not to treat this as a tenth civilization. We will see, however, that Jews actually do present a distinctive profile with respect to secularity.

SECULARITY IN THE WEST

Most of the data summarized in this book pertain to the United States and Western Europe, and we will look more closely at this part of the world in our discussion of secularization. We therefore want to make only a few brief points here to place the West and the rest of the world in perspective.

Nowhere else has a conceptual distinction between religious and secular, believer and nonbeliever, theist and atheist, been quite as sharply drawn, as salient, or as persistent a preoccupation as in the West. Huntington identifies this as one of the defining hallmarks of Western civilization: "God and Caesar, church and state, spiritual authority and temporal authority, have been a prevailing dualism in Western culture. Only in Hindu civilization were religion and politics also so distinctly separated. In Islam, God is Caesar; in China and Japan, Caesar is God; in Orthodoxy, God is Caesar's junior partner."[13]

This may be attributable to the distinctiveness of Christianity, which became—particularly in the form of Roman Catholicism—one of the most highly structured and institutionalized forms of religion in human experience. As religion scholar Thomas Luckman observed,"the church in the Judaeo-Christian tradition of Western history . . . represents an extreme and historically unique case of institutional specialization of religion. It emerge[d] from an extraordinarily sharp segregation of the sacred cosmos from the profane world in Hebrew theology."[14] But, of course, in scope and impact, "Christendom" far outstripped its Judaic roots. It became "a tight conglomerate of civilization, territory and ideology."[15] By the Middle Ages it represented a commingling of political, cultural, economic, institutional, and even military domains on an unprecedented scale. God, wealth, and power merged within an elite societal superstructure—regardless of the variable degree to which common folk were aware of the religious order in which they lived, knew or subscribed to official doctrine, or participated in church ritual.

It was within the framework of Christian theology that the sharp distinction between the realms of God and Caesar, divine and temporal, sacred and secular, emerged. It was perhaps inevitable that the cultural, ecclesiastical, intellectual, and political power of Christendom would eventually elicit critical reactions from within (as in the Protestant Reformation) or without (as among secular "Age of Enlightenment" intellectuals and their descendants). Such sharply drawn secular-religious dualism has not, however, been equally salient everywhere in the world. As a result, attempts to superimpose such constructions elsewhere can be problematic and often misrepresent the character of both "religiosity" and "secularity." Consider, for example, East Asian intellectual, cultural, and societal experience.

SECULARITY IN THE SINIC AND BUDDHIST REGIONS

Naturalistic or materialistic schools of thought have emerged in Chinese intellectual history.[16] Until the introduction of Communist "atheist" or antireligious policy, however, these have been marginal intellectual threads in a pervasive fabric of ritual and belief. The Sinic worldview has traditionally been a syncretic amalgam of a this-worldly social and political philosophy (in Confucianism, at least as originally presented), ethical principles and metaphysical abstraction (in Buddhism and Daoism), and "folk religion" (including "ancestor worship," magic, divination, local deities, demons, and spirits).[17]

Ceremony or ritual has been "the basic social mechanism for consolidating key social groups (such as family, village, and nation) and transmitting key cultural values (such as hierarchy and authority) in a society in which there has been no national church and little standardization of belief."[18] Ritual behavior is arguably more salient than belief.[19] Western expectations for congruence between behavior and expressed beliefs are thus often thwarted. In a sense, Sinic culture has been more "secular" than the West in that Chinese religiosity has—at least until the advent of Communist irreligion—consisted of a "loose tray" of ritual practices imbued with variably magical, superstitious, or supernatural beliefs. This is quite different from the comparatively tighter, exclusively "confessional," doctrinally fixed, authoritative, institutionalized, and (at times) hegemonic character of Christianity.

Within such a cultural context, it has been difficult to draw clear boundaries around constructs such as "God" or "atheism," "religious" or "nonreligious." In Taiwan, where Communism has not been an influence, and fairly reliable data are available, it has been estimated that roughly 88 percent of the population engages in worship of ancestors or local deities, and some 85 percent adhere to magical beliefs or practices (such as fortune telling and feng shui).[20] Some "87 per cent of Taiwanese who claim to have no religious belief actually believe in, or worship gods; only 6.3 per cent of the sampled population have no religious belief and do not believe in or worship gods."[21] And while 53 percent of a sample of Taiwanese college students nominally identified themselves as "atheists," 77 percent of the sample subscribed to traditional Chinese religious beliefs and practices (such as "burning money and incense to the Buddha and Gods and using Taoist magic spells" in order to "relieve one's mind").[22] On this basis, only 12 percent of the full sample consisted of comprehensively nonreligious "atheists." Both the comprehensive "atheists" and the Christians subscribed to folk and paranormal beliefs significantly less than traditional Chinese religionists (61 percent of the full sample) and self-described Buddhists (21 percent). Predictably, the comprehensive "atheists" were least likely to report religious beliefs and practices.

Similar complications appear in Vietnam. In a survey conducted in 2012 by WIN-Gallup International, a minority of Vietnamese described themselves as "religious" (30 percent; down from 53 percent in 2005). Even so, no respondents described themselves as "confirmed atheists." The concept of "atheism" is problematic:

> Traditionally, Vietnam knows neither a single and transcendental God nor its opposite, a radical atheism. Rather, a multitude of non-exclusive divinities co-exist, products of diverse religions. Vietnamese tolerance has often been extolled; in religious matters, this amounts to plain and simple syncretism in practice, sometimes even the absence of any convictions. . . . In such a context, atheism does not take on the radical, Western, form of "all or nothing," but rather a more nuanced and relative aspect. Thus the most common form of atheism is ignorance.[23]

In the 2000 World Values Survey, only 19 percent of Vietnamese respondents said they "believe in God," but 38 percent said they were "a religious person" and believed that "people have a soul."[24] Reflecting a tradition that is not monotheistic, such results depend a great deal upon terminology. If "God" were rendered as Thiên Chúa ("Father God" in a monotheistic or Christian mold), responses would be far less (suggesting substantial secularity) than for Ông Trời (often rendered as "God" but more broadly conceived in polytheistic terms as a primary deity among many).[25] As elsewhere in the Sinic world, "religion" and "God" tend to be viewed narrowly—as reflections of an exclusive devotion to particular named worldviews, typically "imported." "Folk" rituals and beliefs in ancestral (or other) spirits are more prevalent but often are not thought of, or reported, as, "religious" or "theistic."

In mainland China, explicitly antireligious Communist policies have undoubtedly suppressed supernatural beliefs and related practices—whether public or private—but because of strict government control over data collection and information flow, "survey data of religious belief are extremely unreliable."[26] Using similar questions but different sampling methods in 2007 and 2012, the World Values

Survey and WIN-Gallup International found that 18 and 47 percent of Chinese respondents, respectively, identified as "convinced atheists." With some softening of Communist policies concerning religion in recent years, however, investigations have begun to uncover signs of increasing religious identification (with Western as well as Sinic traditions), institutional activity, and "folk" beliefs and practices.[27] Additional evidence is found in World Values Survey data, with 5 percent of Chinese respondents identifying themselves as "a religious person" in 1990 compared with 15 percent in 2000 and 21.8 percent in 2007.[28] But, again, all of these results may well be underestimates for cultural, historical, linguistic, and political reasons. We need to keep in mind that "religion" (and, so, "secularity" or "nonreligion") is comparatively "fuzzy" in Asia (apart from Communist antireligious policy, imported from the West). This is also evident in Japan.

JAPANESE SECULARITY

As in the Sinic world, in Japan, religiosity has generally been inclusive and syncretic. Indigenous beliefs and rites, known collectively as "Shinto," were joined by Confucian social philosophy and Buddhist metaphysics. Christianity was largely held at bay, making limited inroads. As in the Sinic world, Japanese religiosity has been more focused on ritual than belief. "Religious praxis (*shugyō*) and feelings (*kimochi*) and not belief per se form the core of Japanese religion."[29] Exclusive or even dominant devotion to any particular named religion has been the exception rather than the norm. As such, the application of Western notions of religious and secular, theistic and atheistic have been perennially challenging.[30] Michael Roemer distilled the distinctive character of Japanese "religion" this way:

> Japanese religiousness is a syncretistic blend of, mainly, Buddhist, Shintō, and folk traditions, practices, and beliefs. It is important to recognize, however, that despite the multitude of sacred beings, they are not the focus of attention for most Japanese. Often, religiousness is more about the doing and the act of worship than the meaning behind the rituals or the specific objects of veneration or consideration.[31]

The very concept of religion has negative connotations for many or even most Japanese people. It was only in response to Western cultural contact in the late nineteenth century that a Japanese word for religion (*shūkyō*) came into use. It tends to be associated with foreign, "founded," or formally organized traditions, particularly Christianity and other monotheisms, but also Buddhism and new religious sects.[32] As such, many or most Japanese have described themselves as "nonreligious" (*mushūkyō*), but this does not necessarily mean comprehensive, definitive, or principled absence or rejection of all supernatural, metaphysical, or "spiritual" beliefs and ritual activities associated with them. To this point, "when the Japanese identify themselves as nonreligious, most do not mean that they are atheists but rather that they don't have affiliation with any particular individual tradition. . . . [M]any who consider themselves to be *mushūkyō* . . . participate in many aspects of different traditions as they view these as cultural traditions rather than as religious activities per se."[33]

It has been long been difficult to know precisely what the Japanese do or do not believe, or where "religion"—as a coherent behavioral and conceptual system infused with supernatural ideas—fades into "cultural religion" or secular cultural tradition, as exemplified in the case of Michiko, with which we began the chapter.[34] In surveys conducted in recent decades, majorities claim "no personal religion" and "little or no interest" or trust in religion(s) but also report beliefs in "something spiritual"; the existence of spirits, gods, or an "unseen higher power"; and participation in traditional rites with historical, cultural, or religious significance.[35] Only 27 percent said they were "a religious person" in a 2000 World Values Survey, but 53 percent said they "believe in God," and 71 percent said "people have a soul."[36] Similar "fuzziness" is associated with the notion of atheism. In a survey conducted in 1998, "one quarter of those who described themselves as atheists (*mushinronsha* . . . ; 19% of total respondents) also professed some belief in God," indicating that "'atheist' has different connotations in Japan" and is "identified more with a rejection of 'religion' than a lack of belief in the divine."[37]

There has been an intellectual thread of deliberate philosophical irreligion or "atheism" in Japanese culture, but this has been slender, at best. It emerged in, and was largely confined to, the nineteenth century, as Japan grappled with Western ideas, but its popular influence has been difficult to gauge and, most likely, quite limited. Even in intellectual circles, this "never fully emerged as an independent area of intellectual inquiry."[38] The absence of formal secularist movements or organizations in Japan is a reflection of this historical inattention to deliberate philosophical secularism or "atheism."

This said, there is strong evidence of decline in "traditional" religious practices and beliefs. Based in part on the observations of Japanese scholar Kunio Yanagita, Winston Davis recounts many ways in which religious festivals (*matsuri*), shrine and temple rituals, shamanism, and other spiritually imbued phenomena were weakened by economic development, urbanization, and commercialization, or actively suppressed by deliberate modernization policies following the opening of Japan to international contact in the late nineteenth century.[39]

More recently, Ian Reader has documented signs of decline throughout the post–World War II era in beliefs and behavior associated with both indigenous folk religion, or Shinto, and founded or imported religions, such as Buddhism or Christianity, particularly among younger cohorts. Some of this is attributable to a postwar reaction to the role played by "state Shinto," or the adoption of some aspects of Shinto to legitimize the political and military order.[40] But sharper recent declines seem attributable to a broad-based distancing from religiosity in the wake of the sarin gas poisoning of the Tokyo subway by members of the syncretic cult Aum Shinrikyo in 1995. Based on a wealth of survey data, Reader points to many signs of increasing religious indifference or overt antipathy in recent years—particularly among younger, educated, and urban Japanese—including the following:

- greater reported distrust of religious organizations and leaders
- declining beliefs in deities and ancestral or other spirits
- declining reported identification with named religious traditions
- dwindling participation in shrines and temples
- declining performance of Buddhist funerary rituals
- declining household ownership or ritual propitiation at Buddhist or Shinto altars
- a "hollowing" of pilgrimages as touristic entertainment more or rather than devotional or ritual religious activities

The (supernaturalist) religious fabric that was once more tightly and/or pervasively woven through the everyday lives of most Japanese is apparently becoming a looser weave, with more evidence of indifference to, or abandonment of, ritual practices and associated supernatural beliefs. As indicated by the contradictory evidence just cited, however, it remains difficult to conclude that these are dissolving completely into pervasive and deliberate or thoroughgoing secularity or philosophical naturalism. As elsewhere in East and Southeast Asia, adherence to historically traditional religious forms may unravel, but metaphysical, superstitious, paranormal, and spiritualistic threads persist.[41] Moreover, while traditional beliefs and ritual practices may be less frequently invoked in the everyday lives of many Japanese (particularly young, educated urban dwellers), they are re-emerging elsewhere—in the imaginative world of Japanese popular culture, such as anime and manga.[42] There, they are engaged—as they have been in times past—in the perennial endeavor to identify, reinforce, and celebrate the attributes and sources of Japanese cultural uniqueness. In *animanga*, manifestations of "founded," imported, organized, and "New" syncretic (read: alien) religions—as well as scientific secularism and modern skepticism!—are cast as threats to the decidedly (if amorphously) spiritual, metaphysical, or "animistic" (read: Shinto) wellsprings and heart of "Japaneseness." It is not entirely clear what those who produce or consume such materials actually believe. But this ambiguity is nothing new. It may be "symptomatic of that existential drift for which the Japanese have such talent, rather than any disciplined, philosophical commitment to atheism."[43] As Winston Davis also notes, the challenge is "how to conceptualize secularization in a culture in which the sacred and the profane are not understood as categorical opposites."[44]

INDIAN SECULARISM AND SECULARITY

Deliberately skeptical, naturalistic, or irreligious philosophical schools of thought have been somewhat more prominent in Indian history, even if these have been perennially overwhelmed by a preponderance of magical, metaphysical, or religious beliefs and behaviors. The sixth century B.C.E. saw the emergence of the "materialistic and hedonistic" Lokayata or Carvaka schools of thought, in some respects similar to the Epicurean school of ancient Greece.[45] Their posture was decidedly this-worldly and dismissive of metaphysical ideas or spiritualistic ritual. As Jennifer Hecht notes, "the Carvaka proclaimed that there were no gods, and that there was no heaven; the only hell there is, they insisted somewhat gleefully, is here below, caused by normal pain and frustration."[46] Other strands of skeptical—if not comprehensively naturalistic or irreligious—thought may be found in the third-century C.E. Samkhya school, in Jainism, and even in early Buddhist, Vedic, and Upanishadic texts.[47]

The thread of Indian doubt has continued to the present day, but as before, it remains a minority posture in a pervasively religious realm. Reliable data on forms or prevalence of secularity, as well as active irreligious critics, are elusive. In a 2001 census, a majority of Indians claimed specific religious identities, but disbelief was not directly assessed. Only 0.1 percent of respondents gave no specific religious identification or affiliation, but here as elsewhere, nonidentification is not necessarily nonreligion. Then again, "Hindu" (some 80 percent of the population) can be a cultural rather than a religious marker, thus underrepresenting the prevalence of secularity.[48] In the 1990 World Values Survey, 91 percent of Indians believed in reincarnation. In 2000, 95 percent indicated belief in "God," and 88 percent considered God extremely important in their lives (up from 94 and 68 percent, respectively, in 1990).[49]

As elsewhere, secularity is stronger among wealthier and better-educated individuals. Numbers are still small, however, and there are signs that differences between highly and poorly educated individuals have recently moderated. In World Values

Survey data, 2 to 4 percent of respondents with an elementary-level education, and more than 9 percent with university degrees, did not believe in God in 1990, but this narrowed to roughly 4.5 and 5.6 percent, respectively, by 2001.[50] Even among scientists and academics, only 10 percent identified themselves as "atheist" or "no religion" in a 2008 survey.[51]

Membership numbers for atheist, skeptic, and rationalist groups are elusive but are counted (and claimed by such organizations) in the thousands or tens of thousands, at best. As such, they represent fractions of a percent of the total population. Nonetheless, the Indian landscape is dotted with a network of such secularist organizations fervently engaged—like Rajiv in our opening sketches—in debunking magical or pseudomedical claims and challenging religious beliefs and authority.[52]

While it is difficult to establish a direct or continuous historical connection between schools like the *Lokāyātas* and the modern anti-religious movements, many of the latter draw some degree of confidence and cultural legitimacy from the legacy of Indian doubt.[53] Western secularist writers and movements—primarily British and American—have lent more recent and arguably greater stimulus to the methods and messages of contemporary Indian rationalist advocates and secularist groups. Through publications, live presentations, regional conferences, the mass media, and the Internet, such groups promulgate skepticism, empiricism, and scientific reason, but they remain "small in number and of uncertain impact in the face of daunting historical, cultural, and religious forces."[54]

SECULARITY IN THE FORMER SOVIET AND ORTHODOX COUNTRIES

Broadly speaking, while Christian religiosity has been eroding in Western Europe, it has been (re)gaining some strength in Central and Eastern Europe since the retreat of antireligious Soviet Communism.[55] Notably, Borowik, Ančić, and Tyrała begin their review of atheism in Central and Eastern Europe with the case of Valentina—a Ukrainian woman who, following the fall of Soviet Communism, has reasserted a religiosity that she reports she never lost "inside her heart," even as she presented herself as "atheist" while under political duress.[56] She is hardly alone. Apparent membership in or identification with dominant Orthodoxy, Islam, or Catholicism declined substantially in most Soviet countries by 1970, but by 1995, between 30 and 80 percent of the apparent loss had been erased as many (re)affirmed religious identities.[57]

Considerable cultural and national diversity in secularity/religiosity can be found in this region.[58] The Czech Republic, Estonia, and eastern Germany have among the highest rates of atheist self-identification and religious nonaffiliation in the world, whereas Romania, Moldova, and Poland are among the lowest, as are many of the Central Asian states where Islam dominates.[59] At the same time, there are signs in many countries of increased worldview diversity, including growth in New Age and paranormal beliefs—even in the most nonreligious countries like Estonia and the Czech Republic. [60]

Close scrutiny of national cultures and historical experience offers some insight into these differences. In the cases of both the Czech Republic and eastern Germany, secular, freethought, and/or socialist antipathy toward Christianity emerged well before the rise of Soviet Communism. Although historical details differ, in both cases, strong irreligious, anticlerical/antichurch, or atheist/freethought narratives emerged as early as the nineteenth-century in response to perceived associations between Christianity and imperial or government oppression.[61] Soviet irreligion found fertile ground and built upon this (with, e.g., the resumption of secularist/humanist/freethought children's "confirmations"—or *jugendweihe*—in eastern Germany, not unlike the Norwegian humanist confirmations in our opening sketch of Erik).[62] By contrast, in Poland, Christianity—specifically Roman Catholicism—became a symbolic, cultural, political, and institutional bulwark against Soviet Communism.[63] Religion and secularity have had, to paraphrase Steve Bruce, different "work to do" in these countries.

Among predominantly Orthodox countries, there is some basis for Huntington's contention that "God is Caesar's junior partner." In post-Soviet Russia, the Orthodox Church has gained stature. A growing relationship of mutual cultural, national, and political interest has emerged,[64] and atheism has been identified by church partisans as a national threat.[65]

Only 24 percent of Russians identified themselves as Orthodox in 1990, but by 2008, 73 percent did. This is, however, apparently more "cultural" than deeply felt religion, with only 55 percent of nominal identifiers professing theistic belief and less than 10 percent attending services regularly.[66]

The big picture throughout the former Soviet region seems to be one of increasing worldview complexity and diversity following the removal of "state atheism," but pluralism itself has not been responsible for increased religiosity, for the most religious countries are those with one or two dominant religions.[67]

SECULARITY IN LATIN AMERICA

With Spanish and Portuguese colonial expansion, Christianity (overwhelmingly Catholicism) became dominant at the individual, institutional, and political/societal levels throughout Latin America. Despite notable country variations and denominational changes over time, this largely remains true to the present day. Latin America remains more religious than the Latin European countries that colonized the region.[68] In the past decade, forms of evangelical Protestantism have gained substantial numbers of adherents in many countries at the expense of Catholicism, although the election of a pope from Argentina could conceivably help the latter with retention and recruitment.[69]

Despite the pervasiveness of Christianity in Latin America, however, secularity is by no means wholly absent. Uruguay stands out in this regard. It is "as secular as Switzerland or Germany" and similar to liberal European countries in other respects, as well.[70] It has the highest percentage of religious "nones" and atheists, by far, of any Latin American country—"roughly double the share of [religiously] unaffiliated people in any other country in the region."[71] Nigel Barber reported that "only 41 percent of the population see religion as important in their lives, the lowest in South America." He attributed this to Uruguay's distinctive cultural composition—more European than indigenous—and religious history, with comparatively limited Catholic missionary activity due to its small "Indian" population. It has comparatively high per capita GDP and life expectancy; strong healthcare, legal, and educational systems; small family size; low infant mortality; and limited corruption. Constitutional separation of church and state was established in 1917, by which time "divorce had been legalized and religious instruction was banned from state schools."[72]

Argentina and Chile share some of these characteristics, yet their populations are more religious. Anthony Gill and Erik Lundsgaarde suggest that what is most distinctive (and "European") about Uruguay is "the extensive reach of the state's social welfare system."[73] This, they conclude, gives Uruguayans an added degree of personal security which, in turn, reduces dependence upon religious beliefs and services.

While Uruguay is in a class by itself, there are some signs of secularity and modernization elsewhere, including increasing religious diversity, more "nones," liberalization of laws and moral attitudes (contrary to church positions on euthanasia, homosexuality, abortion, nonmarital cohabitation, divorce, and suicide), lower fertility rates, and decreasing family size.[74] Philip Jenkins has suggested that several Latin American countries are "increasingly . . . developing a European coloring." Chile is second only to Uruguay among Latin American countries sampled by the World Values Survey in the number of citizens who describe themselves as "not a religious person" (32 percent) or are "convinced atheists" (3.2 percent).[75] Over the course of four surveys beginning in 1990, Chilean "nones" have increased steadily from 20 to 24 to 28 to 32 percent. It is worth noting that Chile has had one of the more vibrant economies in the region for some time; it is the wealthier individuals and countries that tend, on average, to be less religious.[76]

In El Salvador, 29 percent of people sampled by the World Values Survey have indicated that they are "not a religious person," followed by Guatemala (27 percent), Mexico (22 percent), Colombia (20 percent), and Argentina and Peru (both 17 percent).[77] Ecuador was one of the forty countries sampled by WIN-Gallup International that reported the steepest declines in self-described religiosity, from 85 percent in 2005 to 70 percent in 2012. While the Brazilian population remains substantially religious—with between 85 and 88 percent describing themselves as such—census reports indicate gradual growth in religious diversity, with Catholicism continuing a multiyear decline, evangelical Protestants still on the rise, but also growing numbers of "nones," who increased slightly from 7.3 percent in 2000 to 8 percent in 2012.[78]

Despite Uruguay's Euro-style secularity and some signs of religious decline elsewhere, however, Latin America remains substantially religious, partly as a result of the vitality of evangelical, Pentecostal, and charismatic Christian forms in recent years.

SECULARITY IN THE ISLAMIC WORLD AND AFRICA

Throughout most of the Sunni and Shiite Islamic world, secularity has a limited and uncomfortable presence. Samuli Schielke recounts a thread of criticism and dissent—some overtly atheist or irreligious—throughout Islamic history but notes that "in most Muslim-majority societies today, atheism and nonreligion are strongly scandalized, and often also criminalized." The Qu'ran repeatedly excoriates unbelievers, particularly apostates, laying a foundation for persistent and pervasive disregard for personal secularity. As Schielke further notes:

> In Egypt, for example, there is no legal option of being non-confessional. Believer or not, one must be legally a Muslim, Christian, or a Jew. . . . In Saudi Arabia and Iran, among other places, apostasy (and by implication, atheism) are [sic] considered capital crimes. . . . In most cases, non-believers and atheists have to fear social rejection more than state persecution. In Egypt, being openly not religious at all, or even worse not believing in God, can lead to loss of job, divorce or impossibility to marry, exclusion from the family, and in at least one case . . . assassination.[79]

In the most conservative Muslim countries like Egypt, Iran, and Saudi Arabia (and despite Qu'ranic tolerance for all people of "The Book," encompassing Christians and Jews), de facto tolerance for any competing worldviews is limited. Extending work by Jonathan Fox, Alfred Stepan concluded that Pakistan, Egypt, Iran, and

Saudi Arabia are among the least tolerant states in the world based on multiple measures of legal and political control over other religions and worldviews.[80]

In most substantially or dominantly Islamic countries today (where 80 percent or more identify as Muslim), majorities typically indicate theistic belief and the strong importance of religion in their lives.[81] Given the anti-apostate and anti-infidel ethos of conservative Islam, however, it is reasonable to suspect that these numbers mask at least some covert secularity.[82] Moreover, the countries cited by Schielke are among the most religiously conservative, and there is more variation in forms and degrees of personal, institutional, or political religiosity/secularity among Muslim countries and sects than is often recognized.

For example, Turkish Alevis (25 percent of the population) and Syrian Alawites (12.5 percent) represent parallel Muslim minorities rather different from the surrounding (Sunni and Shiite) Muslim majority.[83] Although they are quite distinct culturally and historically, with little mutual association, both tend to be less conservative in their theological and behavioral approach to Islam; so much so that they are often regarded as heretical by the Muslim majority. Their approach to the Qu'ran is critical and nonliteral; interpretation of and adherence to the pillars of Islam is selective; fewer strictures are placed on women (regarding dress, public activity, or, among Alevis, participation in worship); and consumption of alcohol (in moderation) is accepted. Both have a comparatively tolerant, live-and-let-live attitude toward other sects and religions. Given their minority status, both support political secularism. They are, in some respects, more liberal enclaves of Islam.

Personal religiosity is not consistently strong in all countries where the overwhelming majority considers itself Muslim. Roughly 10 to 30 percent of self-identified Muslims in Iraq, Indonesia, Jordan, Kyrgyzstan, Saudi Arabia, Tunisia, Turkey, and Uzbekistan describe themselves as "not a religious person."[84]

In Algeria, more than 40 percent do not consider themselves religious, and 36.7 percent describe themselves as "convinced atheists."[85] This has been speculatively attributed to the secularizing influence of French colonialism or reactions to civil war involving Islamic militants in the 1990s, when "religion was often invoked to justify violence against citizens."[86]

A majority of respondents in Azerbaijan describe themselves as Muslim, but only 4 to 6 percent are active adherents.[87] More than half of the population describes itself as nonreligious.[88] Despite increasing numbers of mosques and Islamic schools since the Soviet era, Islam is viewed more as heritage—a part of national identity—than religion. Regular attendance at mosque, for example, is extremely low compared with other Muslim countries.[89] "Islam plays only a very limited role in the political sphere . . . due to the long tradition of secularism in Azerbaijan and to the fact that the strong nationalistic movement is secular in character."[90]

Turkey, of course, represents a unique experiment concerning political secularism and personal secularity in the Islamic world, at least with regard to public behavior. "Kemalism"—so named after its architect, Mustafa Kemal Ataturk, the father of modern Turkey—was not the "perfect separation" of church and state envisioned in the West but, rather, a blend of de facto government control or co-option of Islam together with limits placed upon public religious expression, such as female head or bodily coverings. While there is no officially preferred or legally established religion, virtually all Turks identify as Muslim. Substantial numbers, however, consider themselves nonreligious.[91]

Under Prime Minister Recep Tayyip Erdogan and his Justice and Development Party, there have been notable shifts away from Ataturk's enforced public secularity. For example, bans on public religious expression such as the wearing of headscarves have been loosened, and there has also been some tightening of "secular" behavior, such as the consumption of alcohol in public places. The conservative policy shifts by Erdogan and his Justice and Development Party have become a lightning rod for debate within Turkey and beyond, given its real and symbolic status as a "test case" for political secularism, personal secularity, religious expression, and democracy in the Islamic world.

* * *

In Africa, religion is both pervasive and diverse. Africa is widely regarded as the most religious continent on earth, and in addition to predominantly Muslim countries in the North and elsewhere, "imported" religions (most notably Protestant and Roman Catholic) have been laid over indigenous belief systems, many of which persist together with Christian (and Muslim) adherence.[92] Non-Islamic Africa is thus a syncretic mosaic of indigenous tribal and Christian beliefs and practices. The latter include colonial inheritances as well as more recent imports, most notably, Pentecostal, evangelical, and charismatic forms of Christianity.

There is, however, some variability in religiosity/secularity among sub-Saharan countries and tribal groups. South Africa and Botswana, in particular, stand out. Both have among the strongest economies on the continent. And while belief in God remains strong, South Africa contains a comparatively high—and rising—rate of religious "nones"/nonaffiliates, or individuals who describe themselves as "not a religious person."[93]

Botswana also exhibits a comparatively high rate of religious "nones" or nonaffiliates (roughly 20 percent).[94] Although Afrobarometer data indicate this has been declining (from 32 percent in 2012–2013, to 28 percent in 2005–2006, and 27 percent in 2008–2009), rates in 2012 were highest among younger individuals (21 percent among those aged fifteen to twenty-nine; 18 percent among those aged thirty to forty-nine; 17 percent among those aged fifty and older). This said, only 8 percent of respondents indicated that religion is not at all or not very important. It is notable that, like Uruguay, Botswana has exhibited among the highest economic growth rates and per capita GNP throughout the continent, thanks to sound government policy decisions, tribal power-sharing, limited corruption, and effective natural resource management, particularly diamond mining.[95]

Cape Verde is also distinctive, at least based on Afrobarometer data (2012), with 13 percent "nones" and 18 percent who indicate that religion is not at all or not very important—highest among the twenty-two surveyed nations. Other sub-Saharan countries with 10 percent or more religious "nones"/nonaffiliates or those who describe themselves as "not a religious person" in at least one data source include Cameroon, Gabon, Ethiopia, Mozambique, and Swaziland. That said, reports of the personal importance of religion are pervasively high, and theistic nonbelief or atheist identity is consistently negligible across the continent.[96]

As in India, a virtual handful of secularist individuals and organizations are actively challenging traditional and imported religious beliefs and promoting nonreligious worldviews. Some of these are associated with Western-based atheist, humanist, rationalist, and skeptic movements. They maintain websites, hold conferences, and offer educational materials and experiences.[97] But as in India, they operate in the face of daunting religious majorities and forces.

In Ghana—one of the most religious countries in Africa and the world—students surveyed at the University of Ghana knew of no atheist or secular associations on campus or at other state schools. Ninety percent of a survey sample of ninety-six students and others knew of no such organizations in the country.[98] The establishment of a Ghana Humanist Association—formed in 2012 to carry on the work of a rationalist center founded in the 1980s—may help to raise the profile of secularist philosophies somewhat. But it is worth noting that an international humanist conference sponsored by the association in November, 2012, in Accra, Ghana, drew only about fifty-five participants (in a capital city of more than 2 million residents).[99] The International Humanist and Ethical Union, with which the Ghana association is affiliated, lists only six member organizations in African countries.[100]

Despite these indications of modest diversity, secularity remains a minority stance throughout sub-Saharan Africa, with little more than 3 percent of the population that is religiously unaffiliated.[101]

JEWISH SECULARITY

Given the comparatively small size and dispersed nature of the Jewish population, cultural maps of the world do not typically treat Jews as a separate entity or "civilization."[102] With respect to secularity and religiosity, however, Jews— particularly in the United States and Europe—are notably distinctive. Despite the historical connection between ethnic or cultural and religious (or Judaic) attributes of "Jewishness," contemporary Jewry represents one of the most secular(ized) populations in the world, and, through public discourse, societal roles, and scholarly activity, one of the most influential.

Most Jews reside in Israel (43 percent of Jews worldwide) or the United States (40 percent).[103] A quarter or more of American Jews are nonreligious.[104] While more than half of Israeli Jews described themselves as secular in one study, 35 percent reported that they perform some ritual observances; 21 percent (categorized as "antireligious") did not.[105] Among Israelis, "although their standard of observance is low by Orthodox standards, the ostensibly secular exhibit an array of religious acts that would mark them off as fairly religious in the American context. . . . Though the term is misleading, 'secular' is the common label to identify people who do not consistently practice the ritual behavior mandated by Orthodox Judaism."[106]

With respect to political attitudes and religiosity, Jews in the United States resemble religious "nones" substantially more than they resemble Christians. They are much less likely than the average American to believe in a personal God, heaven, hell, an afterlife, or miracles, and less likely to pray, meditate, read the Bible/Torah, or look to religion for moral guidance.[107] They are "more than three times as likely to say their outlook is 'secular'"—with behavior to match. For example, "The percentage of Jews who never attend religious services aside from a family life-cycle event climbed from 27% in 1971 to 35% in 1990 to 41% in 2008."[108]

Jews, particularly in the United States, are distinctive with respect to political and social liberalism, moral thinking, behavioral emphasis, this-worldly focus, and charitable activity, as well. Some of this may be attributable to Judaic religious heritage, which tended to focus on "social connectedness and on behavior" and "less on salvation or eternal life, and more on bringing goodness into this world."[109] But these characteristics have become part of Jewish cultural identity and behavior, with or without religiosity.

Again, like seculars and religious "nones," Jews are more likely than most Americans to value education, intellectualism, and independent thinking in themselves and their children.[110] They are more supportive of civil liberties (especially free speech) and tolerant of minority groups and nonnormative lifestyles, including ethnic or racial minorities, homosexuals, and atheists.[111] In fact, they think about moral issues differently. Jews are more likely than American Christians to perceive abortion as a "women's rights" issue rather than a moral issue. Similarly, they are less likely than Christians to view homosexuality as a moral issue, and more as a matter of personal behavior and lifestyle.[112] And they are strong political secularists—vigilant about breaches in the wall between church and state, and wary of (religiously influenced) government efforts to legislate morality.[113]

Jews also exhibit comparatively strong commitment to community and social capital.[114] In the United States, charitable giving by Jewish individuals and foundations is proportionately far greater than their numbers.[115] Jews are more prone to give to secular than to (Jewish) religious causes, with an emphasis on institutions for public benefit (education and higher learning, museums, libraries, medical research, and the arts).[116]

In sum, American Jews, particularly nonreligious, Reform, and Reconstructionist, tend to exhibit many of the attributes extolled by secularists. As Kosmin and Keysar have concluded:

> The well-educated Jewish masses appear to emulate the secular elites of Europe. Whom do American Jews most resemble from a sociological and demographic perspective? The Dutch or Scandinavians: an affluent population with low fertility, well-educated and emancipated women, low levels of religiosity, strong communitarian values, tolerant social attitudes, liberal outlook, and center-left voting records.[117]

CONCLUSION

The world is a decidedly complicated place when it comes to religiosity and secularity. Human worldviews and behavior make it so. As José Casanova has commented, "Any discussion of the secular has to begin with the recognition that it emerged first as a theological category of Western Christendom that has no equivalent in other religious traditions."[118] The "binary system . . . separating two worlds, the religious-spiritual-sacred world . . . and the secular-temporal-profane world," is unusually sharply defined in Christianity and the West. The degree to which secularity meaningfully applies to other cultures varies with the degree to which similar distinctions are made. Where "the sacred and the profane are not understood as categorical opposites,"[119] or where ritual behavior is more salient than belief, the meanings of "religious," "nonreligious," "secular," "god," and related terms will vary considerably, particularly across languages.

With this in mind, we can still roughly assess the distribution of theistic or supernatural thinking and related behavior—and their absence or overt rejection—around the world. On this basis, it becomes clear that religiosity remains widespread, but that secularity, to varying degrees and in different ways, is unevenly distributed across countries, cultures, and civilizations. It is most prevalent in parts of Western

Europe and the anglophone world, current and (some) former Communist states, and a handful of other locations (such as Japan and Uruguay). To complicate things further, it should be remembered that religiosity, secularity, and the many gradations along this tacit continuum shift over time. It is to this consideration, and the subject of secularization, that we now turn.

3

SECULARITY THROUGH TIME

THE BRIEF GLOBAL survey in chapter 2 makes one thing clear: the world is complex, particularly with regard to secularity and religiosity. Nonetheless, we may ask whether any general patterns or trajectories can be discerned amid the complexity. For example, is humanity tending toward more secularity, or greater religiosity, or do rates of both stay fairly constant over time? This is a question that has been asked for a very long time, with ample data and argumentation to support a wide range of views, many of them contradictory.

Overall, our conclusion is that there is evidence of a *very* broad tendency for religion(s) to weaken or religiosity to become more individualized as countries become more economically developed, as societies become more institutionally complex, and as individuals become more existentially—that is, economically, medically, psychologically—secure.[1] This trend, however, is neither evenly distributed across the globe nor simply unidirectional. It interacts with heritage, history, polity, and culture to produce distinctive local outcomes that run the gamut from strongly secular to (re)assertively religious, and many gradations in between. Not all economically developed countries are equally secular. One size—or pattern—does not fit all. There are "multiple modernities" or pathways in economic and societal development, with varied involvement of religiosity and secularity.[2]

Secularization is but one dimension in the tendency toward increasing economic/technological development and societal complexity. It is important to recognize and understand how this dimension interacts with others in order to truly comprehend what is actually happening around the world over time and why. In this chapter, we will begin with a critical review of the principal arguments that have swirled around the question of secularization for at least a century. This will be followed by our best sense of the most significant forces that affect secularity and religiosity, where these forces have led us thus far, and in what direction they seem to be taking us in the future.

SECULARIZATION THEORIES AND EVIDENCE

The progenitors of what has come to be known as secularization theory or the secularization thesis—including Voltaire, Auguste Comte, Friedrich Nietzsche, Émile Durkheim, Max Weber, Sigmund Freud, and Karl Marx—generally believed that "a modern rational scientific age of enlightenment would replace religion as the basis for understanding and running the world."[3] In this sense, the subject of secularization sprang from the European "Age of Enlightenment." This was not, however, mere presumption or mythmaking, as some critics have asserted.[4] Durkheim, Weber, and other early sociologists made earnest efforts to describe and explain observable developments in the industrializing societies around them.

At least in Europe, there were signs of profound societal change, such as the division or specialization of labor, a shift from intimate community to instrumental association in society, the rise of capitalism and the "disenchantment" (or, to be more accurate, "demagicalization") of everyday life, an erosion of "traditional" morals, an intensification of individualism, and the transformation or decline of the political, societal, institutional, and popular roles of Christianity.[5] In some ways, much of this had been in the works for some time; in others, there seemed to be something new happening. In any event, their views triggered an arguable "over-preoccupation with secularization" in Western sociology for decades to come.[6]

By the middle of the twentieth century, the issue had coalesced into a theory of the relationship between various aspects of economic and societal development—or modernization—and secularization. An incalculable volume of material has been devoted to this subject in Western intellectual circles. Points of view run the gamut, from strong advocacy to substantial or categorical rejection and much in between.[7]

"CLASSICAL" MODERNIZATION-SECULARIZATION THEORY (CMS)

The core of what has been called "classical" or "orthodox" secularization theory has been neatly encapsulated by Peter Ester and Loek Halman:

In premodern societies, religion dominated peoples' lives in all respects. Due to processes of differentiation, specialization, and the accompanying process of individualization in particular, religion was forced to retreat from many important sectors of social life. It has become a highly specialized institution of its own, like other major social institutions such as the family, education, economics, and politics. As a consequence of individualization, individuals are free to choose and practice their own religious convictions, just as they are free to choose their own political ideas, primary relationships, and so on.[8]

The concept of structural, functional, or institutional "differentiation," as Olivier Tschannen observed, has been "absolutely central" to classical sociological theories of secularization.[9] Broadly speaking, it refers to the separation of social activities, functions, or services into separate institutional structures, such as educational, judicial or legal, governmental or political, and so on.[10] More pointedly, it refers to the separation or contraction of one particular function—the religious—into a delimited domain rather than a dimension that pervades all social activity or all levels of society. This observation applied specifically to European experience, where at one time the Christian (Catholic) church was a dominant force that permeated society.[11] As José Casanova summarized it, "The central thesis of the theory of secularization is ... modernization as a process of functional differentiation and emancipation of the secular spheres—primarily the state, the economy, and science—from the religious sphere and the concomitant differentiation and specialization of religion within its own newly found religious sphere."[12] This was, however, one of several aspects of modernization that were identified and emphasized by a series of observers, including rationalization, societalization, privatization, individualization, pluralism, and relativism.[13]

Rationalization, like differentiation, is an elusive construct because its meanings are many and it is not always clearly or consistently defined.[14] This may, at least in part, be attributed to Max Weber, who saw "rationality" as central to an understanding of societal modernization, but who used it (or multiple German linguistic variants of "rational") in several senses.[15] It referred, for example, to the "demagicalization" or "demystification" of modern worldviews (*Entzauberung*); to pragmatic, instrumental, calculated, or means-end decision-making, particularly as this applies to economic activity (*zweckrational*); and to the control or guidance of behavior through political, legal, or ethical—rather than supernatural—means (*wertrational*). In various contexts, he applied it to the behavior of individuals, institutions, or entire societies. Subsequent CMS theorists have tended to focus on "rationalization" first and foremost as the instrumental or calculated means-end approach to decision-making they saw as characteristic of modernizing capitalist economic environments. "Rationality" as a logical, naturalistic, or empirical turn of mind is acknowledged but is generally considered subordinate to structural factors such as differentiation.

"Societalization" grew out of the views of Émile Durkheim and Ferdinand Tönnies and was central to Bryan Wilson's approach to CMS theory.[16] It referred to a shift or expansion of individuals' frame of reference—with respect to personal identity and social intercourse—from family or local community to wider institutions like companies or government bodies, or to society or the nation at large. For Wilson, modernity marked an erosion of community. This tended to undermine religion, which he viewed primarily as a local communal phenomenon.[17]

Pluralism (or "pluralization") has figured prominently in CMS theory, particularly in Peter Berger's early work.[18] In Europe, the Protestant Reformation prompted the fragmentation of a monopolistic Christianity into sects and denominations. This, in turn, initiated a process that undermined the plausibility of any single, overarching "sacred canopy" (as in, for example, Western European Christendom). Industrial urbanization further encouraged worldview pluralism, or relativism, as various worldviews appeared side by side in neighborhoods, workplaces, and cities.

"Autonomization," "individualization," and "privatization" are closely related. As institutions differentiate and worldviews proliferate, each individual confronts increasing opportunity and responsibility for negotiating alternatives. As wealth grows and labor specializes, individuals become more autonomous. The individualism fostered by Protestant emphasis on an unmediated relationship between each individual and God paved the way for each individual to selectively build his or her own identity and worldview. Thomas Luckmann, in particular, suggested that, as a result, religion(s) become increasingly privatized, secularized, and thus "invisible."[19] One's sense of self, existential meaning, social roles, or shared community depended less on participation in institutional religious structures built around supernatural beliefs. "Religion," defined functionally as a principal source of existential meaning, dissolves into secular form(s), such as ideological, political, nationalistic, or passionate personal commitments and interests, including sports, charitable activity, the arts, and so on.

As suggested in our global survey, this view of modernization and secularization emerged from, and is arguably best suited to, Western Europe, which was marked by the emergence of "an absolutist state and its ecclesiastical counterpart, a caesaropapist state church" followed by a critical, fragmenting reaction in the Protestant Reformation.[20] This historical and cultural experience is distinctive. In key respects, it does not apply to what unfolded in the United States, much less in Asia, or most anywhere else. In the United States, *both* political secularism and popular religiosity have been woven together into the cultural fabric from the start, and in non-Communist East Asia, religion has generally not played institutional, political, or societal roles nearly as comprehensive, pervasive, or highly structured as Christianity has in Europe.

As societies have grown in scale and complexity, functional or instrumental associations have undeniably expanded. But whether the expansion of impersonal economic and service interactions has caused a contraction of intimate or communal ones—or of religiosity—is debatable. For every theorist who bemoans the erosion of community, religion, and "social capital," there is another who sees shifting, rather than declining, forms of intimate association and social engagement—whether people are religious or not.[21] Social engagement may become more voluntary and selective, and communities and "networks" may become more fluid, but this does not necessarily mean the wholesale collapse of social relations or community.

One aspect of economic and societal development that has received widespread assent is the emergence of individualization, individualism, or autonomy.[22] The range of phenomena these words denote and the extent to which this is occurring across cultures demand closer scrutiny. Moreover, whether this is responsible for the transformation or personalization of religiosity or its erosion is a matter of debate. [23]

As Christian Smith has argued, CMS theory has suffered to an extent from "over-abstraction" and "under-specified causal mechanisms."[24] It has also arguably suffered from overelaboration. At first blush, many of its constituent theses seem logical and reasonable, but it has become freighted with so many moving parts that, as some of its critics have noted, it has become effectively unfalsifiable.[25]

THE DECLINE OF EUROPEAN CHRISTENDOM

All that said, *something* has been happening to religion in Western Europe over the course of the past several centuries, and especially during the past half century. This, as most theorists are careful to note, is the region to which CMS theory most directly applies. Evidence and arguments both for and against CMS theory are far too numerous and extensive to summarize at length here. Moreover, this has been done repeatedly, from many perspectives, elsewhere.[26] Several key summary points, however, can be made.

First, evidence of de-Christianization, to varying degrees in much or most of Western Europe, is overwhelming. There are several historical frames within which this has occurred. One has been a gradual and long-term decline from the political and societal Christian hegemony of medieval or Renaissance Christendom. Another is from the cultural Christianity of late nineteenth-century ("Victorian") society. Still another is from World War II/postwar Christian nationalism.[27] There has been undeniable erosion of Christian identity or membership, societal and moral authority, institutional influence, and beliefs.[28] At the societal and institutional level, this has been a gradual process over the course of centuries. At the individual level, declines in Christian belief and behavior (such as church attendance and prayer) have been documented for at least a century, and this has accelerated markedly in many countries in the past several decades.[29] The era of the late 1960s seems to have been a cultural tipping point regarding religion, moral perspectives, cultural traditions, attitudes about social institutions in general, and much else.[30]

Some, like sociologist Rodney Stark, have argued that such assessments of decline or de-Christianization presume a "Golden Age of faith" and active—that is, frequent and doctrinally knowledgeable—church participation that engaged all of European society at all levels.[31] In fact, they do not. At the societal and institutional levels, and among the decision-making elite, Christian clerics today enjoy nothing like the power, authority, or influence they wielded throughout much of Europe several centuries ago.[32] When he seeks to dispute the decline of Christianity in Europe, for example, Stark suggests that the erosion of clerical ranks and influence is unarguable but trivial.[33] But his documentation elsewhere of the "triumph" and influence of Christianity in the West (and worldwide) offers ample testimony that in many ways—cultural, intellectual, political, practical, economic, institutional, societal, and civilizational—Christianity was profoundly influential throughout Europe and its colonial and cultural progeny. Church clerics and the ecclesiastical hierarchy surely played significant roles in this process. As Stark himself demonstrates, Christianity was, for centuries, the worldview "environment" within which Western civilization unfolded.[34] It is no more. We need only look at changes in the content of European music and the arts as a palpable reflection of this fact.[35]

Stark argues that it is at the individual or popular level that debates about a "Golden Age" and secularization are nontrivial. At this level, in his view, secularization has not occurred to any appreciable extent—even in Europe. Yet, as we will soon see, he also argues that religious "consumption" and vitality (at the individual level) have been limited in Europe by government constraints and religious monopoly. He therefore agrees that religiosity in Europe is comparatively weak. It is just that, by his account, it has *always* been weak.

Regardless of the prevalence of active and knowledgeable adherence to Christianity in the Middle Ages, the Renaissance, or the Victorian era—which, as Stark rightly observes, was very likely limited and interlaced with "pagan" and magical beliefs—the *presumption* of Christian dominance and identity was widespread among both the elites and the general populace. Christianity, whether nominal or genuine, was the default setting. Within "the context of 'Christendom,'" people "lived in a society where there were close ties between the leaders of the church and those in positions of secular power, where the laws purported to be based on Christian principles, and where . . . every member of the society was assumed to be Christian."[36] Again, this is no longer the case. The mere emergence of sociological legions endeavoring to determine how contemporary Europeans privately perceive or publicly present themselves with respect to worldviews, and what they do or don't believe and do—let alone the increasing religious diversity, syncretism, or indifference their data indicate—is testimony to this fact.

Second, de-Christianization does not mean the triumph of pervasive and comprehensive secularity or, for that matter, complete disappearance of Christian beliefs or rituals throughout Europe. David Voas has presented evidence that weak, selective, or "fuzzy fidelity" to Christian beliefs or practices persists to varying degrees but eventually wanes.[37] Others cite evidence that there remain substantial levels of private or personalized Christian identity, belief, or behavior even as public attendance or "belonging" has declined.[38] By the (survey) numbers alone, there is some truth to this. Even in the most secularized countries, substantial numbers still report private prayer or belief in God. Moreover, even where regular church attendance has waned, participation in life-cycle rites and significant events on the Christian calendar persists. While much of this may be reasonably characterized as "cultural religion," rather than signs of "genuine" religious adherence, this is not necessarily true for all. Moreover, a good deal of non-Christian spirituality and syncretism is evident.[39]

There is, in sum, clear evidence of less exclusive devotion to Christian belief, behavior, and belonging and more selectivity, diversity, and syncretic personalization of worldviews and lifeways assembled from a menu of religious (including, but not exclusively, Christian) and secular philosophical content.[40] This is surely secularization of a sort and de-Christianization to a degree, but it is hardly thoroughgoing disappearance of religions or religiosity.

Steve Bruce and David Voas have presented a compelling argument that the substance and volume of alternative spirituality (such as New Age, Eastern borrowings, and paganism) are not commensurate with the decline in Christianity.[41] This is a difficult judgment to make, but one with which we are sympathetic. Spiritual beliefs and practices tend to be more selective, malleable, or individualized, and less structured, institutionalized, obligatory, or even communal or congregational in nature. On this basis, Bruce and Voas argue that increases in "alternative religion" or "spirituality" represent signs of secularization rather than religious persistence. A good deal of alternative "religiosity" and spirituality is arguably secular in character. Nonetheless, as many post-Christian Europeans continue to seek meaning, it is clear that among the "fuzzy" seculars and indifferents there are many religious syncretics and spirituals, as well. This offers support for arguments of both secularization and religious persistence or transformation.[42]

Amid the volleys of evidence and conflicting interpretations, one fact should not be lost or diminished: if nothing else, worldview diversity seems to be growing at the individual level in much of Europe. This said, our third summary point is that de-Christianization, let alone secularization, is hardly proceeding at the same pace, or to the same degrees, everywhere throughout Europe.[43] Western European countries are not uniformly secular or religious any more than Central and Eastern Europe countries are, as we saw in chapter 2. Rates of decline in religious beliefs and convictions have been most pronounced in recent decades in the Scandinavian countries, the Netherlands, Great Britain, Germany, and France. But in Austria, Greece, Ireland, Italy, and Portugal they either have not declined appreciably or else have held steady at higher levels.[44] As David Martin suggested, in general it is the northern and Protestant countries that have secularized more rapidly and profoundly than the southern and Catholic countries, excepting France.[45] While a general secularizing trend is apparent in Western Europe, the pace and paths of this trend are influenced by local historical, cultural, political, and religious experience. It is worth noting, too, that the economies of the northern Protestant countries have generally been stronger than in the Catholic south, a point to which we will return in a moment.

"SUPPLY-SIDE" THEORY

Part of the ongoing dispute about secularization is attributable to a sociological tendency to overgeneralize based on data overwhelmingly from Europe. Since this part of the world was the first to "modernize" (i.e., industrialize within a capitalist or market framework), it seemed reasonable that as other parts of the world developed economically, they would follow a similar path. This assumption, however, proved increasingly untenable as (1) religion persisted in various forms and places, even as development or "modernization" proceeded outside the "First World"; (2) new data from international survey programs emerged; and (3) one of the most highly developed and modernized societies—the United States—remained stubbornly religious even as Europe seemed to be secularizing.

The American religious "exception" has long been an abiding challenge to the application of classical modernization-secularization theory beyond Western Europe, but this may be changing. There are undeniable signs of religious erosion, and this seems to have accelerated. Church attendance has shown signs of decline, although the evidence is not entirely consistent. There has been marked growth in the number of religious nonaffiliates or "nones," seculars, atheists, particularly among young people.[46]

Despite these developments, however, levels of religious belief, identity, and activity still remain high in the United States—much higher than in much of Western Europe and more comparable to many Third World countries.[47] This and other issues have prompted critiques of, and alternatives or modifications to, CMS theory.

One of the most intensely debated of these is what has variably been called the "rational choice," "religious economies," or "supply-side" thesis put forth by Rodney Stark and his colleagues.[48] Their point of departure immediately sets this approach apart from others in that it holds that *demand* for religion remains roughly constant in the human species. What affects religious vitality is the supply or availability of religious "products" from market to market.

The "rational choice" dimension of the approach taken by Stark and his colleagues was prompted, at least in part, by vocal dissatisfaction with what was viewed as a secular bias among Western intellectuals and social scientists. Because of this bias, critics argued, religion was seen as intrinsically irrational.[49] Stark and others argued, by contrast, that religions offer a class of benefits not found elsewhere: supernatural compensation for rewards expected but not received in this life. The fact that religion is a source of such unique rewards means that it is rational for individuals to choose to be religious. Based on the persistence and prevalence of religiosity through history, the human need for the particular *kinds* of benefits offered by religion seems to be inexhaustible. Aggregate demand for (the unique rewards offered by) religion, they argue, is more or less constant. What changes over time is the composition of the religious marketplace—or the range of religious products available to satisfy continuing demand and shifting tastes.

Where religious markets are "free" or unconstrained, a range of "products" may proliferate, meeting "consumer" interests and thus satisfying demand. Where markets are not free—because of control or constraint of religious "innovation" by governments, dominant or exclusionary religions, irreligious policies, and the like—product diversity is constrained, many consumer interests are not met, and satisfaction (not demand!) wanes. In other words, religious variety stimulates vitality; religious uniformity begets boredom and indifference. This is, of course, the opposite of what CMS theory holds, namely, that pluralism of belief systems will tend to weaken religious vitality by undermining the plausibility of any particular religion.[50]

Some evidence has been presented in support of the supply-side thesis.[51] There is, however, a substantial body of evidence that refutes it.[52] In a critical review of research, Mark Chaves and Philip Gorski analyzed twenty-six direct studies of the supply-side theory. Ten found "mainly a positive relationship" between religious pluralism and vitality (such as belief, religious importance, attendance or other activity), eleven found "mainly a negative relationship," and five found little or no relationship. More telling was an analysis of specific findings produced by these studies. This disclosed that "sixty-nine percent (133) of the published analyses report either a significant negative (86) or a null (47) relationship between religious pluralism and religious participation, while only 31 percent (60) report a significant positive relationship."[53] Moreover, methodological problems undermined the validity of many supportive findings.[54] Excluding these studies yielded only eleven supportive and eighty-two nonsupportive findings.[55] Yet another mathematical problem concerning measures of religious concentration or pluralism dealt the thesis still another blow.[56]

Chaves and Gorski concluded that "the quest for a general law about the relationship between religious pluralism and religious participation should be abandoned. The evidence clearly shows that any such general law, to be accurate, would have to be formulated with so many exceptions and qualifications that its claim to generality or lawfulness would be empty."[57] Crockett, Olson, and Voas concluded that based on available data and the methodological and mathematical problems challenging their validity, they "could find no compelling methodologically unproblematic research that shows a genuine relationship between pluralism and participation," and that "a case can be made . . . that pluralism actually has little or no effect on participation."[58] They hold out the possibility that alternative, nonproblematic methods can be found or devised in order to provide valid tests of the thesis, but they suggest that in light of both the methodological problems and disconfirming evidence, the onus is on proponents to present new data and analyses in support of the theory.

There are, no doubt, circumstances and contexts in which religious competition stimulates innovation, consumer-oriented change, effective marketing, and religious vitality. But it is at least as often the case that where one religion is dominant, religious adherence, identity, and/or activity remains strong, as in Poland and many predominantly Islamic countries.[59]

In some places, religious uniformity may help to reinforce national, political, or cultural identity. This can, in fact, occur where subjective religiosity grows strong (as in Poland, Mexico, and Egypt), as well as weak (as in Norway, Spain, and Azerbaijan). Religious pluralism may thus be associated with religious vitality or with secularization, depending on other historical, cultural, and political factors. It does not, however, seem to be a consistent driver of one or the other.

Overall, as José Casanova has said of the traditional/classical and contemporary supply-side arguments:

An impasse has been reached in the debate. The traditional theory of secularization works relatively well for Europe, but not for the United States. The

American paradigm works relatively well for the U.S., but not for Europe. Neither can offer a plausible account of the internal variations within Europe. Most importantly, neither works very well for other world religions and other parts of the world.[60]

Fortunately, a new entrant has changed the complexion of the debate.

ECONOMIC AND EXISTENTIAL SECURITY THEORY

An alternative theory of changes in religiosity and secularity has emerged in recent years. Supported by analyses of World and European Values Survey (and other) data collected in countries worldwide over the past several decades, this new perspective reveals a robust relationship between the level of economic development and secularity.[61] In short, in wealthier countries people tend to be less religious, and in poor countries, more religious. Rather than a social structural explanation as in classical modernization-secularization theory, Pippa Norris and Ronald Inglehart have presented what may be called an economic and existential security (EES) theory.[62]

As countries become wealthier, their citizens become more "existentially" secure. That is, with improved hygiene, medical care, education, opportunities for meaningful work, social welfare systems, and so on, life becomes less precarious—at least materially. In turn, demand for both substantive and metaphysical forms of support or protection supplied by religion declines. These include communal mutual support, charitable services for those in need, and supernatural beliefs that help to "explain" pain and suffering, offer reassurance of divine protection, or give hope of compensatory rewards in this or another life. As demand erodes, institutional participation and religious influence or authority also tend to decline. Norris and Inglehart readily acknowledge that correlation does not prove causation. As Weber demonstrated, religion and culture can and do undoubtedly influence economic behavior, and sometimes enable significant innovations in economic systems. But it seems likely that, as Marx and other materialist theorists have argued, technological and economic advancement is arguably the "primary" driver of change in human affairs, including religion and culture.[63] In systems as complex as human societies, simple unidirectional causal explanations are often inadequate. It is more meaningful to speak of the degrees to which economic, political, and ideological or cultural systems mutually affect one another, and so, society overall.

To this point, Norris and Inglehart note that one of Weber's convictions—that the rise of science and technology will tend to erode religious belief—does not receive apparent support from World Values Survey data. It is reasonable to expect that regard for science will be comparatively strong in more secular—and presumably more "rational"—countries, but just the opposite is found. Contrary to expectations, there is greater conviction in highly religious countries (like Egypt, Nigeria, and Uganda) that scientific advances will help humankind, and greater conviction in less religious countries (like the Netherlands, Norway, and Japan) that they may do harm.

Another interpretation of these findings is possible, however. People in more economically advanced and less religious countries may tend to *think* more instrumentally, logically, "rationally"—and so skeptically—about *every*thing, including science and technology. They may also tend to take science and technology for granted. Moreover, extensive experience with science and technology may make their limitations and unintended or undesirable outcomes more apparent. Conversely, individuals in more religious (and less economically, scientifically, or technologically advanced) countries may *think* more magically, yet they may yearn for the material benefits that science and technology offer. The apparent appeal of science and technology may reflect such yearning rather than acceptance of a scientific worldview or application of empirical thinking in everyday life.

Norris and Inglehart do recognize that there is not a one-to-one correspondence between country wealth and aggregate religiosity or secularity. This tendency is just that—a *probabilistic trend* that interacts with local heritage, polity, population, and culture, producing distinctive developmental paths. There are "outliers" in their data, one of the most notable of which is the United States. Their explanation for this is that the existential security effect is a product not just of aggregate or average wealth but of the *distribution* of wealth and existential security throughout a society. The United States is a comparatively individualistic, meritocratic society with considerable wealth inequality and a minimal social welfare "safety net" (at least in comparison with European social welfare states). As a result, its citizens are not, on average, as psychologically, economically, or existentially secure as those in economically developed countries with strong welfare systems or more equitable distribution of wealth, such as Sweden or Norway. As we saw in chapter 2, the case of Uruguay—whose cultural complexion, political policies, highly developed welfare system, *and* secularity are unique in South America—is consistent with this thesis.

Note that in contrast to supply-side theory, Norris and Inglehart's approach does not assume constant demand for religion. The fact that individual religiosity is generally weaker in higher EES societies indicates that demand for religion is *not* constant.

Norris and Inglehart present data from a host of sources that indicate significant negative correlations between measures of religiosity and per capita income, measures of human development, urbanization, literacy and education, access to mass communications, number of doctors, access to immunizations, improved water sources, and life expectancy. Correspondingly, there are significant positive correlations between religiosity and measures of income inequality (GINI coefficient), illiteracy, infant and child mortality, and incidence of AIDS.[64]

In a further refinement, Norris and Inglehart distinguish among societies at three phases of development: agrarian, industrial, and postindustrial.[65] As predicted, measures of religiosity are strongest in poorer agrarian, and weakest in wealthier postindustrial, societies, with industrial societies in between.[66]

Additional studies within the past decade provide generally consistent support for an EES effect.[67] Lower religious belief, importance, and participation are associated with diverse measures of security, including economic development, higher education, low prevalence of pathogens and improved medical care, one's own and partners' job security, economic well-being in childhood, physical health, low threat of terrorism, and lack of experience with war.[68] In affluent areas, religiosity is largely unrelated to subjective well-being, but in poor areas, greater religiosity is associated with greater subjective well-being.[69] Even the occurrence of an earthquake reveals "existential security" effects, such that (re)turns to religious faith occur frequently among those closest to the epicenter but not among those farther afield. Moreover, among those most directly affected, individuals who abandon religious faith report greater declines in subjective health than those who retain or (re)turn to it.[70]

Some studies provide evidence that, consistent with EES theory, it is not just aggregate wealth but equitable *distribution* of wealth that is associated with lower religiosity.[71] Frederick Solt and his colleagues go so far as to propose a "theory of relative power" in which "religion may serve as a comfort to the poor … but it is also and more importantly a means of social control for the rich."[72] They concur with Norris and Inglehart that "religiosity is much higher in the United States than in western Europe primarily because inequality is much greater."[73] As Tomas Rees concluded, "Personal insecurity is shown to be at least as important in the determination of national average religiosity as the factors that are conventionally considered important, such as wealth, urbanization, and governmental regulation of religion. … [S]ecularization is greatest among those wealthy nations who chose to spend their wealth in alleviating personal insecurity."[74]

There is, however, something of a demographic irony here: wealthy individuals and nations tend to produce fewer offspring than the poor and religious. As a result, "Rich societies are secularizing but they contain a dwindling share of the world's population; while poor societies are not secularizing and they contain a rising share of the world's population."[75]

MODERNIZATION, SECULARIZATION, AND RELIGIONIZATION

The economic and existential security thesis offers valuable insights into the likely drivers and dynamics of secularization. But with regard to the exceptional persistence of religiosity in the United States, economic insecurity is an important, but incomplete, explanation. There is more to this story, we think.

In a study of evangelical Christianity, Christian Smith critically evaluates several theoretical attempts to explain the persistent strength of religiosity in the United States, including the supply-side theory. The latter is a congenial frame within which to suggest that American evangelicalism is a religious innovation that accepts and thrives on competition and is, in fact, "actively engaged in direct struggle with pluralistic modernity."[76]

It is very likely that individualization, pluralization, relativization, and other concomitants of modernization prompt distinctly *un*secular reactions—given the right conditions—alongside any secularizing trend. This no doubt plays some part in religious revivals, resurgence, "deprivatization," and "desecularization"—or what has been called "religionization"—in many parts of the world.[77]

Smith challenges the notion that pluralism necessarily undermines religiosity, but for slightly different reasons than that proposed in constant demand/supply-side theory. He agrees with Lynn Davidman that "contrary to the assumptions of many secularization theorists, the awareness of choice does not necessarily weaken the plausibility of any religious worldview."[78] In the face of religious diversity and/or prevailing secularity, religiosity can intensify, as in the case of orthodox, fundamentalist, and evangelical forms. These can offer strong communality, "thicker" cultural experience, coherent meaning systems, and so on. Smith suggests that fundamentalisms achieve this by attempting to shut out secularity or worldview pluralism, while evangelicalism does so by engaging the wider (secularizing) social environment head-on.

American culture has been characterized by a deeply held and widely shared commitment to individualism.[79] This has produced a culture that is comparatively "loose" rather than "tight," or "thin" rather than "thick," with regard to shared folkways, obligatory behavior, moral rules and sanctions, rituals, symbols, artistic forms, and so on.[80] Individuals are accorded considerable latitude in choosing many aspects of their identities and lifestyles.

In principle, the United States has been a politically secular state. But culturally, throughout much of US history, many have looked to Christianity for a "thicker" sense of shared heritage, national ritual, and cultural coherence in addition to shared political principles. The paradox of American religiosity may be attributable to the fact that it has been, and continues to be, in religious identity and community that many people find tighter and thicker—or more coherent, communal, and dependable—cultural experiences that are absent in wider American society. This is consistent with Smith's subcultural identity thesis.

Another issue to which Christian Smith has contributed valuable insights is what may be called "intentional" secularization.

INTENTIONAL SECULARIZING FORCES

It is paradoxical that the sociology of secularization has been *so* preoccupied with structural, market, and economic factors purportedly driving secularization that deliberate efforts to promote secularity have been all but neglected as a subject of study.[81] Our ability to assess the influence of intentional secularist activity on the secularity or religiosity of individuals, institutions, and societies is even more limited than our ability to ascertain the course of secularization in general. There are several reasons for this. First, as we noted in chapter 1, the behavioral and social sciences have all but ignored secular individuals, secularist advocates, and their organizations. Second, partly as a result of this neglect, we have precious little systematic data on the size, scope, and activities of secularist individuals and organizations—even in countries where public discourse indicates they are most active. Third, there are no systematically gathered survey data whatsoever that tell us how much people in various countries—or even secular citizens—are aware of, listen to, agree with, or are influenced by secularist advocates and organizations. Anecdotal information and the continuing wholesale neglect of such questions suggest to us that the vast majority of secular individuals, regardless of country, are indifferent not only to religion but also to active secularism.[82] All we have to go on are the self-descriptions and highly unreliable claims of such individuals and organizations themselves (typically in publications or on websites), small-scale ethnographic studies, research sponsored by secularist organizations, and historical analyses of significant advocates or particular organizations.

Given the paucity of data, some have concluded that the effects of intentional secularism (apart from antireligious Communist states) are limited, yet others contend that this influence is greater than generally thought.[83] Colin Campbell documents the liberalizing role played by secularist advocates and organizations over the course of the past century in the United Kingdom, and Christian Smith points to the effects of secular(ist) professionals, educators, and opinion makers on American laws, letters, and popular culture in the late nineteenth and early twentieth centuries.[84] Such advocates and organizations have been much more a feature of Western—particularly anglophone—countries, although there are signs of increased expansion and activity in other parts of the world, such as India and Africa. We will return to this subject in chapter 10.

INGLEHART'S THEORY OF HUMAN AND SOCIETAL DEVELOPMENT

We wish to return briefly to Ronald Inglehart's work, which seems to us to offer the most compelling theory to explain secularization (and religionization) at the societal level. Over the course of four decades, Inglehart and his colleagues have outlined broad shifts in values and lifestyles across cultures, from survivalist to materialist to postmaterialist, from premodern to modern to postmodern, and from agrarian to industrial to postindustrial.[85] As Inglehart and Welzel put it, this "revised version of modernization theory . . . views the growth of human choice as the underlying theme of socioeconomic development, rising self-expression values, and the strengthening of democratic institutions."[86] We think that this view is sufficiently compelling to warrant a brief summary, for it provides a useful theoretical framework for much of what follows in the remainder of this book.

In agrarian, premodern, or preindustrial societies, the dominant focus is on material and physiological survival. In this phase, religion plays important psychological and practical roles: "In most agrarian societies, religion is an overwhelmingly important force."[87] "Culture *is* religion" because

> In the pre-industrial world, humans have little control over nature. They seek to compensate for their lack of physical control by appealing to the metaphysical powers that seem to control the world: worship is seen as a way to influence one's fate, and it is easier to accept one's helplessness if one knows the outcome is in the hands of an omnipotent being whose benevolence can be won by following rigid and predictable rules of conduct.[88]

In the modern, materialist, or industrialist phase, there is a shift toward economic growth and material well-being as societies grow larger and more complex. At this stage of development, religions may persist, grow in scope and complexity, and serve to reinforce "traditional" values and worldviews that increasingly reflect and reinforce the "rationalization" of industrial production and economic exchange. As material well-being and institutional specialization grow, the need for the psychological and tangible forms of support offered by religion wanes. This said,

> industrialization does not increase peoples' sense of individual autonomy because of the disciplined and regimented way in which industrial societies

are organized. . . . Life in industrial society is as standardized as its uniform mass products. The disciplined organization of uniform masses in industrial societies creates a need for rigid codes of conduct. Although it tends to replace religious dogmas with secular ones, industrialization does not emancipate people from authority. The industrial standardization of life discourages self-expression values.[89]

It is in the postmaterialist/postmodern/postindustrial phase of societal development that self-expression values fully emerge:

> Post-industrialization brings ever more favorable existential conditions than industrialization, making people economically more secure, intellectually more autonomous, and socially more independent than ever. This emancipation process gives people a fundamental sense of human autonomy, leading them to give a higher priority to freedom of choice and making them less inclined to accept authority and dogmatic truths. The shift from traditional to secular-rational values linked with industrialization brings a secularization of authority. But the shift from survival to self-expression values linked with post-industrialization brings emancipation from authority.[90]

In other words, a broadly "secular" trend in human development is one component of individualization. Increased personal choice and autonomy vis-à-vis other individuals, institutions, societal authority, and cultural tradition tend to give rise to secularization. But, paradoxically, they may also give rise to individualized forms of spirituality and personalized religiosity. In the absence of overarching mantles of tradition or "sacred canopies," people seek and create fulfillment, purpose, meaning, and wholeness in many ways.[91] As Inglehart and Welzel indicate:

> Although the traditional churches (like most bureaucratic organizations from labor unions to political parties) continue to lose members in post-industrial societies, we find no evidence that spiritual concerns, broadly understood, are losing ground. . . . Religion does not vanish. What we observe is a transformation of religious function, from institutionalized forms of dogmatic religiosity that provide absolute codes of conduct in an unsecure world to individualized spiritual concerns that serve the need for meaning and purpose in societies where virtually no one starves to death.[92]

In this way, Inglehart and his colleagues provide an evidence-based account of human development at the societal, institutional, and individual levels that integrates elements of "classical" secularization theorists with those who have stressed the persistence of religious and "spiritual" forms of thought, behavior, and association, and even with some of the points made by modernization-secularization theory's harshest critics. Both secularization and religionization are aspects of a very broad trajectory. The part played by religious ideas and institutions is but one aspect of a multidimensional process. At the heart of this process is the individualization of choice and expression in everything from the formation of worldviews and lifeways to economic behavior to social relations to institutional and organizational participation.[93]

As all these theorists have emphasized, this trajectory is not neatly linear or universal. The broad tendency—from religiously aided survivalism to religious institutionalization to religious or secular individualization—is subject to interactions with cultural heritage, history, and economic conditions, resulting in distinctive local pathways, processes, developmental paces, and outcomes. Moreover, as Ulrich Beck and Elizabeth Beck-Gernsheim have pointed out, greater personal choice brings new challenges and risks. Individualization brings both creative exhilaration and existential "precariousness." Each individual becomes increasingly responsible for choosing every aspect of her "biography"—of creating her own unique social world and "successfully" negotiating her way through a seemingly infinite welter of choices in the marketplace—even as she becomes more dependent upon society for economic sustenance. Each individual becomes an increasingly autonomous agent responsible for finding her own social and existential niche and developing her distinctive offering in the marketplace. The individual becomes engineer, manufacturer, and marketer of the self-as-product. But by this token,

> the do-it-yourself biography is always a "risk biography," indeed a "tightrope biography," a state of permanent (partly overt, partly concealed) endangerment. The façade of prosperity, consumption, glitter can often mask the nearby precipice. The wrong choice of career or just the wrong field, compounded by the downward spiral of private misfortune, divorce, illness, the repossessed home—all this is merely called bad luck.... [T]he do-it-yourself biography can swiftly become the breakdown biography.[94]

This helps to explain persistent or renewed strength of religiosity, especially conservative and fundamentalist forms, in some places. Authoritative endorsement of firm or absolute rules, requirements, and roles (be these moral, marital, familial, economic, sexual/gender, existential, or sociopolitical) may appeal to individuals for whom the choices and autonomy presented by secular modernity are experienced more as threats than as opportunities. Thus, increasing material security, autonomy, and personal choice spur *both* secularity *and* religiosity to varying degrees and in different ways depending on local historical, political, economic, and cultural experience.[95]

Inglehart and his colleagues have presented a model of human development that is hopefully humanistic and optimistic in tone. But as they acknowledge, the issues they have raised, and the trajectory they chart, touch upon a debate that is as old as political and social theory itself. This concerns longstanding fears of the "corrosive consequences" of individualization and individualism—of the loss or absence of religion and other forces of authority, continuity, behavioral constraint, and stability. Fears about such "corrosive consequences have a long history." There has been among many observers "a widespread fear that self-expression values are inherently egocentric and tend to destroy the community bonds that democracies need in order to flourish."[96]

Such fears inform Edmund Burke's "conservative" and critical reaction to the chaos of the French Revolution, Alexis de Tocqueville's prescription of religion as a necessary constraint and counterbalance to the potentially disintegrative and egoistic tendencies of (American) democracy, Émile Durkheim's concern that the waning of traditional (e.g., religious) moral constraints without equally compelling secular substitutes would yield *anomie,* and Robert Putnam's documentation of the erosion of social capital, among many others. As Eric Klinenberg observed, "Concerns about various forms of alienation and social fragmentation are . . . hallmarks of modern culture."[97]

Inglehart, Welzel, and others observe, however, that secular individualism is not *necessarily* selfish, uncivic, anomic, or societally erosive.[98] It *can* be—and we would be wise to remain vigilant about this potential. But there is also evidence that it may yield new patterns of association, social engagement, social capital, and civic morality.[99] The distinctive properties of secular individualism can be channeled into society-building activity. Human beings remain social beings, but increasingly by choice rather than in conformance with traditional cultural or religious heritage and authority. Social formations and structures become more flexible or fluid. This may make the social scientist's task more difficult as the comparatively more stable or "rigid" social structures of the past become less formal, structured, stable, coherent, or influential.

Robert Wuthnow cautions that we should not "conclude too readily that civic involvement has been declining as uniformly or as dramatically as some have suggested."[100] Traditional social institutions may become more "porous" and "permeable," but "today's loose connections" are nonetheless "real and substantial."[101] Interpersonal and institutional commitments may become more scattered and less formal or enduring in some respects, but they may also be quite focused, thoughtful, energetic, and productive by virtue of the fact that they are elective rather than expected, chosen rather than coerced. While people may increasingly elect to exercise greater personal control over their social environments and lifestyles by, for example, living alone, there is evidence that this can produce stronger rather than weaker levels of social engagement and "capital."[102]

We are not about to resolve this debate—or even attempt such a resolution—here and now. Our aim at this juncture is merely to lay out the issues and suggest that the reader remain alert to them in the chapters that follow. We will revisit the question at the conclusion of the book, having had the benefit of substantial empirical data that have both a direct and an indirect bearing on it—particularly with respect to the question of how secularity may play a part in such developments.

CONCLUSION

The question of whether humanity is becoming less religious or more secular and, if so, how, why, and to what extent, is so complex that a wide range of assumptions, assertions, expectations, and conclusions—many contradictory—have been sustained. There are, however, some broad and noteworthy tendencies.

With greater material and existential security seems to come greater personal autonomy, individualization of worldviews, and concomitant weakening of religiosity. Despite this general tendency, higher birth rates among the more religious mean that the world is currently becoming more religious overall. These tendencies, however, are unevenly distributed around the world. Opportunities for greater self-determination in worldviews and ways of life are mediated by cultural heritage, historical memory, political structure, population makeup, and many other "local" factors. There are diverse reactions to the opportunities and challenges presented by technological and economic development, as well as increasing societal scale and complexity. Some of these reactions are insistently, institutionally, nationalistically, subculturally, individualistically, or syncretically religious. This, in turn, stimulates more ardent secularist advocacy in many places.

The net result, at least at present, seems to be a "marketplace" of worldviews spread all across the religious-secular continuum. Even as the world is becoming more homogeneous in some respects, it remains insistently diverse in others. In some places, religion is weakening (as in parts of Europe). In others it is reassertive (the Islamic world), persistent (the United States and Latin America), or ascendant (sub-Saharan Africa). There is ample evidence to support grand theories of both secularization and religious growth. "Modernity" is giving rise to greater complexity, for human activity is continually changing form and direction in defiance of our theories.

This chapter has sought to lay out, and extrapolate from, the main theories that help us understand how and why certain societies, or certain segments of societies, may become more secular over time. But once they do become predominantly secular, what are they like? In the next chapter, we will look at the degree to which strongly secular societies tend to exhibit some of highest degrees of societal health and well-being.

4

SECULARITY AND SOCIETY

WHEN I (PHIL) was in my twenties, I went backpacking through Europe. This was in the 1990s. At one point on, I made my way up to Scotland, where I stayed for a few days in a pension in the town of Oban. I went to Oban because a Scottish friend of mine, Nigel, was going to be there as well. Nigel was camping on the outskirts of town with a group of his old schoolmates. On the day of my arrival, they invited me to join them later in the evening for some beers. I was more than happy to accept their invitation.

"Where shall we meet?" I asked.
"At the church," they replied.
"The church?"
"Yeah, the big church. Right in the middle of the center of town. You can't miss
    it. See you tonight!"

I wasn't quite sure why we would be meeting at a church. I had never started out a night of drinking at a house of worship. Was it some sort of Scottish ritual: to repent for one's sins of alcoholic indulgence before committing them? Or was the church simply an easy, centrally located landmark? I decided that the latter must be the case; we'd probably be going to many pubs over the course of the evening, so best just to first meet at an easy-to-find building: the big church in the center of town.

So that night I walked from my pension into the city center of Oban. I got to the main square. And there it was: the big, old church. Massive. Imposing. Austere.

I sauntered up the stone steps and stood in front of the thick doors, waiting for Nigel and his friends. They soon arrived, and then directly into the church we went. And the moment we stepped inside, I realized that my two speculations about meeting at the church had both been off the mark.

We had met at the church because we would be staying and drinking at the church. Partying, dancing, and laughing—all inside the church. But the church was actually no longer a church. Not inside. It had been gutted a few years earlier and turned into a large pub. There were two bars on opposite ends of the interior, plenty of long tables and benches, a Celtic-funk band in one corner, hip modern chandeliers drooping from the rafters, lots of happy people, and, well, we stayed in that church until the wee hours of the night.

The fate of this old Scottish church is not totally out of the ordinary. Over the last few decades, many churches throughout Scotland—and throughout wider Great Britain—have met a similarly secularized fate. With church attendance dwindling dramatically in Britain, many church buildings have been sold and converted into pubs, discos, laundromats, carpet stores, and apartment complexes. Although many people in Britain still identify as "Christian" in a distinctly cultural sense—invoking heritage, custom, and national identity—the fact remains that, according to eminent sociologist Steve Bruce, contemporary Britain "is one of the most secular countries in the world."[1]

The evidence of this widespread withering of religion is abundant. The title of historian Callum Brown's book *The Death of Christian Britain* says it all. According to Brown, "A formerly religious people have entirely forsaken organized Christianity in a sudden plunge into a truly secular condition."[2]

As evidence of the secularization of Britain, consider the following:

- In the 1930s, about 17 percent of Scots said that they never attended church; today, nearly 60 percent claim to never attend church.[3]
- In the 1960s, the majority of marriages in Scotland took place within the Church of Scotland, but today only 19 percent of marriages do, and three out of five wedding ceremonies are nonreligious.[4]
- In the late nineteenth century, approximately 60 percent of British adults attended church on any given Sunday, but today, fewer than 10 percent do.[5]
- In the 1930s, about three-fourths of English children were baptized, but by 2006, only 14 percent of English children were.[6]
- In 1900, only 15 percent of English weddings were civil/secular (performed by a nonreligious officiant in a nonreligious setting), but by 2006, more than two-thirds of all English weddings were civil/secular.[7]
- In 1900, 55 percent of British children regularly attended Sunday school, but as of 2002, only 4 percent do.[8] In the 1950s, only 2 percent of British adults

said that they did not believe in God, but that figure was up to 27 percent in the 1990s.[9] According to a 2008 study, 37 percent of British adults said that they either did not believe in God or thought God's existence was impossible to make judgments about either way.[10]

• Today, more than half of all people in Scotland claim to have no religion.[11]

These trends show no sign of abating. Thus, in the words of David Voas and Siobhan McAndrew, "British society is becoming progressively more secular as each generation emerges and remains less religious than the one before."[12]

SECULARIZED SOCIETIES

The point of all this is to illustrate that Phil's personal experience in Oban is indicative of just how strongly secularity has emerged in certain societies. The fact is, many other countries have experienced a trajectory of secularization similar to that of Scotland over the last hundred years. While the populations of most nations on earth are quite religious, a growing number of nations now contain large proportions of their population that are secular. In these societies, religion has little impact on personal, social, family, recreational, political, or economic life; religious rituals and holidays either are losing popularity or are far more cultural than spiritual in practice—done for tradition's sake, not for the sake of one's soul; and a significant percentage of the population lacks a belief in God or anything supernatural. This situation is—historically speaking—relatively new. While there have always been secular individuals of varying stripes throughout history, here and there, even thousands of years ago,[13] never before have we seen secularity so widespread, and never before have we seen such huge chunks of whole societies that can be characterized as largely secular.

Thus, for the first time in history, there are some societies where millions of people live their lives without religion, and even some where secularity is more widespread, mainstream, and normative than religiosity.

What are such strongly secular societies like? And how do they compare to strongly religious societies?

METHODOLOGICAL COMPLICATIONS

Before answering such questions, a quick discussion of methodology is necessary. As already broached in chapter 2, determining just how many secular people there are in the world is no easy feat, and neither is determining just how secular a given society is. There are many quandaries that attend any attempt to objectively and accurately ascertain such information.

To begin with, there is the problem of how to even define secularity/religiosity within a given society. The nuanced, socially constructed, and historically rooted meanings of both "religious" and "secular" vary greatly from society to society, and there really is no single, universally standard way to characterize, let alone measure, either of them.[14]

Is it all simply a matter of belief in God, or the lack thereof? For instance, if the majority of people in a given country do not believe in God—as is the case in Estonia—does that mean it is a secular society? But what about other super-natural beliefs, such as beliefs in spirits, jinn, ancestors, or ghosts—how might they factor into our assessment? Or maybe the degree of religiosity/secularity in a given society is less about belief in God, and more about participation in reli-gious rituals and/or holidays. If this is the case, then if a majority of people in a given country celebrate Christmas—as is the case in Canada—does that mean it is a religious society? What if the celebration of that holiday is devoid of any supernatural content? And what about the matter of self-identification—that is, how people label themselves? If a majority of citizens in a given country identify themselves as "nonreligious"—as is the case in Japan—does that mean it is a secu-lar society? Maybe, maybe not. For example, what if we find a society that is low in theism but high in participation in religious rituals—or the reverse? Or what if we find a society that is high in religious self-identification (e.g., a majority of its citizens claim to be "religious" or "Christian" or "Buddhist") and yet members of this society simultaneously don't hold supernatural beliefs and rarely participate in religious rituals? Is such a society to be deemed secular or religious? And who's to say? Or what if a society is officially, constitutionally secular, but the majority of its citizens are very religious in terms of both belief and practice, as is the situ-ation in Turkey?

These questions all point to the obvious main question: By what indicators or measures do we designate a society secular or religious?

SOMETHING AMBIGUOUS IN THE STATE OF DENMARK

One in-depth example will illustrate the briar patch a social scientist faces in deter-mining whether or not a given society is secular. Consider the case of Denmark. On the one hand, the majority of Danes self-identify as Christian and are taxpaying members of the National Church of Denmark. So Denmark could be considered a religious society, right? Not so fast. Yes, a majority of Danes may identify as "Christian"—but what does that designation mean to them, actually? Rarely does it mean that they believe in Jesus Christ as their savior, nor does it usually mean that they believe that Jesus was the son of God, or that he died and was resurrected. In fact, the vast majority of Danes *don't* believe such things. Rather, for most Danes, being Christian simply means "being a good person and treating others well." Or for many other Danes, identifying as Christian serves as a de facto ethnic-national marker, indicating allegiance to Danish heritage and culture—as opposed to being a Muslim immigrant, for example. But it generally does not mean anything spiritual or theological. And although the majority of Danes are taxpaying members of the national church, very few ever actually *go* to church. In fact, Denmark exhibits the lowest rate of church attendance in the world, with less than 7 percent of the population attending church on a weekly basis. So in terms of nominal membership, Danes appear to be religious, but in terms of actual church attendance, they are remarkably secular. What about theism? When Danes are asked whether they believe in God, a majority will say yes.[15] But extensive fieldwork and in-depth interviews further reveal that many, if not most Danes—even when they say "yes" to belief in God—are actually much more passively deistic or even agnostic in orientation, rather than typically theistic in an American Christian sense.[16] That is, they may say "yes" to belief in God, but their image, understanding, or construction of God is extremely nontraditional, amorphous, and downright inchoate. Furthermore, when Danes are asked, "How important is God in your life?," only 21 percent say "very"— and this is among the lowest rate of people declaring the importance of God in their life in the world.[17] So what are we to make of theism in Denmark? It's hard to say. A case could readily be made that it is prevalent, while another equally strong case could simultaneously be made that it is anemic.

The secular/religious situation of Denmark is clearly unique—but so is every other nation's secular/religious identity. That's the soup we're in.

CHARACTERISTICS OF SECULAR SOCIETIES

While acknowledging the methodological challenges sketched here, we still *can* make relatively reliable estimates concerning the secularity of given societies. These estimates are not airtight or unassailable, but they are the best we can do as we try to discern and make sense of broad patterns concerning the prevalence of secularity in the contemporary world, and how that secularity affects, influences, or interacts with various aspects of society. Thus, based on national and international surveys with random samples and acceptable response rates, as well as rich ethnographic/

qualitative research from within various societies, we can readily identify some of the most secular societies on earth today, because these societies generally share the following characteristics or traits:

- *Separation of church and state*: governmental powers are decidedly secular and not beholden to religious authorities in most areas of governance; religion is not a legally prominent, institutionally privileged, or authoritatively hegemonic pillar of the political landscape.
- *Secular self-identification*: a majority of the members of the society do not consider themselves religious, nor do they consider religious faith or participation a strong or significant aspect of their personal identity.
- *Weak theism*: belief in God is lower or weaker than in most other countries in the world, with significant swaths of the population being atheistic or agnostic in orientation.
- *Low levels of religious belief*: only a minority of people hold religious or spiritual beliefs concerning such things as life after death, miracles, the efficacy of prayer, the divinity of Jesus, the supernatural feats of Muhammad, the existence of spirits, devils, or angels, and so forth.
- *Low rates of religious participation*: only a minority of people attend religious worship services on a regular basis or are active in religious congregations.
- *Low rates of religious ritual observance*: only a minority of people engage in religious rites and rituals.

Of course, not every relatively or even highly secularized society exhibits every single characteristic listed here. But they all exhibit most, to varying degrees.

Given these criteria, and drawing on the best available data, we can estimate that the most secular nations on earth today—that is, those countries with the highest levels of atheism and agnosticism among their populations, and the concomitant lowest levels of religious participation and identification—are the Czech Republic, Estonia, Sweden, Denmark, Norway, Finland, China, South Korea, France, Vietnam, Russia, Bulgaria, Japan, the Netherlands, Slovenia, Germany, Hungary, Great Britain, New Zealand, Canada, Australia, Belgium, and Latvia.

SOCIETAL HEALTH AND WELL-BEING

So, when we look at that list of nations, we can ask: How are they faring? According to certain traditional views, they shouldn't be faring well. After all, it has long been postulated by various pundits, politicians, and philosophers that religion is a uniquely necessary ingredient for a healthy, successful, and well-functioning society, and that without religion, society is doomed.

For example, in his classic *Democracy in America*, Alexis de Tocqueville argued that religious faith is "indispensable" for a well-functioning society, that irreligion is a "dangerous" and "pernicious" threat to societal well-being, and that nonbelievers are to be regarded as "natural enemies" of social harmony.[18] Even Voltaire, the celebrated Enlightenment philosopher who was highly critical of the Catholic Church, nonetheless maintained that without a widespread faith in God, society could not function properly, and thus people must have "profoundly engraved on their minds the idea of a Supreme being and creator" in order to maintain a moral social order.[19]

Contemporary articulations of such sentiments abound. For example, former Republican congressional leader Newt Gingrich argues that a secular society would be hellish, riddled with all kinds of social problems.[20] Secularism, according to Gingrich, is as dangerous to society as Nazism.[21] Pundit Bill O'Reilly has similarly asserted that a society without religion would inevitably be anarchic, chaotic, weak, and lawless.[22] And in the succinct words of syndicated radio talk-show host Dennis Prager: "No God, no moral society."[23]

However, reality paints a very different picture. By and large, the most secularized countries in the world today are in fact not bastions of depravity or immorality. In the prescient words of University of London professor Stephen Law: "If declining levels of religiosity were the main cause of . . . social ills, we should expect those countries that are now the least religious to have the greatest problems. The reverse is true."[24]

With the exceptions of China and Vietnam (both nondemocratic nations), the majority of the most secular countries in the world today are actually doing quite well. Indeed, many of them are among the most successful, healthy societies on earth. For it is generally among the most secular societies today that we find the greatest levels of social harmony, civility, freedom, equality, peacefulness, and prosperity. The greatest levels of inequality, oppression, crime, corruption, and destitution can be found in highly religious nations.

Let's consider some specific examples. Take motherhood. Which countries today are the best for mothers? Taking into account many variables (e.g., the percentage of births attended to by skilled personnel, maternity leave benefits, infant mortality rates), the nonprofit Save the Children Foundation publishes an annual "Mother's Index," which ranks the best and worst places on earth in which to be a mother. According to the foundation's ongoing reports, of the best nations on earth in which to be a mother, all are highly secular, with most being among the least theistic nations on earth. Of the worst places on earth in which to be a mother, nearly all are highly religious nations such as Yemen, Mali, Niger, Bangladesh, Uganda, Sierra Leone, Senegal, and Nigeria.

What about peacefulness? Which countries today are the most peaceful? Not the very religious ones. Rather, it is the most secular societies today that tend to enjoy the greatest levels of peace. The nonprofit organization Vision of Humanity publishes an annual "Global Peace Index," which calculates numerous variables, such as levels of safety and security in a given society, levels of violent crime, warfare, ease of access to dangerous weapons, and so forth. According to this organization's rankings, among the top ten most peaceful nations on earth, *all* are among the most secular nations in the world. Conversely, of the least peaceful nations, most of them are extremely religious, such as Sudan, the Philippines, Colombia, Zimbabwe, and Pakistan.

How about murder? Which countries have the highest and lowest murder rates? According to the United Nations 2011 *Global Study on Homicide*, those nations with the highest intentional homicide rates all are very religious, such as Colombia, Mexico, El Salvador, and Brazil. But of those at the bottom of the list—the nations with the lowest homicide rates—nearly all are very secular, with many being among the least theistic nations, such as Sweden, Japan, Norway, and the Netherlands. Additional research by criminologists such as James Fox, Jack Levin, and Oablo Fajnzylber shows that murder rates are significantly lower in the more secular nations, where atheism and agnosticism are more common, and higher in the more religious nations, where faith in God is widespread.[25] Robert Brenneman, a sociologist who studies gangs in Central America, is clear: among the most violent, brutal barrios of El Salvador, Honduras, and Guatemala, atheism and agnosticism are virtually nonexistent.[26]

In short, when we look at just about any standard measure of societal well-being—such as levels of corruption in business and government, sexually transmitted disease rates, teen pregnancy rates, literacy rates, quality of hospital care, quality of roads and highways, rates of aggravated assault, degree of freedom of speech and freedom of the press, environmental degradation, pollution, sanitation, access to clean drinking water, voter turnout, and so forth—more secular nations fare markedly better than the more religious. As Tomas James Rees sums up, "Those countries with shorter life expectancy, higher infant mortality, higher violent crime, more corruption, higher abortion rates, and less peace also tend to have higher average levels of personal religiosity."[27] And this is surely why the United Nations' Human Development Index—the most well-known multivariate index for ranking nations in terms of their overall health and well-being—consistently ranks the more secular nations higher than the more religious, year after year.

SUCCESSFUL SOCIETIES SCALE

Just to drive home the point, we can look at the work of independent scholar Gregory Paul, who has constructed a Successful Societies Scale, a thoroughly impressive multivariate index that measures societal success and overall well-being.[28] It considers a plethora of factors—including some of, but also going well beyond, those on the Human Development Index—such as life satisfaction, incarceration rates, fertility rates, alcohol consumption rates, per capita income, inequality, and employment rates, and correlates them with religiosity/secularity. Paul's findings strongly support what has been presented earlier in this chapter: aside from the important exception of suicide (religious societies have significantly lower suicide rates than more secular societies), on just about every other single measure of societal success, the nations with the highest rates of atheism, agnosticism, and religious indifference and the lowest rates of religious participation and involvement fare markedly better than those more religious nations with higher rates of religious belief and participation.

WITHIN THE UNITED STATES

Does the strong correlation of high rates of secularity with societal success and well-being that we find internationally remain equally strong when we look within our own country? Yes. For when we compare the most religious states (those with the highest rates of church attendance and belief in God) with the most secular states (those with the lowest rates of church attendance and belief in God), we find that, yet again, it is the more secular that tend to fare better, on average, and on just about every societal indicator.

According to the Pew Forum's Religious Landscape Survey, the ten most religious states are Louisiana, Arkansas, Alabama, Mississippi, Georgia, South Carolina, North Carolina, Kentucky, Tennessee, and Oklahoma (tied with Utah). The bottom ten—that is, the most secular states—are Maine, Vermont, Connecticut, New Hampshire, Rhode Island, Massachusetts, New York, Alaska, Oregon, and California.[29] Of course, the most secular states are not totally or completely secular; in all of them, a majority of residents still believes in God, and a certain percentage is religiously active, to varying degrees. But weekly church attendance rates, as well as the rates of theism, are dramatically lower than in other states. For example, 91 per-cent of people in Mississippi and 86 percent of people in South Carolina claim to believe in God "with absolute certainty," but only 54 percent of people in Vermont and 59 percent of people in Maine do so. Only 1 percent of people in Kentucky explic-itly claim to not believe in God, compared with 9 percent in Oregon. And while 52 percent of people in Alabama and 57 percent of people in Utah report attending religious services on a weekly basis, only 30 percent of people in Massachusetts and 23 percent of those in Maine do so.

As is the case when comparing countries the world over, when it comes to nearly all standard measures of societal health—such as homicide rates, violent crime rates, poverty rates, domestic abuse rates, obesity rates, educational attainment, funding for schools and hospitals, teen pregnancy rates, rates of sexually transmit-ted diseases, unemployment rates, and domestic violence—the correlation remains robust: the most secular states in America tend to fare much better than the most religious.

To take one glaring example, consider child abuse fatality rates. Perhaps there is no greater affront to a moral social order than the murder of children, especially at the hands of their caretakers. Well, on this particular indicator of societal health and well-being, we see that the rates of children being beaten to death by their own parents are markedly higher among the most religious states and significantly lower among the most secular. For example, the child-abuse fatality rate in Mississippi is twice that of New Hampshire, and Kentucky's rate is four times higher than Oregon's.[30]

As these data reveal, high levels of secularity in society do not result in communal decay or contribute to societal degradation. Conversely, high levels of faith or religi-osity don't seem to produce impressive levels of societal well-being either.

CORRELATION OR CAUSATION?

We have to be careful, of course, not to confuse correlation with causation. The pre-ceding discussion in no way proves that secularity *causes* positive societal outcomes, in and of itself. It is conceivable—if not more than likely—that the success/failure, well-being/depravity, or unhealthiness/healthiness of various societies today have little to do with the secularity/religiosity of their populations, but rather, are more likely the result of a host of various and disparate historical, political, and economic factors, perhaps related to colonialism, the exploitation of foreign labor, access to natural resources, resilience to disease, weather, and so forth.[31] Or, as a fair amount of data seems to suggest, perhaps both secularity and societal success are caused by some third variable, such as rates of educational attainment.[32] Or perhaps both levels of secularity and societal well-being are causally linked to welfare expenditures.[33] These are all interesting, plausible possibilities.

However, the correlation/causation story that appears to make the most sense—and currently has the best data to support it—comes from the work of Pippa Norris and Ronald Inglehart, discussed in chapter 3. As you will recall, Norris and Inglehart show that it is not necessarily the case that religion causes societal disarray, nor that secularity causes societal well-being. Rather, it is just the opposite. According to their analysis, in countries characterized by high degrees of societal health, where most people live relatively secure lives, having easy access to food, shelter, health-care, and education, and living peaceful, supported, and unthreatened lives, we tend to find the highest rates of secularity, atheism, agnosticism, and theistic indifference. Conversely, in those countries most beset with societal ills, we generally find the highest rates of religiosity and theism. Thus, atheism and societal well-being are indeed most likely causally linked, but it is the latter (societal well-being) that most likely causes the former (secularity), and not the other way around. Independent researcher R. Georges Delamontagne's research reveals just that: it is not a lack of secularity that causes societal dysfunction, but societal dysfunction that impedes secularity.[34]

BENEFITS OF SECULARISM TO SOCIETY

While we readily admit to all of the preceding, it would be mistaken to completely dismiss secularization as utterly inconsequential for societal progress. Secular values and secular people *have* played roles in shaping society for the better, and many successful societies today owe at least some aspects of their well-being to secularism. In many instances, secularism—being a conscious, nonspiritual, rational ideology for social betterment in the here and now—has unmistakably been a key factor spurring and advancing various forms of societal goodness and contributing to societal well-being.

One of the biggest ways in which secularism has been of direct benefit to many societies has to do with the major historical-political movement that transformed government away from divine-right monarchies to modern-day democracies. This transformation was largely spearheaded by secular philosophies and Enlightenment humanistic ideologies.[35] No society on earth today that is led by a religious dictator is faring well, and simultaneously, and the most successful societies on earth today tend to be secularized democracies. Secular ideas, secular values, and secular people have all played a decisive role in shaping this reality.

The progress in women's rights, status, and overall well-being is yet another clear societal improvement that has been specifically pushed by secular political and cultural forces. In fact, just about wherever secularism has become a strong presence in society, the health, wealth, and overall status of women have all dramatically improved.[36] Secularism has also played a key and ongoing role in the fight against caste in India.[37] It has played a leading role in the development of effective sex education.[38] And the creation of the enviably successful welfare state in Scandinavia was constructed by decidedly secular social democrats.[39]

SECULAR DICTATORSHIPS

When discussing some of the ways in which secularism has been societally beneficial, and when laying out the strong secularity/societal health correlation that we find both internationally and within the United States, we must also acknowledge a less rosy aspect of the story: all those brutal atheist regimes of the twentieth century, regimes that hardly produced models of societal goodness and well-being.

The first ever officially declared atheist nation in the world was Albania under the rule of Communist dictator Enver Hoxha (1908–1985). For several decades, atheism was brutally enforced. All religions were outlawed; religiously based city names were changed; religious names for all newborn babies were banned; religious leaders were exiled, and those who remained were imprisoned, tortured, and killed, and religious buildings were destroyed or converted to secular use.[40] Life in this officially atheist nation was downright depressing: no democracy, gross human rights violations, widespread poverty, lack of adequate health care, and more. Although literacy rates did skyrocket under Hoxha, atheist Albania was definitely not a model of societal health. It was an isolated, underdeveloped, poor nation held hostage by a paranoid, avowedly secular tyrant.

The leaders of the former Union of Soviet Socialist Republics were also flagrantly atheistic. In the late 1920s, the Communist regime of the USSR created the League of Militant Atheists, which had the explicit, state-sanctioned mandate to destroy religion, disseminate atheistic propaganda, debunk religious belief, and replace religious rituals and holidays with newly minted secular versions. Simultaneously, the Soviets attempted to eradicate religion by arresting, torturing, and killing religious leaders and closing or destroying religious buildings.[41] The USSR was ultimately a failure—economically, politically, and morally. The Soviets did not manage to establish a workers' paradise based on principles of fairness and equality. Instead, they created a totalitarian nation plagued by poverty, famines, surveillance, suspicion, gulags, and corruption.

And Cambodia in the 1970s, under the bloody and secular reign of Pol Pot—an atheist killer of grisly distinction—was a land of starvation, repression, and genocide.

Finally, there is North Korea, one of the worst nations on earth today in just about all respects—from the lack of freedom to the lack of electricity. Plagued by poverty and starvation, and characterized by the entrenched denial of basic human or civil rights, North Korea maintains a state-sanctioned and enforced atheism, with the only "religion" permissible being that of the worship of the dictator.

Clearly, atheism plus totalitarianism makes for an ugly, repressive combination. There is no question that some of the worst governments of the twentieth and twenty-first centuries have been explicitly atheistic. But perhaps atheism is not the main culprit here. Maybe totalitarianism is. After all, some of the world's most tyrannical, corrupt, and bloody regimes during the same time period have also been explicitly religious, with God-believing leaders at the helm: Idi Amin in Uganda, "Baby Doc" Duvalier in Haiti, Augusto Pinochet in Chile, the ayatollahs in Iran, Francisco Franco in Spain, Ferdinand Marcos in the Philippines, the strongly Catholic Hutus in Rwanda, and so forth.

But before going any further, we need to ask ourselves: What good is tallying up corrupt dictators and noting if they were atheistic or theistic? Does it really matter? The fact is, we find plenty of brutal tyrants in both camps. And when seeking to measure levels of societal well-being, we know that, by and large, when power is held undemocratically, the result will always be less than ideal. That is, *all* nondemocratic, tyrannical governments of the past century have been oppressive. Fascism, totalitarianism, communism—all such forms of political dominance have been based on repression. They have all hindered societal progress and curtailed societal well-being, be they theistic or atheistic in orientation. So one way to control for this factor is to simply exclude nondemocratic societies from our analysis and look only at democracies in assessing the correlation between religiosity, secularity, and social well-being. And this is exactly what Gregory S. Paul has done.[42] His research has consistently shown that the least religious democracies fare better on nearly all indicators of societal well-being.

ORGANIC VERSUS COERCIVE SECULARIZATION

When looking at examples of both well-functioning, highly secular societies such as Sweden or Japan and poorly functioning, repressive secular societies such as the former Albania or Cambodia under Pol Pot, it helps to simply recognize and understand that just as religion comes in all shapes and sizes—some vicious, others benevolent—so it goes with secularity. In some instances its presence in society can be brutal and repressive; in other instances, benign or beneficial.

It is thus essential to always differentiate between secularity that emerges organically in a free and democratic culture, and state-enforced secularism that is aggressively imposed upon a nation by totalitarian regimes. In totalitarian regimes, religion is demonized and often outlawed, believers are vilified or worse, and the whole situation is not only repressive and inhumane but generally quite untenable.[43] But in more organic secularization—and this is what we are witnessing in much of the world today—many people who are living in open, democratic societies simply stop finding religious beliefs viable or compelling; they lose interest in participating in religious congregations or rituals; and they maintain values, exhibit virtues, find meaning, and develop a sense of identity outside of the sacred canopy of religion. And as the data presented in this chapter show, this cultural, organic manifestation of secularism is not a threat to society but, rather, is highly correlated with positive societal outcomes.

While readily granting that correlation is not causation, and while soberly acknowledging that some of the worst societies in recent history have been led by atheist tyrants (as well as religious tyrants), we are still left with the undeniable reality that today, when we compare nations, as well as states within the United States, the more secular are faring qualitatively and quantitatively better than the more religious.

CONCLUSION

There have always been secular men and women throughout history, even in the most religious of cultures and eras. What is new today is that, for the first, time we have a plethora of large societies containing significant swaths of secular people. And in some cases, these secular people outnumber the religious—so that secular culture is dominant rather than marginal. From Scotland to South Korea, from the Netherlands to Japan, and from Sweden to Australia, highly secularized societies abound.

Contrary to the claims of those who insist that religion is necessary for a good society, or that secularization spells societal decay, we know that those nations that are the most secular tend to also be among the most successful. Whether this is mere correlation or not, the state of the world today allows us to reject—with a high degree of certainty—at least two widely held hypotheses: (1) that religion is a uniquely necessary ingredient for a sound, successful society, and (2) that secularism is a detrimental, destructive threat to social order. Concerning the latter hypothesis, while it is true that some aggressively atheistic regimes of the past century have committed extensive atrocities, such coercively secular states are qualitatively different from societies in which secularity emerges freely and organically. It is in just such democratic, highly secular societies that we find the greatest degrees of peacefulness and prosperity.

5

HOW AND WHY PEOPLE BECOME SECULAR

WHEN LESLIE WAS in sixth grade, in early 1980s, she had a friend named Jeremy. Leslie and Jeremy were in the same class at school, and they lived in the same neighborhood. They spent quite a few afternoons at each other's houses, eating little, prepackaged ice cream sundaes in plastic cups and listening to the soundtrack of the movie *9 to 5*. One weekend, Jeremy's family invited Leslie to a college football game: UCLA versus Stanford. During the halftime show, the Stanford marching band performed various antics on the football field, and at one point during one of the skits, the band members all stood in a certain configuration so as to spell out the words "Adam" and "Eve." The biblical reference was funny—and fittingly irreverent given the nature of the musical skit. Leslie laughed. But Jeremy didn't. He didn't understand. He turned to his dad and said, "What is Adam Eve?" Without a moment's hesitation, Jeremy's father said, "Oh, nothing, nothing." So Leslie then said to Jeremy, "You know—from the Bible." Jeremy nodded, but Leslie could tell he had no idea who or what Adam and Eve were. She was surprised and actually quite puzzled. How could he not know about Adam and Eve? Many years later, as an adult, Leslie ran into Jeremy's father. She told him that she always remembered that time at the UCLA-Stanford game when Jeremy asked about Adam and Eve. Jeremy's dad nodded knowingly and said, "My wife and I made a very intentional decision that we would raise our children without any religion." Leslie reconnected with Jeremy on Facebook a few years ago, and as she fully expected, he is secular. His parents' decision to raise him as a nonreligious person worked. It almost always does.

SECULAR SOCIALIZATION

The overwhelming majority of religious people were raised that way. Indeed, this is one of the precious few things that sociologists of religion know for sure: children generally soak up and internalize the religiosity of those who raise them. As Rodney Stark and Roger Finke have posited, "Most people remain within the religious organizations into which they were born," and "children usually adhere to the faith of their parents and relatives."[1] A leading expert on religious socialization, Darren Sherkat, has similarly concluded that when it comes to the shaping of religious beliefs and religious organizational attachments, "parental influences dominate," and "the family remains the primary influence on religious preferences and choices."[2] For at least seventy-five years, social scientists have observed the unparalleled power of religious socialization, documenting in a plethora of studies the degree to which the religiosity of children is strongly determined by the manner in which they are raised.[3]

It should then come as no surprise that socialization also accounts for why many people are secular: they were simply raised that way. They were reared, loved, fed, disciplined, encouraged, supported, and nurtured by parents who were either nonchalantly secular or actively, affirmatively irreligious. And when children are raised in such families, they tend to remain secular as they grow into adults.[4] Various studies have documented this phenomenon. For example, according to Joseph Baker and Buster Smith's analysis, of those Americans born after 1970 who were socialized secular, over 70% remained nonreligious as adults.[5] And in his multigenerational study of religion and family across generations, Vern Bengtson found that approximately six out of ten nonreligious adults come from families where their parents were also nonreligious.[6]

Stephen Merino found, in his longitudinal analysis of religiosity/secularity in the United States, that "those with religiously unaffiliated parents as children are significantly less likely to express a religious preference as adults."[7] These recent studies bolster what Hart Nelsen observed back in the 1980s: that the secularity of parents has a strongly determining influence on their children. According to Nelsen's analysis—among American families in the 1980s—if the father was secular but the mother was religious, then about one-sixth of the children of such unions grew up to become secular. If the mother was secular but the father was religious, then about half of such children grew up to be secular. And if *both* parents were secular, then about 85 percent of such children grew up to be secular themselves.[8] As sociologist Steve Bruce concludes, "If you did not learn a faith from your parents, you are unlikely to acquire one later in life."[9] According to

Bruce, if someone was not raised in a particularly religious home, the chances of such a person becoming religious later in life are remarkably low. How low? "About 5%."[10]

Studies conducted outside of the United States further confirm just how durable secular socialization can be. For example, in their study of Canadian college students, Bob Altemeyer and Bruce Hunsberger found that people who are brought up in secular households and then end up being religious are extremely rare; in their sample, less than 1 percent of people raised without any religion ended up as confirmed religious believers later in life.[11] Steve Bruce and Tony Glendinning found that children in the United Kingdom raised without religion almost never grow up to become religious themselves,[12] and according to David Voas, less than 10 percent of Scottish children raised without religion went on to become religious as adults.[13] All of this supports the frank words of social psychologist Bob Altemeyer: "If you (correctly) believe that very religious offspring tend to come from very religious upbringings, you can see why a nonreligious background can lead to nonbelief. Socialization usually works."[14]

So socialization definitely helps explain why many people are secular. But we must remember that—in most countries, and especially in the United States—only a small proportion of families are secular. That means that only a distinct minority of secular people were initially raised as such. Indeed, of Americans born between the years 1925 and 1943, less than 4 percent were raised with no religion; of those born between the years 1956 and 1970, 7 percent were raised with no religion; and of those Americans born between 1971 and 1992, almost 11 percent were raised that way.[15] So while their numbers are clearly on the rise, secular families are still a clear minority. And this means that, since most American children have been raised with some kind of religion, then those who today identify as secular or "none" in America were, much more often than not, brought up in a religious tradition.[16] Thus, socialization does not explain how or why most of the people who currently identify as secular got to be that way.

For example, people like Zayneb. She is now secular, but she wasn't always. For most of her life, Zayneb was a devout Muslim. While she was growing up, her parents taught her to earnestly believe the teachings of Islam and to dutifully recite the Qu'ran. And it took; she was a true believer and a pious Muslim for many years. She felt good wearing gender-appropriate attire and covering her hair, and she routinely prayed to Allah for strength, comfort, and guidance. Although raised in Orange County, California, Zayneb lived within a small subculture of immigrants originally from Pakistan and Islam permeated nearly every aspect of her life: it undergirded various holidays such as Ramadan, it affected what foods she could and could not eat, it set certain parameters concerning who she felt comfortable socializing with, and it created a strong sense of community and identity.

However, by the time Zayneb was in her early twenties, she was an atheist. Today, she considers herself an "ex-Muslim." What happened?

My mom passed away very suddenly from pneumonia. I was a junior in college. It just kind of happened suddenly. She got sick all of a sudden so we took her to the hospital and she was there for six weeks. And then she passed away, and right after she passed away I did a lot of prayers. . . . I thought I should pray, because everybody's telling me to pray. I did it for maybe a week and then I kind of just prayed at night, just hoping that she's safe in heaven. Then all of a sudden, I don't know why, but I was just like: I don't feel anything. I don't feel that she went anywhere. I thought that my prayers were useless—I'm just wasting my time. And I remember that all my questions about heaven and the afterlife and everything when I was younger just were unanswered. At that moment, maybe over the span of three months, I all of a sudden let go of religion. I guess my brother did too, because we talked about it later, maybe that summer. We both just kind of asked each other if we believe in Allah anymore and we said no we don't believe in religion and Allah. Because I just didn't feel anything, you know. I didn't believe that she went anywhere else. I think the belief in an afterlife is central to religion, and that part I just didn't feel it and I didn't believe in it, so I let go of religion. I think, slowly, I would have still started kind of moving away from it just because there were so many unanswered questions. I wouldn't understand why, if there was a God, why there would be so much suffering among the most innocent and the poorest people, you know?

So, for Zayneb, becoming secular was something that occurred as a development, shift, or change—rather than something that she had been all her life. Zayneb is thus what is generally referred to as an "apostate." This term is not without its problems; some might feel that it has a pejorative ring to it, or that it is biased because it has traditionally been employed by religious authorities to stigmatize those who have strayed, and are thus no longer in good standing within a given religious group.[17] Given such concerns, perhaps the terms "exiter," "disaffiliate," "disidentifier," or "religious leave-taker" are more objective or carry less baggage. But those terms are rarely used in most relevant studies. Because the term "apostate" is most widely known and much more frequently employed in the social sciences,[18] we will stick with that here.

APOSTASY

David Caplovitz and Fred Sherrow define apostasy as "the relinquishing of a set of religious beliefs,"[19] but they further add that apostasy not only involves a loss of faith but also often entails a rejection of a particular community that previously provided a sense of identity and belonging. Benjamin Beit-Hallahmi defines apostasy as "disaffection, defection, alienation, disengagement, and disaffiliation from a religious group."[20] David Bromley defines apostates as "individuals who once held a religious identity but no longer do so."[21]

In essence, if secularization can be understood as the diminishing or weakening of religion at the macro-societal level, taking place over the course of many decades or even centuries, then apostasy can be understood as the loss of religion that occurs at the micro-individual level, in the course of an individual's lifetime.[22] Or, as Beit-Hallahmi and Argyle have put it, apostasy can be understood as "a private secularization."[23]

Given that apostasy comes in various shades and shapes—and given that it can be the result of a variety of dynamics—several typologies of apostasy have been constructed over the years. For example, Armand Mauss has put forth a three-type classification, based on the reasons underlying individuals' withdrawal from religion: intellectual apostasy (i.e., people just don't believe anymore); social apostasy (i.e., a disintegration of social bonds with coreligionists or the formation of social ties outside one's religious community); and emotional apostasy (i.e., one has psychological reactions to perceived church hypocrisy, or one comes to apostasy as an outgrowth of an unhappy family life).[24] Merlin Brinkerhoff and Kathryn Burke offer another three-type classification: "ritualists," who have lost some or all of their religious beliefs but continue to identify with a religious community and participate in various ceremonies and rituals; "outsiders," who maintain clear religious beliefs but no longer identify with a religious community and don't participate in its activities; and finally "true apostates," who have both lost their religious beliefs and become totally disaffiliated with a religious community.[25] Kirk Hadaway has labeled five types of apostates: "successful swinging singles" (single young adults experiencing social or financial success); "sidetracked singles" (pessimistic single adults who are not experiencing "the good life"); "young settled liberals" (adults who have a positive outlook on life but are dissatisfied with traditional values); "young libertarians" (people who reject religious labels but not necessarily religious beliefs); and finally "irreligious traditionalists" (older, conservative, married people who maintain some religious moral traditions despite their nonattendance and nonaffiliation).[26]

More recently, Phil Zuckerman has distinguished "early apostasy" from "late apostasy";[27] the former refers to individuals who were raised in a religious home but then went on to reject their religion as soon as they became teenagers or young adults, while the latter refers to individuals who drop or abandon their religion much later in life. Of the two, early apostasy is much more common; the majority of apostates leave their religion in their late teens or early twenties.[28] For example, in two separate studies, both David Roozen and Everett Perry found that "maturational" processes often correspond with the timing of apostasy, and that many people stop being religious once they are no longer under the direct auspices and/or influence of their parents.[29] In a study of American Catholics, Dean Hoge found that of those who leave the religion, most do so between the ages of sixteen and twenty-five.[30] And in a study of affiliates of secular-humanistic groups in the Pacific Northwest, Frank Pasquale similarly found that the majority of people knew they were nonreligious by the time they were twenty-two, and 25 percent of them knew they were nonreligious in their teenage years.[31] Research on apostasy from the United Kingdom reveals similar conclusions: the late teenage years are, without question, the ripest period for the rejection of religion.[32]

Zuckerman additionally distinguishes between "shallow" and "deep" apostasy. The former refers to the phenomenon of people rejecting their religion but still considering themselves strongly spiritual, or at least not wholly or completely secular. The latter refers to individuals whose break from religion is total and absolute; they no longer consider themselves religious in any way, shape, or form. Nor do they consider themselves even spiritual. They are avowed nonbelievers and are totally uninterested in participating in anything religious.

Finally, Zuckerman distinguishes "mild" apostasy from "transformative" apostasy. The former refers to individuals who rejected their religion but were not all that religious in the first place, so letting it go entailed few personal life consequences, little social disruption, and no real psychological turmoil. The latter refers to individuals who were deeply, strongly religious before they rejected their religion. For such people, apostasy is a true personal revolution, a life-altering transformation. It not only involves a massive psychological reorientation from a religious worldview to a secular worldview but also often entails a loss of close friendships, alienation from a strong community, and even rejection by one's family. Indeed, Simon Cottee's study of Muslims living in the West who reject their Islamic faith is replete with harrowing accounts of apostates being castigated, condemned, and even disowned by their families.[33]

PREVIOUS RESEARCH ON APOSTASY

What do we know about contemporary apostasy? More specifically, who is most likely to become an apostate? Various social scientific studies conducted over the previous fifty years offer some clues, for instance:[34]

- Apostates are generally more likely than nonapostates to have higher educational attainment and higher grade point averages, to be "very bright," and to self-identify as intellectuals.
- Apostates are much more likely to be liberal, progressive, or left-leaning politically than their religious peers.
- Men are more likely to become apostates than women.
- Jews are more likely to become apostates than Protestants and Catholics.
- Students who describe their relationship with their parents as "poor" have higher rates of apostasy than students who describe their relationship with their parents as "good."
- Apostates tend to be less conventional in their social and political outlook than nonapostates and are more likely to have smoked marijuana and to have engaged in or support sexual experimentation.
- Compared with people who remain religious, apostates are more likely to support abortion rights, welfare for the poor, and environmental protections, and they are less likely to be ethnocentric or support the death penalty.
- College-attending apostates tend to be less likely to describe themselves as happy or having high morale than religious students.

This body of research is not without its shortcomings. First off, the majority of samples were made up solely of college students. Second, many of the studies were done in the 1960s and 1970s, when society was qualitatively different in many respects, and apostasy was much rarer and more stigmatized. Third, there are a few important discrepancies/contradictions within the extant literature. For example, some studies found that apostates tend to have less positive relationships with their parents, while others found no such correlation. However, while we acknowledge these shortcomings of—and discrepancies within—the existing research on apostasy, the majority of the studies on apostasy over the decades have nonetheless identified some clear and consistent patterns: a greater tendency toward apostasy appears to be correlated with being male, intellectually oriented, and politically left-leaning. But these correlations—while sociologically significant—do not spell out the actual, specific reasons that propel given men and women to reject religion. For that, we must ask apostates themselves.

REASONS FOR REJECTING RELIGION

Why do some people reject their religion in favor of a secular worldview or identity? The reasons are, understandably, numerous. As Colin Campbell has asserted, "The factors which actually give rise to the irreligious response are likely to be as complex and diverse as the causes of religious commitment."[35]

Perhaps the most common explanation, and one consistently offered by apostates themselves, is what Zuckerman has dubbed "acquired incredulity syndrome,"[36] which refers to the process by which an individual somehow loses her faith, finding herself unable to accept or believe what her religion teaches or expects her to believe. This loss of faith is seldom sought out or actively chosen; for most apostates, it is just something that happens. As Altemeyer and Hunsberger report, most apostates "simply found it impossible to believe their religious beliefs were true . . . they could not make themselves go on believing what seemed to them false."[37]

In his book *Leaving the Fold*,[38] Edward Babinski provides a collection of personal essays written by people who were once fundamentalist Protestants but are no longer. Many of these former fundamentalists had been preachers before leaving the fold—they were true believers and active promoters of their religion. And then they let go. What many of them emphasize in their accounts is an irrepressible inability to continue to believe some of the basic teachings, creeds, and ideas of their religion. For example, some of these individuals came to find it hard to believe that we are all born sinners and that God had to have his son killed in order to save us all from everlasting torment. Others started to find specific problems with the Bible, discovering stories and passages that were factually incorrect, manifestly contradictory, or simply implausible. A good example of this latter phenomenon is Edward Babinksi himself. He started to realize that the Bible was full of errors, unsound science, and intractable contradictions, that present-day events actually *aren't* fulfilling ancient biblical prophecies, and that the biblical account of creation was baldly implausible in light of the evidence from geology and evolutionary biology. He spent many a night wondering whether his strongly held beliefs "might not be too narrow or even wholly false."[39] He concluded that it was indeed the latter, and this conclusion led him to his eventual state of agnosticism.

Ibn Warraq's *Leaving Islam: Apostates Speak Out*[40] contains numerous personal testimonies and autobiographical essays by ex-Muslims from a variety of cultures and national backgrounds. While the reasons the many individuals who contributed to the book give to explain their rejection of Islam are manifold and numerous—witnessing genocide in Bangladesh; taking issue with Muhammad's marriage to a nine-year-old girl; feeling alienated or oppressed as a female; having trouble with passages in the Qu'ran that are intolerant, hostile, or inhumane; objecting to teachings that caution against being friends with non-Muslims or suggest that nonbelievers will burn in hell—many former Muslims also stress an unavoidable inability to simply believe certain pillars of the religion that just didn't make sense to them.

In his study of Muslim apostates, Simon Cottee observed three forms of doubt that were central to his informants' decision to leave their religion: espistemological doubt (suspicion that Islam's claims about how the world is or came to be are false), moral doubt (being ethically opposed to the teachings or practices of Islam), and instrumental doubt (reservations over the practical utility of certain Islamic commands or prohibitions).[41]

Finally, in his study of secular group affiliates in the Pacific Northwest, Frank Pasquale found that, when individuals were asked what caused their loss of faith and rejection of religion, a majority cited their basic inability to continue to believe.[42] Their explanations included things like "absurdity of religious teachings," "the Bible didn't seem logical," "internal inconsistencies," and "contradictory claims." All of this lends credence to the arguments of Hood, Hill, and Spilka, who state that "cognitive factors are probably involved in apostasy to some extent, since apostates are more likely to question, doubt, and debate religious issues earlier in their lives than are nonapostates."[43]

In addition to this basic, fundamental loss of faith—this acquired incredulity—Zuckerman found, in a study based on in-depth interviews with nearly ninety American apostates from various ages, class backgrounds, religious backgrounds, and parts of the country, that several reasons for apostasy showed up again and again:[44]

Education. Increased educational attainment can make people look at the world differently, forcing them to ask questions that they had never wanted or even thought to ask, and causing them to scrutinize their own values and beliefs. The natural sciences can certainly be corrosive to religious faith—especially its fundamentalist forms—and it comes as no surprise that nearly 41 percent of American physics professors and 41 percent of American biology professors do not believe in God.[45] However, it isn't just the natural sciences that can dilute religious faith. In Zuckerman's interviews, it was often philosophy classes, religious studies classes, and the social sciences—sociology, psychology, and anthropology—that triggered doubts, eventually leading to apostasy. Various studies have confirmed the degree to which increased educational attainment can be correlated with increased secularity and apostasy.[46]

Personal Misfortune. Many people who experience loss or pain seek out religion and embrace the comfort of theism.[47] For others, however, loss, pain, and other life difficulties can cause them to question religion's utility, God's goodness, or even God's existence. The untimely death of a parent, the tragic loss of a child, a bitter divorce, or even the loss of a beloved pet can all lead people to question God. And when those who have been religious experience such difficult loss or pain, they don't understand how it could be happening to them. Their confusion is all the more confounded when their prayers go unheeded. Rather than cling to God, they feel forsaken, and can sometimes let go of God altogether.

Other Cultures, Other Religions. Moving to a new country—even if only for a short while—and being exposed to different ways of life, new values, and other ways of looking at the world can cause some people to question or doubt their own religious convictions and traditions. For others, questioning or doubting can arise in the wake of becoming acquainted with other religions. Experiencing, witnessing, or learning about other people who do things differently or believe different things can stir up a process of critical self-reflection that can potentially be corrosive to one's religious identity.

Friends, Colleagues, Lovers. If it isn't our parents who affect and influence us—as discussed earlier—then it is those people closest to us in our social world who do.[48] Many apostates cite the direct influence of a friend, colleague, lover, or spouse in significantly affecting their rejection of religion. Thus, it is often one's social intimates—through their direct argumentation or mere life example—who can spur one's eventual apostasy.

Political Disagreements. In the United States, over the past thirty-five years, an increasing number of politicians on the right have embraced a conservative Christian agenda, and more and more outspoken conservative Christians have allied themselves with the Republican Party. With an emphasis on seeking to make abortion illegal, fighting against gay rights (particularly gay marriage), supporting prayer in schools, advocating "abstinence only" sex education, opposing stem cell research, curtailing welfare spending, opposing gun control, and celebrating the war on terrorism, conservative Christians have found a warm welcome within the Republican Party, which has been clear about its openness to the conservative Christian agenda. But this has turned off a lot of people who were left-leaning or moderate politically.[49] Many American apostates cite their support of gay marriage, their opposition to the US invasion of Iraq, and their overall disagreement with the Christian Right's agenda as prompting their apostasy.

Moral Qualms. For many people, it is the perceived immorality of God that initially kindles their doubt. That is, God's apparent lack of righteousness or fairness becomes deeply problematic, triggering their personal skepticism. The fact that God punishes nonbelievers or sinners in hell for eternity strikes many as flagrantly immoral. Or they are morally troubled by the apparent reality that God is all-powerful and yet does not prevent natural disasters that kill millions, or halt diseases that cause endless suffering, or intervene in human affairs to prevent genocide or child abuse. Or they object to passages in the Bible in which God commands his people to kill others, or passages in the Qu'ran in which God seems particularly vindictive or malevolent, or passages in the Book of Mormon in which God seems unambiguously racist and sexist. Such scriptural information is hard to reconcile with a deity they want to conceive of as all-good, all-wise, and supremely moral. Doubt ensues.

Sex and Sexuality. Sex and sexuality can be contributing factors in apostasy in several ways. The first has to do with desire. Some people, as they reach their teenage years or early twenties, want to have sex, but this desire to have sex is condemned by their religion.[50] They thus feel themselves caught between what their bodies and hearts so desperately want to do, and what their minister or their God so stridently commands them *not* to do. Many people are able to successfully deny or sublimate their sexual urges. Many others secretly engage in sexual activity, while simultaneously upholding a pious front. But still others take a third route: they choose to engage in sexual activity and subsequently let their church attendance—and even their faith—dissipate.[51] Another way in which sex can contribute to apostasy has to do with guilt. Many religions spend a lot of time and energy making their adherents feel shame and guilt about sexual urges, desires, and experiences. Sex becomes heavily associated with sin, uncleanliness, and moral depravity.[52] This emotional linkage of healthy sexual desire/experience with guilt/shame can leave a bitter taste in some people's mouths as they grow older and more mature. They come to resent what they had been taught. A distancing from their religion can result, coupled with a flowering skepticism. Finally, there is the matter of homosexuality. Being gay or lesbian can definitely contribute to someone's apostasy. Within many religious circles, gays and lesbians learn early on that their sexual identity is unwelcome, unacceptable, and downright unholy. So many leave—and they go on to embrace secular values and secular worldviews that confirm and celebrate who they are. Indeed, Thomas Linneman and Margaret Clendenen report that homosexuals and bisexuals are nearly three times more likely to be atheist or agnostic than heterosexuals.[53]

Satan. Fear can be one of the most powerful motivators of human behavior. Many religions—particularly conservative or traditional versions of Christianity and Islam—contain a heavy element of fear. They teach that there is a Devil, that there are demons, and that a fiery hell awaits the disobedient. Such teachings can motivate many people to stay within their religious fold, to be faithful followers of a God they believe will protect and save them. However, some people—particularly those who had been raised in conservative Protestant denominations or strongly Catholic households—found that their fear of Satan was an ugly, damaging, and disturbing element of their life for many years. As they got older, they began to resent it, hate it, and eventually question it. At some point, they just want to get away from the source of those feelings, namely, their religion.

Malfeasance of Religious Associates. Most religious people, at one time or another, come into contact with less-than-moral people who should not, given their outward religiosity and ostensibly moral orientation, lack such integrity. Perhaps it is their fellow congregants, who act in unprincipled, deceitful, or selfish ways. Or maybe it is their priest, pastor, or minister, who does something one might describe as unethical, criminal, phony, or merely hypocritical. Such malfeasance on the part of religious leaders or coreligionists can often spur shock, resentment, and disappointment—which can, in some instances, result in apostasy. In fact, in their study of apostates, when Brinkerhoff and Mackie asked individuals what was the initial source of their doubts about religion, a significant proportion (38 percent) cited hypocrisy of fellow church members.[54]

Suffering, Cruelty, Injustice. For some individuals, witnessing or even merely learning about suffering, cruelty, or injustice in the world can trigger doubts about God's power, love, or even presence. Watching a loved one suffer for years from a degenerative disease, touring a children's hospital, working with sexually abused children or rape victims, learning about the Holocaust or Rwandan or Cambodian genocides, or the devastation of a tsunami in Thailand or an earthquake in Haiti, seeing reports of famines on television—and so on—can, for some, lead to a loss of faith and an eventual rejection of religion.

* * *

While the preceding ten factors are among the most common put forth by apostates in explaining their rejection of religion, it is important to stress that for most men and women, it is seldom only one of these factors that undergirds their apostasy. Rather, it is usually a combination of several such reasons, occurring together, in varying degrees. Consider Zayneb, whom we met earlier. While the untimely death of her mother certainly triggered her loss of faith, it is important to note that this also occurred while she was in college (increasing her education) and while she was developing friendships with non-Muslims and people from a variety of backgrounds (influence of others).

Additionally, it is important to note that rarely does apostasy occur instantaneously or quickly. While Zayneb's loss of faith took only a matter of months, and while some apostates may experience instantaneous "A-ha!" moments that quickly shatter their religiosity in favor of secularity, for most apostates, their rejection of their religion is a relatively slow process, and their eventual break with religion is a prolonged, fairly drawn-out shedding, taking place in languid but poignant increments, usually over a period of three to five years. Other researchers have confirmed this.[55] For example, Helen Ebaugh has described the doubting process that can lead to eventual exiting from religion as, more often than not, a gradual and slow development,[56] and Brinkerhoff and Burke concur, describing apostasy as a "gradual, cumulative" process.[57]

Finally, it must be acknowledged that while the explicit reasons that apostates offer in explaining their apostasy are subjectively true, they must not be mistaken for objective *causes* of apostasy, in and of themselves. That is, although the personal reasons apostates give as the underlying factors in their rejection of religion are honest and valid causes of apostasy *for them*, in the unfolding of their own individual lives, these same reasons are not necessarily things that would independently, objectively—in and of themselves—lead to apostasy for anyone or everyone. For example, most individuals who struggle with sexual desire, or who witness a natural disaster, or who are friends with someone from a different religion do not go on to become affirmatively secular. Even most gays and lesbians—many of whom certainly grow up to reject a specific religion that condemns them as sinners—will still choose to continue within their religious traditions and simply ignore or rationalize its failure to accept homosexuality. Others will go on to find an alternative religious tradition that accepts them for who they are.[58] But the point is that they don't all become godless or secular.[59] Thus, when it comes to the various subjective reasons apostates give for their rejection of religion, the best we can say is that these reasons may *increase the likelihood* of apostasy. When several of them occur simultaneously in a given person's life, they can probably become cumulatively corrosive to religious faith and identity.

Clearly, a variety of life circumstances, personal experiences, and/or social dynamics can increase the likelihood that certain individuals will go on to reject their religion. But there is no one single "thing"—be it an experience, event, or relationship—that always, in and of itself, causes apostasy. Thus, while subjective reasons for apostasy are easily discernible, objective causes are much more difficult to uncover, and perhaps impossible to prove, given the complex factors at play in any single human's life, including, but not limited to childhood experiences, socialization, physiological makeup, cultural imperatives, genetic predispositions, emotional predilections, intellectual capabilities, social circumstances, family relations, media influences, and peer-group dynamics.

BECOMING AN ATHEIST

For those apostates who go on to become avowed atheists, what is that process like? In his qualitative analysis of in-depth interviews with forty self-identified atheists living in Colorado—the majority of whom had once been religious—Jesse Smith found that the process whereby a person embraces an atheist identity consists of four main elements or stages.[60] The first refers to a basic recognition—as well as experience—of the ubiquity of theism in American culture. The "starting point," then, for most American apostates who become atheists is their own theism, which they experienced as children. They grew up believing in God, and they saw such belief all around them—exhibited by friends, relatives, and neighbors, all or most of whom seemed to be believers. However, most such apostates look back on their childhoods as a time when their theism was actually something imposed upon them, something they had no choice about. Thus, the second stage is the conscious questioning of theism. This usually tends to happen when individuals are in college, away from their families. Thus, just as Zuckerman found in his interviews with apostates discussed earlier, Smith also found that increased education—specifically, college attendance—and developing friendships with nonreligious people weakened individuals' theism and strengthened their emergent skepticism toward religion. The third stage is the period of actually rejecting theism—coming to a place where one's questioning ends, and a verdict results: there is no God. The fourth and final stage is "coming out" as an atheist—letting others know of one's loss of faith, rejection of religion, and atheism. As Smith writes: "Although an individual may think of him/herself as an atheist, acknowledging the consistency of their views with that label, it is only when this label is voluntarily applied in concrete social interaction that it takes on its full social significance."[61]

Some apostates whom Smith interviewed experienced distress in coming out as atheists, especially friction with friends and family. Altemeyer and Hunsberger also found that some apostates reported experiencing estrangement or alienation from family and friends in the wake of their rejection of religion.[62] Zuckerman's interviewees recalled similar experiences and further expressed feelings of loss in the wake of their apostasy: loss of community, loss of the surety of God's love. Yet most apostates, in all three of these studies, ultimately found their apostasy to be an overall positive experience, using words like "liberating," "feeling free," and "empowering" to describe it. A fairly typical example from Altemeyer and Hunsberger's study is Pete, aged nineteen, and a former Catholic. He told them, "I don't feel I have to believe anymore. I'm happy to have it finally out that I don't believe any more. . . . I can look inside me and find out what I want and not what people think I should want."[63]

A typical example from Zuckerman's sample of informants is Jayme, aged thirty-seven, a wife and mother of two, and a former Protestant. Here's how she describes her rejection of religion and her adoption of a secular identity:

> It was so powerfully liberating and now it feels like a fabulous loss, while at first it felt like a sad loss. . . . it was a bit frightening and a bit sad to lose something that had been such a part of my life. It also felt like a loss of something that I had going with my parents who I feel connected to and to take that stuff

away from them—that felt like a loss. . . . But it was liberating because suddenly you're not in a box of beliefs with like a finite set of rules and thoughts and expectations of who you are to be and what you are supposed to do and who you are to associate with. Yeah, if anything, you can take the best from all the religions in the world or you can take nothing and rely on whatever is internally yours of how to be a good person in the world. Suddenly—well, definitely not suddenly—but life became—living became so much more expansive after kind of suffering that loss, I'll say. So I'm glad for the loss. . . . the best thing is that you have—I have—the freedom to draw from so many different traditions and the—I think a greater ability to be accepting of people and beliefs in a way that I don't think Christians are allowed to. So, I think it gives a more open-heartedness and open-mindedness.

APOSTASY IN SOCIAL CONTEXT

The vast majority of the research summarized here—the findings from both quantitative and qualitative studies—was based upon examinations of North American individuals, some from Canada, but most from the United States. There is no question that the socioreligious culture of North America shapes and influences the ways in which religious rejection is recalled, explained, justified, and experienced by individuals within that culture.

To be sure, apostasy is a deeply psychological matter, relating to a given individual's personality, emotional disposition, neurological wiring, and more. Apostasy is also surely related to a given individual's family circumstances and relations with parents and others. But beyond these psychological, individualistic, and familial factors there undoubtedly exists a social or cultural level of influence. That is, although apostasy is a personal transformation, the culture/society in which a person lives will greatly shape his or her experience—not only of religion but of rejection of religion.

For a clear example that serves to illustrate this assertion, Zuckerman contrasted American apostates with Scandinavian apostates and found significant qualitative differences between the two.[64] One major difference has to do with the process of individuals' loss of faith and the experience of their personal rejection of religion. For Scandinavians, their experience of apostasy was no big deal. It was a relatively mild, minor, almost insignificant experience. In fact, religion was rarely something that they had outright "rejected," but more like something that they had "casually left behind." That is, for most contemporary Danes and Swedes, losing their faith in God was just something that happened almost naturally, as they grew older. Their rejection of religion was thus an almost matter-of-fact experience, about which they had little to say, and little to explain or recall. Hardly anyone could recount some dramatic moment when his or her faith was shattered. Few could recall some specific event or instance that caused them to become a nonbeliever. None could recount any negative reactions from friends or family. Instead, what they claimed, nearly to a person, was that their belief in God and interest in religion simply withered with age, undramatically, and without much to-do.

By contrast, most nonreligious Americans described their apostasy as being quite intense. It entailed a real personal struggle. It was a dramatic, transformative, life-changing experience that they recalled as being very significant and even painful. And unlike Scandinavians, Americans have a lot to say about it. They tend to talk about their loss of religious faith with great personal reflection. They recall key events, specific causes, important details, reactions of family and friends, and so forth. Furthermore, American apostates tended to be much more critical of the religion that they rejected, whereas Scandinavians did not exhibit such an orientation. For most Danish and Swedish apostates, religion was simply something quaint, benign, and uncompelling—not something to be critical of.

Thus, for most secular Americans, apostasy is a dramatic, significant personal experience, while for most secular Scandinavians, it is hardly memorable, and of little personal significance. How do we explain this discrepancy? The sociocultural context is key. First, religion is much more widespread and pervasive in the United States than it is in Scandinavia. In the United States, politicians wear their religion on their sleeves, fundamentalism is alive and well, biblical literalism is prevalent, and sports events often begin with prayers. In stark contrast, religion is relatively weak, subdued, and marginal in Scandinavia.[65] Religious fundamentalists are virtually nonexistent, religion is not trumpeted or championed by politicians, and faith in God tends to be a very personal, very quiet thing. Because religion is so widespread and overt in the United States, while it is so weak and personal in Scandinavia, this helps account for the different flavors of apostasy we find in each society. When religion is widespread in a given culture, as it is in the United States, rejecting it will be a much bigger deal in the lives of individual apostates than when religion is weak. Clearly, then, apostasy manifests itself differently in different sociocultural contexts.

A SIGNIFICANT PREDISPOSITION? GENDER AND SECULARITY

No discussion of being and/or becoming secular would be complete without some acknowledgment of the most consistent, ubiquitous finding about the nonreligious, at least demographically speaking: the fact that men are more likely than women to reject religion or be secular. Of course, this is just an average, just a correlation, but it is about as robust and universal as averages and correlations get within the social sciences. Although there are a handful of outlying exceptions[66]—for example, among certain Muslim and Jewish enclaves—in just about every study, and on nearly every measure of religiosity/secularity, and for nearly every racial, ethnic, or religious group, nationality, age range, educational level, and class standing observed, men tend to be, on average, less religious than women. In the summarizing words of Tiina Mahlamäki:

> Statistics conducted in countries all over the world, for as long as statistics on religion have been collected, confirm that women are more religious than men. This concerns every dimension of religion. Women participate in religious ceremonies more often than men; women pray more often than men; they more likely than men believe in God, a Spirit, or Life Force; they hold matters of faith and religion more important than men do. Women are more committed than men to their religious communities and are less willing to resign from them. Although older women are more religious than young ones, women of all ages are more religious than coeval men are. Women are members of both traditional religious communities and new religious movements more often than men. Young, urban men are the least religious of all groups.[67]

Contemporary survey findings back this up. The Pew Forum reports that, of Americans who claim to be religiously unaffiliated, 56 percent are male and 44 percent are female; of those who self-identify as atheist or agnostic, 64 percent are male and 36 percent are female.[68] According to the American Religious Identification (ARIS) survey, of those Americans who claim "none" as their religion, 60 percent are male and 40 percent are female;[69] of those who self-identify as atheist or agnostic, 70 percent and 75 percent are male, respectively.[70] Similar differences between men and women have been found all over the world for many decades,[71] leading Paul Sullins to acknowledge that the finding that women are more religious than men—on nearly every measure of religiosity—comes as close to a universally accepted truth as may be possible within the social sciences.

Why are men more likely to be secular than women? How do we explain such a nearly universal pattern? Possibilities abound.[72] Some of the more plausible ones include the following: (1) perhaps because men generally have more power, wealth, and agency in society than women, they have less of a need for the comfort or security that religion can provide to some people who may feel vulnerable or insecure;[73] (2) perhaps the religious realm is one of the only social spaces in which women can experience a sense of empowerment and self-actualization, whereas men have greater opportunities to experience such things more readily in various nonreligious realms;[74] (3) perhaps young boys are raised or socialized to be more "independent-thinking," distanced, or rebellious than girls, who are more often raised or socialized to be more dependent, cooperative, and relational toward others;[75] (4) perhaps men, who are far less likely than women to have responsibilities of child care and eldercare, have less of a need for the communal and social support that comes with religious involvement;[76] (5) perhaps it is the result of genetic, physiological, or bio-evolutionary factors;[77] and, related to this, (6) perhaps it is the result of innate personality differences between the sexes.[78] Most likely, it is a combination of some or all of these explanations.

CONCLUSION

As discussed in the introduction, rates of secularity have been increasing in recent decades in many societies all over the world, from Uruguay to Norway, from Canada to Japan, and from the United States to the United Kingdom. The two micro-level phenomena that undergird this macro-level secularization are secular socialization and apostasy. Children who are raised secular generally remain secular as adults. Additionally—at least in recent decades—we are seeing that many children who were raised religious go on to reject religion later in life, usually as teenagers or young adults. When such apostates remain secular, and then go on to have children of their own, we can expect rates of overall secularity to continue to rise as secular socialization takes its course.

Any understanding of cultural secularity or historical secularization must consider the underlying, micro-level, "on-the-ground" social dynamics and personal processes outlined in this chapter, and perpetually seek to account for how and why contemporary men and women choose to embrace, or simply manifest, a secular orientation and identity.

In the next chapter, we consider existing sociological and psychological data that help shed light on secular people today, specifically concerning their demographic characteristics, personality traits, and family relationships.

6

PERSONALITY, COGNITION, AND FAMILY BEHAVIOR

SECULAR PEOPLE COME in all shapes and sizes. There are secular people of every race, ethnicity, gender, personality type, sexual orientation, educational background, cognitive proclivity, income level, and marital status. There are, however, certain observable and significant correlations, averages, and patterns which indicate that some people—or some groups of people—are more likely to be secular than others. And there are certain personality traits, as well as family associations, which do seem to be more common among secular people when compared with their religious peers.

So what are secular people like, on average, when it comes to personality? And what do we know about the demographic characteristics, cognition, and family relationships of the nonreligious?

Before presenting and discussing what we know about the social and personality characteristics of secular people, it bears repeating that one pervasive problem in the literature to date has been the failure to distinguish completely nonreligious individuals from the weakly or nominally religious, the merely unaffiliated, or the "nones." As we have said, there are good reasons to believe that those who self-identify as nonreligious (e.g., atheists, agnostics, secular humanists) differ in significant ways from those who are indifferent to religion—much as the strongly devout or fundamentalist differ from the indifferent or nominally religious. Another problem in existing scholarship is the relative lack of emphasis on those raised from childhood in secular households. As discussed in the previous chapter, we know relatively more about those who grew up religious but subsequently have abandoned religion. This discrepancy exists partly because the proportion of the population with a nonreligious upbringing has historically been quite small, such that many of those who identify as nonreligious in adulthood grew up in at least nominally religious contexts. Another reason apostates have received greater scrutiny is that, because religiosity has been the norm in our society, those who have deviated from that norm have been deemed more worthy of close examination, much as the "abnormal" receive disproportionate attention in the field of psychology.

When considering the various ways in which the nonreligious are distinct, whether demographically or psychologically, it is important to keep in mind that certain variables may not necessarily reflect the absence of religiosity per se. We will discuss throughout this chapter the distinct patterns of demographics, personality, marriage, divorce, and childbearing among the nonreligious. These patterns are correlational, however, and do not necessarily mean that they are caused by (or themselves contribute to) secularity. It is possible that any given factor (e.g., personality traits) and secularity itself are both caused by yet another, more basic, underlying characteristic or some other combination of influences. Therefore, it is important to distinguish correlation from causation. However, in some cases, we have deeper knowledge that enables us to determine with more certainty why a given trait is related to secularity.

BASIC DEMOGRAPHICS: SEX, AGE, AND RACE

As discussed in the previous chapter, men are overrepresented among the nonreligious. According to large-scale surveys such as the General Social Survey, 15 percent of women versus 22 percent of men self-define as "not religious." The same figures from the World Values Survey are 21 percent and 27 percent for females and males, respectively. It is interesting that the gender gap is narrower within broader groupings such as "none" or "unaffiliated" than it is within more specifically nonreligious designations. For example, whereas approximately 60 percent of "nones" or the unaffiliated are male, more than two-thirds of those self-designating as agnostic, and more than 70 percent of those identifying as atheists or nonbelievers are male.[1] It therefore appears that the more strongly or affirmatively nonreligious a given demographic category is, the more likely it is to be disproportionately male.

Another clear demographic pattern is that the nonreligious are overrepresented among the young.[2] The religiously unaffiliated, or "nones", are the fastest-growing major religious segment; one in three "Millennials" (eighteen to twenty-nine years old) is religiously unaffiliated.[3] Historically, when assessed over the course of their life span, people typically have shown a decline in religiosity in adolescence followed by an increase during the family formation stage.[4] However, the current cohort of young adults is less likely to be affiliated or to attend religious services than earlier generations were at the same age, indicating that the current generation of young people is coming of age in a milieu in which secularity is increasingly normative.[5] This also means that much of the information in studies done even as recently as five or ten years ago may be outdated.

In addition, the proportion of those *within* the nonreligious who label themselves atheist is higher among younger people than among older ones (who are more likely to call themselves humanists).[6] That is, the average age of a self-identified humanist is older than the average age of an atheist, indicating that the younger nonreligious individuals are "trending atheist." One possible explanation for this trend is that the actual metaphysical beliefs are shifting in society to such a degree that substantial or affirmative nonreligiosity is displacing other forms of belief. There is also evidence of changing trends in nonreligious descriptors, such that "humanism" has been on the decline while "atheism" has been on the upswing, possibly encouraged by the "New Atheist" authors and movement.[7] This may also reflect a greater willingness to assert a sociopolitical identity that was previously stigmatized (i.e., atheism) rather than any shift in actual belief. The point, though, is that the things that characterize one cohort of the nonreligious, who came of age during a specific time period, may not characterize subsequent cohorts. Some notable studies of organized atheist groups, such as Hunsberger and Altemeyer's, found disproportionately older membership, but this may have had more to do with the type of person who is likely to join organized groups in general rather than something specific to atheism.[8]

Another significant demographic effect pertains to race and ethnicity. In the United States, European Americans and Asian Americans are overrepresented among the nonreligious, whereas African Americans and Hispanic Americans are underrepresented. As discussed in chapter 2, Asian American secularity may be attributable to inheritance of very different (and muted) conceptions of, approaches to, or attitudes about "religion" compared with those associated with immigrants from monotheistic cultures, most notably Euro-Christian or Muslim.

As is the case with the gender gap, the ethnic or racial gap is greater among strongly or affirmatively nonreligious groups than in broader categories, such as religious nonaffiliates. For example, around 70 percent of "nones" are white, which is proportionate to their representation in the general population, but 82 percent of affirmative atheists, agnostics, and nonbelievers are white. There is also some indication that the growth in the unaffiliated has occurred disproportionately among whites; the increase in religiously unaffiliated between 2007 and 2012 was 5 percent among whites but 2 percent among blacks.[9]

In short, demographic indicators show that the nonreligious are disproportionately young, white or Asian, and male.

EDUCATION

One of the most consistent findings in the social science literature is that secular men and women are disproportionately well-educated. Although 27 percent of the US population has a college degree, 42 percent of agnostics or those claiming "no religion" have a college degree, as do 32 percent of atheists.[10] Furthermore, 11 percent of the US population has some form of postgraduate education, whereas 21 percent of atheists and 20 percent of agnostics are similarly educated.[11] In one recent survey of members of organized nonreligious and secular groups, fully 41 percent had a graduate degree.[12] As with gender and ethnicity, the education "gap" varies with nonreligious grouping. Although the general category of "none" or "unaffiliated" does not differ substantially in terms of education from the general population, those who are affirmatively secular, agnostic, or atheist have significantly higher levels of education.[13] And while several variables—gender, ethnicity, age—correlate with secularity, it has long been theorized that education itself is a causal contributor to secularity.

It is widely assumed that universities are hotbeds of godlessness, and politicians do their part in reinforcing this assumption. During the 2012 US presidential campaign, Republican candidate and former senator Rick Santorum called President Obama a "snob" for encouraging all Americans to seek a college education. Santorum suggested that Obama was promoting not only education but also atheism. According to Santorum, "As you know, 62 percent of children who enter college with a faith conviction leave without it." A similar notion was voiced by other Republican candidates. Newt Gingrich mentioned in a speech to pastors, "I for one am tired of the long trend towards a secular, atheist system of thought dominating our colleges."[14] Despite such assertions, identifying the causal direction of the relationship between higher education and secularity is actually more complicated than it may first appear.

Although longitudinal studies indeed indicate that religiosity decreases during the transition to adulthood, and that college students report being less religious than when they were adolescents, this decline is even greater for those who do not attend college than for those who do.[15] Roughly three-quarters of young adults who do not attend college decrease their frequency of church attendance. The association between obtaining a college education and becoming less religious has diminished over the past half-century largely because of the increasing access to higher education.[16] The proportion of the population attending college has more than doubled in the past forty years, which has reflected a more utilitarian view of higher education and a greater representation among college attendees of the religious. However, Santorum may have (inadvertently) expressed some aspects of the actual effect of college education on religiosity. One of these is the decrease in religious attendance or affiliation during the college years, although this is often temporary and recovers after graduation when many begin careers and form families. Another is that although the experience of attending college does not decrease overall religiosity, there is some evidence that it has a corrosive effect on fundamentalist views such as exclusivist, literalistic, and sectarian religious beliefs.[17]

There is also evidence of self-selection in the choice of field of study; nonreligious or secular individuals are more represented in, and may seek out, certain disciplines. This likely overlaps with individuals' social and political views, in that more conservative individuals are found in applied fields such as education, business, or nursing, as opposed to social or natural sciences or the humanities (and thus political conservatism versus liberalism is likely one of the previously mentioned "third variables" that confounds a clear effect of religion itself). However, the content of the field of study may also influence students' religiosity over time. For example, students who major in the social sciences and humanities become less religious over the course of their college education, whereas those who study educational or clerical fields become more religious over the same time frame, and those who study biological or physical sciences remain as religious after college as they were before, on average.[18] This is consistent with a reciprocal process; less religious individuals seek out fields of interest and careers that further solidify or polarize their secularity. As a result, the proportion of nonreligious individuals is greater at successively higher levels of education and in more elite institutions.

Perhaps not surprisingly, then, the nonreligious are heavily overrepresented among scholars, professors, and scientists.[19] Surveys of elite scientists in various disciplines have long indicated high (and increasing) levels of disbelief in a personal God (53 percent in 1914; 72 percent in 1998).[20] However, secularity within educational institutions varies substantially depending on the selectivity of the university. The proportion of professors who are atheists and agnostics is greater in the more elite, PhD-granting universities.[21] There also is a wide range of beliefs among the professoriate; some two-thirds of psychology professors and biology professors claim to be atheists, whereas those in more applied disciplines such as nursing, social work, education, accounting, and finance show levels of religious belief similar to those of the general public.

Several factors could be contributing to these patterns and trends. Interestingly, although the proportions of atheists and agnostics are higher in the elite versus nonelite schools, it is the orientation of the professor toward research versus teaching that is more predictive of atheism and agnosticism. It therefore appears that those professors who emphasize research, whatever their field of study, will be more likely not only to be nonreligious but also to self-select into the type of school where they can pursue their research. The effect of the specific academic discipline and the emphasis on research both illustrate that disbelief in God is not merely associated with higher education in general (since all the professors in these studies have equivalent levels of education). Furthermore, being a member of any scientific discipline is not uniformly associated with secularity; for example, professors in electrical engineering and computer science have higher levels of religiosity than those in the social sciences. Rather, the disciplines that focus on the study of humanity and our belief systems (i.e., the social and biological sciences) and that emphasize research-oriented scholarship, are the ones most associated with low levels of religiosity.

Why do we see this association of secularity not only with higher education and scientific disciplines but also with a research-oriented mindset? On the one hand, many have stated that there is no inherent conflict between science and religion. Stephen J. Gould has declared these domains "non-overlapping magisteria," meaning that they are two separate belief systems whose domains do not overlap. Indeed, the head of the National Institutes of Health, Francis Collins, is an evangelical Christian. Clearly, not all scientists are nonreligious. On the other hand, the rates of secularity in some scientific fields are markedly different from those in the general population. Many nonreligious individuals specifically mention that scientific concepts (e.g., evolution, geologic time spans, neurology) have had a corrosive influence on religiosity.[22] Indeed, recent experiments have indicated that the domains of science and religion compete as worldviews or ultimate explanations, even at an unconscious level.[23] It is therefore possible that for many secular individuals the magisteria of science and religion do overlap, and that some forms of scientific content tend to undermine religious belief.

INTELLECT AND COGNITION

Intelligence refers to a general ability to reason, to solve complex problems, to think abstractly, and to synthesize information.[24] Cognition refers to the process of thought or application of knowledge. Commensurate with their relatively higher levels of educational attainment, the nonreligious tend to score high on measures of general intelligence and cognition.[25] More broadly, those who have engaged in religious questioning tend to have superior performance on elementary cognitive tasks, such as reaction time and general world knowledge.[26] This tends to be true at younger ages as well; levels of adolescent intelligence predict later adult espousal of atheism, and adolescents who are "not at all religious" have higher levels of verbal intelligence than other groups.[27] Similarly, verbal SAT scores are higher among those with no religious identification than among both moderate and conservative Protestants.[28] However, as with education, there is some evidence that the relationship may be stronger with specific forms of religiosity. For instance, verbal SAT scores are higher among those who reject the authority of the Bible relative to those who believe the Bible was "inspired by God" or biblical inerrantists. Because intelligence itself is highly correlated with levels of education, it is plausible that either of these could be driving the relationship with religiosity/secularity. However, the use of statistical controls for factors such as education does not eliminate the relationship between higher intelligence and lower religiosity.[29] This explanation also accords well with the evidence that cognitive functioning develops quite early and is more likely to precede than result from both educational achievement and exposure to religious influences.

Among adults, the values and behaviors of the nonreligious also tend to reflect intellectualism (e.g., low valuation of obedience, high valuation of freedom of scientific inquiry, tolerance, membership in literary groups).[30] However, there is still the question of cause and effect. There is some evidence that cognitive factors contribute to a transition from higher to lower religiosity, indicating a possible causal role for intellectual abilities.[31] Altemeyer and Hunsberger found that "Amazing Apostates" (secular students who had grown up in religious households) reported higher grade point averages than "Amazing Converts" (those who had transitioned from nonreligious childhoods to highly religious adulthood).[32] And as seen in chapter 4, one of the best predictors of apostasy itself is considering oneself to be "intellectually oriented" (e.g., enjoyment of debating religious issues).[33] This is consistent with the finding that those who are likely to become more nonreligious over time tend to exhibit stronger or more analytical cognitive faculties.

Other findings suggest that what distinguishes the nonreligious from others is not overall intelligence or education but, rather, specific types of cognition; individuals who have become nonreligious engage in greater complexity of thought or "divergent cognition" (i.e., examining issues from multiple perspectives).[34] This is similar to another trait associated with religious doubting—so-called quest religiosity. Quest religiosity refers to religiosity that is open-ended and incorporates contradictions and problems, as opposed to a closed and exclusivist approach.[35] Those who have developed doubts over time, or who have transitioned from greater to lesser levels of religiousness, are likely to score higher on measures of quest.[36] Such findings suggest that what distinguishes individuals whose religiosity decreases from those who maintain beliefs over time is that the former tend to cognitively process religious information in a more complex and critical manner.[37] This process has been described as a "polarization," in which individuals tend to "snowball" such that those with lower initial levels of religiosity tend to further decrease in belief over time in contrast to those stronger in religiosity who increase in belief over time.[38] Those with greater initial levels of religious doubt tend to seek out information from belief-inconsistent (e.g., nonreligious) sources, whereas those with fewer religious doubts restrict information-seeking to sources that support belief.[39] Therefore, these studies suggest that aspects of intellect or cognition may play a causal role in relinquishing religious beliefs over time.

ANALYTICAL VERSUS INTUITIVE COGNITION OR "MENTALIZING"

Consider the following problem: "A bat and a ball cost $1.10 in total. The bat costs $1 more than the ball. How much does the ball cost?" The intuitively obvious answer given by most individuals is "10 cents," but upon more careful consideration of the phrasing, the correct answer must be "5 cents" (.05 plus a $1.05 bat equaling $1.10). Or consider this question: "In a lake, there is a patch of lily pads. Every day the patch doubles in size. If it takes forty-eight days for the patch to cover the entire lake, how long would it take for the patch to cover half of it?" The intuitively obvious answer to this question given by most people is often much lower than the correct answer: forty-seven days. Such questions are tricky because they require a certain degree of mental effort to suppress an initial, often misleading, tendency to "shoot from the hip." For this reason, these problems are optimally solved using analytical, as opposed to intuitive, cognition. That is, they require the ability to think deliberatively and resist premature fixation on an intuitive (but incorrect) answer. Based on performance on such problems, individuals tend to fall on a bell curve–like continuum of analytical versus intuitive cognition.

As it turns out, greater analytical thought is also related to disbelief in supernatural concepts, even when the test items themselves do not contain religious content.[40] For example, atheists use more analytical words (e.g., "thought," "idea") on Twitter, whereas Christians use more intuitive words (e.g., "know," "feeling").[41] More interestingly, even beyond a mere correlation with nonbelief, encouraging analytical thought subsequently lowers individuals' belief in God, at least temporarily.[42] In essence, analytical thought appears to reduce belief in the supernatural.

Consider another type of problem:

In a study, 1,000 people were tested. Among the participants there were 995 nurses and 5 doctors. Paul is a randomly chosen participant of this study. Paul is thirty-four years old. He lives in a beautiful home in a posh suburb. He is well-spoken and very interested in politics. He invests a lot of time in his career. What is most likely? (a) Paul is a nurse; (b) Paul is a doctor.

This personality description conveys a stereotype ("wealthy doctor") that nonetheless conflicts with the overwhelming statistical probability (99.5 percent) that Paul is, in fact, a nurse. This type of problem also assesses analytic cognition. The secular are more likely to accurately detect such conflicts between stereotypes and the actual probability of occurrence and provide the correct answer.[43] Another type of problem requiring analytical thought is syllogistic reasoning, which involves using a series of premises to reach a conclusion. For example, "All philosophers are Greek. Socrates is a philosopher. Therefore, Socrates is a Greek." Again, secular individuals tend to more accurately solve such reasoning problems, and do so more slowly and deliberatively than the more religious.[44] In all these studies, the researchers controlled for general cognitive ability, so the results are not attributable to overall intelligence. Rather, there is substantial evidence that secular individuals are distinguished by their *way* of thinking. They are more likely to think deliberatively when processing information, overriding their initial impressions.

Another dimension of cognition refers to the tendency to, at one end, empathize (identify and respond to others' emotions) versus, at the other end, to systemize (analyze nonsocial relationships). Empathizing includes the tendency to "mentalize," or to represent and think about others' thoughts, often referred to as having a "theory of mind." Theory of mind enables humans—and some nonhuman animals—to transcend mere behavioral observations in determining courses of action based on what others' inner intentions might be. Again, individuals vary on a continuum in their type of processing. On the high end of the mentalizing spectrum are those who are very adept at gauging others' intentions and emotional states. However, sometimes overactive mentalization causes us to "overshoot," that is, to project mental states (i.e., anthropomorphize) onto nonhumans such as animals or objects. Those on the other end of the dimension, strong systemizers, often have difficulty thinking about others' thoughts and are sometimes said to be on the "autism spectrum"; in some cases they may be diagnosed with Asperger's syndrome.[45] These people are less able to interpret others' intentions and emotions, and are less adept with nonverbal or emotional cues. However, they may be better at gathering and organizing factual information and discerning patterns and logical relationships that are unnoticed by low systemizers. Studies using this empathizing-systemizing continuum indicate that there is a sex difference such that, on average, men tend to use systemizing cognition, whereas women are more adept at empathizing and mentalizing.[46] This is reflected in the overrepresentation of males among high systemizers such as those with Asperger's syndrome. This dimension of cognitive style also has relevance for religious belief and the lack thereof.

Religious individuals tend to show, on average, greater tendencies to mentalize, whereas secular people, especially atheists, tend toward the systemizing end of the continuum.[47] This pertains to the religious "gender gap" as well; the lower religiosity of males relative to females may be attributable to males' tendencies toward lower mentalizing and greater systemizing thought.[48] That is, atheism may be disproportionately represented among males because males disproportionately rely upon systemizing rather than mentalizing.

Such differences between the religious and secular are not limited to mental states but may also extend to the projection of human-like physical qualities. For example, compared with skeptics, religious believers not only are better at identifying face-like visual stimuli but also have a higher "false alarm" rate and identify faces where none exist.[49] Such findings may also explain the compensatory or "hydraulic" connection between religious belief and the desire to socially connect with others. People who have been made to feel temporarily lonely or disconnected from others respond with greater tendencies to anthropomorphize onto objects and animals, and such procedures even lead to (temporarily) increased belief in supernatural entities such as gods.[50] At the other end of the continuum, individuals with lower mentalizing tendencies may find it difficult to maintain beliefs in supernatural agents to the extent that they do not readily generate and project intentionality.[51] In effect, a lack of religious belief may be a consequence of lower metacognition; those whose cognitive processes tend toward high systemizing do not readily think that an external agent (such as God) is thinking about them.

PERSONALITY

The concept of personality refers to stable individual differences that persist across situations. The current, predominant model of the basic dimensions of personality is called the five-factor model, which suggests that the basic variation in normal personality can be described most concisely as consisting of five traits on which individuals can vary. These traits each resemble a bell-type curve in that most people are moderate, whereas a few are extremely high or low.[52] An acronym used to summarize these dimensions is CANOE (or OCEAN). Probably the most familiar of these dimensions is Extraversion (versus Introversion at the other end). Those high on Extraversion tend to prefer more social contact, whereas introverts prefer less social contact. Another dimension is Negative Affect (or Neuroticism) versus Emotional Stability. High Negative Affect reflects the presence of various negative emotional states such as anxiety, depression, or anger, as opposed to their absence at the stable end. (Because the Negative Affect dimension overlaps substantially with constructs involving mental well-being and mental illness, discussion of this factor will appear separately in chapter 7.) The dimension of Agreeableness refers to warmth, compassion, or trust in others, as opposed to suspicion or cynicism. Conscientiousness refers to the tendency to be organized and goal-driven as opposed to being lazy or disorganized. Finally, Openness to Experience (or Intellect) reflects curiosity, active imagination, and aesthetic sensitivity as opposed to conventionality, traditionalism, and preference for simplicity. Personality traits appear relatively early in psychological development and thus precede exposure to religious tenets, beliefs, and concepts.

As discussed earlier, nonreligious individuals tend to describe themselves as interested in intellectual matters and cognitive complexity. This is also reflected in the personality trait of Openness to Experience. Among the five factors, this trait most distinguishes nonbelievers from believers.[53] For example, in a comparison of secular group members with members of liberal church groups, Openness was the characteristic that best distinguished the former from the latter, even when controlling for key demographics.[54] Those who have deconverted from religion—apostates—are also significantly higher on Openness than those who maintain their religiosity.[55] However, other work has suggested a more complex relationship between religiosity, or the lack thereof, and Openness, such that it may correlate more strongly with the *type* of religious views rather than the mere presence or absence thereof. Openness is inversely related to religious fundamentalism, but it is *positively* related to spirituality.[56] Therefore, Openness may be more accurately described as reflective of whether one views religious content as symbolic and metaphorical versus literal, rather than simply being religious or not.[57] More broadly, Openness is connected not only to nonbelief but also to a variety of shared characteristics, including attitudes, cognition, and metaphysical worldviews. Those high in Openness tend to be nonconforming, antiauthoritarian, and politically liberally minded.[58] Openness is indicative of divergent cognition (that which does not simply reconfirm previous belief), which leads to processing religious material in a critical way.

There has been a general consensus that nonreligious individuals tend to also be characterized by lower Conscientiousness and Agreeableness, relative to those high in religiosity. Vassilis Saroglou states, "One may find it interesting to know that if he has to select a partner for business or marriage, there is a 60% chance that a religious partner will be non-individualistic, warm and straightforward (A), conscientious and methodical (C), compared to only a 40% chance with a nonreligious partner."[59] Because these two traits are associated with interpersonal characteristics such as trust, diligence, and orderliness, some researchers have suggested that religiosity itself increases these "prosocial" personality qualities associated with Agreeableness and Conscientiousness.[60] However, when interpreting any personality factors that differentiate the nonreligious and religious, several things must be kept in mind.

First, comparisons are frequently made between religious group members and those who are unaffiliated—rather than with affirmatively secular individuals who are also group members. Therefore, some personality traits may be more reflective of differences in characteristics such as preference for socialization and group membership, rather than anything specific to religious beliefs or the lack thereof. Also, some traits may reflect strongly committed worldviews—of any sort—rather than specifically religious beliefs. For example, nonbelievers who are members of secular groups display a level of Conscientiousness (diligence and dutifulness) equivalent to that of religious church members. This trait actually shows a curved relationship, such that those who are strongly religious *or* strongly nonreligious score higher on Conscientiousness than those who are only somewhat religious or indifferent.[61]

Another problem with interpreting personality characteristics of nonreligious individuals pertains to stereotypes often assumed to accompany nonbelief or religiosity. As we have discussed elsewhere, in many societies secularity is perceived as amoral and deviant. When individuals self-report on their personalities, there may be a tendency to project an impression based on what that person presumes he or she "should be like."[62] Thus, the responses to such personality measures may partly reflect internalized religious stereotypes. Religious people are more likely to rate someone as being more agreeable and conscientious if that person is depicted as being religious compared with an identical person depicted as being an atheist, thus demonstrating a "prosocial" personality stereotype.[63] A stereotyping effect may also play a part in the divergent ways in which religion is viewed in different cultures. The association between religion and responses to personality measures in a positive and socially desirable manner is greater in the United States than in less religious contexts, such as the United Kingdom.[64] Also, the association between nonbelief and low Agreeableness is greater in the United States than in Europe.[65] Communal traits such as warmth—as opposed to independence—are correlated with religiousness only within predominantly religious cultures. For example, in a study conducted in the United States, when participants were asked to form impressions of personal characteristics based only on photographs, smiling faces were judged to be more religious than nonsmiling faces. However, a study conducted in the United Kingdom (where religiosity is less normative) found the opposite was true. This is consistent with a normativity effect in which the greater cultural presence of the nonreligious (such as in Europe) is associated with a more positive stereotype as opposed to contexts, such as the United States, where atheism is considered deviant.[66] These findings indicate that at least a portion of the relationship between personality and religiosity may depend on what is normative in a particular cultural context. If someone is a social "joiner" of normative groups, in a religious society, that person is likely to be drawn to religion. Likewise, in religiously predominant contexts (like the United States), those with less communal personality characteristics are more likely to become or remain identified as nonreligious. In nonreligious contexts, these patterns are reversed.

DIFFERENCES IN PERSONALITY BETWEEN NONRELIGIOUS TYPES

Are the personalities of those who describe themselves as atheists or agnostics different from those who describe themselves as "spiritual, but not religious" or "secular humanist"? The answers to such questions have implications for debates about whether differences between nonreligious types are more a function of style than of substance. In one study, in which the nonreligious were asked to self-label, four main types emerged: atheists, agnostics, humanists, and "spiritual-but-not-religious."[67] The personality differences between types of nonreligious individuals mirrored some of the trends along the spectrum of religious belief and nonbelief. For example, spirituals scored higher on Agreeableness than humanists, who in turn were more agreeable than atheists and agnostics. However, spirituals were also higher on Negative Affect (i.e., less emotionally stable) than atheists and humanists—who were relatively more emotionally stable. Differences in Agreeableness may indicate greater willingness among the spirituals to try to "get along with" or trust others; for example, spirituals also reported having more close confidants than atheists, for whom there seems to be greater willingness to go against the social grain. These personality findings suggest that atheists place less emphasis on sociability, or pleasing and trusting others, than do humanists and spirituals.

Part of the difference between nonreligious "types" may also reflect the underlying certainty or confidence that individuals have in their beliefs and worldviews. Agnostics may be more cautious or muted than atheists in terms of general personality.[68] This hints at the possibility that differences between those who self-identify as spirituals compared with agnostics or atheists are due more to presentation or style than to differences in metaphysical beliefs. Perhaps spirituals privately hold views identical to those of atheists but outwardly "tone it down," which would reflect in traits such as Agreeableness. In one survey of the nonreligious, 83 percent reported on a measure of certainty of belief that they were "mostly" or "absolutely certain that God does not exist."[69] Of this segment of "de facto atheists," 67 percent self-labeled as atheist, 26 percent as humanist, and 7 percent as agnostic. This allowed a comparison between self-labeled atheists and agnostics. "Agnostic atheists" (i.e., those who disbelieve in God but self-label as agnostic) were lower on Openness to Experience and higher on Negative Affect or Neuroticism, and were also older and more educated than "atheist atheists" (those who disbelieve in God and self-label as atheists). In contrast, the spiritual-but-not-religious individuals were higher in Agreeableness than the others. This lends some empirical support to the hypothesis regarding a stylistic differentiation. That said, it should be acknowledged that the overall differences in personality between atheists, agnostics, and humanists in this study were small. One reasonable hypothesis is that the more affirmatively nonreligious (rather than noncommittal) an individual, the less likely that person is to perceive him- or herself as being agreeable, although, as mentioned earlier, this is contextual as a function of cultural norms. Personality traits that correlate with attitudes and beliefs such as religiosity are of particular interest to social scientists because of their implications for the causes or origins of religiosity itself.

GENETICS AND EVOLUTION

One inescapable feature of religion (and secularity, as noted in chapter 5) is that it seems to run in families. The best predictor of an individual's religiosity or secularity is his or her family background. However, it is also true that even people who share nearly identical upbringings (e.g., siblings) can still hold divergent religious views upon maturation, and they often can diverge markedly from their childhood religious teachings (e.g., the stereotypical "preacher's kid" who grows up to reject religion). How can we account for such variability in outcome given similar family environments? One explanation is that no two individuals, even siblings from the same family, share exactly the same experiences. Rather, they likely have different friends or are exposed to different teachers in school. Another explanation is that the genetic makeup of siblings also varies. Although social scientists, for many decades, presumed that the degree to which individuals are religious must be entirely attributable to the social environment, it is now recognized that genetic variation plays a part.[70]

In the past decade, increasing attention has been devoted to viewing religion—and by implication, irreligion—through the lens of possible biological and genetic influences. One method used to determine the level of genetic contribution involves comparing identical twins (who share 100 percent of their genes) with fraternal twins (who share, on average, 50 percent). Several studies have found that identical twins tend to be more religiously similar than fraternal twins, despite the two groups sharing the same environment.[71] Clearly, one does not inherit a "gene" for religiosity or secularity, or for theism and/or atheism, so by what mechanism would genes exert an effect?

This question is directly relevant to the mediating role of personality.[72] Personality traits are genetically influenced, manifest at an early age, and are predictive of later religiosity.[73] The role of genetic factors is relatively smaller at a younger age, due to the constraining role of the environment, but this genetic influence grows over time as individuals mature, consistent with a more active role of temperament in adults.[74] An individual high in Openness to Experience may have devoutly attended church at a younger age due to social or parental influence. However, upon maturation, this individual would find greater latitude to express any religious skepticism (e.g., through education, peer selection, or career choice) consistent with the expression of a trait such as Openness to Experience. Though personality traits are not likely to influence rejection or endorsement of specific religious concepts, they may nonetheless influence broader patterns of values, such as the tendency to be individualistic and unconventional, as opposed to traditional and obedience-oriented. Studies using twin comparisons indicate that religiosity, authoritarianism, and political conservatism (the so-called Traditional Moral Values Triad) all reflect a central underlying heritable trait.[75] This indicates a genetically influenced component, not only in the degree to which one is secular versus religious, but also in more general sociopolitical worldviews, such as the tendency to conform versus reject social convention. Such putative genetic influences bring up deeper questions of purpose and function.

Much as some researchers argue that the ubiquity of religion indicates that it may be "natural" in an evolutionary sense, others have suggested that some traits related to an absence of religious belief could themselves be adaptive, indicating that there may be "born atheists."[76] For example, the tendency toward analytical and systematic thought mentioned earlier could have conferred fitness-enhancing benefits over the course of human evolution.[77] However, these theories are in their infancy and await further study.

MARRIAGE, COHABITATION, AND DIVORCE

Marital patterns can tell us a great deal about people. Whether to get married, and to whom, are arguably the most important decisions one makes, and they provide a window to important personal proclivities, values, and worldviews. Some earlier studies indicated that secularity was associated with a lower likelihood of getting and staying married and a higher likelihood of divorcing.[78] Consequently, religiosity itself was thought to strengthen marriages and families. One study, however, found that the nonreligious are actually *less* likely than the religious to be divorced.[79] To add to the complexity, national surveys are fairly consistent in showing that religious adults are overrepresented among both married *and* divorced segments, whereas the nonreligious are more likely to be either single/never-married or cohabitors.[80] How can we make sense of all this?

One explanation may lie in the specific categories or types of nonreligious individuals used in comparisons. The category of "divorced" is a good example of this. In a Pew Forum survey, 12 percent of unaffiliated individuals were divorced—the same incidence as in the overall US adult population, and the same rate found among main-line Protestants. As with the vast majority of studies, however, this survey used the unaffiliated as a catch-all category. Within this group, the rate of divorce for the religious-yet-unaffiliated was 13 percent, whereas the figures for atheists, agnostics, and secular unaffiliated were 10, 10, and 11 percent, respectively. Other large-scale surveys such as the General Social Survey also indicate that the completely nonreligious, such as atheists, have a lower rate of ever being divorced than the broader grouping of "nones" or those not certain of God's existence.[81] These broader categories of "none" and "unaffiliated" actually consist largely of religiously indifferent people (e.g., believers who don't attend church), who have higher divorce rates than the narrower groups of atheists or agnostics. Therefore, although those within a general "no religion" category have less stable marriages than religious individuals, it is unclear to what extent this is reflective of religious beliefs themselves (or the lack thereof), as opposed to something about those who are religious but are less committed.[82] Given that a lower divorce rate has a greater association with church attendance than with religious belief per se, it is likely that self-selection or social factors (e.g., group involvement) are involved.[83] That is, those who are religious and also functioning well socially, as reflected in church attendance, are also likely to have more stable marriages. But why would atheists and agnostics have a lower rate of divorce, on average, than religious people?

The strongest predictors of the likelihood of divorce are demographic rather than religious, namely, younger age at marriage, lower education levels, and lower socioeconomic status.[84] Atheists and agnostics differ from the broader category of "nones" and the unaffiliated in being relatively more educated and being older at first marriage, which accounts at least in part for their lower divorce rate. Also, obviously, divorce presumes marriage. In the Pew Forum survey, 37 percent of atheists, 36 percent of agnostics, and 26 percent of secular unaffiliated had never been married, compared with 19 percent of the overall US population. From the perspective of survey data, a delay in marriage, or an extended period of cohabitation, lowers the chances that one will be divorced at any given point in his or her life. This may partially explain why the nonreligious are both more likely to be single *and* less likely to be divorced.[85]

Secular people are more likely than the religious to cohabit without marriage. Typically, cohabitation is said to place one at higher risk for divorce. However, this is due to the underlying differences between those likely to choose cohabitation prior to marriage more than it is an effect *of* cohabitation. That is, those with a less traditional approach to marriage—and who are less religious—tend to self-select into cohabitation, whereas those with more traditional views proceed more directly to marriage.[86] These groups differ in ways unrelated to the act of cohabiting itself. Cohabitors are more liberal and may see marriage as more ephemeral than do those with more conservative views. Putting these factors together, we can see that predictors of marriage and divorce can contain complex and competing influences.

The overall picture that emerges is that the nonreligious are more likely than the religious to delay marriage, to defer it entirely, and to cohabit prior to marriage. Taken together, these trends constitute a more drawn-out "social clock" of milestones in development.[87] This likely emerges from several broad influences, including familial factors, personality traits, and values such as beliefs about gender roles. For example, in a cross-national comparison, those with no religious identification had a less traditional attitude toward the family; they were less supportive of marriage, more accepting of divorce, and so forth.[88] This is reflected in the relatively greater distinction seculars make between the onset of sexual activity, completion of educational or career goals, age at marriage, and childrearing. They are more likely to view personal independence as the goal of maturation. By contrast, those who are more religious tend to have a social clock that more closely associates the onset of sexuality, childbearing, and age of first marriage, with the latter constituting the goal of maturity.[89] In effect, seculars tend to delay marriage and have a lower divorce rate because they prioritize individualistic values such as personal and career achievement—a so-called strategic orientation, referring to deliberate planning—rather than framing these values in moral terms. That is, premarital sexuality, unwanted pregnancy, and out-of-wedlock births are undesirable to seculars not because they are "sins" but because they threaten personal independence and achievement. Paradoxically, the effect of specific moral or religious sanctions against cohabitation and sex outside of marriage (which consequently increase pressure to marry soon after sexual initiation) may actually increase the risk of divorce by decreasing the age of first marriage. These tendencies are also reflected in values regarding family formation.

CHILDBEARING

As is the case with marital patterns, the age at family formation and the optimal number of children in a given family are influenced by a variety of social factors, religion—or the lack thereof—being one among many. Numerous studies in the United States have found that nonreligious and religiously unaffiliated couples tend to have fewer children than the religious.[90] One possible explanation may be related to differences in religious content or theological emphases, such as scriptural encouragement of fertility. Others have suggested that because religion may serve a social binding function, the lack of any religious belief frees atheists from societal obligation, including family obligations. Bainbridge points to atheists' lower rates of fertility and greater tendency to be single or cohabit rather than marry as evidence that atheism is linked to a lower sense of social obligation.[91] However, controlling for demographic factors disproves this explanation.[92] As we saw in the previous section, secular individuals tend to have a drawn-out separation of the onset of sexual activity, marriage, and childbearing. As a consequence, this often means that the window of childbearing is narrower than with those (more often religious) who marry and begin family formation at a younger age.

On a societal level, the association of a high proportion of secular citizens with a lower birth rate appears to vary. It is more characteristic of the United States than Europe, for example. Studies in the United States find that those with no religious affiliation have low fertility and that this gap is present even after controlling for demographic factors such as age and education.[93] One theory is that religious and secular family behaviors differ in regard to "fertility intentions," that is, the number of desired children.[94] Women in the more secular countries of northern and Western Europe have equivalent or even higher fertility than women in the United States, and higher fertility than women in southern Europe.[95] Evidently, factors other than religion contribute to family size, such as child and family policies in a given country or region, or the support given to both fathers and mothers to take time off from work to contribute to child care. For instance, countries like Sweden, which offer generous family benefits, have higher fertility rates than countries like Italy or Spain, which offer fewer benefits.

As we have seen elsewhere in this chapter, differences between secular and religious individuals may be attributable not so much to religiosity per se but to underlying characteristics that may influence both religious views and, in the present case, values pertaining to family formation. For example, those who score higher on the personality trait of Openness tend to have lower fertility, a relationship that has been increasing over generations. This also interacts with sociopolitical conditions in that, if there is an economic trade-off between pursuing work and education, those who value such goals will delay parenthood.[96]

CHILDREARING

Another factor that distinguishes the familial patterns of nonreligious individuals involves childrearing philosophies and behavior. Obviously, parents differ in their strategies for childrearing, and these differences are—to varying degrees—related to their broader views about human nature. According to an influential model, parenting consists of two independent dimensions.[97] On one axis, parents can exhibit high or low demandingness; on the other axis, they can exhibit high or low responsiveness. Parents can also vary in the relative valuation of children's autonomy, as opposed to obedience. Those who value traits such as obedience, respect, and good manners in children are themselves higher in authoritarian tendencies. Conversely, those who value independence, self-reliance, curiosity, and nurturing in children tend to be nonauthoritarians.[98]

As we have seen, secular people are distinguished by an aversion to authoritarianism, and this is evident in their attitudes and approaches to childrearing. For example, those who believe the Bible is a "book of fables" are more likely to encourage autonomy in their children. Those who believe the Bible is the word of God place greater emphasis on obedience. In general, lower religiosity in parents is associated with an emphasis on children's self-reliance, curiosity, and tolerance rather than obedience and respect for authority, themes that can also be seen in the "strategic orientation" mentioned previously.[99] Secular parents emphasize that children's priority should be to become educated and self-sufficient, rather than to marry and start a family. The emphasis on autonomy rather than obedience in childrearing extends to methods of discipline; nonreligious parents are the least likely to support the use of corporal punishment on children. At the other end of the continuum are conservative Christians, who are noted for their emphasis on obedience in their children, as well as a more general authoritarian worldview.[100]

According to one typology, individuals' sociopolitical worldviews can be categorized according to a "nurturing parent" versus "strict father" dichotomy.[101] The secular tend toward the former, more likely viewing the world as essentially benevolent; they believe that children should be taught with respect and compassion rather than relying on strict discipline. Thus, secular parents may view authoritarian parenting as counterproductive because of children's essential goodness, which necessitates the encouragement of autonomy and independence. By contrast, parents who view humanity as being essentially flawed tend to view children as willful and in need of correction.

Although secular people are sometimes pejoratively accused of "believing in nothing," particularly with regard to the purported absence of values imparted to their children, secular parents actually use a wide range of methods to instruct children about religion, values, and religious values. Christel Manning has developed a categorization based on interviews with parents of no religious preference.[102] According to her research, some types of parents, such as the "unchurched believer" and the "indifferent," were not specifically secular but, rather, had some religious beliefs. The "indifferent parents" essentially ignored the issue of religion altogether and were the only group that did not incorporate any elements of instruction on religion, spirituality, or secular philosophy into the upbringing of their children. By contrast, "Secularist" parents proactively inculcated values such as humanism and skepticism, viewing the goal as education about religion. Another parental type, the "Spiritual seeker," also instructed children pluralistically about a range of religions because they viewed several approaches as equally valuable. For example, there is a growing number of worldview education programs that cater to families who are not traditionally religious, such as the "Tapestry of Faith" curriculum offered through the Unitarian Universalist Association. In this way, the seekers resembled the secularists because both types of parents chose instructional methods that provided information about all religions. However, the secular parents' goal differed from the pluralists' in that they sought to promote skepticism rather than ecumenism. Another reason that secular parents wished to provide this type of education was the desire for a supportive community.

In general, the nonreligious tend to allow other individuals to make up their own minds about religious issues. This "nonzealous" approach distinguishes nonreligious parents from their religious counterparts. When Altemeyer and Hunsberger asked formerly religious "apostates" how they would raise their own children, none of them indicated that they raised or would raise their children specifically to be nonbelievers. Half said they would send their children to church to learn from believers, and the other half said they would let their children learn from other sources such as peers; additionally, these formerly religious individuals said they would not disparage religion in front of their children.[103] Similarly, Hunsberger and Altemeyer found that, of a sample of atheist parents from Canada, 11 percent reported that they would influence a hypothetical "questioning teen" to adopt their own nonreligious beliefs; the remainder supported letting the teen make up his or her own mind.[104] Therefore, only a small minority of atheist parents indicate that they have raised their children specifically to adopt atheist views. Instead, in accordance with the value of autonomy in childrearing, nonreligious individuals most often favor exposure to numerous religious points of view and then allowing children to choose.[105]

CONCLUSION

We asked at the beginning of this chapter: What are the nonreligious like? We found some general patterns. Demographically speaking, the nonreligious tend to be disproportionately young, white, and male. They tend to be better educated and more intellectually oriented, and to think in a complex, analytical and critical manner, and they are found in disproportionately greater numbers in elite institutions and in fields requiring graduate-level education, particularly in the sciences. The personalities of secular people tend toward nonconformity, independence, and antiauthoritarianism. Finally, secular people tend to base their maturational goals on personal independence, and their childrearing philosophy emphasizes autonomy rather than obedience to authority. We can see continuity here. For example, one hypothesis that unites the areas of intelligence and personality is that the high analytic and intellectual performance of the nonreligious is related to their nonconforming personality. In a religiously normative society, sustained cognitive effort is required of those who have rejected these beliefs. Another overarching trait that appears in many of these characteristics is that the nonreligious are more individualistic in orientation.

What we have seen in this chapter, then, is a mixture of not altogether surprising findings, together with a significant amount of ambiguous or unknown information. It is perhaps not surprising that secular individuals tend to be more educated, nonconforming, and open to new experiences. But there is much we do not know, for example, about why some individuals accept and carry religious teachings into adulthood, whereas others question and challenge such teachings. We do not know which, among the many factors, are the most "fundamental" or basic, in a causal sense. For example, does childrearing or early personality contribute to later adult positions on religious and existential issues? It is very difficult to separate cause and effect in processes that may reciprocally influence each other. Given the rising numbers of completely secular households, however, we may have to substantially revise the existing literature on nonreligious individuals based on much-needed new information.

7

SECULARITY AND WELL-BEING

JUSTIN GRIFFITH, A sergeant in the US Army, was taking a required military survey designed to measure the well-being and mental fitness of soldiers. On this questionnaire, Griffith was asked to agree or disagree with statements such as "I am a spiritual person," "I believe that in some way my life is closely connected to all of humanity," and "I often find comfort in my religion and spiritual beliefs." Because Griffith was an atheist, he answered in the negative. When his computerized interpretation of the test was returned, it said: "Spiritual fitness may be an area of difficulty"; "You may lack a sense of meaning and purpose in your life. At times, it is hard for you to make sense of what is happening to you and others around you. You may not feel connected to something larger than yourself. You may question your beliefs, principles and values"; and "Improving your spiritual fitness should be an important goal." Griffith was angered by this experience because he did not see what these items had to do with his fitness as a soldier. He complained about the situation, and his complaints successfully drew public notice to this issue.[1]

Although this is just one example, many researchers, as well as clinicians, regularly use such measures of spirituality to predict mental health. In fact, such measures often *do* correlate with emotional adjustment—at least when they are used with religious participants. In this chapter, however, we will take a different approach by reviewing what we know about the mental and physical well-being of secular individuals like Justin Griffith. Griffith's story hints at the potential problems in extrapolating findings pertaining to religion and well-being based on religious samples to secular men and women.

DEFINITIONS

The terms "mental health" and "mental well-being" can refer to a wide range of phenomena. These concepts can refer to the absence of obvious pathology, such as depression, anxiety, or more serious diagnosable disorders. Beyond this easily categorizable yet simplistic definition, there is a wider range of concepts, including subjective well-being (i.e., happiness), strong social support, and emotional stability. According to these broader definitions, individuals who are mentally healthy tend to have greater life satisfaction and a higher sense of purpose or meaning, qualities that are often referred to as "self-actualization." Recognizing that mental well-being can refer to a broad range of characteristics is crucial because, as we will see, its relationships with secularity vary substantially, depending on the definition used for both sides of the equation.[2]

We know a great deal about mental health and religiosity. The scholarly literature that pertains to this issue is truly voluminous, reaching back across the past century, with entire journals devoted to the topic. The consensus is that greater religiosity is associated with modest but significant mental health benefits, but that the relationships vary depending on the type of mental health and type of religiosity in question.[3] For example, church attendance is more closely associated with lower depression and greater happiness than is strength of religious belief.[4]

However, as indicated earlier, we know much less about what implications these findings have for secular individuals. And much research can be misconstrued as suggesting that the greater mental health among the highly religious must stem from religious faith, content of beliefs, or religious practices such as prayer.[5] This extrapolation can occur when the assumption is made that these religious components contribute to a "dose-response" relationship, such that if a high degree of religiosity is associated with the best mental health, then moderate levels would be associated with moderate mental health, and the lowest level of religiosity with the lowest levels of mental health. For example, some research has suggested that being religious provides mental health benefits (e.g., positive coping mechanisms).[6] This could be misconstrued as implying that nonreligious people must lack these benefits and resources. As we will see, applying findings in this vein to secular individuals can be quite problematic.

EXTENDING STUDIES OF RELIGION
AND MENTAL WELL-BEING TO SECULARS

One problem in applying this "dose-response" relationship between mental health and the religiosity continuum is the difficulty in determining what is the opposite of "highly or devoutly religious." That is, to test the hypothesis "more religious people have greater mental health," we have to ask: Greater than whom? In the vast majority of studies, the typical group at the bottom of the religiosity scale consists of those who are comparatively less religious, religious nonidentifiers, nonaffiliates, or "nones." Some studies, in fact, specifically exclude nonreligious individuals yet refer to the results based on the residual (less religious) sample as evidence for better mental health among the "more religious" or worse mental health among the "nonreligious."[7] Although most studies do not distinguish the completely or affirmatively nonreligious from the unsure or nominally religious, there is evidence of important differences between these populations.

The "nones" (those who do not specify any particular named religious identity) are mostly religious individuals who are unwilling to join a church or are indifferent believers. By contrast, about a third of the unaffiliated are secular atheists and agnostics who differ markedly from the unaffiliated on a wide range of important variables.[8] Similarly, the most commonly used measure of behavioral or participatory religiosity is the frequency of attendance at services. In many studies, the category of "seldom or never attending church" is used to represent the complete absence of religious belief, belonging, and behavior. For example, David Myers reported that the proportion of "very happy" people was roughly twice as great among those who frequently attended church as among those who never attended.[9] Often the language used to frame these results implies that a contrast was made with the complete absence of religiosity, even though a "never-attender" is not equivalent to someone who is completely or affirmatively nonreligious. A more accurate description of such findings would be that "committed or devout religious individuals tend to have lower incidence of depression than uncommitted or uninvolved religious individuals." These types of methodological and typological problems are widespread in the mental health literature, and so a great deal of existing data does not really address whether truly secular people are more or less mentally healthy than those who are truly, or even moderately, religious.

Separating supernatural beliefs from this-worldly factors—such as group participation—is also important because collective group involvement, such as church attendance, is more strongly related to mental health than are personal religious beliefs.[10] Frequent church attenders tend to have greater social contact and denser social networks than nonattenders.[11] In fact, relationships between religious faith or supernatural beliefs, alone, and individuals' sense of well-being or life satisfaction often diminish or disappear when factors like social ties are accounted for.[12] Therefore, what studies of well-being are likely detecting in the distinction between attenders and nonattenders is not belief itself but characteristics such as the ability to conscientiously commit to groups, the desire for social integration, social support, life stability, and other similar social/psychological characteristics. This means that for religious and secular individuals alike, the most reliable positive influence upon mental health is social integration. This said, as indicated in earlier chapters and as we will consider further in chapter 10, among seculars an emphasis on autonomy or individualism may result in lower rates or "density" of social participation, and among the religious, avowed beliefs likely play a role in strengthening social participation and communality.

MENTAL HEALTH IS GRADED ON A CURVE

Once we consider that mental health may best be predicted by factors such as coherent worldviews or being a member of a supportive community, then this suggests an alternative way of understanding and analyzing relationships between religiosity or secularity and mental health. Simply put, there is some evidence that *both* strongly or affirmatively committed religious *and* secular individuals experience better mental health than those whose religious or philosophical views are weakly developed or indecisive. In other words, we sometimes see a "curvilinear" relationship between religiosity/secularity and mental health. Data from the World Values Survey, representing fifty nations, indicate that those for whom religion is "very important" as well as "not at all important" report a greater level of happiness than those for whom religion is "rather important" and "not very important."[13] An increasing number of studies, though not all, have detected such a pattern. The highest levels of mental distress are often found among the weakly religious or nominal believers, whereas affirmatively nonreligious individuals, like atheists, exhibit or report mental health comparable to that of the highly religious.[14] This relationship seems to occur in all age groups and across a range of mental health measures, such as life satisfaction and coping with stress.[15]

Despite indications that greater worldview certainty, commitment, or coherence—whether religious or nonreligious—is associated with greater psychological health or lower distress, this pattern is sometimes not accurately reported, even in studies that purport to provide evidence for it.[16] For example, a Gallup-Healthways poll found curvilinear effects for several measures of mental health.[17] The authors suggested that ambivalence or lack of commitment in moderately religious groups may have adverse effects compared with those with strong religious or nonreligious commitments. Yet the report was titled "Very Religious Americans Report Less Depression, Worry," and the authors concluded that "the best explanation for the observed relationship between religion and more positive states of emotional health may be the most straightforward—that being religious in fact produces a salutary effect on one's mental health." There has been, then, a tendency to minimize, to not test for, or simply to not report such curvilinear patterns. There is, however, sufficient reason to wonder what may account for such a pattern.

One possible explanation is that greater certainty or commitment in people's beliefs or worldviews, whether religious or secular, may result in greater emotional stability, comfort, or acceptance compared with persistent ambivalence or uncertainty.[18] Those who are "fence-sitters," or who have uncertain views, may be at greater risk for anxiety. There are indications, for example, that those who are "spiritual but not religious" exhibit or report more anxiety, phobias, neurotic disorders, and drug dependence than those who have "a religious understanding of life" or are "neither religious nor spiritual."[19] Similarly, individuals whose religiosity fluctuates over time, such as "seekers" or those who are "on a quest," tend to report more mental health problems than those whose views have remained firm and consistent.[20]

The phenomenon of religious doubting is pertinent. There is evidence that religious people who have doubts about their beliefs or their religion experience more symptoms of distress, anxiety, and depression than peers who have fewer doubts.[21] However, doubts may be problematic only for those whose degree of religious involvement was greater in the past, or who remain in environments where religious doubt is discouraged. Rather than being inherently psychologically problematic, lower levels of religiosity are associated with poor mental health if there is an expectation that this is a sign of inadequate faith, and so, unusual or shameful. Among seculars, where skepticism is expected or encouraged, doubt is less likely to cause anxiety, guilt, or shame. Worldviews, whether religious or secular, tend to be associated with mental health if they are perceived to be normative and consensually validated by others.

SOCIAL AND FAMILIAL NORMS AND CONTEXT OF SECULARITY

The earliest and most basic social context is the family of origin. Those who grow up with strong familial religiosity but who subsequently become nonreligious (i.e., apostates) have attracted a great deal of attention, vis-à-vis mental health. Overall, those who reject familial religion tend to report more emotional difficulties than those who maintain familial religiosity. One straightforward explanation of this is that the loss of religiosity deprives individuals of its previously functional benefits and causes friction between the apostate and his or her family. It is perhaps also not surprising that individuals who often view themselves as having caused pain for their parents or others should experience some guilt and/or anxiety.[22] However, the idea that the loss of religion inevitably leads to maladjustment requires some caveats. Some studies have failed to uncover definitive patterns of maladjustment or have yielded only mixed evidence of family conflict.[23] The relationship undoubtedly depends on factors such as the centrality of religion to the family of origin and the family's specific religious denomination. The effects of rejecting familial religion in a conservative or fundamentalist household are likely quite different from rejection in an indifferently or weakly religious one. In one survey of secular group members, those who experienced a change in beliefs reported negative effects on family relationships, but only if they had strongly religious upbringings.[24] Secular individuals who came from nonreligious upbringings reported fewer family conflicts or other effects. These results are consistent with results from other surveys of nonreligious individuals. Therefore, it does not appear that simply being nonreligious is correlated with family conflict, such as having difficult relationships with parents. That is only the case if one's family is strongly religious to begin with.

Another qualification concerns the causal direction of the relationship. Although it is likely that the rejection of parental or familial religion sometimes results in conflict with parents, siblings, and others, it can also be the case that parental conflict or parental loss can precipitate a weakening or relinquishment of religious beliefs.[25] In fact, there is evidence that apostasy results more often from families in which parents have different religious commitments.

There is additional evidence that the relationship between apostasy and family relations or mental health may change as social or family norms, prevailing attitudes about secularity, or broader cultural factors change. Although some early research suggested that apostates were delinquent or maladjusted, much of this work was conducted during the tumultuous 1960s and 1970s, when parental and political rebellion by the Baby Boom generation was widespread.[26] For example, there is evidence that secular students were more actively engaged in antiwar protests than conservatively religious ones. But more recently, the growing prevalence of secularity and apostasy may have rendered the rejection of family religion more common or normative, and thus less rebellious. Also, in recent decades, a greater portion of the "nones" were raised in nonreligious households, and thus the rate of parent-child similarity in secularity has increased (in contrast to the religious, for whom this has remained stable). One study found that in 1970, 40 percent of those with no religion grew up with nonreligious parents, compared with 63 percent in 2005, indicating an increase in intergenerational transmission of secularity over time.[27]

When discussing any putative mental health consequences of becoming nonreligious, it is important to tease out effects that are attributable to the loss of beliefs themselves both from subjective effects, like guilt and anxiety, and from more external or "objective" effects such as social ostracism and discrimination.

Apostasy and religious disaffiliation may trigger the loss of social support or even excommunication from a religious community or group. Many secular people report having experienced negative reactions from others, including slander, coercion, social ostracism, denial of opportunities, goods, and services, and even hate crimes. A nationally representative survey in the US found that 41 percent of atheists reported experiencing discrimination in the previous five years as a result of their lack of religious identification.[28] The extent of discrimination appears to be a function both of the degree of identification or "outness" of secular individuals and of the level of religiosity of the families or religious communities they have abandoned. For example, self-identified atheists and agnostics are three times as likely to report experiencing discrimination as are those who identify as "nones." Those who grew up with stricter familial religious expectations report experiencing more ostracism.[29] As is the case with other marginalized minority groups (e.g., gay/lesbian/bisexual/transgendered), higher rates of mental health problems are directly related to factors such as minority stress and a lack of acceptance from the community or families.[30] Therefore, a portion of what may appear at first glance to be related to apostasy may actually be attributable to factors other than the abandonment of religious beliefs, in this case, normative acceptance. However, there is also likely to be a very real immediate impact surrounding the loss of faith in an all-powerful, all-loving deity.

Beyond the familial context, communities and societies vary in the degree to which they consider secularity acceptable or normal. Being nonreligious in Sweden is not socially "deviant" the way it is, for example, in Mississippi. Broader cultural or contextual differences of this kind have mental health implications. Cross-cultural comparisons indicate that where religiosity predominates, secular people do indeed tend to be less mentally healthy on average, but where religiosity is not dominant, either no relationship exists or seculars report or exhibit fewer mental health problems than the religious.[31] Greater life satisfaction tends to be associated with personal religiosity in societies where religiosity is the norm.[32] There is even evidence from outside religiously predominant contexts that the relationship between religiosity and well-being is reversed.

One study found that rates of depression and suicide were negatively correlated with religiosity for American college students but positively correlated for Chinese students.[33] There may be several reasons for this. There is an obvious stigma—accompanied by stress and mental health effects—attached to being nonreligious where this is widely viewed as "deviant," as in the United States. In such contexts, secular people report being treated as minorities often are—unfairly or disrespectfully. In countries where secularity is more prevalent or accepted, this is less likely to occur, and so, psychological problems are less likely to be correlated with secularity.[34] The relationship between religiosity or secularity and well-being may be a function of the alignment between individuals' orientation and the prevailing social milieu. For example, in a study conducted in more secular Norway, religious and nonreligious middle-aged adults did not differ in their levels of social support, and secular older adults reported higher levels of social support than the religious.[35] This normativity effect also extends beyond social groups, into the domain of how such concepts are measured.

METHODOLOGICAL AND CONCEPTUAL EFFECTS

We started this chapter with the story of Sergeant Justin Griffith, which gave some indication of the problems he and others like him are likely to encounter when the mental health of the nonreligious is assessed using tools developed on a religiously normative population. There are practical, methodological problems with using such psychological measures with secular participants to predict well-being. In fact, biases inherent in many studies may artificially exaggerate a positive relationship between religiosity and mental health among the religious, and a negative relationship among seculars.

One bias involves how religiousness or spirituality is conceptualized. This can be seen most clearly with the definition of spirituality, which often includes not only transcendent aspects such as belief in a "higher power" but also nontranscendent components such as having a coherent sense of meaning, self-efficacy, and purpose in life.[36] Several conceptualizations include a sort of "transcendentless spirituality" without reference to life forces or a search for truth beyond the natural world.[37] Many atheists actually endorse this nontranscendent spirituality item content. For example, in response to items inquiring if they have ever felt wonderment or felt as if they were part of something greater than themselves, approximately three-quarters of atheists responded affirmatively, citing nature, science, music or art, and human cooperation.[38] This becomes problematic when such concepts are assumed to reflect religiosity or spirituality and are used to predict mental well-being that is itself conceptualized as having a strong sense of purpose or meaning (e.g., "self-actualization"). In their book on positive psychology, Christopher Peterson and Martin Seligman have enumerated several areas of virtue and component character strengths.[39] One of these, the virtue of "transcendence," includes the character strength of "religiousness," defined as "having coherent beliefs about the higher purpose and meaning of life." In methodological terms, it is problematic when the use of one domain (in this case religiosity or spirituality) is used to ostensibly predict another domain (in this case, mental health) but the definitions of the two domains blend together. In effect, such studies establish a tautology along the line of "well-adjusted individuals are well-adjusted."

Unfortunately, this problem is quite widespread.[40] Many measures of spirituality combine clearly transcendent domains with others such as "universality" ("I believe there is a larger meaning to life") and "connectedness" ("It is important for me to give something back to my community"; "I believe that humanity as a whole is basically good"; "I am concerned about those who will come after me in life").[41] It is not inherently problematic to focus on such domains that assess individuals' level of functioning, combining beliefs with mental health such as "religious or spiritual well-being." This is reflected in items such as "I believe that God is concerned about my problems" or "How much comfort do you find in religion or spirituality in times of suffering and distress?"[42] However, it is problematic when such studies are used to imply that religious belief—in and of itself—is related to well-being, as is the case when secular individuals take these questionnaires. Religious individuals are lumped together with completely nonreligious who do not endorse "religious well-being." Such a conflation prevents the study from testing whether religious belief itself is related to prosocial outcomes in a way that nonreligious belief is not. As a result, such studies are in effect finding that "non-depressed religious individuals are not depressed." In fact, once content that is nontranscendent is separated from that which is transcendent (i.e., spiritual and faith-based), the latter beliefs add little to the prediction of well-being, indicating that past results may have been entirely due to items that could equally be endorsed by well-adjusted religious and secular individuals alike.[43] This is consistent with work suggesting that, although the type of belief in God (e.g., images of God as benevolent versus punitive) is related to psychiatric symptoms, overall belief in God is not.[44]

Recall from earlier in this chapter that the relationship between religiosity and mental health appears to be more robust when the latter is conceptualized as a stronger sense of purpose or meaning, or greater satisfaction in life as opposed to merely the absence of overt pathology (e.g., diagnoses of depression or anxiety). Although the degree of personal religious devotion does predict concepts such as "self-actualization," religious belief itself does not predict straightforward measures of mental health such as low depression and anxiety. The conceptual overlap between religiosity and mental health may explain this pattern, namely, that mental health, when conceptualized more abstractly such as self-actualization, is more associated with spirituality and secular existential concepts.[45] Because of this conceptual confusion, the nonreligious are not disadvantaged regarding mental health, as some studies may imply. Rather, a secular individual with a sense of purpose, meaning, and satisfying social contact is as well-adjusted as a comparable religious individual.

EXISTENTIAL COPING: SECURITY, MEANING, AND COMPANIONSHIP

Whether religious or secular, people are motivated to believe that they live in an orderly world—one where things are under control, events have clarity, and lives have purpose and meaning. Both the religious and the secular share many coping mechanisms (self-distraction, venting, positive reframing) and sources of meaning.[46] However, secular people do differ from the religious in some ways of coping with psychological challenges. One example already mentioned is that the nonreligious often experience rejection or stigmatization from others, which can lead to a lack of social support. Another obvious difference is that seculars do not perceive that there is an external agent such as God who will protect them from harm or who can be counted on to provide a sense of meaning. Interestingly, although seculars report having fewer coping resources than the religious, the impact of this may not be consequential for their mental health. That is, although atheists report the experience of external meaning in their lives less frequently than their religious counterparts, this is not perceived as a crisis of meaning, nor does it affect their overall happiness or life satisfaction.[47] Rather, meaning for atheists varies as a function of their commitment and engagement levels. This indicates that perhaps the perception of objective, external meaning is not as essential for the life satisfaction of atheists and agnostics as it is for the religious. This research has found that atheists and believers did not differ on their level of satisfaction with social support, even though the atheists and agnostics reported fewer actual sources of social support. It may be that nonbelievers tend to identify less with social groups and institutions, instead seeing themselves individualistically and as relatively less dependent on validation from the existing social framework (see the previous chapter on personality). These findings are what one would expect for those whose individualistic values are derived less from reference to external sources or in unison with other groups.[48] Again, this shows that the objective presence of coping resources may not be as relevant to mental health as one's subjective need for, or satisfaction with, these resources.

In some religious worldviews, belief in an external god provides an explanation for existence and a sense that no matter what happens, someone or something is in control, and that life has a superordinate purpose. Therefore, when life is challenging and these existential needs are threatened, one of the functions of religion is to compensate for the perceived lack of control, certainty, meaning, and companionship. This raises questions about how secular individuals are similarly compensated. Upon what sources do the nonreligious rely to maintain their self-esteem in the face of threats? A sense of control can be derived both from personal sources, such as an internal will or drive, and from external systems.

One external source of control and order for seculars is the existence of a system of competent sociopolitical institutions. Experiments in which individuals' sense of control or order is temporarily threatened reveal that people compensate by bolstering beliefs in an orderly worldview. The relationship between different sources of control is "hydraulic" in the sense that threats to one source of control cause a compensatory reliance on alternative sources of control. Experimental threats to personal control cause people to become more supportive of their government and more resistant to changing it.[49] Conversely, increased personal control leads to a higher level of comfort criticizing the government. Also, threats to one source of external control (e.g., government corruption) cause individuals to "shift" their reliance to other forms of external control (e.g., capitalism). Therefore, even in the absence of a religious worldview, secular individuals rely on other equivalent external and internal resources to meet existential needs.

Such findings have implications for how secular individuals view the relationship between religious and governmental systems of control. Events that challenge a sense of control (e.g., electoral chaos) cause individuals to feel anxiety about lack of stability, which in turn lowers faith in these external systems (i.e., the government), which is balanced by subsequent increases in faith in other sources of control (e.g., God).[50] In the opposite direction, threatening religious systems of external control leads to increased faith in government. Individual factors can determine which method of control is preferred. Those with independent methods for construing themselves rely more on their own beliefs or on sources of external control.[51]

As mentioned earlier, the nonreligious are often derided for "not believing in anything." However, in light of these findings, we see that existential insecurities can be managed without reference to religious worldviews. Just as with religion or governmental institutions, a sense of order and predictability can also be derived from a belief in scientific knowledge and/or societal progress. For example, an affinity for logic and science can bring happiness to secular individuals.[52] This gives us intriguing insight into the oft-discussed conflict of "science versus religion" in that, rather than a merely factual dispute, belief in these competing worldviews conflicts on a deeper and more existential level. Not only does belief in science tend to be negatively correlated with religiosity, but to the extent that one worldview is valued, the other one decreases in value.[53] In experiments wherein scientific theories were depicted as insufficient explanations, there was a simultaneous increase in individuals' evaluations of God, and vice versa, so that faith in God does in fact decrease faith in science.[54]

Endorsing scientific progress helps people regulate threats to order and control, as long as these theories and beliefs also imply that the world is (or will be) an orderly place.[55] For example, one problematic aspect of science for many religious—and even some nonreligious—individuals is Darwin's theory of evolution by means of natural selection. Although this conflict is often framed as one in which scientific accounts of human origins contradict biblical literalism, the conflict also occurs at a more abstract level, because of the contrary implications of naturalistic evolution for a sense of orderly, goal-directed progress; in pure Darwinian selection, there is no agent "in charge" and no ultimate goal. In one study, a temporary threat to a sense of control reduced people's belief in evolution and induced a relative preference for theories of life that promote order, either by stressing the role of a controlling God (intelligent design), or in a form of evolution that emphasizes inevitability and progress. Moreover, in this study, increased preference for intelligent design over evolutionary theory disappeared when the latter was framed in terms of an orderly process with inevitable outcomes. Thus, even for secular individuals, psychological threats can enhance belief in external agency, but only in the absence of other options that help to create order in the world.[56]

DEATH AND SUICIDE

Perhaps the ultimate existential threat to control, certainty, meaning, purpose, and social connection is the inevitability of death. In his book *The Denial of Death*, Ernest Becker suggested that awareness of our own mortality threatens our self-esteem and causes anxiety, but our belief in the validity of our cultural worldviews allows us to symbolically—or, in the case of religion, literally—transcend our own mortality. Given that, for seculars, there is no comfort of literal immortality, does this mean that cultural worldviews do not play the same death-denying function for them? According to Becker, the transcendent basis of symbols forming our worldview (or "hero systems") functions similarly:

> It doesn't matter whether the cultural hero system is frankly magical, religious, and primitive, or secular, scientific, and civilized. It is still a mythical hero-system in which people serve in order to earn a feeling of primary value . . . of unshakable meaning. . . . "Civilized" society is a hopeful belief and protest that science, money, and goods make man count for more than any other animal. In this sense, everything that man does is religious. [57]

For seculars, self-esteem and symbolic immortality may be derived from cultural accomplishments (such as writing a book!), artistic work, material possessions, or an ideology such as humanism. But are these forms of immortality less satisfying than eternity itself? The evidence on whether overt anxiety surrounding death differs as a function of religiosity is mixed. Most studies have shown that religious individuals have less death anxiety, with other studies finding no difference, and still others find that religious individuals are more anxious about death.[58] As with other areas of the literature, these findings are difficult to apply to the nonreligious because of the religiously predominant samples. Experiments in the field called "terror management theory" have tested some of Becker's ideas about the compensatory role of cultural worldviews in fending off mortality fears. Results suggest that anxiety about death, when made more conscious or salient, causes individuals to reinforce or bolster their cherished worldviews; conversely, any threat to the validity of their worldviews causes an increase in death anxiety, often on an unconscious level.

This raises the question of whether seculars show similar reactions to death reminders as the religious. It appears that, contrary to the "no atheists in foxholes" theory, atheists do not increase their belief in God in response to mortality threats, and thus religion does not serve a death-denying function for the nonreligious.[59] However, evidence regarding whether secular individuals increase secular beliefs in response to mortality, a "worldview defense theory," is inconsistent. In one study, when reminded of their own mortality, the nonreligious exhibited a defensive reaction, denigrating those who threaten their worldview, whereas religious individuals did not, implying that even nonreligious worldviews can function to ameliorate the awareness of death.[60] Other work finds that when they are reminded of death, all participants, regardless of religiosity or secularity, explicitly polarized and defended their own worldviews (i.e., atheists becoming even more strongly disbelieving), implying that all worldviews, regardless of supernatural content, may be protective against mortality threats. Interestingly, there is some evidence that agnostics, but not atheists, increase their religiosity when death is made salient, indicating that their lack of certainty is more reactive to death anxiety.[61] This would again imply a curvilinear relationship between religiosity/secularity and death anxiety, such that moderately religious individuals experience or report greater fear of death than either strongly religious or nonreligious individuals.[62] This is consistent with a view that confidently held worldviews, whether religious or secular, may help in dealing with existential threats. Clearly, this emerging area needs further research.

As mentioned previously, secular individuals' worldviews often focus on science or competent governance in order to provide a sense of control and meaning. Those who hold such secular worldviews also have reactions to mortality threats. In one study, individuals prompted to contemplate their own death report greater belief in science compared with those who are not under such stress, indicating that a scientific worldview may serve a compensatory death-denying function.[63] Similarly, as mentioned earlier, the unguided process of Darwinian evolution may be particularly threatening to religious individuals. For example, reminders of participants' own mortality increased participants' acceptance of intelligent design theory and rejection of evolution, regardless of their religiosity or preexisting attitude toward it.[64] However, these effects were reversed when naturalism itself was presented as a source of existential meaning (and also among natural-science students, for whom evolution may already provide existential meaning). These reversals suggest that, beyond any scientific merits, attitudes toward evolution or intelligent design can also function as a source of existential meaning and purpose for seculars.

When faced with death, religious and secular alike often search for meaning. In a study about end-of-life concerns, atheists expressed a desire to find meaning in their own lives, to maintain connection with family and friends, and to experience the natural world through the experience of dying.[65] However, some differences are also apparent. In places where religiosity is common, seculars become concerned that care providers respect their nonbelief by not introducing religious elements into their treatment. Another distinct difference is that, relative to the religious, the nonreligious are more open to the use of physician-assisted suicide in the instance of potentially futile suffering. Interestingly, secular individuals show lower preference, relative to the religious, for aggressive measures to extend life.[66] Those who use religion to cope with advanced cancer are more likely to receive intensive life-prolonging medical care near death.[67] It is possible that certain religious beliefs (i.e., the view that life is sacred and can only be taken by God) influences religious individuals' beliefs about the role of medicine at the end of life. A substantial proportion of the general public also believes that divine intervention or a miracle could resolve a persistent vegetative state when physicians believe treatment is futile, leading to an unrealistically optimistic expectation of survival (which itself is linked to requesting more aggressive medical measures).[68] In contrast, many seculars evidently wish to retain, via their physicians, control of the dying process.

The openness to terminating their lives in the eventuality of suffering extends outside the narrow situation of an illness with little hope of recovery. It has long been noted that countries with lower levels of religiosity tend to have higher rates of suicide.[69] On an individual level, more frequent participation in religious activities is associated with a lower risk of suicide. Conversely, those who never participate in religious activities have higher odds of dying by suicide than those who participate.[70] Because greater religious attendance is associated with decreased odds of a suicide attempt, even controlling for greater social supports, it may not be the social contact inherent in some forms of religious participation that decreases suicide risk but something more specifically intrinsic to religiousness.[71] Religious individuals may have more hopefulness for the future, or secular individuals may lack fear of divine retribution for having taken their own lives.

PHYSICAL HEALTH

In many ways, what we know about the physical health of secular individuals resembles what we know about their mental health; on balance, those with lower religious engagement have poorer physical health than those with greater religious engagement—although the majority of studies do not find a difference either way.[72] For example, longevity and life expectancy are higher in those with greater as opposed to lesser religious involvement.[73] The link with religious attendance appears to be stronger for health or longevity rather than for recovery from already-existing illness.[74] As is also the case with mental health, the strongest association with physical health is with public, participatory faith (i.e., religious activity and attendance) rather than privately held beliefs. Although some have concluded that the transcendent content of religious and spiritual belief systems contributes to greater health,[75] there is little support suggesting that these specific aspects of religiosity are protective against physical illness, or that depth of religiosity is a factor.[76] Therefore, even though simple group comparisons indeed indicate that those with no religious preference are disadvantaged when it comes to mortality risk, studies controlling for demographics and religious service attendance eliminate much or all of this effect.[77] This suggests that demographic characteristics, psychosocial influences, and the lack of attendance at services account for the higher mortality of those with no religious preference.

Why would a lack of religious engagement be linked to a lower quality of physical health? The most plausible mechanisms may involve the absence of the benefits of religious attendance in (1) promotion of healthy practices, (2) social support, (3) psychosocial resources (e.g., self-esteem and self-efficacy), and (4) belief structures fostering a sense of coherence.[78] The role of religious attendance in promoting healthy lifestyles (e.g., avoidance of smoking, regular exercise, moderate alcohol consumption) has received mixed support.[79] Although greater attendance is related to increased rates of female preventive service utilization (e.g., yearly exams, Pap smears), the relationship with religious identity or belief, alone, is inconsistent and dependent on the aspect of religion measured and the type of preventive service in question.[80] This does not necessarily follow a linear "greater attendance is better" pattern. Evidence is also mixed regarding diet and physical activity (e.g., lower prevalence of smoking in the religious but greater prevalence of obesity).[81]

It may be that differences in healthy behaviors, as a function of religious attendance, are actually due to some sampling variable—perhaps those with less conscientious personalities are also less likely to attend religious services, whether or not they believe in God. One fundamental influence on diligent health-promoting behaviors (e.g., diet, exercise) and resulting longevity is having a conscientious personality.[82]

As discussed in the previous chapter, those with more conscientious personalities may also gravitate toward organized religious groups in religiously normative communities. Therefore, greater religious attendance acts as a proxy for conscientious health behaviors, and this may explain why less conscientious individuals have both relatively poorer health and lower religious attendance.

Another possible health mechanism present in religious groups that is less readily available to unaffiliated seculars is social support. Meaningful group activities are encouraged by religious organizations, which are well-known for providing support to members who are ill.[83] Studies find that the connection between religious attendance and ability to cope with illness is not direct but indirect, via greater perceived social support from one's community.[84] Obviously, social support is not a uniquely religious mechanism. In fact, when religious and nonreligious group members with equal levels of group participation are directly compared, their physical health is equivalent.[85] This indicates that the ostensible positive health effect of religious participation is attributable to the "secular" factor of general group participation and the resulting social support, rather than to religious content or the supernatural power of faith.

Just as with flawed research into religion's effect on mental health, some ways of improving physical health that are ostensibly "spiritual" actually rely on secular processes used by the religious and nonreligious alike. Meditation and relaxation to address stress-related diseases are not necessarily spiritual, although they are often categorized as such.[86] Similarly, although spiritual concepts such as having a sense of reverence improve health, secular reverence—being in nature, playing sports, enjoying music or art, being loved or supported, and serving others—does so as well. For example, in patients awaiting surgery, reverence in a secular sense ("feeling or attitude of deep respect, love, and awe, as for something sacred") rather than the religious/spiritual sense predicted shorter hospitalization.[87] Many of the effects traditionally attributed to "spiritual" forms of reverence do not add discernible benefits to secular forms of reverence. The connection often seen between the use of positive religious coping and better functioning may be largely due to basic—and often secular—factors like social support and hope.[88]

Although concepts such as religious doubt and spiritual struggles are associated with poorer physical health, as was the case with mental health, these are difficulties faced by those with uncertain or conflicted religious beliefs, rather than the completely or firmly secular. It is well-established that the use of positive religious coping (e.g., "God is by my side helping me") or having a "secure relationship with God" has been linked to better self-rated physical health among people facing stressors.[89] Compared with parallel secular methods of coping with illness such as hope, self-control appraisals, and active coping, religious methods of coping are related to greater subsequent stress-related growth.[90] It may be the case that religious world-views provide religious individuals with a cognitive framework that lends itself to reappraising a random, threatening event as beneficial. However, this sort of finding has little applicability to secular individuals for the same reason that the poorer physical health of those who feel distant from God is not relevant to those who do not endorse any conception of God at all.[91] Conversely, religious and spiritual struggles (e.g., "God has abandoned me," "the Devil made this happen") have also been predictive of declines in physical recovery in medical rehabilitation patients and greater risk of mortality following a medical illness, and yet these are also not applicable to secular individuals.[92] Therefore, physical health difficulties are more common among those with religious doubts and struggles, or among those who use religion for negative coping, but this does not imply that the lack of religiosity, in and of itself, is detrimental.

Overall, then, physical health does differ between secular and religious individuals. But beyond this relatively broad finding exists a more complicated and complex picture.

CONCLUSION

Given the exceptionally broad and complicated field of mental and physical health, and with all the possible methods of determining outcomes, any brief summation is by necessity going to be an oversimplification. However, some conclusions have emerged. On the one hand, there may be domains of mental well-being in which the nonreligious are at a disadvantage. The strongest case for this is the evidence contrasting those nonreligious who do not attend organized groups with engaged religious individuals. In this case, the engaged religious believers appear to function better across a wide range of domains, including lower depression and anxiety and better physical health. However, the most relevant question quickly narrows to: "What are the mechanisms of this association?" The vast majority of findings in the religion and health domain are not applicable to completely nonreligious individuals. There is emerging evidence that atheists and agnostics, particularly those involved with organized secular groups and who are embedded within their community, are no different than engaged religious believers with regard to mental or physical health. Additionally, any connection between secularity and mental well-being must be considered within its cultural context. In religiously predominant societies, the nonreligious appear to have poorer mental health than they do in contexts where secularity is more normative. In fact, some of the strongest factors affecting physical and mental health relate not to religious belief itself or the lack thereof but to having a coherent, functional worldview and being a member of a normative and socially supportive group. Put a different way, there is no strong evidence that confidently secular individuals who are engaged in their communities differ in any substantive way from similarly engaged religious individuals in terms of mental or physical health.

8

SECULAR MORALITY AND ETHICS

SAMANTHA IS IN her thirties. She lives with her boyfriend and their three dogs. Every now and then, while walking her dogs around the neighborhood, she runs into a neighbor—a woman in her fifties—who also walks her dogs along the same route. The two of them have become dog-walking friends. And so, about twice a week, they end up walking their dogs together, talking about this and that.

But recently, their friendship hit a snag when the topic of religion came up. The neighbor asked Samantha what church she goes to. "I don't go to church," Samantha said.

"Why not?"

"Well, I don't believe in God."

"What? But if you don't believe in God, then how can you be a good person?!"

Samantha tried to explain that she doesn't think one has to believe in God in order to be moral, but her neighbor wasn't buying it. She just couldn't fathom how anyone could be a good person without belief in God.

* * *

Morality is perhaps the one, single topic that most frequently surfaces in any discussion of religiosity and secularity. Rare is the atheist who has never had to field a question like Samantha did. What nonbeliever has never heard the backhand compliment along the lines of "You're an atheist? But you seem so nice."?[1] If one makes even the most cursory search on the Internet using terms such as "atheism" and "religion," one is almost always led to some discussion of how these domains relate to moral or ethical decision-making.

146

Given all of this, it is useful to step back and more deeply consider the domains of religion, secularity, and morality.

ATTITUDES AND STEREOTYPES REGARDING SECULAR ETHICS

One obvious reason that morality is linked to religiosity is because religions have often claimed to be the source of moral rules and precepts, despite the fact that other sources of morality clearly exist. After all, nonhuman animals living in groups also exhibit forms of proto-morality such as empathy and reciprocity that promote cooperation.[2] Likewise, successful human social groups often develop ethical codes that have nothing to do with transcendent justification or supernatural monitoring. Religious institutions themselves may have an interest in the notion that one cannot behave morally outside of their influence, or that a rejection of divine authority is tantamount to a rejection of common ethical tenets (e.g., "the Golden Rule").

Regardless of the origin of the association, however, the stereotype of the immoral atheist is entrenched.[3] Atheists are often seen as "other," simultaneously a moral threat from the lower social rungs (e.g., as criminals) and/or as the snobbish elite (e.g., self-interested materialists). These stereotypes are so widespread that common reactions to atheists include distrust and disgust.[4] In one poll by the Pew Forum, about half of US respondents report that a belief in God is a necessary prerequisite to living a moral life.[5] Even many social scientists suggest that religious individuals are more "prosocial" (e.g., helpful, altruistic, empathic) than nonreligious individuals, and that without religiosity, society would suffer a lack of self-control.[6]

The pervasiveness of these stereotypes can create problems for attempts to actually ascertain any relationship between religion and morality in an unbiased manner.[7] Common methods used to measure morality, such as self-reports and peer reports, can be biased or contaminated by what is presumed to be the case: that atheists "must be less moral." Even when two individuals behave identically, the nonreligious one is labeled as less moral, personable, and conscientious than the religious one.[8] Interestingly, many nonreligious people themselves subscribe to this stereotype, although to a lesser extent. Even exhibiting symbols of secularity, such as a "Darwin fish," can cause people to assume one's immorality. This may thus become a self-fulfilling prophesy. For example, individuals are less willing to cooperate with nonreligious than religious individuals, which itself could elicit lower cooperation.[9] The stereotype of the immoral atheist is widely held, but it is endorsed more strongly by religious people.[10] Studies that use economic sharing tasks indicate that religious individuals trust their fellow religious in-group members and are more generous to them than toward nonreligious individuals.[11] By contrast, the nonreligious tend to not discriminate on the basis of group identity and show little preference for other nonreligious individuals over religious ones.[12]

The overall effect of this stereotype makes the assessment of actual, objective morality all the more difficult. Self-ratings on personality measures or estimates of hypothetical moral behavior are colored by stereotypical expectations, with the potential result being that religious people will rate themselves as being more moral than nonreligious people rate themselves.[13] And while there is a tendency for all individuals, regardless of religiosity, to respond to such measures in a way that is socially desirable and that will enhance their image, this tendency to "look good" appears to be stronger among the religious, whereas self-image is less likely to be enhanced among the secular.[14] As a result of these effects, any attempt to accurately assess morality must weigh objective measures of actual behavior more heavily than self-reports or estimates of hypothetical prosocial behavior. However, before we get to the findings on actual moral behaviors as a function of religiosity/secularity, we need to start with the fundamental question: "What is the definition of morality?"

DEFINING MORALITY

What is morality? How does it develop? Which domains of behavior does it encompass? As it turns out, the answers to these fundamental questions are complicated, and each answer affects how one approaches subsequent questions; there is disagreement regarding which domains constitute morality not only among philosophers but also among sociologists and psychologists. Making matters even more complicated, an individual's sociopolitical and religious worldview systematically biases what he or she regards as moral and ethical, rendering elusive any common agreement about which issues fall under the domain of morality.

Some suggest a "postmodern" or relativistic approach to morality, maintaining that it is subjectively defined and dependent on a given culture or era, whereas others assert that there are core characteristics of morality that transcend time and context in a truly universal way. For example, consider two individuals, one who assists the needy without prejudice yet has a casual sex life and enjoys recreational drugs, whereas the other person is not generous toward the poor, perhaps even blaming them for their plight, yet leads a chaste sexual life and is a teetotaler. Further, one of these individuals is scrupulously honest with business transactions, yet lies to the government regarding personal income taxes; the other pays what he owes in taxes but has lied on his résumé.

Which one is more moral? Judging the overall level of morality obviously involves trade-offs. Using the preceding example, one method is to distinguish between personal or ascetic morality as opposed to social morality.[15] The former involves issues of restraint regarding sexuality, alcohol and drug use, and the valuation of conformist attitudes toward "offensive" behavior and language. Social morality refers to behaviors that more directly affect others, such as charity, prejudice, and attitudes such as forgiveness and tolerance.

Although morality can be approached by studying specific behaviors, there are other ways to conceptualize morality such as a focus on the process or rationale by which individuals arrive at moral conclusions.

MORAL REASONING

One model of morality that has been influential for several decades is based on the work of Lawrence Kohlberg.[16] Kohlberg suggested that moral reasoning develops and matures through successive stages. He hypothesized that earlier stages of moral reasoning, characteristic of young children, focus on self-interest or the mere avoidance of punishment. That is, something is thought to be "wrong" if it results in punishment or disadvantages the child. Kohlberg suggested that adolescents and some adults developmentally proceed to "conventional" moral reasoning, making judgments based on social conformity, "law and order," or obedience to authorities. Some people later develop postconventional moral reasoning based on broad underlying principles such as justice or fairness. Postconventional morality is complex and relativistic, balancing competing interests and possibly rejecting social norms. Take the classic example of a poor man named Heinz whose wife is dying of a rare disease that can only be treated by a drug that must be purchased from a rich man who is only willing to sell it for large sums of money. In this case, a conventional line of reasoning may be that Heinz should not steal the drug because stealing is wrong and Heinz is not a criminal. However, according to postconventional reasoning, stealing the drug may be acceptable because the life of his wife outweighs the illegality of stealing. Using such scenarios involving trade-offs, researchers have developed methods of determining individuals' level of moral reasoning, which can then be cross-referenced with other characteristics such as religiosity.

Studies have found that the religious—particularly conservative and more literalistic religious individuals, such as fundamentalists—tend to act based on rules or obedience to social norms or authority, whereas secular individuals more often make decisions on the basis of delineating an underlying principle.[17] As a result, more liberal individuals tend to reason at the postconventional level, leading some to allege that the Kohlbergian moral system is liberally biased, antiorthodox, and even antireligious because complex and relativistic reasoning is judged to be of a higher developmental level than conventional rule-based morality.[18] Although a categorization on the basis of these stages does result in "lower" scores for those whose morality is reliant upon divine authority, religious authority is not the only limiting factor on moral develop-ment. Rather, reliance upon any external authority for moral claims not accessible to disputation or inquiry can prevent the extension of moral reasoning to general prin-ciples. Aside from the controversy regarding whether one form of moral reasoning is superior to another, Kohlberg's system can still prove valuable on a descriptive level in its recognition that there are identifiable differences in moral reasoning.

Despite the focus in popular culture on the role of religion in morality, empirical evidence indicates that religion is often secondary to other broader and more influen-tial characteristics, such as age and education, in predicting the development of moral judgment.[19] For example, experience gained from training in ethical philosophy is associated with more complex moral reasoning than that derived from religious training.[20] Although studies indicate that those who are not religiously affiliated judge a wider range of actions as less morally serious than the religiously affiliated, the quality of moral reasoning itself does not differ between these groups.[21] Meaningful real-world altruistic behavior is better predicted by factors such as moral reasoning than by religiosity itself.[22] Furthermore, reasoning based on conventional religiosity (e.g., "Thou shalt not steal") often does not generalize to complex real-world actions requiring flexible principles and contextualization (e.g., "Is a tax shelter equivalent to theft?"). Aside from these practical problems, more recent approaches to moral psychology have posed a challenge to the study of moral reasoning, via evidence that much of morality is actually based on nonrational processes.

MORAL INTUITION

The field of morality has shifted over time from a Kohlbergian approach emphasiz-ing moral reasoning to one based on unconscious processes with deep evolutionary roots.[23] This "social-intuitional" model suggests that morality is based principally on emotional "gut-level" responses that are then rationalized or justified by higher-order processes. One such model that has been gaining in popularity in recent years is that proposed by Jonathan Haidt. According to Haidt, there are five general domains of moral concerns, each of which can be amplified or attenuated as a function of indi-vidual or cultural differences. These domains of moral concern are (1) harm/care, (2) fairness/reciprocity, (3) authority/respect, (4) in-group/loyalty, and (5) purity/sanctity. A given moral action can be addressed using a mixture of different domains.

For example, one's reaction to abortion could be based on harm concerns such that "abortion is wrong because a potential life is harmed." Alternatively, restricting abortion could offend one's sense of fairness in that "banning abortion unfairly penalizes women, especially poorer ones." The social-intuitional model of morality is not necessarily incompatible with models emphasizing moral reasoning; indeed, the moral domains of emphasis are also reflected in moral reasoning levels. Those who stress individuating factors (empathy and fairness) also tend to use postconventional moral reasoning, such as delineating underlying principles, whereas those who use binding morality (including in-group, authority, and purity concerns) tend to determine morality based on conventional reasoning stages.[24] Overall, evidence suggests that morality is influenced to a large extent by intuitive, noncultural, possibly evolutionarily based instincts.

IS SECULAR MORALITY DIFFERENT?

The nonreligious are generally indistinguishable from the religious on most moral issues. There is little difference as a function of religiosity on issues regarding honesty, helping, violence, or forgiveness. College students differing on religious involvement do not significantly differ on social attitudes such as gun control, capital punishment, or affirmative action.[25] The exception is on issues of personal or ascetic morality.[26] That is, domains such as restraint regarding hedonism or sexuality (e.g., premarital sex, abortion, homosexuality, alcohol and drug use) and attitudes toward "offensive" behavior and language tend to elicit the largest discrepancy as a function of religion, whereas religiosity does not strongly predict "cooperative" or social morality such as lying, cheating, and hurting others.[27]

Researchers have found that moral intuitions can vary systematically as a function of broader religious and sociopolitical worldviews. Liberals and seculars tend to disproportionately focus on care and fairness ("individualizing" morality) and use an "ethics of autonomy," namely, that people ought to be allowed to live as they choose as long as others are not harmed.[28] Conservatives, and those who are more religious, tend to emphasize all five areas roughly equally and thus give the moral domains of purity, in-group, and authority ("binding morality") equal consideration with harm and fairness. A religious individual is likely to view gay marriage as violating purity or normative standards (i.e., "it seems unnatural," "it is deviant"), whereas secular individuals are more likely to view it as a fairness and care issue ("in the absence of harm it is discriminatory to restrict someone's right to marry"). Interestingly, the most self-evident moral domain for a given issue is not necessarily the one that actually best predicts moral views. Despite the

rhetoric on issues such as abortion, euthanasia, and stem cell research being dominated by arguments about potential harm, moral disapproval of these issues is actually better predicted by individuals' moral sensitivity to purity than by their stance
on harmfulness.[29] This suggests that rationales given for or against a given moral
position may sometimes be only loosely connected to the intuitions that motivated
the attitude in the first place.

The values and social attitudes of nonreligious individuals most likely stem as
much from underlying personality traits as from any specific religious or nonreligious
effects. As we saw in chapter 6, the nonreligious tend to have personalities marked
by higher levels of Openness to Experience, which is itself correlated with liberal
patterns of moral concerns. Also, as we will see throughout this chapter, because the
nonreligious tend to be quite low on the trait of authoritarianism, secular morality tends to reflect nonauthoritarian themes, such as independent autonomy, rather
than obedience to convention, as well as tolerance of unusual yet harmless "deviant"
behaviors.[30] The nonreligious are also more likely to reject the idea that morality
should dictate loyalty based on arbitrary characteristics such as shared group identity, nationality, or family ties.[31] These values reflect a general worldview that diversity is not a threat to social cohesion, and that other individuals and the world in
general are fundamentally benevolent and not to be feared.[32]

Another reason that secular morality may differ is related to systematic differences
over the source of morality. While religious people tend to view moral rules as transcendent and established by God, secular people's moral rationale does not involve
transcendent sources. One's stance on the source of moral authority (e.g., religion
versus institutional science) is the strongest predictor of whether one believes homosexuality is chosen or innate, which is also related to one's moral judgment on the
matter.[33] This may be because the nonreligious are generally more likely to use criteria such as "ethics of individual autonomy" as based on rational evaluation of the
social and human consequences of actions (i.e., "Who would be harmed if I acted
in such a way?").[34] By contrast, religious individuals tend to offer more rule-based
moral arguments (e.g., "Does my religion forbid this action?") rather than utilitarian
arguments grounded in the consequences of behavior.[35]

In short, seculars and religious individuals disagree about the substance, nature,
and origin of morality.

MORAL DOMAINS

Up to this point, we have discussed general moral attitudes. But this does not tell us
how secular and religious individuals actually behave. Therefore, it is informative to

look more closely at some specific domains of morality to determine whether any pattern emerges.

Honesty, cheating, and contextual influences. One of the ways to determine whether individuals will behave ethically is to place them in situations where they do not know they are being monitored and then offer an opportunity to cheat. This is easier said than done, of course, because, ironically, it requires a level of deception. Some standard paradigms include offering students a chance to grade their own test on the "honor system" or to have research participants engage in laboratory tasks in which they can be observed cutting corners. Although earlier studies often took the easier route of obtaining the subject's self-report of hypothetical honesty (e.g., "Would you be likely to cheat on a test?"), these hypotheticals are obviously flawed because they are vulnerable to individuals "faking good" or engaging in self-deception. Reviews of the many studies of honesty and cheating have indicated that religious individuals are more likely than nonreligious individuals to report that they value honesty and to say they would be less likely to cheat. When actual behavior is assessed, however, few differences are observed.[36]

In fact, studies find scant evidence of any predictors of honesty in general. Although it is common to conceptualize ethical behavior as a reflection of some innate quality analogous to a personality trait, the general consensus is that moral behavior is largely driven by situational or contextual factors. Despite the tendency to designate and distinguish "good guys and bad guys," most studies show rather weak behavioral relationships across domains (i.e., moral behavior in one situation does not strongly predict whether a given individual will behave morally in another situation), and people can be influenced, for good or for ill, by situational demands.[37] Again, controlled laboratory studies measuring behavioral honesty have found participants' level of religiosity to have no effect. However, some research has used experimental conditions to activate or "prime" concepts in order to influence individuals' behavior. Flashing words with a particular meaning on a visual display, or asking participants to solve word anagrams featuring subtle semantic content, often influences behavior on a nonconscious level. This is relevant to morality because many studies have shown that priming with religious content leads to greater prosociality, such as increasing generosity or inducing more fair play in economic games. In one example, when experimenters used words like "bless" and "cross" to activate religious concepts, participants interacted more generously and honestly with partners than did those who were presented with neutral control words.[38] This has often been referred to as evidence that religiosity has a general prosocial effect, but this explanation must be questioned on several counts.

Prosocial effects of religious primes often occur regardless of the individuals' religiosity, such that even nonreligious individuals tend to be influenced by religious priming. This may be due to the activation of stereotypical associations (as mentioned at the beginning of the chapter) endorsed by most individuals. It may also be due to activation of the perception of being under social surveillance—whether by God as a supernatural monitor or by other third-party observers, real or imagined. Rather than religious content in general, particular theistic concepts may have greater influence on moral behavior. Some work has indicated that activating belief in a punitive, stern god may be associated with greater honesty than either no belief in any god or belief in a loving, forgiving god.[39] Although religiosity has little consistent behavioral effect on honesty, religious precepts and concepts may serve a situational activating function (e.g., commandments against stealing), reminding individuals of ethical standards.[40]

Another qualification to the supernatural monitoring explanation is that religious concepts are not the only stimuli that prime prosocial behaviors. Secular prosocial primes (e.g., words such as "civil" or "court"), indeed any prime with a positive, reward-based content, have been shown to produce responses similar to those of positive religious primes, such as increases in honesty and generosity.[41] In the nonreligious, like the religious, this may function by activating the concept that others are monitoring them or by increasing self-awareness.[42] A range of nonreligious stimuli can do this. Participants become more honest when the experiment is conducted in a room containing a mirror or pictures of eyespots or even when being told that a dead student's ghost might haunt the laboratory.[43] Also, priming with the category of superhero increases future volunteering behavior.[44] These findings indicate that situational reminders that activate morality are not uniquely contingent on a transcendent or religious source. Rather, regardless of religious belief, individuals are affected by situational cues that remind them of how they ought to behave.

Religious priming can also have negative or non-prosocial effects, such as inducing participants to behave in a prejudicial or aggressive manner or generally increasing in-group favoritism.[45] This likely reflects the fact that religiosity is associated with both prosocial content and in-group favoritism and authoritarianism, both of which are activated by different aspects of religious priming (e.g., "religion" priming in-group loyalty versus "God" priming out-group altruism). There have been no studies of whether any form of secular priming has a similar negative effect on nonreligious individuals.

As mentioned at the beginning of the chapter, the belief that the nonreligious are morally suspect because they do not endorse a supernatural monitoring authority undergirds a stereotype of secular immorality. However, one interesting feature of such a stereotype is that religious people can be reassured that there are secular authorities that can function for the nonreligious in a manner analogous to the monitoring role of gods for the religious. One study has found that when secular authority concepts (e.g., police or courts) are primed, distrust of atheists is reduced, because individuals are reassured that atheists are being somehow monitored.[46] This accords with the general principle that well-functioning secular institutions that can provide rules and supervision are seen by secular and religious individuals alike as ways of ensuring prosocial behavior and even as alternatives to religious prosociality.[47]

Criminality, delinquency, and the problem of comparison groups. If religious beliefs are viewed by many as the foundation for moral behavior, it follows that the complete absence of religiosity would be associated with the greatest deviation from social norms—criminality. However, determining whether there is a consistent relationship between secularity/religiosity and criminality has turned out to be quite difficult. Although some reviews of research have found that religiosity has a negative association with crime, the relationship often fluctuates—or even reverses—depending on how both domains are conceptualized and/or measured. Similarly, the apparent association between youth delinquency and low religiosity is also inconsistent.[48] Some forms of deviance may be higher in the nonreligious (e.g., drug use), but other major forms show no pattern (e.g., violence).[49] This inconsistency is also reflected at a cross-national level; for example, church membership and attendance are associated with low property crime (e.g., theft) rates, whereas religious belief itself shows little association with serious crime, such as violence or drug offenses.[50] This "type of crime" phenomenon is an example of a hypothesized role of religion as a deterrent only for minor forms of deviance.[51] That is, in situations wherein secular institutions already emphasize the deterrence of significant crimes (e.g., assault, major theft), religion is thought to extend additional deterrence only for non-victim-oriented criminal behavior. As a result, some have argued that in environments where there are already secular norms, the effects of religiosity are redundant and weak.[52]

According to a "moral community" perspective, religiosity has been hypothesized to deter deviance and reform offenders by instilling a sense of guilt or shame. But, much as with the previously mentioned contextual priming of honesty and generosity, religiosity is not unique in this respect. Much as criminals have used religious narratives to reform themselves, those outside a religious framework use an analogous type of secular "conversion narrative" of personal transformation.[53] Unfortunately, as is also the case with the negative effects of religious priming on some behaviors, religious offenders just as often selectively use religious content to rationalize their behavior as to condemn it.[54] Therefore, although religiosity is often presented as uniquely transformative of deviant behavior, its role is neither unequivocally positive, nor qualitatively different from positive secular influences.

One problem with the literature pertaining to deviant or criminal behaviors is that studies are almost always unequipped to determine whether secular individuals differ from their religious counterparts in any meaningful way. On the one hand, many researchers have suggested that religiosity results in prosocial and antideviant effects that are unavailable to seculars. For example, David Myers draws attention to the fact that, relative to those who never attend church, "religiously engaged" Americans are "half as likely to be divorced and about one-fourth as likely to be smokers or have been arrested."[55] However, such comparisons of those who never attend church with frequent attenders reflect not only differences in metaphysical belief but also differences in group membership, social belonging, and even personality traits (e.g., conscientious diligence) required for stable membership in groups. This is related to the problem, mentioned in chapter 7, of defining religiosity or spirituality ("feeling connected to others") in such a way that ensures a relationship with other positive variables. In the same manner, many studies define religiosity as behavioral commitment (e.g., frequent prayer, group attendance), thus increasing any relationship with positive outcomes. As a result, it does indeed appear that the behavioral dimension of religiosity (i.e., religious participation) is associated with lower deviance, although measures of beliefs themselves are less consistently related to deviance.[56]

What does this tell us about religiosity and secularity? One hypothesis is that the deviance-reducing effect of religious belief is primarily a function of immersion in social networks—a "community of believers." Importantly, when the most frequently used measure of religiosity—church attendance—is anchored by "never" at the low end, such a study is actually addressing the hypothesis that *among religious believers*, those with low frequency of church attendance have more deviant behavior than the religiously devout.[57] Again, what is often interpreted as the apparent effect of religion appears to be a proxy for general motivation, conscientiousness, and engagement in programs or social events rather than simply believing in God.[58] Therefore, the relevance of any study using religious attendance to extrapolate conclusions onto secular individuals is questionable.

This lack of discrimination between low religious attendance and complete nonbelief is also reflected in the comparison groups, which often use "none" or "unaffiliated" to represent the absence of religiosity. Interestingly, out of the few studies of actual criminal behavior that have included categorizations clearly separating the nonreligious, most have found that those with no religious affiliation have lower crime rates than the religiously affiliated.[59] Surprisingly, there is a dearth of information regarding the religious makeup of incarcerated offenders. In one such study, 6 percent of inmates did not believe in a higher power—a figure identical to that for the general population (including those stating they did not know or there is no way to find out if God exists).[60] In one recent response to a Freedom of Information Act request, of federal prisoners willing to provide an answer (i.e., not all prisoners in the system), 17 percent report no religious preference, and 0.07 percent self-identify as atheists.[61] Similar figures for the proportion of atheists in the general population run between 0.7 and 1.6 percent.[62] Therefore, contrary to the expectation of a high rate of irreligion among criminals, there is not an overrepresentation of the nonreligious in prison.

Within-prison evidence is inconsistent regarding whether the absence of religiosity predicts institutional misconduct or the recalcitrance of the offender.[63] One study found that incarcerated adult male sex offenders who were lifelong religious stayers had more sexual offense convictions, more victims, and younger victims, relative to atheists.[64] Religiosity in the form of behavior such as attendance at services is associated with less deviant behavior in prison, although this is largely because prisoners with greater levels of self-control are more likely to engage in religious behavior. That is, problems with deviance are due to deficits of self-control, not deficits of religiosity.[65]

When comparing religious and nonreligious individuals on attitudes toward deviance, it is difficult to link any detectable differences to actual religious effects themselves. As mentioned in chapter 6, the nonreligious tend to be demographically distinctive (e.g., more often male, lower likelihood of being married, higher educational attainment). Therefore, many associations between religion and social deviance may actually be due to demographic or social influences (e.g., family structure or social embeddedness). Studies that control for such variables frequently find that the religiosity-deviance relationship is substantially diminished, often to nonsignificance.[66] For example, regarding youthful deviance, Benson et al. concluded, "After accounting for whether they have friends who engage in deviant behaviors, the adolescents' closeness to their parents, and how important it is for them to do what their parents say, religion contributes little independent constraining effect."[67] Such methodological difficulty in linking effects specifically to religiosity (or the lack thereof) presents interpretive problems for studies of social deviance.

Behavioral self-control and substance abuse. One domain that encompasses criminality together with a broader range of behaviors such as substance use is self-control. This is relevant to the topic of morality because it involves not merely general knowledge or attitudes about right and wrong but also the ability to plan future goals and exert restraint over impulses or temptations to deviate from those intentions. Some have suggested that the most relevant connection between religiosity and moral or ethical behavior is through its ability to assist in self-control. [68] The relationship between religiosity and lower crime has been found to be an indirect one, via the association between religiosity and greater self-control.[69] In a manner similar to the effect of activating religious concepts on honesty, exposing individuals to religious themes or concepts with priming causes them to exert greater self-control (although this effect is the same regardless of the personal religiosity of the participant, again indicating a generally held stereotype between religion and restraint).[70] The relationship between self-control and secularity exhibits a pattern similar to other concepts that we have seen throughout this book. We have a clearer picture that some forms of religion (notably, behavioral commitment) play a role in assisting in greater self-control relative to weaker religious commitment, but we have less information regarding whether this is relevant to nonreligious individuals. For example, one study found that, compared with evangelical Protestants, adolescents who do not identify with any religion exhibit greater self-control.[71]

One set of behaviors thought to be influenced by self-control is the use of substances. There is a modest relationship between overall religiosity and alcohol consumption: religious people, on average, drink less than secular people.[72] However, alcohol consumption does not linearly and smoothly increase as a function of lower religiosity. Rather, the relationship is driven largely by substantially lower consumption among conservative Protestants, the highly devout, and denominations or sects that specifically prohibit alcohol consumption. There tends to be less evidence of a difference in alcohol consumption or attitudes between the religiously unaffiliated and liberal or moderate religious (at least Christian) populations.[73] A negative relationship between religiosity and drug use or abuse is stronger and more consistent than between religiosity and alcohol, likely because of the "deviant" status of drug use, although again, data on the affirmatively secular are limited.[74]

Interestingly, there is some indication that the religion-alcohol relationship is curvilinear, with greater consumption levels found in the mildly or weakly religious than among the strongly religious or nonreligious.[75] In the broader US population, in regard to abusive or problematic drinking, although the very religious have the lowest number of negative social consequences as a result of alcohol use (e.g., job or legal problems) and the lowest levels of binge drinking, the heaviest drinking occurs among the "not really" religious, as opposed to the "not at all religious," group.[76] A similar phenomenon has been found among those participate in Alcoholics Anonymous programs , such that atheist and agnostic nonbelievers have equivalent rates of abstinence to those of strongly spiritual and religious members. Those with weak or uncertain beliefs about God report a higher frequency of drinking.[77] As with the general deviance literature, however, it is difficult to further dissect such curvilinear effects because most studies tend to lump together the nonreligious with the weakly religious or tend to use church attendance as a measure of religiosity.

Many studies suggest that religiosity seems to have a preventive effect on drinking among youth, and so less religious youth lack its "buffering" benefits. However, the effects of religion are themselves tied to other effects (e.g., peer, family, academic influences). When such variables are held constant, although religious effects do not consistently disappear entirely, they are frequently diminished. Secular factors such as parental constraint and peer behavior tend to be more predictive of drinking than personal religious belief.[78] Even less religious youth who are involved in secular but religion-supported programs drink less, an effect largely due to peer influence.[79] Social, not private, religiosity is associated with decreased substance use and delinquency, suggesting once again that it is communal religiosity rather than private belief alone that can act as a preventive force against deviance.[80]

As with criminality, greater religious commitment appears to reduce substance use because it is associated with self-control. Engagement in forms of religious commitment (e.g., daily prayer) contributes to greater self-control, which translates into lower substance use.[81] Those who demonstrate religious commitment tend to monitor their standing regarding personal goals, and they also feel monitored by others.[82] In sum, there is evidence that strongly communal forms of behavior, such as religious belonging, can have some preventive effects on deviance, delinquency, or substance abuse compared with weaker, private, or unaffiliated religiosity because of the effects of self-control. Limited data on strongly or affirmatively secular people suggest complex patterns depending on specific behaviors, but no evidence overall of consistently deviant or amoral behavior compared with (more) religious individuals. Exceptions typically regard attitudinal differences about behaviors that are of questionable moral relevance (like moderate alcohol consumption). In fact, there are once again some indications in the research literature of greater similarity between strongly religious and nonreligious individuals, compared with those who are less strongly committed either way.

Sexual attitudes and behavior. For many people, one of the domains of behavior most closely associated with concepts of morality is human sexuality. Indeed, the domain of purity (from Haidt's five moral dimensions described earlier) contains many references to sexuality. Historically, all human societies have regulated sexual behavior, a sign that these behaviors have been of perpetual concern.[83]

An overview of sexual attitudes and behavior reveals that the traditional association between lower religiosity and liberalized sexual behavior and between religiosity and sexual restriction is partially correct. Overall, seculars do appear to have a greater expression of sexuality relative to the religious. The average age of onset of sexual behavior in youth ("sexual debut") is younger for the more secular than for the more religious.[84] Similarly, youth with no religious affiliation and no religious service attendance have more oral sexual experiences and sex partners than people who are religiously affiliated.[85] Conversely, strong religious devotion appears to inhibit or delay premarital sexual activity relative to lower religious devotion, primarily by shaping sexual attitudes.[86] Interestingly, some of this may be qualified by differences between types of nonreligious individuals. For example, in one study, agnostics, but not atheists, had more liberal sexual attitudes relative to Christians.[87] Clearly, more information is needed on sexuality among the nonreligious. Overall, it appears to be a safe statement that low religiosity is associated with greater sexual expression relative to high religiosity on a variety of dimensions.[88]

However, there are significant caveats here. Self-reported attitudes toward sexuality as a function of religiosity/secularity show closer relationships than measures of actual behaviors. Also, simply self-identifying as secular or religious is less related to sexuality than degree of belief or religious attendance.[89] Although nonreligious youth are likely to view premarital sex and sexual fantasies as more acceptable than religiously devout youth, there are few actual behavioral differences as a function of religious affiliation or the lack thereof.[90] In another domain, those who never attend church consume more pornography than high church attenders, but the relationship is modest and, again, is more strongly related to church attendance rather than to beliefs.[91] In one study, when controlling for religious attendance, unaffiliated college-aged women were actually less likely than Catholic women to have engaged in casual sex ("hooked up") at school, such that the likelihood of "hooking up" was explained by church attendance rather than subjective religiosity.[92] Therefore, the relevance of most of the literature for the nonreligious is limited because most studies have defined nonreligiosity as the absence of church attendance, or low religious importance such as "religiously disengaged," and many studies omit the low end of the religiosity continuum entirely.[93] These issues are important for determining what, precisely, differentiates the sexuality of secular from religious individuals.

It is often difficult to directly link patterns of sexuality to secularity or religiosity per se as opposed to other proxy factors. As we have discussed in other chapters, the nonreligious often differ demographically, or in their personalities, from the religious. Many studies find that associations between religiosity and sexuality disappear once such characteristics are controlled for (e.g., parents' education or race/ethnicity). Religiosity is more related to sexual restraint in females than in males and in whites than in African Americans.[94] For example, religiosity may decrease consumption of pornography by shaping more conservative sexual attitudes and self-control, but this "restraining effect" of religiosity does not appear to be uniform across all demographic groups.[95] Therefore, it appears that secular youth display a lower level of sexual restraint relative to more religiously engaged youth, but it is not evident that this is connected with religious belief itself.

The relationship of religion to constraint of sexual expression is also complex because factors that influence the initiation of activity may not affect activity once it is initiated (i.e., a "threshold effect"). Despite the lower age of sexual debut among secular youth, religiosity has little association with sexual behaviors once intercourse occurs and appears to be less protective against unsafe sex among those who are already active.[96] This phenomenon can also be seen in the case of religiously motivated, abstinence-oriented sex education and associated "pledge" programs. These programs tend to enroll religiously motivated youth who pledge to delay sexual onset until marriage, although some four-fifths of them fail to do so. A more worrisome association is that those who pledge but do become sexuality active are more likely to have unprotected sex, and therefore are more likely to have sexually transmitted diseases, thus losing any tangible benefit of a delay in sexual onset.[97] Another potential negative effect is that greater religious participation has been associated with less sexual and reproductive health service use among sexually active young women.[98] One likely mechanism at play here is that secular youth may more pragmatically prepare for the onset of actual sexual behavior, whereas religiously devout youth may not even entertain the possibility, and thus are caught unawares and unprepared when sexual onset occurs.

In the domain of pornography, religious restraining effects may induce shame or guilt without necessarily attenuating the actual behavior, leading to cognitive dissonance or the perception of loss of control.[99] This may be related to the finding concerning the greater number of online pornography subscriptions in conservative "red" states, and that such subscription rates do not differ between areas with regular religious attendance and less religious areas.[100] Overall, it appears that secular individuals differ from religious individuals mainly in earlier onset of sexuality.

ABORTION, DIVORCE, AND INFIDELITY

Sexual onset and activity form part of a broader trajectory of marriage and childbirth—or, in some cases, the termination of pregnancy, cohabitation, or divorce. As we saw in chapter 4, in addition to earlier sexual debut, less religious and more liberally religious youth tend to stretch out the time between onset of sexual activity, marriage, and childbearing.[101] This is likely due to the "strategic orientation" of nonreligious youth, who are more likely to see the achievement of higher education rather than initiation of childbearing as the indicator of full maturity,[102] although, as we have seen, this orientation itself appears to function for nonreligious youth as an alternative to religious sanctions intended to delay pregnancy and marriage. For example, states with lower aggregate religiosity tend to have lower teen birth rates, even after controlling for income.[103] Overall, religiously based moral sanctions against certain sexual activities (e.g., premarital sex) tend to be less effective than the stronger influence of demographics, most notably age at marriage, education, and socioeconomic context.[104]

The topic that is seen as most representative of the disjunction between secular and religious morality, abortion, is more complex than it first appears. The likelihood of pregnancy termination is indeed higher in less religious individuals.[105] This is related to the previously mentioned strategic emphasis on educational and occupational goals rather than early family formation. Unintended early pregnancy and early marriage are seen as potentially threatening to education for the career-minded; therefore, more liberal secular youth have a higher abortion rate. Given that one obvious precursor to abortion is an unintended pregnancy, among women who conceive out of wedlock, religiosity increases the likelihood of subsequent marriage before birth, thereby reducing the probability of abortion. However, among women who conceive out of wedlock and do not marry before birth, religiosity is unrelated to the probability of having an abortion. In other words, it is not that religiosity itself directly decreases the chances of abortion; rather, it increases the likelihood of getting married subsequent to pregnancy, whereas pregnancy without marriage is more likely to end in abortion. In fact, religiously based abortion attitudes are less related to abortion behavior for those pregnant outside marriage than other factors such as economic and educational goals.[106] Therefore, the overall effect of religiosity (and the lack thereof) on abortion appears to be indirect via its influence on the probability that a woman will react to an out-of-wedlock pregnancy by deciding to marry. The characteristic that most sets secular individuals apart in the domain of sexuality is a preference for older age at first marriage. Most other decisions regarding sexuality and family formation are subordinate to that, illustrating the greater influence of demographic factors such as education and family-formation attitudes relative to religious attitudes.

An example of a sexually related moral domain in which seculars are not sharply distinguished from the religious is infidelity. As we have seen, religious effects tend to be greater for "threshold" or illicit behaviors (e.g., premarital sex, homosexuality) than for those behaviors with general social sanctions.[107] Although the nonreligious are more likely to have had, and to view as acceptable, premarital sex and same-sex sexual experiences, they do not differ from the religiously affiliated in nonmonogamous (i.e., cheating) sex.[108] Once again, the effects of behaviorally based religiosity (i.e., church attendance) on infidelity are stronger than the influence of religious belief itself, indicating that personal commitment and perhaps the effects of social support are more relevant to morality than are metaphysical beliefs.[109] Therefore, given the tangible effect on others involved in behaviors such as cheating or affairs, any additional religious sanction yields little incremental deterrence. By contrast, sexual behaviors that are more "personal" in their impact, such as sexual debut, are more strongly correlated with religiosity.

CHARITY AND VOLUNTEERING

Studies of self-reported charitable donations indicate that seculars report lower levels of giving than do the religious.[110] The Gallup World Poll reports that 39 percent of those for whom religion is highly important and who have attended services in the past week have donated to charity in the past month, compared with only 28 percent of the less religious; the figures for volunteering in the past month for those groups were similar—29 percent versus 18 percent.[111] Such findings have led many social scientists to conclude that there is a generalized prosocial effect of religious belief on giving and volunteering. As Robert Putnam and David Campbell stated in their book *American Grace: How Religion Divides and Unites Us*, religion makes "good neighbors."[112]

When this issue is examined in more detail, however, more complexity is revealed. In order to use charitable giving as a comparative measure of the generosity of religious and nonreligious individuals, it is also necessary to take into account the recipient or target of such giving. In the United States, religious organizations are the largest sources of charitable giving, with only a fraction of donations to churches being allocated to actual charitable programs or benevolences, the majority going toward personnel salaries or maintenance.[113] Although charitable giving to churches is fairly easy to identify, most of the existing literature does not clearly separate nonchurch giving into proportions directed toward religious versus secular programs. Many sources designated as "nonreligious" or "secular" often refer to groups or programs with religious ties, including religious education, summer Bible school, or missionary work. For example, in one major study, the category of "religious giving" referred narrowly to houses of worship or congregations, whereas all other forms of what was termed "secular giving" also included gifts to a school, program, or hospital run by a religious organization or those "that many would agree embodies spiritual values."[114] Therefore, because recipients of aid, though not themselves a house of worship or congregation, are frequently religiously affiliated or advance a religious agenda, it is in most cases difficult or impossible to distinguish assistance that is primarily religious in essence (e.g., church maintenance, proselytizing missionary work) from assistance consisting of a mixture of religious and secular benefit (e.g., faith-based counseling, medical missionary work).

Similarly, in many studies the religious identity of the giver is not properly identified. In his book *Who Really Cares*, Arthur Brooks argued that religious individuals are more generous than secular individuals.[115] However, his study categorized individuals as "religious" if they attended church once a week or more and as "secular" if they reported no religious preference or if they attend less than a few times per year. This has the effect of bundling "secular" individuals together with those who are religious but uncommitted or indifferent. Clearly, it is difficult in real-world contexts to cleanly separate religious and nonreligious givers and receivers of charity.

Why is it relevant to identify the religious or secular identity of both the givers and the recipients when determining relative generosity? One point of view is that all forms of charitable giving or volunteering, regardless of the beneficiaries, are equally helpful. Consider two agencies that both provide international aid: Samaritan's Purse and Doctors Without Borders. On first glance, both groups perform identical medical relief tasks (e.g., caring for patients stricken with Ebola) such that either group could be considered unambiguously prosocial and equally secular. However, Samaritan's Purse is considered by its directors as being primarily a Christian organization, and secondarily a relief organization. It also engages in proselytization (e.g., Bible distribution even in predominantly Muslim countries) and has addressed the HIV crisis by promoting abstinence-only sex education and opposing condom distribution. In another example, religiously affiliated hospitals or aid programs often base aspects of patient care on religious doctrine rather than on the medical needs of the patients. Similarly, many groups such as the Salvation Army or Catholic Social Services provide a mixture of relief work together with religious promotion that excludes recipients deemed inconsistent with religious values (e.g., same-sex parents).[116] Therefore, the religious character of a charitable organization is relevant to the types of services that it offers. Groups providing services are not all equally secular; thus support for them is not unambiguously prosocial because it is intertwined with the promotion of religious ideologies and proselytization as well as the provision of services.

A comparison of the religious identity of the organization with the religious identity of those providing support or charitable giving is important in determining qualities about the giver such as motivation or generosity. That is, any assessment of moral or ethical qualities necessitates a determination of the underlying reasons for the behavior, which also allows predictions to be made regarding how individuals will behave in other contexts. The factors that motivate charitable assistance can often be inferred through the pattern or exclusivity of this help. If assistance shows little relationship between the religious or secular identity of the giver and that of the receiver, we can infer that the motivation is more universalist and communal, directed primarily at assisting those in need. However, assistance provided only in conjunction with proselytization, or offered only to those sharing a religious identity rather than to non–group members does not represent generalized dispositional generosity operating independently of religious identity or motivation. Rather, we may infer that the underlying motivation is ideological or group-based and not universally prosocial. An individual who will give money to a soup kitchen but only if the assistance is offered within a religious context can be assumed to have less universalist motivation than one concerned solely with the provision of assistance.

As we have seen earlier in this chapter and in other chapters, religion appears to increase "parochial altruism"—a tendency toward greater concern for one's own group members combined with greater hostility toward out-group members. This is commonly found in a range of human social groups but can vary in strength of exclusivity.[117] Because a focus on the former component—greater prosocial behavior toward in-group members—has the initial appearance of benevolence, it is important to also determine whether such prosociality is extended equally to those outside the immediate group in order to distinguish generalized helping from parochial favoritism (for the same reason that selectively giving employment to family members is considered nepotism rather than disinterested helpfulness). Although some research has argued that religious individuals display greater charitable giving than the nonreligious even to secular charities, other studies find little effect of religiosity on nonreligious giving, indicating that the religious "giving gap" is the result of greater religious giving to religiously affiliated recipients.[118] Christians and the nonaffiliated are equally likely to give to "basic necessity" organizations (i.e., ones that help people in need of food, shelter).[119] Similarly, although some research suggests that religious individuals perform more community volunteering than nonreligious individuals, other work suggests no relationship between religiosity and volunteering for secular causes.[120]

A more apt description is that the more religious individuals are, the less their charitable giving and volunteering is directed toward general secular community causes.[121] For example, Boston College's Center on Wealth and Philanthropy stated, "As families become highly committed to their religion their giving becomes more concentrated in their church, synagogue, temple, or mosque and less concentrated in secular causes."[122] As with charitable giving, some studies find that those who are more religious (particularly conservatively religious or fundamentalist) show more exclusivity or insularity in their communal volunteering than seculars.[123] The Portraits of American Life Study found that the proportion of the unaffiliated who report volunteering at least one hour in a month (61 percent) was roughly equivalent with other major religious denominations such as Catholics (62 percent) and main-line Protestants (59 percent). However, the differences were greater for volunteering that was not with a religious organization, with 81, 68, and 73 percent, respectively, for those same categories. This suggests that religiosity is not necessarily associated with general community volunteering in the United States, but it does guide where people volunteer, such that the religious spend more time volunteering in churches, whereas the nonreligious spend more time volunteering outside churches.[124] Given the range of results and the ambiguity of separating religious and secular charities and volunteer beneficiaries in such naturalistic studies, one plausible conclusion is that religious people have reliably greater charitable giving than seculars and, to a lesser extent, a willingness to volunteer. However, this advantage in generosity extends primarily to situations in which the recipients themselves are religious; to the extent that the charity or volunteering recipient is not religious, seculars do not reliably differ from the religious.[125]

This pattern can be seen more clearly in controlled contexts wherein factors such as the group identity of the various "helpers and helpees" can be clearly identified. Rather than relying on naturalistic studies, a variety of experimental paradigms have been developed to study prosocial behaviors such as generosity, trust, and cooperation in laboratory settings that allow for more control over giver and receiver characteristics, including religious identification. For example, in economic interactions such as the "Dictator Game," generosity is assessed by giving one member of a pair an amount of money that is to be split with the other player. Other games, such as "Common Goods," enable players who trust each other to mutually profit. Some fairly solid conclusions have emerged from various reviews of this type of research.[126] First, there are few differences between secular and religious individuals regarding generosity and sharing in controlled interactions. Controlled studies manipulating the religious or secular identity of potential charities evidence no relationship between religious attendance and secular giving.[127] Second, religious individuals tend to share or cooperate more than nonreligious participants, but again, more with others who share their religious identity. Compared with secular people, Christians favor religious charities and are more trusting and generous with other religious people.[128] Third, studies appear to be detecting religious differences that are a function of group identity rather than religious beliefs. Controlled studies of prosocial behavior show that religious individuals appear to be more influenced by indicators of shared religiosity than are seculars.

In fact, this tendency to be influenced by shared group identity may be one of the key distinguishing factors between overall secular and religious morality. More broadly, the differences observed between seculars and religious individuals in prosocial behavior, rather than being due to differences in religious beliefs, are most attributable to differences in organized group membership and activities—obviously, the most relevant of these are religious group-related factors like church attendance. Other demographic differences between religious and secular individuals also complicate the relationship with prosociality. For example, women are found in greater numbers than men in religious groups, and they are also more likely to engage in prosocial behavior such as charity and volunteering. Controlling for the greater proportion of women has been found to diminish or eliminate the relationship between religious denomination and prosociality.[129] Beyond simple demographic characteristics, however, the general trend is that group-related factors such as church attendance or having a robust social network are typically stronger predictors of prosocial behaviors than is religious belief.[130] Social embeddedness in church-based networks, rather than religious belief, more accurately predicts behaviors such as charitable giving.[131] Likewise, membership in church groups simply increases the likelihood that one will be asked to donate money or time, or that social activities, accompanied by peer influences, and interactions will be structured around charitable activities.[132]

The lack of relationships between prosociality and belief is evidenced by findings that even nonreligious individuals, if they are socially linked to active members of religious congregations, display more volunteering.[133] In *American Grace*, Putnam and Campbell found that even unaffiliated or secular individuals who report attendance at religious events also report more prosocial behaviors. When controlling for frequency of church attendance, the authors found that "religious beliefs ... turn out to be utterly irrelevant to explaining the religious edge in good neighborliness." Rather, it was the religiously based social network that predicted prosociality, such that "even an atheist who happened to become involved in the social life of a congregation ... is much more likely to volunteer in a soup kitchen than the most fervent believer who prays alone."[134] However, this can be further qualified in that the group providing such benefits does not have to be a religious one in order to yield similar positive effects. Secular group involvement also has social benefits equivalent to those of religious groups and is motivated more by generalized trust values rather than by insular values.[135] Therefore, seculars are at a disadvantage in regard to communal prosocial behaviors such as charitable work and volunteering not because they do not believe in God but rather because they are not engaging in social networking within some of the most ubiquitous social institutions in the United States (i.e., churches). As a result, they are not being exposed to the factors that most facilitate community participation such as requests and opportunities to engage in these activities.

Another factor that is almost never mentioned in the conclusion of studies on religious and secular differences in charitable giving is that there is a systematic difference related to religiousness, as well as political conservatism, regarding preferences for types of prosocial generosity. Less religious individuals—who also tend to be politically liberal—are more supportive of government programs and services paid for by taxation than they are of private charitable giving.[136] Nonreligious and liberal religious individuals are more likely to favor government intervention in reducing inequality.[137] In a revealing survey item, respondents were asked this question: "In the Bible, when Jesus and prophets were talking about helping the poor, they were primarily talking about: A) our obligation to create a just society; or B) charitable acts by individuals."[138] Grouped by religious denomination, 60 percent of Hispanic Catholics, 54 percent of black Protestants, and 46 percent of the unaffiliated responded with "a just society," whereas only 36 percent of white Catholics, 33 percent of main-line Protestants, and 32 percent of evangelical Protestants did so. In other words, these latter groups interpreted their religious beliefs as mandating private charitable solutions rather than collective social justice. Similarly, societies with greater religiosity tend to have lower levels of taxes and hence lower levels of spending on both public goods and redistribution.[139] Therefore, the vast majority of studies characterizing generosity only in reference to charitable giving are actually assessing the particular form of prosocial generosity preferred primarily by more religious individuals, rather than other forms such as collective taxation and redistribution favored by the nonreligious. The more theoretically interesting question is why secular individuals prefer to engage in prosociality via public redistribution whereas religious individuals prefer to direct it via private charitable activity. This topic will be addressed further in the next chapter.

AGGRESSION, PREJUDICE, OBEDIENCE, AND AUTHORITARIANISM

Aggressive behavior does not appear to be strongly related to religiosity, although those with higher religiosity self-report as being less aggressive than those with lower religiosity.[140] Similarly, as will be covered in greater detail in the following chapter, the nonreligious have the lowest levels of racial, ethnic, and sexual minority prejudice among the major religious and demographic groups.[141] One of the reasons for these relationships is low authoritarianism, a trait sharing a substantial correlation with both religiosity and negative attitudes or behaviors such as prejudice and aggression.[142] That is, seculars tend to be, on average, quite low on traits that involve submission to authority, distrust of social out-groups, conformity, and the tendency to be aggressive toward perceived threats. For example, frequent church attenders and those with a denominational affiliation are more supportive of the use of torture against suspected terrorists than are non–church attenders and the unaffiliated.[143] In some ways, we have come full circle here, because we are again discussing broader moral emphases such as (using the Haidt system of five moral domains) authority-based and in-group-based morality. The nonreligious and liberally religious tend to reject morality based on these elements.

We also saw, earlier in this chapter, that activation of religious concepts (by conceptual priming) can lead both to greater generosity and honesty but also to greater in-group prejudice, most likely because religiosity is stereotypically associated with these tendencies. Such experimental priming research also shows that activation of religious concepts has the capacity to elicit prejudicial and aggressive responses from individuals, particularly those who are submissive to authority.[144] Although exposure to religious stimuli does not appear to have aggression-inducing effects on nonreligious individuals, the concept of religiosity for at least some individuals is evidently associated with greater obedience to authority. Another related pattern, discussed at the beginning of the chapter, is that seculars show a resistance to rule-based morality in favor of more consequentialist morality.[145] To use an example attributed to Socrates, what is "good" for seculars is independent of what is "good to God." Therefore, seculars are likely to consider disobedience to authority as being morally preferable if the authority is judged to be arbitrary or illegitimate. The individualistic values of seculars thus manifest themselves as a lack of conformity to moral norms that they deem to be based on mere social conventions.

Classic studies on obedience to authority, such as the Milgram paradigm, in which participants believe they are administering electric shocks to others at the request of the experimenter, are well-known for their demonstration of the power of situational and contextual variables relative to dispositional traits like authoritarianism.[146] However, one variant of this paradigm found that the relationship between obedience to the experimenter (i.e., delivering higher shock levels) and the participants' religiosity level was actually curvilinear.[147] That is, both the highly religious and least religious participants disobeyed (i.e., refused to shock), whereas moderately religious participants obeyed and gave higher levels of shock. The experimenters interpreted this as a conformity effect: that the religious extremes consisted of the types of people who act more on individual conscience rather than social conformity. Although somewhat informative regarding the issue of religiosity and obedience, the experiment cannot address what would have resulted if the authority requesting the violent action had been religious rather than secular (e.g., a minister versus a professor in a lab coat). However, we do have other studies regarding the relationship between moral conformity (and the lack thereof) and religiosity (and the lack thereof). The connection between some forms of religiosity and prejudice may depend on conformity to the social norm regarding the particular target group. For example, one meta-analysis found that racism was tied to religious conformity and traditionalism, and that although the relationship with overt racism has declined in recent years, true racial humanitarianism tends to be largely confined to in-groups; only agnostics were consistently tolerant.[148]

We mentioned earlier the theory that religion decreases deviant behavior by assisting with self-control. However, we are now seeing that the relationship may be more complex once we consider factors such as what happens when authorities may actually approve of aggression or situations in which social or personal constraints are removed. For example, in one laboratory study on the effect of alcohol intoxication on aggression, atheists did not differ from those with religious affiliations on aggression.[149] More interestingly, although religiosity predicted lower aggression when participants were consuming a placebo beverage, it predicted more aggression for the religious who were intoxicated. In other words, intoxication made normally restrained religious people more violent. This suggests that the "boost" offered by religiosity to self-control could backfire when inhibitions are compromised. Such findings indicate that the type of self-control enabled by religious devotion may not always lead to uniformly positive behavior. In fact, this heightened sense of personal control can actually lead people to take more risks or "leaps of faith."[150] This induced risk-taking can be caused by a sense of divine sanction or by increased susceptibility to the influence of others. The infusion of religious values can exacerbate group conflicts by "sanctifying" disagreements, making compromise less likely and obedience to authority more likely.[151]

SPONTANEOUS HELPING AND ALTRUISM

In contrast with planned behaviors such as charitable donations or volunteering, some forms of helping are "spontaneous"—in the sense that individuals unpredictably find themselves in situations where they are called upon to help. A typical behavioral study of spontaneous helping is staged by allowing someone to be exposed to a bystander who is in need of assistance.[152] Interestingly, this type of helping does not always correspond to the tendency to be nonspontaneously helpful, such as with planned giving, and may in fact show opposing relationships to these other forms of helping as a function of religiosity. In general, higher religiosity is more strongly related to planned helping, and lower religiosity is more related to spontaneous helping.[153] One study found that students who rated higher in Christian belief self-reported that they volunteer to help more than did those low in Christian belief, although they were not more willing to *actually* volunteer to help in nonreligious contexts.[154] Because of the issues raised earlier about the unreliability of self-reports, spontaneous helping tends to be less affected by self-presentation concerns and biases. When an individual is planning to make a donation or to volunteer time, this is more of a conscious decision to "be a helpful person"; when one is spontaneously caught unawares and asked to help, there is little time to deliberate on the implications of what this means to one's self-image.

A more fine-grained analysis has indicated religious differences in the type of assistance offered (and subsequently the underlying motivations) as opposed to the overall likelihood of spontaneous help. A series of programmatic behavioral studies has demonstrated that those who are high in religiosity tend to have a desire or need to appear helpful, whereas those who are less religious tend to be more interested in the stated needs of the "helpee" or victim.[155] That is, because those higher in religiosity may associate helping with external rewards, they tend to offer a "preset" plan, whereas those low in religiosity base their plan of helping on empathy for the person who is being helped. Such findings are consistent with other work suggesting that those low in religiosity are more likely than the religious to express prosocial behavior that is driven by compassion.[156] It is worth noting that the strongest predictors of real-life spontaneous helping are almost always contextual and situational (e.g., number of people present, being in a hurry or not) rather than dispositional, such as one's personality or level of religiosity/secularity.

One might argue that psychological studies of helping behavior are relatively trivial and confined to artificial situations and experiments. By contrast, it would be difficult to find more meaningful types of altruism than that which typified those who helped hide or rescue Jews from the Nazis during the Second World War. In a fascinating examination of altruistic helping, Samuel P. and Pearl M. Oliner identified and interviewed rescuers who risked their lives hiding Jews, along with non-rescuer controls who were not known to have assisted Jews during the war.[157] The interviews inquired about a variety of subjects, including not only the individuals' motivation for helping and family background but also their religiosity. The results indicated that the proportion of rescuers to nonrescuers was greater among both the highly religious and the nonreligious, with the nonrescuers predominating in the moderately religious. In a result consistent with religiosity in the Milgram obedience paradigm, individuals at the religious extremes refused to conform to general social norms but rather acted out of inner conviction. In fact, one of the principal characteristics that distinguished the rescuers from the nonrescuers was family background and the example set by parents. The parents of rescuers modeled high standards for caring behavior, rarely used physical punishment, preferring instead lenient discipline accompanied by reasoning about consequences to others, and encouraged their children to formulate their own value systems. Although the nonrescuers placed a greater emphasis on the value of benevolence (to friends and family), it was the rescuers who endorsed greater universalism, lower obedience, and an ethic of caring. This pattern has also been supported by other studies contrasting verified altruistic rescuers with nonrescuers, finding that the most important characteristics in the former are (1) higher moral reasoning level, (2) greater empathy, and (3) greater sense of social responsibility.[158] Therefore, in general we see that altruistic behavior stems from having high internal convictions, which often includes nonconformity to social norms if these norms are not judged to be prosocial.

CONCLUSION

At the beginning of this chapter, we discussed one obvious difference between secular and religious people: a belief that morality requires an external transcendent source. After viewing various moral domains, we have approached a deeper question: Does the perceived source of morality relate to the manifestation of moral behavior? That is, if one individual perceives morality as stemming from a transcendent authority, would this individual's actions be observably different from those of another individual who believes that morality can be derived from naturalistic sources or rational methods? Many believe that the absence of religiosity leads to relativism and moral turpitude. That hypothesis would seem to indicate that those who reject transcendent morality should be manifestly distinct in some way.

If secular morality is distinguishable from religious morality, it is not primarily in specific domains that are universally regarded as good (e.g., helping, honesty) or bad (e.g., crime, cheating). Rather, the primary differences are found in a subset of behaviors. In accordance with a sense of individualism and nonconformity, seculars are most distinct from the religious in domains that are thought to affect only themselves. For example, the domains of sexual debut and drug use could be classified as hedonistic in the sense that, whether pleasurable or immoral (or both), any consequences are limited to the individual engaging in the behavior. These are matters of "personal morality" and tend not to be judged by seculars as being necessarily harmful or unfair to others. This may be indicative of what differentiates the nonreligious from their religious counterparts. This overall distinction must also be qualified in that the differences are often not primarily between nonreligious and religious individuals but between conservatively religious individuals and both nonreligious and liberally religious individuals. That is, in many moral domains, such as charity and helping behavior, liberally religious individuals are indistinguishable from seculars. For example, a "Quest" religious orientation (i.e., open-ended and flexible), which resembles agnosticism, shows a different pattern from religious fundamentalism in domains such as helping or prejudice. In Haidt's schema, the "group-binding" moral domains are more meaningful to conservatives than to liberals. Therefore, many moral domains differ more as a function of type of religiosity as opposed to the mere presence of absence of religiosity.

In philosophical terms, the nonreligious tend to be consequentialists rather than deontologists; that is, they determine the relative morality of a given action based on its actual impact rather than its inherent goodness or badness. Major harmful behaviors like criminality or cheating do not show large differences as a function of religiosity. Similarly, some behaviors such as helping anonymous bystanders tend to be judged universally as beneficial. However, differences as a function of religiosity emerge in regard to the reasons for helping and the types of help offered. Religious individuals show greater engagement in areas such as planned helping and charitable giving, but this appears to be related to a greater desire to select the beneficiary of help rather than an intrinsically greater level of universal generosity. We will see in the next chapter that these differences are reflected in broader social and political values.

Our knowledge of secular morality is sorely handicapped by the failure of most studies to incorporate design features that would allow a clearer comparison of affirmatively nonreligious and religious individuals. Interestingly, those that have separated the effect of religious belief from behavior (e.g., organized group attendance) indicate that when secular and religious individuals differ, it is primarily driven by differences pertaining to involvement in an organized group. Therefore, most studies to date have established that those individuals who are socially integrated with a group tend to behave more prosocially than those not involved in groups, regardless of personal religiosity. Future studies will provide more explanatory mechanisms for the patterns of moral behavior that have been identified. The questions yielding the most interesting answers will likely be those such as "Why are the differences between nonreligious and religious individuals more evident in domains such as planned charitable giving but not in domains such as spontaneous helping?" "Are situational influences on morality such as characteristics of the recipient or the presence of an audience differentially influential on religious or secular individuals?" Given the relative power of situational contexts, such as priming compared with dispositional factors, we are likely to see the discussion shift from the latter to the former. For example, why are both religious and nonreligious individuals made more honest and generous by religious priming? Studies need to include secular contextual influences as a comparison to address whether religious effects are uniquely beneficial as opposed to merely a subset of prosocial influences. These are merely some of the deeper and theoretically interesting issues pertaining to the ultimate motivation and sources of morality.

SOCIAL AND POLITICAL ATTITUDES AND VALUES

ARTICULATING A SOCIOPOLITICAL worldview based on secular principles may appear at first glance to be quite straightforward. In some contexts, however, notably the United States, there has been a historical pattern of describing overarching political views through the lens of religious values. Consider two presidents who grappled in similar ways with the tension between religiously versus secularly based rhetoric. In 1862, Abraham Lincoln was lobbied by different groups, including religious ones, regarding how best to memorialize the Emancipation Proclamation. He wrote:

> I am approached with the most opposite opinions and advice, and that by religious men, who are equally certain that they represent the Divine will. . . . I hope it will not be irreverent for me to say that if it is probable that God would reveal his will to others, on a point so connected with my duty, it might be supposed he would reveal it directly to me. . . . These are not, however, the days of miracles, and I suppose it will be granted that I am not to expect a direct revelation. I must study the plain physical facts of the case, ascertain what is possible and learn what appears to be wise and right.[1]

Thus, one secular alternative to religious inspiration involves referring to objective and relevant facts in formulating a political course of action. Consider a quote from another president, Barack Obama, wrestling with religious versus secular ways of basing policy:

Democracy demands that the religiously motivated translate their concerns into universal, rather than religion-specific, values. It requires that their proposals be subject to argument, and amenable to reason. I may be opposed to abortion for religious reasons, but if I seek to pass a law banning the practice, I cannot simply point to the teachings of my church or evoke God's will. I have to explain why abortion violates some principle that is accessible to people of all faiths, including those with no faith at all. . . . in a pluralistic democracy, we have no choice.[2]

What do we know regarding the social and political views of secular individuals? Predicting an individual's position on many political issues, based on knowledge of his or her religious or secular views, is often not terribly difficult for anyone with a cursory exposure to current events. However, the relationship of secularity to other social attitudes is not as straightforward as it may seem. For example, there are different nonreligious subtypes—such as atheists versus spiritual-but-not-religious—that may exhibit different patterns. Also, in many cases, a shared political outlook transcends any difference in religious views; religious progressives are often indistinguishable from seculars on social issues. We know relatively less about how secularity is associated with sociopolitical views outside a Western, monotheistic context. Almost all our information on this front comes from North America and Europe, which may indicate that any observed relationship between secularity and political orientation may not generalize beyond that context.

The chapter will begin with views on specific social and political issues that characterize secular men and women. Then it will proceed into what is arguably a deeper and more interesting question: Why are these views associated with being secular? There is no required set of tenets for secular people, no necessary ideological checklist. Why, then, would we see similarities in sociopolitical worldviews among such people? It may be useful to keep in mind other, related questions, including: How do individuals go about forming a coherent sociopolitical worldview? What is the causal direction of these relationships? In other words, do we formulate religious or secular views early in life and then set about identifying what we "should" think about various political issues, or does the direction run the other way—from our sociopolitical views to our metaphysics? Are both religious and sociopolitical attitudes manifestations of some broader ideological and value systems? Although the variety of such potential issues would seem to be so numerous as to defy classification, some consistent patterns have emerged.

POLITICAL ORIENTATION

The most familiar way of categorizing people sociopolitically is along a liberal-conservative continuum. When views across the range of specific topics are reduced to essential underlying characteristics, two fundamental meta-issues emerge. One involves acceptance of, or resistance to, change in the existing order, with conservatives on the political right favoring stability or resisting change, and liberals on the political left favoring change.[3] The other element of political orientation is an acceptance of, or resistance to, social and economic inequality.[4] A recent survey in the US indicated that Republicans (relative to Democrats) tended to endorse the statement, "It's not really that big a problem if some people have more of a chance in life than others," whereas Democrats more often feel that "one of the big problems of this country is that we don't give everyone an equal chance in life."[5] Thus, a given individual's view on specific political issues is largely shaped by the way that person conceptualizes change and equality.

Others have argued that sociopolitical differences are better classified by using more than one axis or dimension, such as economic views (left-right) distinguished from social views (authoritarian-libertarian), yielding multiple quadrants.[6] For example, Josef Stalin would probably be classified as an extreme combination of authoritarian leftist, whereas Mohandas Gandhi would be a more libertarian leftist. Ronald Reagan would probably be in the authoritarian right quadrant, whereas Ayn Rand would be on the libertarian right. There have been many other attempts to categorize and distill patterns in how people view social and political issues, all of which have some combination of advantages and disadvantages.

If our question is "How do nonreligious and secular individuals view social and political issues?," we already run into a problem. Being secular does not, in and of itself, compel or require a particular political orientation. As we will see, despite indications that on many issues the nonreligious appear to frequently hold traditionally liberal political positions, at least in the United States, this is not necessarily always the case. As has been mentioned at various points throughout this book, there are many different kinds of nonreligious individuals, and some secular individuals hold diametrically opposing sociopolitical worldviews. Two notable examples are Objectivists versus Marxists. Proponents of Objectivist philosophies, exemplified by Ayn Rand, occupy the libertarian end of the political spectrum, favoring unfettered free markets and few social constraints. Objectivists are typically atheists who believe societies function best with minimal governmental intrusion. However, dialectical materialism associated with Marxist thought—also emphasizing atheism—views religion as merely another tool used by capitalists to control the proletariat. These two examples of atheist political philosophies demonstrate that simply knowing that a given individual is an atheist does not necessarily indicate his or her position on any given sociopolitical issue.

It must be said, however, that at least in contemporary Western contexts, most secular individuals do not hold either of these views, which lie at the ends of the political spectrum. Despite accusations that all atheists are "godless communists," and although the nonreligious tend to lean in the liberal direction, the number of outright communists is negligible, and many communists are not atheists.[7] Also, despite some contemporary Americans paying homage to Ayn Rand's libertarian vision, the popular political movements that use her economic ideas are actually, on average, more religious than those on the more liberal end of the political spectrum. For example, the Tea Party has been touted as a libertarian movement, but most of its adherents are actually Christian conservatives.[8]

In terms of party affiliation and voting, the nonreligious in the United States are much more likely to be Democrats or Independents, and less likely to be Republicans.[9] Indeed, one survey found that only 21 percent of people claiming "no religion" reported voting for Republican candidates in recent elections, and only 10 percent of atheists, and 15 percent of agnostics, claimed a Republican affiliation.[10] Therefore, the numbers within the "none" or unaffiliated religious grouping mask even stronger tendencies among the completely nonreligious (because many religiously unaffiliated or "nones" are not completely nonreligious). Although 63 percent of the religiously unaffiliated claim Democratic affiliation or lean Democrat, 73 percent of atheists do so, with only 18 percent of atheists claiming a Republican affiliation.[11] Strong secularity is also overrepresented among left-wing political perspectives; conversely, the nonreligious are the segment that is least supportive of the conservative Tea Party movement.[12] Over the past half-century, this "God-gap" difference between parties has become quite large.[13] Generation X voters with no religious affiliation have shifted; they were divided evenly between parties in 1990, but by 2008 Democrats outnumbered Republicans two to one.[14] In the 2008 US presidential election, 76 percent of atheists and agnostics voted for Barack Obama, and only 23 percent voted for John McCain.[15] Although religious and political alignment in the first half of the twentieth century was largely along ethnoreligious lines, such that main-line and moderate Protestants tended to vote Republican, whereas Catholics (many of whom were of Irish, Polish, and Italian ancestry) voted Democrat, this changed with the political realignment of the 1960s and 1970s. In the second half of the twentieth century, the differences in political affiliation became more marked between liberals and conservatives within religious denominations, such that conservative Catholics, Protestants, and Jews increasingly shifted to the Republican Party, and liberals from these denominations shifted to the Democratic Party.[16] One reason for the growth of the nonreligious or "nones" in the last decades of the twentieth century has been the intertwining of religion with conservative politics. As a result, moderates and liberals with little attachment to religion migrated farther to the "no religion" category in reaction to the rise of Christian conservatives.[17]

Because of the strong association in current US politics between secularity and progressive or liberal positions, it is necessary to keep in mind this overlap when discussing the underlying reasons for individuals' position on any given issue. It is often unclear whether political liberals tend to hold certain views on issues because they tend to be less religious, or whether seculars tend to hold social views because they tend to be liberals—or whether both secularism and liberalism are expressions of a common underlying disposition. In many instances, it turns out that religious content itself (or the lack thereof) has little to do with a position on a given issue. For instance, although the role of some forms of religion (or the lack thereof) may be fairly straightforward on some issues, such as abortion, it is less clear why some forms should correlate as strongly as they do with views on global climate change. Thus, a religious affiliation—or lack thereof—in some cases is directly and causally related to views on social issues, but in other cases, a left-right political orientation itself, or other demographic factors, may be the primary influence.[18] Obviously, the simplistic notion that religion itself dictates views on social issues, independently of political worldviews, cannot explain why, to use one example, liberal and conservative Catholics differ in their views of homosexuality and gay marriage. Using other issues as examples, white Catholics are more supportive than Hispanic Catholics of both the death penalty (47 percent versus 30 percent) and legal abortion (56 percent versus 43 percent).[19] It is more likely that secularism and liberalism co-occur because they share a common way of viewing the world that is reducible to a core set of essential values, a point that we will revisit at the end of the chapter.

CIVIL RIGHTS, GAY RIGHTS, GENDER, AND ETHNIC MINORITIES

Historically, the rejection of religious authority has tended to co-occur with support for progressive social causes, including civil rights.[20] Major figures in the early women's rights movement such as Elizabeth Cady Stanton, Jocelyn Gage, Susan B. Anthony, and Margaret ("No gods, no masters") Sanger were either freethinking agnostics or outright atheists. Supporters of labor unions and workers' rights, such as Emma Goldman and Clarence Darrow, were openly nonreligious. As Susan Jacoby has documented in her book *Freethinkers*, the strongest white supporters of the latter twentieth-century civil rights movement were a mixture of the liberal religious (such as Quakers and Unitarians) and the completely secular (such as liberal college students, members of the American Civil Liberties Union, and secular Jews). In fact, civil rights activity often resulted in coalitions of the highly religious, such as African Americans who drew sustenance from churches, together with the nonreligious. (A similar coalition exists in the Democratic Party today.) As Jacoby describes it, those who sought broader acceptance and respectability for the movement often wanted to downplay any element of secularity due to the association with social radicalism and communism. Additionally, individuals accustomed to framing the struggle in religious terms may have had difficulty understanding their equally dedicated secular partners. Even Martin Luther King Jr. could not believe that his closest white friend and lawyer, Stanley Levison, a secular Jew, was not motivated by any religious belief. King often teased Levison, saying, "You believe in God, Stan. You just don't know it."[21]

Studies have shown that secular individuals tend to be low in racial prejudice and ethnocentrism.[22] For example, in one survey, the unaffiliated were most likely to endorse interracial marriage as a "good thing for society."[23] In an international survey, nonreligious people had lower ethnic prejudice than Catholics and Protestants.[24] However, it must be pointed out that the link between religiosity and prejudice differs as a function of the particular type or dimension of religiosity in question. Although fundamentalism and more "extrinsic" (i.e., utilitarian) religiosity is reliably associated with greater prejudice, "intrinsic" (i.e., internalized or salient) and "quest" (i.e., open-ended or liberal) religious orientations are associated with lower prejudice.[25] Likewise, the relationship between religiosity and prejudice is stronger among some denominations and nonexistent in others. For white Evangelical Protestants, particularly those in the South, religion has an ethnoracial component that contributes to opposition to interracial marriage and the belief that discrimination against whites is more pervasive than that against blacks.[26] More liberal religious denominations tend to have lower levels of prejudice on a par with the nonreligious.

Studies also show that the unaffiliated and seculars tend to display high degrees of support for gender equality, egalitarianism, and women's rights and are less likely to endorse traditional gender roles (e.g., negative views of women working outside the home).[27] These relationships exist internationally as well, with seculars having a less traditional attitude toward the family in general and valuing the option of divorce in the case of a bad marriage.[28]

Seculars are also supportive of gay rights and gay marriage and more accepting of homosexuality than the religious.[29] The vast majority of atheists and agnostics favor allowing gays to serve openly in the military.[30] However, this is set against a background of a general societal shift. Opinions on homosexuality and gay marriage across most demographic groups in the United States have moved toward increasing acceptance over the past two decades. The US population as a whole is roughly evenly split on the issue of gay marriage; however, the rapid increase in support for gay marriage in recent years appears (as of this writing) to have solidified above the majority level.[31] An examination of statistics—subdivided by religious subgroup—reveals one of the largest divergences across religious groups of any social issue. In one survey, 60 percent of religiously unaffiliated Americans support gay marriage, compared with roughly 26 percent of Protestants and 42 percent of Catholics. But even within the unaffiliated, the differences are quite wide, with 78 percent of atheists and agnostics supporting same-sex marriage. Similarly, although 71 percent of the unaffiliated say that homosexuality "should be accepted," 81 percent and 83 percent of atheists and agnostics, respectively, endorse that view.[32] This divide is also increasingly separating religious groups along liberal-conservative lines. That is, support for gay rights is much higher among main-line Protestants and liberal Catholics than among evangelical Protestants and conservative Catholics, with the former denominations more closely resembling the nonreligious and the latter ones diverging from them.[33]

As mentioned at the beginning of the chapter, it is often difficult to untangle the influences affecting views of political and social issues that are attributable specifically to religion (or the lack thereof), and this is the case with views of homosexuality and gay rights as well. Those with no religion are unlikely to view homosexuality as morally wrong, although the broader acceptance of civil rights for gays is partially independent from moral views of homosexual behavior.[34] For example, although the nonreligious clearly exhibit a greater approval of gays relative to the religious, secular conservatives oppose gay marriage for ostensibly nonreligious reasons. Therefore, evidence indicates that both religious and conservative political factors have independent influences on opposition to same-sex marriage.[35] Also, the nonreligious are more likely to view homosexuality as being a disposition one is born with, rather than a behavioral choice; the latter of these attitudes is associated with opposition to marriage and civil unions for gays.[36] Therefore, there are a number of factors, including, but not limited to, a lack of a religious worldview, that contribute to attitudes toward civil rights issues on the part of seculars. Essentially, seculars appear to be supportive of gays both because of a rejection of religious moral sanctions and simply because of progressive social views in general (e.g., tolerance and "live and let live" attitudes about personal lifestyles). Thus, with the possible exception of Jewish Americans (many of whom tend to be quite secular as well), the nonreligious are the major "religious" demographic most supportive of egalitarian policies regarding race, gender, and sexual orientation.[37]

FOREIGN POLICY, THE MILITARY, AND DEFENSE

In line with the more liberal/progressive stance on social issues, secular people tend to be less likely to own guns, to hold militaristic attitudes, and to advocate military force.[38] For example, only 38 percent of secular Americans favored the 2003 invasion of Iraq, compared with 68 percent of evangelical Protestants, 57 percent of main-line Protestants, 58 percent of Catholics, and 47 percent of Jews.[39] Similar figures were found when the issue was framed as support for the justified use of force and the general unilateralist tenets of the "Bush doctrine."[40] Other than Muslim Americans, the nonreligious are the group most likely to think that targeting and killing of civilians is "never justified."[41] Interestingly, when the topic of foreign policy is expanded to include nonmilitaristic intervention, such as humanitarian efforts, the distinction between seculars and other religious affiliations is less stark. On the "New Internationalist" issues of famine assistance, disaster relief, or the promotion of human rights, secular support for these policies is generally comparable to that among mainstream religious groups because the attitudes among these affiliations do not fall along a strict liberal-conservative dimension.[42] Only a few percentage points separate atheists and agnostics from the religious regarding whether the United States should be more involved with world affairs, likely due to the unspecified nature of this involvement.[43]

As with other political views, the question arises whether these views are primarily a function of their secularity, or merely the reflection of a liberal political affiliation. On the one hand, with respect to views on militarism and warfare, seculars appear to be quite similar to several other ethnic and religious groups with traditionally liberal social stances, including Jews, African Americans, and Hispanic Americans.[44] Still, when political effects are statistically separated from those stemming specifically from religious affiliation, some studies still find that views on issues such as the Iraq War and whether Islam is a violent religion are shaped by religious factors, independently of political views or sociodemographic variables, indicating at least some independent effect of both. In other words, seculars tend to be less militaristic because of both their lack of religious views and their more liberal political orientations. [45]

ABORTION, PHYSICIAN-ASSISTED SUICIDE, AND STEM CELL RESEARCH

Seculars in the United States tend to be more supportive of abortion rights, on average, than are religious people. The "God gap" on this particular issue is substantial, with religious affiliation showing one of the strongest divergences when compared with the usual demographic categories such as race or education. According to one poll, only 19 percent of the nonreligious identified as pro-life, compared with 54 percent of Catholics and 57 percent of Protestants and other Christians.[46] In another, 84 percent of atheists and agnostics favored legal abortion in most or all cases.[47] Indeed, abortion is the social issue that reliably elicits the strongest differences of opinion between individuals as a function of religious engagement.[48]

The nonreligious are also more accepting than any other major religious group of physician-assisted suicide for incurable patients.[49] In a Gallup poll, those who seldom or never attend church were more likely to say that when a person cannot be cured, doctors should be able to legally end the patient's life (84 percent) than were those who attend church monthly (70 percent) or weekly (47 percent).[50] In another study, secular people had three times the approval rate for assisted suicide relative to the religious.[51] Seculars also show strong support for embryonic stem cell research.[52] According to one survey, 84 percent of nonreligious Americans supported stem cell research, compared with 55 percent of very religious Americans.[53] Again, some of this effect may have to do with extrareligious factors such as scientific knowledge or general liberal worldviews. For example, with regard to embryonic stem cell research, religion plays a conditional or "moderating" role. Those with low knowledge or awareness regarding this research, no matter what their level of religiosity, tend to show strong initial opposition to it. But for nonreligious and moderately religious individuals, greater awareness and knowledge of the issue are related to greater support for research. By contrast, highly religious individuals do not support such research, regardless of levels of knowledge and awareness.[54]

LEGAL AND CRIMINAL JUSTICE ISSUES

Studies consistently show that the nonreligious have some of the least punitive attitudes regarding treatment of those accused of crimes; seculars and religiously unaffiliated Americans are the least supportive of harsh sentencing, the death penalty, and the governmental use of torture on suspected terrorists.[55] There is, however, some debate regarding whether seculars significantly differ from liberal religious groups such as Jews and moderate Protestants and Catholics. For example, some studies have focused on specific elements of conservatism such as fundamentalism and views of God as vengeful as the specific forces within religion that drive more punitive attitudes. Other studies simply have found that those from any religious background are, on average, more punitive than the nonreligious.[56] Part of the problem, as we have seen throughout the chapter, is that religiosity consists of opposing elements that may directly conflict. In this case, the more harsh and authoritarian elements lead to more punitive views on crime and punishment, whereas forgiving and "turn the other cheek" religious elements have the opposite effect.[57]

Seculars are also much more likely to support the legalization of marijuana than are religious people.[58] For example, those who seldom or never attend church are more supportive (49 percent) of legalizing marijuana than those who attend almost weekly or monthly (30 percent) and weekly (17 percent).[59] Although support for legalization follows a fairly uniform conservative-to-liberal continuum, with only a third of evangelical Protestants supporting versus nearly half of main-line Protestants, the unaffiliated, with two-thirds favoring, are still the segment most supportive of legalization.[60]

VIEWS OF SOCIAL PROBLEMS

What are the underlying factors that explain why seculars have less punitive views but instead have more favorable attitudes toward marginalized groups such as minorities and criminals? One answer may be that seculars occupy one end of a worldview continuum on which social problems and personal misfortune are explained with reference to situational factors such as social context or luck rather than individual character. In contrast, religious fundamentalists occupy the opposite end of this continuum, believing that events such as misfortune occur because of personal responsibility, and they are therefore more likely to blame victims even in the absence of any evident culpability. For example, on average, the nonreligious are more likely than the religious to state that "hard work and determination are no guarantee of success for most people."[61] In contrast, religious fundamentalists tend to view victims of natural disaster, the poor, and criminal delinquents as being personally responsible for their situation.[62] Although these tendencies are observed to differ between liberal and conservative religious groups, some studies have still found differences between the religious and nonreligious even controlling for political orientation.[63]

This begs the question regarding why differences in attributions of responsibility or blame for social problems should vary as a function of spiritual and religious views. One reason for this discrepancy may be related to the content of religious beliefs, or the lack thereof. Some have suggested that certain religious principles, particularly found in forms of Protestantism, posit a characterological "essence" embodied in the concept of a soul that emphasizes individuals' personal responsibility for the condition and outcomes of their lives.[64] Seculars are less prone to endorse such dispositional views. Nonreligious individuals also discount the religious conception of a teleological or purposeful universe in which divine forces mete out consequences commensurate with individuals' actions.

In some religions, belief in a "just" afterlife is associated with expectations for equity in this life, such that one's actions in life are associated with predictable outcomes.[65] Such beliefs are thought to reduce anxiety in that they contain a clear formula: proper living is eventually rewarded. Religious individuals endorse a "belief in a just world" more often than the nonreligious. This bias holds that good outcomes must have been preceded by good deeds, and bad outcomes are punishment for misdeeds, so that individuals "get what they deserve."[66] This tendency is also common in conservative or fundamentalist worldviews, which may explain why individuals who hold these views tend to have a relatively greater acceptance of inequality of outcome. For example, conservatives attributed more responsibility than did liberals to the victims of the earthquake in Haiti.[67] By contrast, the religiously unaffiliated do not believe that all outcomes are deserved. The nonreligious and liberal religious groups tend to believe that it is problematic that not everyone has an equal chance in life.[68] Therefore, seculars may be better characterized by the belief that "stuff happens" to individuals on many occasions, without regard for personal responsibility or blame, and that "the rain falls on the just and on the unjust alike." Because of these tendencies, their sociopolitical views are less likely to include attributions of blame or responsibility toward victims of misfortune or injustice.

THE ENVIRONMENT, EVOLUTION, AND ANIMAL RIGHTS

Most studies find that, relative to the religious, secular individuals tend to have more pro-environmental attitudes, support more environmental spending, and be more knowledgeable about environmental scientific evidence.[69] Atheists and agnostics exhibit even stronger support for environmental regulation.[70] In one survey, 69 percent of the unaffiliated felt that stricter environmental laws and regulations were "worth the cost," while 75 percent and 78 percent of atheists and agnostics, respectively, agreed.[71]

On the issue of global warming, polls indicate that secular Americans are more likely to believe that there is evidence of human-caused global warming and that this is a serious problem (62 percent) than are Catholics (52 percent), main-line Protestants (48 percent), and evangelical Protestants (37 percent).[72] Similarly, religious adults are less likely than the nonreligious to report beliefs consistent with the scientific consensus.[73]

There is, however, some controversy concerning the precise role of religion in shaping environmental attitudes. Differences between the nonreligious and religious may be due to factors such as demographic characteristics, liberalism, education, and scientific knowledge more than religion per se.[74] Further, the overall relationship between religion and environmentalism is fairly weak because of contrary influences within religion itself.[75] Some aspects of religion associated with political conservatism work against environmentalism, and the presence of fundamentalist eschatological beliefs also affects attitudes (e.g., viewing the planet as nearing the end of days).[76] However, other aspects of religion may compete with these influences to promote pro-environmental views, such that liberal religious groups may share seculars' environmental concern but frame it as "creation care" or "stewardship."[77] Therefore, the environment may be an issue upon which environmentally minded nonreligious and religious individuals may find common cause.

The subject of evolution by means of natural selection in general, and the implications for human origins in particular, has been seen as a central and fundamental issue that divides secular and religious individuals. This is partly due to the problems it presents for the biblical literalism of some Christian conservatives but also to deeper issues regarding the purpose and meaning of life itself, and even the source of morality. The United States stands out from nearly every other industrialized nation in its high levels of support for creationism—typically in the 40 to 50 percent range, depending on phrasing of survey questions.[78] These figures have changed little in the past thirty years. Views of evolution also elicit one of the widest gaps of any issue between the nonreligious and the religious in the United States. In one survey, 83 percent of seculars accepted evolution compared with 59 percent of Catholics and 62 percent of main-line Protestants.

Within the general idea of evolution, there are several specific components, including the common ancestry of all organisms, an extended time frame consisting of millions of years, and the role of chance versus divine intervention or purposefulness in the process. The latter component particularly separates nonreligious from religious individuals. When the question is posed as one of evolution guided by a supreme being versus by natural selection, only among seculars does a majority accept natural selection without divine intervention.[79] In a separate Gallup poll using church attendance as a religious indicator, the proportion of those who seldom or never attend church who endorsed the idea that "humans developed over millions of years, God had no part" was 26 percent, but among those who attend church monthly or nearly every week, the percentage endorsing that option was only 10 percent, and for those attending weekly, only 3 percent.[80] However, it appears that support for evolution in general (although not God-guided evolution) is specifically lower for those with fundamentalist and conservative political views rather than the religious per se.[81] In other words, it is not merely religiosity that distinguishes evangelical Christians from the nonreligious on this issue but rather something intrinsic to religious fundamentalism and conservative ideology that creates this "gap" in worldviews. Therefore, the nonreligious share beliefs similar to those of the moderately religious on the topic of evolution in general, although these groups still differ substantially regarding the component pertaining to overall purposefulness.

With regard to evolution in the classroom, students without religious beliefs show a greater ability to acquire knowledge about evolutionary theory subsequent to instruction than do the religious.[82] A straightforward theory would suggest that nonreligious individuals have simply been exposed to or instructed in evolutionary theory in a way that religious individuals have not. However, these differences in knowledge are predicted by factors other than religiosity (or the lack thereof) or even the explicit exposure to these theories in the classroom. One reality is that even students in public schools are often exposed to a mixture of creationist and evolutionary theory. Surprisingly, explicit instruction in evolutionary theory seems to result in little change among students or teachers.[83] Even those students who are exposed to evolution in school may have a tenuous grasp of the theory.[84] Rather than deriving evolutionary knowledge from explicit classroom instruction, the best predictors of human origin beliefs are individuals' overall intellectual preferences, such as whether the student reads books outside of school, watches science shows on television, or simply gets better grades.[85] Therefore, the ability to benefit from instruction on the theory of evolution may be less related to what students know about it beforehand and more to the way they think. Those students who exhibit a more reflective (as opposed to intuitive) reasoning ability are able to acquire knowledge about evolution to a greater extent and are less committed to scientific misconceptions. This may also be related to the findings (discussed in chapter 6) that the nonreligious tend to show a more analytical rather than intuitive thinking style. Thus, it may be that nonreligious students endorse evolution not simply because they are nonreligious (and thus without religious qualms) but because of a thought process underlying both human origin beliefs and the metaphysics of nonbelief.

This is an important illustration of some influences that may underlie secular worldviews, yet by themselves may not be specifically secular in content. Belief in evolution is associated with other scientific beliefs such as pro-environmental attitudes, possibly because those with a belief in Darwinian principles may view humans as part of, rather than above, nature.[86] Those who accept evolution are more likely to view nonhuman animals as similar to humans in their mental and emotional lives.[87] Those with less frequent church attendance generally have less exploitative or utilitarian attitudes toward animals, and individuals with no religious affiliation or participation are more supportive of animal rights than the religious.[88] Atheists and agnostics are overrepresented among animal rights activists.[89] Again, there is reason to believe that this is partly due to the view that humans share a common ancestry with animals.[90] These foundational existential beliefs, such as acceptance of evolution, rather than being merely a repudiation of biblical literalism, are actually components of broader sociopolitical attitudes and worldviews that influence epis-temology and ethics.

NATIONALISM AND PATRIOTISM

The nonreligious, at least in the United States, tend to be remarkably unsupport-ive of nationalism and exclusive patriotism, or American exceptionalism. When the Pew Research Center asked respondents whether the United States was the "greatest country in the world," only one in five of the unaffiliated agreed, with an equal per-centage agreeing that "there are other countries better than the U.S."[91] Evangelical Christians were at the other end of this continuum, with 40 percent agreeing that the United States stands alone as the greatest country. (This was referred to as a "patrio-tism God gap" by *Christianity Today* magazine.) The religious tend to show greater overt patriotism than the nonreligious, such as displaying the American flag on their clothing or at home.[92] Although it would appear that nonreligious individuals iden-tify less with their country than do religious individuals, it is important to also view this in terms of any and all types of group identification, using relative comparisons. The nonreligious are less inclined to claim *any* source of group identification. In one survey pertaining to national, ethnic, and religious identification, the proportion of nonreligious Americans saying they "extremely strongly" or "very strongly" identi-fied as a citizen of the United States was 76 percent, and the proportion of those strongly identifying with their ethnic identity was 36 percent (not surprisingly, iden-tification with religion was in the single digits). By contrast, Protestant Christians strongly identified with their citizenship (91 percent), with their ethnic identity (57 percent), and with their religious identity (70 percent). Catholics responded similarly except for slightly lower religious identification. Therefore, although in absolute terms it appeared as if Christians tended to identify more closely with the nation than did the nonreligious, the latter group did not identify with *any* of these groups relative to the religious. This captures another theme in secular sociopolitical worldviews: emphasis on a sense of universality (a broader connection with human-ity in general) in contrast to group binding.

VIEWS OF SOCIETY: THE ROLE OF RELIGION, THE STATE,
AND POLITICAL TOLERANCE

Most secular individuals believe that religion should be kept separate from other key spheres of an individuals' communal life, such as politics.[93] For example, the unaffiliated believe that it is not important for a presidential candidate to have strong religious beliefs or to talk about his or her faith, and almost two-thirds say that there has been too much expression of faith by political leaders.[94] This attitude is not unique to the nonreligious. The unaffiliated (and other liberal religious groups, such as Jews) are opposed to organized school prayer.[95] This is in line with a general decline over time in support of the mixture of religion and politics among religious moderates.[96]

Although there is evidence that most Americans are reluctant to overtly mix religion with policymaking, this view coexists with a view that religion has some role to play in politics, typically providing some overall moral compass for decision-making. As we saw in chapter 8 (on morality), the majority of Americans (although not Europeans) use religiosity as an indicator of personal morality. So it is not surprising that the majority of religious Americans say that it is important that a presidential candidate have strong religious beliefs. More surprising, however, is that a third of unaffiliated Americans agree—although this may be because many "unaffiliated" individuals are still religious.[97]

According to a standard question posed by the Gallup organization over the past several decades, there has been some change in the willingness of the general public to vote for an otherwise qualified atheist for president. The most recent figures indicate that 54 percent of Americans would do so, an increase of 36 percent since 1958.[98] The strongest demographic shift in this question has been as a function of age, with some 70 percent of "Millennials" (aged eighteen to twenty-nine) reporting that they would vote for an atheist. However, it is still notable that almost half of Americans would *not* vote for an atheist, and this does not differ greatly between Democrats (42 percent would not) and Republicans (52 percent). The view that religiosity is a necessary attribute of elected officials likely contributes to the largest discrepancy between a religious category in the US population in general and that represented in the US Congress. Although one-fifth of adults are not affiliated with any particular faith, only one member of the 113th Congress stated that she was religiously unaffiliated (Kyrsten Sinema, D-AZ).[99]

Secular individuals (by definition) believe that the sphere of religion should be separated from venues where there is a potential for the coercive effects of institutional endorsement (e.g., courts or schools). However, that does not mean that seculars believe that religion has no "role in the public square," if that means that religious institutions or private individuals are kept from exercising religious rights in public. Rather, the nonreligious tend to support religious speech as long as it is separate from governmental endorsement. One-third of the unaffiliated agree that churches should express views on politics.[100] The key line for seculars is the use of institutions to proselytize or espouse religious views to a captive audience.

The nonreligious also disapprove of nonreligious proselytizing to a greater extent than religious individuals disapprove of religious proselytizing. For example, in Hunsberger and Altemeyer's study of atheist organization members, almost all atheists and agnostics disapproved of laws requiring schools to teach *against* religion.[101] This was in contrast to religious fundamentalists who approved of laws promoting religion in the schools. Thus, most atheists and agnostics consistently support having schools be religiously neutral, not actively antireligious. Similarly, in the personal domain, seculars show less willingness to proselytize their views to others relative to the religious. Very few apostates try to convert others to irreligion.[102] In Hunsberger and Altemeyer's study respondents were asked how they would handle a hypothetical teenager with religious doubts who comes to them seeking advice. Respondents then indicated whether they would either encourage the youth to give up religion (or, at the other end of the continuum, encourage them to listen to their religious parents) or advise the teen to make up his or her own mind. In contrast to 98 percent of religious fundamentalists who would try to lead the teen to become more religious, less than half of the atheists reported that they would tell the teen to adopt nonbelief. Although the US atheists expressed a greater acceptance of influence than the Canadians, their level of zealotry was still lower than the fundamentalists'. It appears that although atheists are firm in their own worldviews and do not anticipate ever changing them, there is little evidence that they have greater levels of personal zealotry—that is, a desire to convert religious individuals to secular views. It remains to be seen whether this tendency will still apply when more people are openly secular.

Outside of the coercive power of government-sponsored ideas, compared with the religious, the nonreligious tend to promote the free expression of controversial ideas in general. Compared with the major religious groups in the United States, the unaffiliated are least likely to approve of banning "dangerous" books.[103] Secular Americans support the extension of civil liberties and willingness to allow speech to dissident groups, even those that may not share liberal views.[104] For example, along with more liberal religious groups, such as Jews and Episcopalians, the "nones" consistently report greater tolerance than conservative religious groups toward "deviants" such as militarists, homosexuals, communists, and racists.[105]

This is not to say that nonreligious individuals are all neutral regarding their general social contact with those who share their worldviews, as opposed to other groups. But studies reliably indicate that as religious engagement increases, the degree of tolerance for different groups decreases and level of parochialism increases (although this is more characteristic of fundamentalist religions than of liberal forms).[106] Nonreligious individuals tend to dislike religious individuals less than religious individuals dislike the secular; that is, their "preference gap" is smaller.[107] Of course, some differences in tolerance as a function of religiosity may be limited to Western or

US contexts. For example, in a Korean sample, atheist university students did not differ from religious students on a variety of measures including nationalism, patriotism, internationalism, respect for civil liberties, and tolerance of dissent.[108] However, in general, cross-nationally, members of a range of religious denominations have lower levels of political tolerance compared with those with no religion.[109] Why would this be the case? One explanation is that religiosity contains opposing forces, such that in some contexts, it facilitates intolerance, but in others it does not. For example, although religious behavior is associated with greater support for democratic principles, religious belief is associated with opposition to democracy.[110] Likewise, some studies indicate that although support for theocracy promotes intolerance, this can be attenuated through social liberalism.[111] This would account for the similarities in political outlook between seculars and the liberal religious. Therefore, liberalism may be a more fundamental underlying trait for many nonreligious people, rather than atheism or secularity per se. But this runs the risks of becoming circular. Why is it that many (but certainly not all) nonreligious individuals are socially liberal, and why do socially liberal religious individuals share many sociopolitical views with seculars? Are there more basic characteristics that subsume these tendencies?

UNDERLYING TRAITS

It should now be apparent that nonreligious worldviews transcend individual issues. And as mentioned earlier, it is often difficult to determine whether a view on any given issue exists *because* an individual is secular or nonreligious. Another possibility is that broad tendencies—such as liberalism—develop prior to any religious/nonreligious views, and thus the social views endorsed by seculars may not actually be causally related to any underlying nonreligious reason.

We now turn to some of the core cognitive, personality, developmental, and moral characteristics discussed in the preceding chapters to see whether they help to explain the social and political views of the nonreligious. In chapter 8, the "individualizing" moral factors based on Haidt's five dimensions, such as empathy and fairness, were said to be more characteristic of secular individuals, whereas "binding morality" factors, such as an emphasis on purity, in-group concerns, and authority, were shown to be relatively more common in religious individuals. As we discussed, Haidt found that liberals' individualizing morality emphasizes an "ethics of autonomy," which holds that morality allows people to act in accordance with personal freedom—as long as others are not harmed and the consequences are fair for everyone. In the case of a given social or political issue, such as gay rights, secular individuals support gay rights and gay marriage because they see the issue as one of fairness and are not swayed by appeals to moral purity, traditionalism, or scriptural authority. Thus, the political views of seculars may be related to an underlying worldview that encompasses moral and sociopolitical elements.

It is widely assumed that a given individual's sociopolitical worldview is held together by "team loyalty" that drives individuals' stance on a range of issues. However, this still raises the question of what ultimately determines which team we identify as "ours." There is increasing evidence that our worldviews are broadly influenced by early-developing moral dispositions and basic-level personality traits that precede exposure to specific religious or political information. In one study, participants' positions on the moral foundations (based on Haidt's conceptualization), particularly moral purity (i.e., perceived importance of cleanliness, sanctity, and avoidance of symbolic violations), predicted judgments about "culture war" issues over and above other factors including ideology, religious attendance, and interest in politics.[112] Despite the rhetoric on issues such as abortion, euthanasia, and stem cell research being dominated by arguments about (potential) harm, in this study, moral disapproval of these issues was better predicted by individuals' moral sensitivity to purity than by their stance on harmfulness. Thus, it may not be the absence of religious belief among seculars that motivates their ideology but rather lower moral sensitivity to issues of sanctity, self-transcendence, and self-control.

We return briefly to a similar pattern, mentioned in more detail in chapter 6, that cognitive and personality-related traits underlie and contribute to not only sociopolitical views but also a secular worldview. In that chapter we saw that personality dimensions of the "Big Five," such as Openness to Experience, distinguish secular from religious individuals, as well as separating those who view religion literally from those who see it symbolically. Openness is also relevant to political ideology, tending to be higher among liberals than conservatives.[113] Thus, some of the familiar patterns, such as nonreligious support for liberal political candidates, a rejection of moral traditionalism, and support for the disadvantaged, are collectively related to underlying personality dispositions, such as greater Openness (as well as lower Conscientiousness).[114] This is relevant to the development of secularity over one's life span (covered in chapter 5) or rejection of a religious worldview (i.e., "apostasy") because, in many cases, core characteristics such as personality and temperament precede religiosity.[115] There is evidence that temperament characteristics beginning in early childhood (obviously prior to an articulation of mature sociopolitical worldviews) are predictive of later political views.[116] Youths with personality traits such as high Openness become less religious over time, whereas those with high Conscientiousness in adolescence are likely to increase in religiosity in young adulthood.[117] To put it colloquially, this suggests that people are secular and politically liberal because of their temperament and personality, rather than being liberal because they are secular.

Another quasi-personality trait (but not one discussed in chapter 6), relevant to sociopolitical views, is dogmatism, which refers to an unwillingness to give up one's beliefs upon encountering new evidence—usually juxtaposed against open-mindedness and cognitive flexibility. Political liberals tend to be lower in dogmatism and higher in open-mindedness (or tolerance for ambiguity) than conservatives.[118] One occasionally hears in popular discourse a stereotype that atheists are similar to religious fundamentalists in that they are rigid and inflexible in their views. However, the nonreligious, even atheists, tend to score very low on measures of dogmatism. One caveat is that US atheists who were members of secular groups have been found to score higher on a measure of dogmatism relative to US agnostics or atheists from Canada.[119] In one study, half of the US atheists agreed that nothing would change their mind and cause them to believe in religion. However, these American atheists scored much lower than religious fundamentalists, creating a "fishhook" pattern of dogmatism as a function of religiosity, rather than a U-shaped curve.

There are other core psychological characteristics that appear to underlie and contribute to both religious and political views, including those relevant to cognition. For instance, we saw in chapter 6 that the less religious tend to exhibit higher integrative complexity of thought (i.e., ability to integrate multiple perspectives).[120] In the political domain, liberals also show less of a need for certainty, order, structure, and closure than do conservatives, who tend to be lower in integrative complexity of thought and desire clear structure and certainty.[121] Such general cognitive preferences, it has been hypothesized, influence individuals' religious views—or lack thereof. Religious dogmatism and conservative morality may themselves be understood as attempts to provide clear and unambiguous responses in an attempt to manage uncertainty.[122] Similarly, conservatives tend to be more sensitive to negative or threatening stimuli such as viewing the world as a more dangerous place or being more motivated by fear, relative to liberals.[123] According to these theories of political psychology, general sociopolitical worldviews including secularity are based on very basic, core elements of cognitive functioning.

Although a full discussion of political psychology is beyond the present scope, suffice to say that these core psychological dispositions are associated not only with religious and political views but also with general approaches to existential issues such as morality, the nature of humanity, and overall worldviews, secularity being merely one facet of such a worldview. For example, it has been found that those who believe the world is a dangerous place tend to develop binding morality (e.g., based on in-group, purity, and authority concerns), and this in turn leads to a conservative political orientation.[124] Many people, whether or not they were raised religiously or secularly, may find a certain worldview more compelling as a result of these psychological preferences. Further, as is the case with religiosity, there is also evidence of a substantial inherited component to political orientation, and this genetic variation in political orientation is itself mediated by personality traits.[125] According to such theories, religiosity may be part of a cluster of traits that also include social (but not economic) conservatism and authoritarianism, reflecting an underlying "Traditional Moral Values Triad."[126] This may at least partially explain why individuals come to different religious and metaphysical conclusions despite contrary environmental influences; individuals' early cognitive preferences place them on a "trajectory" of later religious and political worldviews.

Another core personality trait that encompasses a set of specific religious and political views together with cognitive dispositions is authoritarianism. This trait is characterized by an emphasis on obedience and submission to a variety of sources of authority (e.g., religious, governmental), strong valuation of social conformity, and a willingness to use aggression against outsiders.[127] It is also believed to play a significant role in things like intolerance of diversity, racial prejudice, militarism, and xenophobia. Religious conservatives and fundamentalists tend toward authoritarianism, whereas seculars tend to be low on authoritarian characteristics, although most "low authoritarians" are still somewhat religious.[128]

It is perhaps more accurate to conceptualize authoritarianism as a way of viewing the world that may include religion as only one component, because measures of authoritarianism often include little overt religious content. Given that strong authoritarians place an emphasis on traditionalism, if this happens to be embodied in a religious cultural milieu, then authoritarians will strongly defend that religious tradition. In the domain of cognition, low authoritarians typically seek out many sources of information from multiple points of view on religious issues whereas high authoritarians tend to seek only information that reinforces their original point of view.[129] In one interesting comparison, Altemeyer gave his students (bogus) "archaeological" scenarios of supposed ancient scrolls purporting that Jesus of Nazareth actually did rise from the dead.[130] He also used a comparison scenario (also fake) that revealed the Gospel stories of Jesus to be a fraud. Altemeyer found that the nonreligious low authoritarians were much more persuadable by the authentic resurrection scenario—that is, willing to reconsider their previous views when confronted with contrary evidence—than the religious high authoritarians were to the Jesus-was-fraudulent scenario. Thus, low authoritarianism, with its component of open-mindedness and de-emphasis on traditionalism, characterizes how the nonreligious approach religion.

Individuals' views on childrearing may be a reliable indicator of political ideology and, as such, also reflect the authoritarian continuum.[131] As we saw in chapter 6, those who value traits in children such as obedience, respect, and good manners over independence, self-reliance, and curiosity also tend to show authoritarian political views. In essence, strong authoritarians view humans as essentially flawed and in need of strong social control (lest they "get out of hand"), whereas low authoritarians see individuals as essentially benevolent, requiring minimal control and greater freedom and autonomy. In general surveys, secular (and Jewish) Americans score significantly lower on authoritarian childrearing views than do other major religious groups.[132] This suggests that the nonauthoritarian sociopolitical views of the nonreligious, shared with the liberally religious, could be seen as a manifestation of this underlying trait.

VALUES AND PERSONAL IDEOLOGIES

As we noted in chapter 1, individuals' ideologies and values expand beyond the confines of morality and ethics. They are broader worldviews that contain sets of core or central beliefs about what is desirable or what priorities motivate people and societies.[133] As such, they function as "oughts" in determining social and political attitudes and describe what individuals "want" or are motivated to do. Whereas religiosity is associated with values such as traditionalism, certainty, and conformity (restraint of actions likely to upset others or violate social expectations or norms), secularity has been associated with valuing hedonism (e.g., pleasure or gratification), achievement (success via demonstrating competence), stimulation (novelty and challenges), and self-direction (independent thought and action).[134] Religious individuals, across many different cultures, tend to value benevolence (enhancing the welfare of the people with whom one is in frequent personal contact) more highly than seculars. However, secular people tend to rank universalism (protecting the welfare of all people) more highly than the religious.[135] That is, religious people report valuing kindness to friends and family to a greater degree than seculars, but seculars tend to value fairness toward those outside their own group more than the religious. This may partially explain the pattern of results seen in group-based versus individually based morality (chapter 8). For example, we saw evidence for relatively stronger preferences for planned or nonspontaneous helping, as well as the in-group favoritism among the religious, contrasting with the spontaneous or nonplanned assistance, even to out-group individuals, among the secular and the liberally religious.

As we have seen, though, religion's relationship to values can also be viewed in a multidimensional manner. Those who view religion more symbolically (as opposed to literally), like the nonreligious, are also more likely to value elements such as universalism and benevolence.[136] However, other values are reliably associated with a nonreligious exclusion of the transcendent, namely, a rejection of traditionalism and conformity.

As with values, personal ideology transcends and subsumes specific social issues and produces a broader philosophy of how life should be lived and a broader interpretation of what forces influence human life. According to one such system, an ideology can range along a dimension from humanism to normativism. Humanistic ideology views humankind as an end in itself, posits that humans are essentially good-natured, and emphasizes equality, open-mindedness, personal expression, and unconditional love. Conversely, a normative worldview maintains that reality exists prior to and independent of humankind and that, because humanity is not inherently good, we should conform to normative rules, valuing constraint, social approval, and politeness.[137] The nonreligious are likely to view particular sociopolitical issues as a function of an underlying value system that stresses humanism. This may explain why they value hedonism, stimulation, achievement, and self-direction more than do religious individuals—because they see these as ends in and of themselves rather than potentially negative goals.

CONCLUSION

We have proceeded from specific sociopolitical views and linked them to underlying core characteristics. The themes on which we have concluded show a pattern reminiscent of many of the same psychological, moral, and personality-based themes that we have seen throughout this book. Therefore, we can see how the sociopolitical attitudes of the nonreligious interconnect with themes we discussed in previous chapters to form a coherent worldview.

Take, for instance, the relatively higher level of tolerance that seculars show for minorities, disadvantaged groups, and even those considered "social deviants." The mere absence of religion itself is insufficient to fully account for such high levels of social tolerance. What core secular characteristics account for this? One answer is that because seculars tend to be nonauthoritarian, they do not view the world as a dangerous place that necessitates a fear of diversity or the new. Rather, they tend to see humans, even those who are different, as being fundamentally good and nonthreatening. They also value personal independence and nonconformity over obedience to norms and therefore are less willing to aggress against outsiders simply because these groups are not familiar.[138] The relative prioritization of universalism (the welfare of all humanity) as a value can be seen as an outgrowth of these individualistic influences.[139] We also saw that the nonreligious display less group allegiance in the form of nationalism and patriotism, and they disagree with narrow or parochial views that favor particular ethnic, sexual, or national in-groups. This is reflected in their moral values, which place a lower emphasis on shared group ties.[140]

We also saw that the social attitudes of the nonreligious tend toward the liberal end of the political spectrum, for example, viewing events such as social strife as stemming from situational factors (e.g., poverty) rather than from more fixed dispositional tendencies (e.g., lack of moral character). In fact, a humanistic worldview is more likely to compel such social attitudes because circumstances are not seen as necessarily inevitable or dictated by divine will. In contrast to a religious worldview in which the world is seen as operating via a system of transcendent, fixed principles, humanists are more likely to view events as caused by chance or humans and therefore amenable to change. A lenient view of criminal justice and a belief in an active governmental role in combating social inequality both require at some level a view that an individual's fate is not always inevitably dictated by, or attributable to, character defects. The nonreligious hold views on the role of government that are similar to those of religious progressives. For example, more than three-quarters of both these groups believe that the government should do more to reduce the gap between the rich and the poor, whereas only a third of religious conservatives endorse this view.[141]

Liberal social attitudes such as these tend to be more complex and difficult to articulate than more straightforward conservative positions.[142] The higher levels of cognitive complexity among seculars, as well as a personality style marked by Openness to Experience, are associated with such views. Thus, the political positions shared by the liberally religious and seculars can be seen as the result of their viewing the world as complex and nuanced. Because seculars do not have epistemic needs for order, certainty, coherence, and purposefulness satisfied via invoking a transcendental source, they may instead seek other forms of external control such as civic, governmental, and scientific institutions.[143]

Future studies of the sociopolitical views of the nonreligious are likely to see the continuance of several trends. In recent decades we have seen an increase in the numbers of the unaffiliated, particularly in North America and Europe.[144] With the increased size of this segment, however, is likely to come greater diversity. For example, will self-described "antitheists" approach issues in a different manner from those who are "apatheist" (i.e., those who do not care about religion either way)? Will those emphasizing ethical humanist values clash with libertarian objectivists on the proper role of government? The answers to these questions are not clear. Another trend that is likely to continue is the growing political coalition between religious progressives and the nonreligious. Despite the absence of shared metaphysics, these groups share remarkably similar social views. The most theoretically interesting work yet to come will lend insight into how affirmative secularity itself works in conjunction with other influences to shape the social and political views of the nonreligious.

10

SECULAR SOCIAL AND ORGANIZATIONAL BEHAVIOR

THROUGHOUT THIS BOOK, we have introduced people who illustrate various aspects of secularity. Let's meet a few more who offer a glimpse of the social and organizational activities of secular people.

Consider Mel, who is in his sixties. He was raised in a Jewish household, but by the time of his bar mitzvah he was neither a religious believer nor a participant. Throughout his life, Mel has been actively involved in cultural affairs, community service, and politics (local, regional, and national). He has served on boards and committees of innumerable civic organizations through the years and is widely recognized and admired for his many philanthropic and voluntary service activities. He has an unparalleled friendship network. And among his many monetary contributions, he gives modest amounts to secular humanist, freethought, and atheist groups, even though he has consistently declined active membership in such organizations. Although he thinks of himself as secular and humanistic, he says that he is wary of getting involved or doing anything "on the basis of doctrine—religious or irreligious." Nor does he "surrender blindly" to any group—even those in which he is deeply involved. He always maintains a "degree of detachment" that enables him to judge whether the organizations he supports live up their commitments and his ethical standards. Violation of these standards, in fact, once caused him to resign membership in a well-known civic group in a widely publicized protest of new policies he found objectionable.

Claire, in her fifties, "gave up God and Santa Claus around the same time" in her youth and has never looked back. Unlike Mel, however, she is "not a joiner." She is not antisocial; she just doesn't like being "immersed in groups." She has a family and a circle of friends and a "comfortably active social life"—which does include a small book discussion group. One friend has spoken to her repeatedly about a local secularist organization that she finds rewarding. Claire attended a meeting once to please her friend, but "that was it—not for me!" She prizes her autonomy and the freedom to choose "who to spend time with, when, and where."

Jon, also in his fifties, has been actively involved in a secular humanist group that he helped to found nearly three decades ago. Membership has waxed and waned over the years, but in recent years growth has accelerated. Where it was once difficult to assemble more than twenty in an audience or discussion group, now eighty to a hundred people regularly fill the meeting room of a community center to hear lectures and discuss a wide range of subjects pertinent to secular humanism, the nonreligious, the community, the country, and the world. Members frequently organize and host potluck dinners at their homes. The group actively participates in charitable, community, and civic activities, such as food banks, beach and roadway cleanups, public broadcasting fundraisers, and homeless shelters. Now that Jon is retired, he spends most of his time directing the group.

Jill, in her sixties, has been nonreligious all her adult life. She raised her daughter single-handedly following her husband's death. She has been involved in professional organizations related to her career through the years—sometimes as board member, treasurer, or secretary. Her personal passion is art, and so she has been a docent at the local art museum, although work has prevented her from devoting as much time to this as she would like. When she retires, she plans to become more active in the arts and also volunteer in elder care or hospice—whose value she learned firsthand as her father approached death. But between career and professional associations, some docent work, a few lifelong friends, and quite a few local ones, she doesn't have enough time or energy to be involved in anything more than she is at the present time.

* * *

There is a long-standing view in Western history that religion is essential to the social character and coherence of societies. "Religion is," as Edmund Burke asserted, "the basis of civil society."[1] In this view, secularity is a threat to social cohesion or solidarity, for, among other things, the nonreligious are substantially asocial. Colin Campbell has noted that "Although most people no longer tend to view the irreligious as friendless, tortured souls, prone to suicide and deathbed repentance, as did the Victorians, the remains of this attitude linger on in the tendency to assume that the irreligious are social isolates, existing in anomic situations and likely to be agres[s]ive or psychologically disturbed."[2]

Some social scientists have concluded, much as Campbell suggested, that the less religious people are, the less socially engaged they are. For example, some researchers have suggested that an

important explanation for religious disaffiliation is social marginality. Religious disaffection is stimulated when people have weaker ties to society. Religion, of course, represents an important part of a person's total connection to society. . . . When people are less tied to society they feel impelled to sever their religious ties more readily, and as religious connections fade, so too, may one's overall social participation.[3]

Similarly, in a widely cited study of American college students in the 1960s, apostates were characterized as socially maladjusted, alienated, and rebellious compared with religious identifiers.[4] And more recently, it has been hypothesized that atheists and agnostics do not believe in God or life after death because they are "people who lack intimate, personal obligations" or "strong social bonds." They therefore do not require the reassurance that deceased loved ones will be well taken care of in the afterlife.[5]

It is frequently said that secular people are "not joiners." The fact that explicitly secularist organizations and movements have remained small throughout history is taken as evidence of this. Even those involved in secularist groups habitually complain that engaging and organizing atheists or agnostics is "like herding cats." But as the cases with which we began this chapter indicate, reality is a good deal more complex than this. Apart from categorical comparisons with religious people, seculars are not uniformly or abjectly asocial. They become involved in a wide range of groups and organizations, but most shun those that focus primarily on metaphysical beliefs—whether religious *or* nonreligious. Relatively few seculars become involved in secularist groups (those that espouse or advocate nonreligious worldviews).

Some, like Mel, are exceptionally socially and institutionally engaged. Some formally identify or affiliate with secularist organizations, like Jon, but it is true that most do not. The overwhelming majority is more like Mel, Claire, and Jill, for whom secularity is a passive or private absence or abandonment of religion rather than a conscious identity, a public mission, or an active commitment to a like-minded community or movement. Most participate in a wide range of social relationships, activities, institutions, networks, and communities. But the profile or pattern of social participation does differ somewhat between secular and religious people— particularly the more devoted and congregationally engaged of the latter. Among the former, social relations and organizational involvements tend more to be subject to personal interests, needs, and choice.

One could certainly be forgiven for concluding that seculars are asocial based on the voluminous and growing research literature on religiosity and social attitudes and behavior. In countless studies, compared with strongly religious people—in most research, Christians, particularly active churchgoers—those who are less or not at all religious generally report or exhibit

- fewer friends, smaller social networks, or lower frequency of social contact[6]
- lower subjective sense of connection with others or support from those in their social networks[7]
- less membership or participation in fewer groups or organizations[8]
- less volunteering or community involvement[9]
- less charitable giving[10]
- in sum, less "social capital," or a metaphorical aggregate of the social, communal, and institutional "linkages" among people that benefit individuals, groups, and society.[11]

There are, however, several things that need to be kept in mind about this growing body of data. First, as we mentioned in chapter 3, there has been a very long-standing debate—particularly in the Western cultural and intellectual tradition—about the relative merits and drawbacks of individualism and communality. There are many who conclude that religiosity is an indispensable force for restraining a purportedly natural human tendency toward selfishness and thus ensuring desirable social life and societal welfare. A great deal of the data on social capital and related subjects, and the manner of interpreting the findings, proceed from and reinforce this view.[12] There is an alternative view that "modern" and "postmodern" changes in the character of social thought and behavior—at the individual and societal levels—are just that: shifts toward a different, but not necessarily or significantly less social, moral, ethical, or desirable model of human life.[13] Rather than "come down" on one side or the other of this debate, our point here is that findings—and their interpretation—regarding religiosity and secularity must be carefully evaluated with respect to the overall philosophical or sociological assumptions underlying this research.

As we have seen in earlier chapters, the relevance of some of these findings for understanding secularity may be limited for methodological reasons. These include limited participation of affirmatively or substantially nonreligious individuals in many studies, reliance on self-reports and attendant biases, or failure to check for curvilinear results across a *full* spectrum of research participants from profoundly secular to religious.

Seculars are not all the same with regard to social behavior any more than the religious are. Close analysis repeatedly finds that many of these results (on the religious side of the comparison) are attributable to those who are strongly committed to their religion and actively involved in their churches. As we will see in this chapter, seculars also differ in levels of social "commitment"—high or low. Even though this would not change *average* differences between secular and religious people, had prior research investigated such a difference, findings for high and low commitment seculars on numbers of friends, social support, or volunteering would likely differ much as they do for degrees of religious commitment.[14]

It is also worth noting that a great deal of the research on religiosity and social or charitable activity has been conducted in the United States. Interpretation of findings must take account of that country's distinctive cultural complexion. There is, particularly among many who are religiously and politically conservative, a strong conviction that assistance for the poor or disadvantaged should be voluntary rather than governmentally administered. Church-based or "faith-based" giving is voluntary in that church affiliation itself is (at least theoretically) by choice, and although churches exercise various mechanisms to induce charitable contributions, these are "ultimately" personal choices, as well. Charitable giving and volunteering, particularly in US Christian churches, thus receive a comparatively strong cultural boost. This cannot help but strengthen the link between religiosity and social capital.

Finally, even though those who are actively religious tend to report or exhibit comparatively strong measures of sociality, this does not mean that the less religious people are, the less sociable they are. There is not a one-to-one correspondence between religiosity and sociality. As the biographical sketches with which we began this chapter remind us, secular people, like human beings everywhere, are social creatures. Social contact and engagement obviously do not decline to "zero" as religious beliefs, behavior, or belonging do.

Despite all these cautions, however, this vast body of evidence cannot be summarily dismissed. Broadly speaking, strong religious adherence and involvement (of certain kinds) encourages distinctive attitudinal and behavioral patterns. But in a sense, this conclusion is unsurprising. It reflects active engagement in church groups that tend to be strongly communal thanks, in part, to shared symbols, rituals, and beliefs.

Most of the findings concerning religiosity and "social capital" are attributable to active participation in religious communities rather, or more, than to beliefs alone. On this basis, some dismiss belief as a causal factor. But shared religious beliefs and associated symbolism play a part in strengthening community and conviction. They help to bind individuals into strong and often mutually obligatory and supportive relationships. This tends to motivate both in-group bonding (with a concomitant tendency toward ethnocentrism or group-centrism, prejudice, and out-group intolerance) and universalistic bridging (reflected in efforts to transcend in-group solidarity) at least in some forms of religion and religiosity.[15]

Some argue, as we discussed in chapter 8, that most religious charity and voluntarism is directed toward religious causes (or in-groups), and so it is not "truly" a prosocial contribution to the social capital in society at large. While there is some evidence for the former, the latter does not necessarily follow. Motivations and intended recipients for prosocial behavior (charitable giving, volunteering, mutual aid, and so on) are many and complex among both religious and secular individuals. Psychological motives do not nullify sociological effects; contributions made to and through religious institutions can benefit the wider community and society, regardless of the psychological mechanisms that prompt them.

When the broad categories of religious and less or not at all religious are compared, there are undeniable differences in the character of social behavior to be explained. Much of the explanation for this, we think, is to be found in the observation that religiosity skews toward communality, while secularity skews toward individualism, at least in Western societies where most of the relevant data have been collected. [16] By individualism we mean the conception of the person as a socially and intellectually autonomous agent, origination of choice within each person, and maximization of options (or freedom) available to each individual to make one's own choices (regarding worldview, social relations, work, lifestyle, gender identity, and so on). Secular social and organizational behavior tends to be more individualistic or personally selective, less all-consuming or group-immersive, and more vigilant (about organizational influences on members' attitudes, thinking, or behavior).

This does not mean that all religious people are communalistic and all seculars are individualistic. There are, for example, forms of religiosity (such as "quest," "seekership," "spiritual but not religious," and New Age) that tend to be more individualistic and, so, share some characteristics with seculars.[17] And, of course, there are many seculars who are very socially and institutionally engaged. What this does mean, however, is that in the religious category we find more cases of strong group devotion or immersion, group solidarity or obligation, subordination of personal to group interests, or submission to authority. In the secular category we find greater emphasis on personal choice or volition, autonomy or independence, and rights or freedoms.

There is a noticeable tendency among seculars to view mass social behavior of certain kinds with caution, discomfort, or even suspicion.[18] This may help to account for the fact that most secular people tend to distance themselves from *both* religious and overtly secularist organizations or movements. As one of our research interviewees—an 86-year-old woman and self-described atheist—once said about the very idea of atheists gathering in organized groups:

I think it defeats its own purpose. Once you get into a group, then you want everyone to think the same way, and then one thing comes [to another].

I mean, we started with twelve apostles and look what's happened. I just can't imagine being part of a group and saying, "We're all atheists. Aren't we swell." You see, that's the next thing that happens. We're smarter than the rest of these guys. And if only they thought like us, there wouldn't be all these wars, and all this trouble. See what happens!?[19]

The observation that secularity and individualism are related is not a new one. The weakening of religion has long been associated with increasing personal autonomy and choice. As we saw in chapter 3, theories of modernization, postmodernization, and secularization have frequently made reference to individualism or individualization as an integral aspect of such changes. The emergence of Protestantism, in particular, has widely been viewed as an important contributor to the emergence of individualism in the West insofar as it represented a diminution of Christian church and clergy as intermediaries between individuals and God.[20] In Luther's Christianity, each individual has a unique and personal relationship with God. As such, and perhaps paradoxically, by removing "the institution of the church as a source of authority between God and man," the Protestant Reformation gave way to unintended consequences such as religious fragmentation and secularization. Individualism was explicitly identified by Steve Bruce as a key element in his account of modernization-secularization theory.[21] The fragmentation and pluralization of religion gave way to religion more as a personal choice than a cultural or environmental "given" (or, in Peter Berger's terms, a "sacred canopy").[22]

These observations are consistent with many of the phenomena we have described thus far in this book, including secular tendencies toward social liberalism, tolerance or acceptance of "alternative" lifestyles, autonomy of moral judgment, encouragement of self-determination and independence in children, universalism, democracy, and so on. It is also consistent with patterns of social behavior and institutional or organizational engagement, which is our focus for the remainder of this chapter.

EVIDENCE FOR SECULAR INDIVIDUALISM

There are many indications that secular individuals tend toward individualism—attitudinally, behaviorally, and socially.[23] One of the most obvious is that they tell us as much. Using Shalom Schwartz's values scheme and survey instrument, for example, it has consistently been found that greater religiosity is correlated with conformity, tradition, security, and benevolence, whereas secularity is correlated with self-direction, hedonism, stimulation, and achievement.[24] This is consistent with earlier work employing other values assessment methods in Israel, the Netherlands, and the United States.[25]

In a meta-analysis of studies that used Schwartz's values model in twenty-one countries, religiosity was found to be positively correlated with conformity and negatively correlated with self-direction, indicating that those who are less religious tend to be more self-directive and less conforming.[26] These studies reflected multiple measures and religions (mostly Christian—Protestant, Catholic, and Orthodox—but also Muslim and Judaic), strengthening the generalizability of these results.[27]

In studies employing David Wulff's distinction between the inclusion or exclusion of transcendence in people's worldviews, it has consistently been found that the inclusion of transcendence was correlated with tradition and conformity, while exclusion of transcendence (a measure of secularity) was correlated with self-direction, stimulation, and hedonism. A similar pattern has emerged elsewhere.[28]

In a study of Protestant, Roman Catholic, and nonreligious college students in Hong Kong, nonreligious students ranked personal achievement, autonomy, and enjoyment higher than did the religious (specifically, freedom, independence, self-respect, ambition, capableness, broad-mindedness, pleasure, happiness, having an exciting life and—ranked lower—a comfortable life). Values ranked higher by religious students were obedience, loyalty, self-control, forgiveness, and honesty, as well as family security, mature love, and salvation.[29]

Employing another approach, Steven Reiss and his colleagues found that the "desires" of nonreligious individuals also emphasize independence. They identified sixteen "basic desires" or "intrinsic motivators." Samples of American adults and college students self-rated their religiosity (as "very," "somewhat," "not at all," or "atheist"), but due to limited numbers, those who responded "atheist" and "not at all" religious were aggregated into a "not religious" category. The nonreligious valued independence (or a desire for self-reliance) most, but honor (or loyalty to heritage and family) least compared with the very religious; the somewhat religious were middling. Interestingly, status (or social standing) was desired significantly less among both the nonreligious and very religious compared with the somewhat religious.[30]

In Reiss' work, those who were not religious also indicated a preference for independence, but this apparently did not mean a desire for social isolation, for they and the "somewhats" expressed significantly greater desire for social contact—or the companionship of peers and others—than the very religious. It may be, of course, that the very religious are more satisfied with levels of social contact and support (that come with greater involvement in churches) than those who are less or somewhat religious. Additionally, the desire for raising a family was significantly lower among the nonreligious than others. There were no differences among religious levels regarding acceptance (desire for inclusion) or power (desire to influence people).

And the very religious indicated less desire for vengeance than either the "some-whats" or the nonreligious, consistent with stronger scores on benevolence and forgiveness.

In a study that carefully distinguished degrees of religiosity and secularity among US adolescents, significantly more atheists (44 percent) felt that "it is not important to fit in with what teens think is cool" than peers of varying degrees of religiosity (between 19 and 24 percent), once again indicating an emphasis on autonomy, independence, or nonconformity.[31] This is consistent with the fact that, as we saw in chapter 6, secular parents tend to value independence and devalue obedience in their children. This is further reflected in literature on secular childrearing, where these values—and parental methods for fostering them—are stressed.[32]

In other research, the decline of Christian affiliation in the Netherlands over the past half-century has been linked to increasing "moral individualism," defined as low authoritarianism, sexual permissiveness, and postmodern expressive values.[33] This has not been accompanied by increasing "rationalization" or increasing belief in the truth of scientific knowledge or value of technological progress, giving rise to a simultaneous increase in *both* nonreligious and New Age orientations. "Individualistic values of freedom and self-assertion" are evident among both New Agers and the nonreligious in England, as well.[34] Both were "higher on values of Hedonism, Self-direction, and Stimulation, which emphasize autonomy of the individual," in comparison with Roman Catholics, who put greater stress on tradition and conformity.[35] New Agers, however, exhibited a "holistic individualism" that involves a sense of connection (often diffuse or abstract) within a larger human, natural, or existential sphere. These findings are consistent with the self-expressive postmaterialist/modern/industrial trend identified by Ronald Inglehart, which we discussed in chapter 3.

Overall, the data paint a fairly consistent picture. Seculars tend to be strongly desirous of autonomy and independence, strongly egalitarian and meritocratic, yet desirous of social contact. They are also less compliant, conforming, obedient, family focused, and socially "forgiving," on average, than strongly religious people. Emphasis is placed on making their own choices in many aspects of life, including worldview formation, social relationships, and group or institutional involvement. The degree to which this is equally true in cultures that are less individualistic, or those that are characterized by very different religious or secular complexions, such as China or Japan, remains to be determined. As we suggested in chapter 2, there is ample reason to believe that the social and group dynamics of secularity are quite different in these societies from those in the West, particularly the United States.

SECULAR SOCIAL AND ORGANIZATIONAL CHOICES

The *types* of organizations in which secular people become involved, and their motivations for doing so, provide more indications of the individualistic character of secularity. Apart from overall differences in reported levels of social involvement, survey data from the United States and other countries indicate that the types of organizations in which theists and nontheists say they are involved differ.

Based on General Social Survey data, atheists and agnostics report greater involvement in professional societies, literary or arts organizations, political organizations, and hobby clubs (table 10.1). Strong theists (primarily Christian in the US context) report more involvement in service-providing organizations (general and

TABLE 10.1

Reported group membership, General Social Survey (US), cumulative 1972–2010

	Belief in God					
	Don't Believe	Don't Know	Some Power	Sometimes	Believe with Doubts	Know God Exists
Average memberships reported	1.66	1.72	1.87	1.50	1.85	1.79
Percent reporting membership in:						
Professional societies	24.6	29.4	22.9	16.7	17.9	13.5
Sports clubs	20.0	20.5	23.8	23.3	24.7	16.2
Literary or art groups	15.4	11.8	17.5	8.3	6.9	9.9
Hobby clubs	15.4	14.2	12.1	12.5	12.4	10.9
Political groups	4.6	10.2	4.6	7.5	4.1	2.9
Labor unions	10.8	15.0	14.3	10.0	13.0	10.0
Youth groups	10.8	7.1	7.1	10.0	10.4	10.4
Fraternal groups	9.4	7.1	13.4	5.8	10.6	7.5
Veteran groups	6.2	3.9	9.2	8.3	8.4	7.1
School fraternity	4.6	4.0	4.2	3.3	6.7	4.6
School service groups	7.1	15.1	11.2	9.2	14.2	15.0
Service groups	4.6	9.5	15.9	7.6	11.9	10.6
N	65	127	240	120	510	1,790

school-related) than atheists, but not agnostics. This is consistent with Christian encouragement of charitable giving and support. Differences are small or nonexistent with regard to membership in labor unions, school fraternities, or sports, youth, fraternal, and veterans groups. In general, seculars tend to be more involved with organizations pertaining to careers and personal interests, while the religious tend to be more involved with charitable or service organizations.

These results are consistent with much of the data reviewed earlier. Those who are strongly religious (particularly Christians, who have been most intensively studied) tend somewhat more toward communality in churches and activities in service to others. Some, but by no means all, of these activities take place within their own religious communities.

Much the same is true in World Values Survey data for eighty-five countries (table 10.2). Religious respondents tend to report greater involvement in religious and service groups (elder, youth), but nonreligious and atheistic respondents report greater involvement in a wide range of organizations, including sports, labor, professional, political, and consumer and animal rights. Involvement in human rights groups and the peace movement is roughly the same among religious and atheistic respondents.

Close inspection of some of these findings suggests the curvilinear relationship we have mentioned in previous chapters. Those who are not religious report lower membership in several kinds of organizations compared with those who describe themselves as religious *or* convinced atheists.

QUANTITY AND QUALITY OF SOCIAL SUPPORTS

Given the deliberately communal or congregational character of some religions (such as many Christian churches), it is hardly surprising that the reported size and density of social networks among strong adherents or attenders tend to be greater than among those who are less devoted or active.[36] In several studies, highly religious people reported talking to more people each day than less frequent attenders, having more non-kin, face-to-face, and telephone contacts with others, and having larger support networks or more close friends.[37] Most of this earlier research, however, either did not include samples of substantially or explicitly secular, atheist, or agnostic individuals, or combined them with weakly or moderately religious individuals. Moreover, much of this work was conducted prior to the past decade's upsurge in secular numbers, public presence, and increased use of the Internet as a medium for social contact and support.[38]

Nonetheless, even in more recent research that included samples of atheists and agnostics, the religious reported more supportive social relationships in their lives. Sheena Horning and her colleagues found that among older American adults, highly

TABLE 10.2

Reported group membership, World Values Survey, cumulative, 1981–1999

	A Religious Person?			Believe in God?	
	Convinced Atheist	Not Religious	Religious	No	Yes
Sports, recreation	17.7	17.9	14.2	20.1	14.3
Labor groups	19.3	20.3	13.9	24.4	13.4
Educational, arts, music, culture	12.5	9.7	10.8	11.0	10.5
Professional	9.7	7.2	7.1	7.7	6.8
Political party	13.7	6.8	6.7	8.2	6.5
Environment, animal rights	7.1	4.9	5.4	6.6	4.9
Consumer group	5.4	2.4	1.6	4.0	1.5
Environmental conservation	5.4	4.6	4.4	6.0	3.9
Animal rights	1.2	.9	.9	3.6	2.5
Other	6.3	5.6	5.7	6.7	5.6
None (no groups)	42.9	48.5	49.1	43.6	50.8
Human rights	3.8	2.1	3.1	1.2	1.7
Peace movement	2.6	1.4	2.3	2.0	2.1
Religious	2.9	6.9	24.0	4.2	22.1
Elder service	5.6	5.2	8.2	5.8	7.8
Youth work	5.2	4.5	6.0	5.0	5.9
Women's	3.1	2.8	5.1	3.2	4.8
Political action	4.7	3.2	4.9	2.8	3.4

religious individuals—those indicating strong religious devotion and activity—reported significantly more social supports than atheists and agnostics; less religious individuals reported more supports than atheists, but not the agnostics.[39] Again, given the strongly communal nature of many (Christian) churches, it is not surprising that those who are most actively involved would report many supportive relationships or a general sense of strong social support in their lives. What may come as a surprise to some is that this does not necessarily mean that seculars are any less *satisfied* with the supportiveness of their social networks than actively religious people.

Horning and her colleagues also found that "despite the fact that atheistic and agnostic older adults have fewer numbers of social supports, it [does] not negatively affect their social support satisfaction level."[40] In other research, no correlation was found between the religiosity of students at a southern US college and the quality of social support (carefully assessed with questions about people to "take you to the doctor," "have a good time with," or "share your most private worries and fears with").[41] Yet another study found no differences among Boston high school students who were Roman Catholic, Protestant, Jewish, or self-identified atheists and agnostics in perceived mutual support and social connectedness with friends, siblings, parents, or their families.[42] And in a comparison of nonreligious members of a secular humanist group with those of a Christian church in the same Michigan community, while the latter perceived "a greater degree of social support from their social network" than the former, there was no difference in reported numbers of social contacts or overall life satisfaction.[43]

The strong communal character of many churches may increase the chances that when assistance is needed it will be available, producing a generalized perception of social support, but this does not consistently result in greater social *satisfaction* than among seculars. People's satisfaction with their social lives is no doubt, in part, a reflection of their social expectations or needs as well as the quality, rather than sheer quantity, of social contacts. It may be that with the emphasis on personal autonomy or individualism among seculars comes more moderate needs and expectations for social contact and support compared with those who seek strong religious community. At the same time, we need to stress again that even though most seculars do not look to either religious or secularist groups for a sense of community, this hardly precludes them from seeking and finding this elsewhere. This is suggested by research on the phenomenon of "going solo."[44]

Eric Klinenberg has documented a growing trend for people in Europe, the US, and elsewhere to prefer living alone. He found that in Sweden—with one of the highest rates of solo living and secularity—such individuals do not generally experience social isolation, but instead become *more* involved in social activities and groups (other than churches) outside the home. There are, to be sure, cultural differences in such behavior, but he concluded that in the absence of social engagement within the home, "solos" tend seek and find satisfactory levels of social engagement in the wider community. Data on the individualistic values and social behavior of seculars suggest that the phenomenon of "going solo" is likely to be pronounced among them, as in (highly secular) Sweden.

At the same time, it is worth remembering that secularity is not a homogeneous category (any more than religiosity is). As we saw in the vignettes with which we began this chapter, seculars vary considerably in degrees and styles of sociability.

This fact is underscored by an insightful piece of research by Tatjana Schnell and William Keenan.

DIFFERENCES IN "COMMITMENT" AMONG SECULARS

Schnell and Keenan administered a "Sources of Meaning and Meaning in Life" questionnaire to church-affiliated religionists, religious "nones" or nonaffiliates, and self-described atheists in Germany.[45] This consisted of 151 questions that assessed twenty-six "sources of life meaning" in four groups: self-transcendence (including, e.g., social commitment, religiosity, union with nature, self-knowledge, and spirituality); self-actualization (individualism, power, achievement, freedom, and creativity); order (tradition, practicality, morality, and reason); and well-being and relatedness (community, love, care, attentiveness, and harmony).

Overall, the atheists reported less meaningfulness in life than the "nones" or religionists. But upon closer analysis, three distinct types of atheists became apparent: broad-commitment, low-commitment, and self-actualization. "Commitment," in this context, meant the degree to which respondents embraced various sources of meaning, or what some would call values. The specific commitments (or values) that distinguished these three types from one another were: well-being and relatedness, order, horizontal self-transcendence (or taking responsibility for worldly affairs beyond one's own concerns), self-actualization (or using and developing one's own abilities), and spirituality (a nontheistic orientation toward "something" greater than oneself).

Broad-commitment atheists might best be characterized as progressives who are committed to relatedness. They exhibited stronger commitments than the other atheist types on all of these dimensions except for self-actualization, on which they and the self-actualizers did not differ. They were also stronger than religionists and "nones" on commitment to individualism, freedom, knowledge, self-knowledge, challenge, and comfort. Notably, they were similar to religionists and "nones" on commitments to attentiveness, care, harmony, and social commitment, but higher on community.

The self-actualizing atheists, like the broad-commitment atheists, stressed individualism, freedom, knowledge, self-knowledge, and comfort, but unlike the latter, "these self-centred commitments [were] not broadened or balanced by an interest in relatedness" (including attentiveness and harmony). They also showed "little interest in cultivating relationships (love, care, community, fun)" or in horizontal self-transcendence.[46]

Low-commitment atheists exhibited the lowest meaningfulness scores of all groups and seemed "generally disengaged." They were less committed than the "nones" and religionists on all but four sources of meaning (knowledge, freedom, achievement, and health). Moreover, they were the only group that reported significantly more experiences of crises in life meaning.[47]

Low-commitment atheists, then, draw substantially less meaning in life from social or relational sources. Broad-commitment atheists draw substantially more meaning in life from these sources, but at the same time exhibit greater emphasis on personal autonomy and individualism than do religious individuals. Self-actualizing atheists find more meaning in life than low-commitment atheists, but they draw less of this meaning from social and relational sources than the broad-commitment atheists. The self-actualizers seem to be quintessential individualists or seekers, while the low-commitment types seem to be loners, and the broad-commitment atheists—if we may borrow from Yiddish—are mensches. It seems to us as though Mel, in our opening vignettes, would be a broad-commitment atheist (and it so happens that the "real" Mel was Jewish).

It would be useful to apply Schnell and Keenan's scheme to the study of social networks among religious and secular people. One would expect the broad-commitment atheists to report greater social connections and support, like the highly or actively religious. In any event, it is useful to keep these types in mind when evaluating research on differences between the undifferentiated categories of "religious" and "secular." Just as we find important differences associated with kinds or degrees of religiosity, so it is at the secular end of the spectrum.

SECULARIST ORGANIZATIONAL AFFILIATION

In an effort to explain why atheists and agnostics generally report fewer supportive relationships than the religious, Sheena Horning and her colleagues suggested that atheistic and agnostic adults "do not have the advantage of utilizing the religious community for networking. Support groups and organizations, like the American Atheists or the Atheist Alliance International" do exist, but they "may not be available in every community, especially those living in primarily rural areas."[48] This seems to suggest that

a) if there were more secularist organizations where the study was conducted more seculars would belong,
b) the secularist organizations would be as communal as religious ones, so
c) the gap between religious and secular people in the average number of supportive relationships reported would narrow or close.

There are good reasons, however, for doubting that premises (a) and (b) are true. Based on available evidence and our observations over the course of many years, the vast majority of secular people do not affiliate with secularist advocacy or mutual support organizations, and the character of most such organizations is generally not the same—or as communal—as religious congregations.[49] As we said at the beginning of this book, secularity and religiosity are not directly parallel phenomena in many ways. This is true of secular and religious organizations and organizational behavior.

In a survey in the United States by The Pew Forum on Religion and Public Life it was found that "the religiously unaffiliated place far less importance . . . on belonging to a community of people who share their values and beliefs" than do the religious. Self-described atheists and agnostics were least likely to say that belonging to a community of people who share their values and beliefs is very important (22 percent) and most likely to say this is not at all or not too important (35 percent)—even compared with those who described their religious identity as "nothing in particular" (30 percent). By contrast, 53 percent of all Christian respondents said that belonging to such communities was very important and 34 percent said that this was somewhat important.[50]

Perhaps even more telling, a Public Opinion Research Institute study found that "only 12 percent of secular Americans report that being secular is very important in their lives, and only 13 percent of atheists and agnostics report that being atheist or agnostic is very important in their lives."[51]

For the vast majority of secular people, the absence or abandonment of religiosity is passive or implicit rather than active or explicit in nature (as in the cases of Claire and Jill in the vignettes that opened the chapter). Their secularity may play a part in how they think about themselves and about life (as in Mel's case). But for most secular people, their secularity is not a central or defining aspect of their personal identities, activities, or associations (as it is for Jon).

There has undeniably been something of an "atheistic awakening" within the past decade or more, most notably in the US.[52] This has resulted, in part, from a reaction to public resurgence of religious conservatism and political involvement in the US and elsewhere, religion-related acts of violence and terrorism around the world, and the books and public statements of "New Atheist" authors and advocates (Richard Dawkins, Christopher Hitchens, Sam Harris, and Daniel Dennett). This has attracted increased attention to secularity, under many banners, as a worldview or "lifestance," ideology, movement, and personal identity (increasingly public rather than private). There has been a marked increase in secularist advocacy, public discourse, networking, and organizational activity. Despite this, the scale of secularist organizational affiliation and activity remains small relative to the total secular population. It has been noticed several times before that during periods when the secular population has grown, secularist group affiliation has not kept pace and has failed to "capitalize" on this growth.[53]

It is unusually difficult to secure reliable affiliation or membership totals for most secularist organizations. In many cases, this is carefully guarded information. When it is not, there is reason to believe that claimed numbers tend to be inflated, as is often the case with minorities seeking to elbow their way into public consciousness. There is, as well, some degree of duplication or overlap in membership counts due to some individuals' affiliation with more than one of these organizations. And the nature of membership, levels of affiliation, or modes of participation vary widely from group to group. As a result, much as we said at the beginning of this book concerning the number of seculars around the world, we can only estimate orders of magnitude.

Our best estimate, based on available data, is that secularist organizational membership or affiliation around the world measures in the hundreds of thousands or low millions, at best, while the total secular population measures in the tens or hundreds of millions (and religious affiliation, in the billions). By and large, quite simply, most seculars are not affiliated secular*ists*.

In the United States, for example, William B. Williamson made a valiant attempt to estimate total secularist organizational memberships in 1993. He concluded that at the time this was 178,000 people.[54] The situation has changed considerably since then with the virtual explosion of secular(ist) activity on the Internet and through social media—a subject to which we will return shortly. This has blurred the very meaning of secular(ist) "affiliation" and made the work of estimating how many seculars actively associate with one another *as* seculars that much more difficult. Even with regard to claimed or reported "memberships" or "affiliates" in named or established secularist organizations and associated student groups, estimation is frought with peril. Nonetheless, our best guess based on available evidence is that in the US this number is most likely measured in the mid-hundreds of thousands.[55]

Outside the United States, the story is much the same. In the United Kingdom, which has had a particularly long history of atheist, freethought, rationalist, secular humanist, and related organizations, growth in numbers of secular individuals has far outpaced growth in secularist advocates and associations. The scale of the former is measured in the millions or tens of millions, while the latter is likely measured in the hundreds of thousands.[56] As Steve Bruce and others have stressed, the character of secularity in the United Kingdom and in Western Europe is more indifferent than assertive or militant.[57] Our conclusion is that this is generally the case, particularly when religion has receded and secularity has achieved a more accepted status in a society.

In Scandinavia, among the most secularized populations in the world, organized secularism varies considerably. In Denmark, for example, the size, social visibility, and impact of such groups are negligible.[58] But in Norway, the dominant secularist organization—Human-Etisk Forbund (the Norwegian Humanist Association, or HEF)—has achieved a unique place in that society and, arguably, the world. It grew out of the Association for Civil Confirmation, formed in 1950 to conduct coming-of-age ceremonies—or "civil confirmations"—outside the state-sponsored (Lutheran) Church of Norway. The first of these took place in 1951. The Norwegian Humanist Association, formed in 1956, assumed responsibility for the confirmations (and other rites of passage, such as births, weddings, and funerals). Its stated priorities also included ethical reflection and education, and criticism of religion and religious privileges in society.[59] HEF actively promoted church-state separation, urging the nonreligious to opt out of church membership and the government to end state-sponsored religion, which it did in 2012. Its government-recognized and monetarily supported status helped to set HEF on a strong growth trajectory beginning in the 1970s, and at present more than 84,000 members are claimed.[60] Even so, this represents less than three percent of nonreligious or nontheistic Norwegians.[61]

In India, secularist and skeptic groups (particularly those aiming to debunk magical, superstitious, or pseudoscientific folk and religious beliefs) have grown markedly in recent decades.[62] Johannes Quack, who has studied some of these, has found that reliable data on nontheists, the nonreligious, or philosophically naturalistic are simply not available. The membership claims made by such groups cannot be corroborated, and there are good reasons to believe that many of these are inflated. This said, these most likely measure in the tens or low hundreds of thousands in a population that exceeds one billion.[63]

In Norway and India, secularist and skeptical activism has had work to do. In Norway, this has been to combat, and offer a humanistic alternative to, an established church. In India, it has been to combat entrenched religious and superstitious beliefs and practices that undermine medicine, scientific understanding, personal safety, or public welfare. In the United States, secularist organizations have focused a great deal of their energy combatting such things as religious challenges to evolutionary theory, scientific understanding and education, personal or "moral" liberties, and constitutional separation of church and state. In places where there is less or little of this "work" to be done, secularist activism and organization is weaker or non-existent. In France, which has had a strong atheist and secular tradition—culturally, intellectually, and politically—such activity is comparatively weak. And in Japan and China, to the best of our knowledge, secularist activism and associations of the kind we have described in the West are virtually unknown.

But even where secularism *has* had work to do, we still find that the majority of those who have abandoned religion do not replace it with deliberately secular identities, activity, advocacy, or organizational affiliation. Rather, the acceptance, importance, or relevance of religion in their lives simply fades and they get on with the business of building lives and families and communities without it. As we have said before, following Steve Bruce, if one imagines an endpoint to secularization, this would not be active irreligion or militant secularity but indifference or neglect.[64] This seems to apply to equally well to individuals as well as to societies.

DIVERSITY OF SECULARIST ORGANIZATIONS

Secularist associations, particularly in local groups, can and do offer their members opportunities for social contact and engagement, camaraderie, purposeful activity, lasting friendships, and a measure of comfort that comes from associating with likeminded others. There are some signs that interest in this kind of experience may be on the rise in the latest generation of religious "nones" and seculars. This is evident, for example, in the apparent popularity of The Sunday Assembly—a secularist "congregational" phenomenon not unlike secular humanistic Unitarian fellowships of a previous generation.[65] But many, if not most, of the principal secularist organizations have historically focused on religious criticism, critical thinking, intellectual stimulation, and advocacy of science or church-state separation more (or rather) than fostering strong communal experiences.

Like secular people themselves, diversity is evident among secularist organizations.[66] Colin Campbell, for example, distinguished between "substitutionist" and "abolitionist" or "eliminationist" forms of irreligion. Substitutionists "are still attracted to the religious model."[67] They seek philosophical systems, rituals, and/or organizational forms that parallel religious models, but without supernatural beliefs or references. A classic, if extreme, example was Auguste Comte's Religion of Humanity, which, in its brief existence, was "modeled entirely on the traditional [Christian] religious pattern, even including a full-blooded ecclesiastical system with pontiff and priesthood."[68]

Selected church or congregational practices are apparent in substitutionist forms, such as secular "celebrants" who perform rite-of-passage rituals (as in some humanist groups); weekly "congregational" meetings (such as The Sunday Assembly, Ethical Culture, and many humanist groups); sermon-like sessions or inspirational readings; alternatives to religious seasonal celebrations; and even traditional "holiday" rituals stripped of theistic or supernatural references (as in Humanistic Judaism).

Some secularist (and skeptic or rationalist) organizations are more directly or aggressively critical of religion, and so, ultimately abolitionist or eliminationist (such as American Atheists, Freedom from Religion Foundation and, as just mentioned, secular humanist organizations to varying degrees). But based on our experience and observations, none are, or can afford to be, exclusively so.[69] Rather, religious criticism accompanies a positive or affirmative focus on, for example, critical or skeptical thinking, scientific understanding or education, evolutionary theory, or church-state separation. Some are, however, undeniably more critical than others. There is, in fact, a history of debate and mutual criticism between "moderates" and "militants" in this respect. Militant secularists (or "atheists" in much of this discourse) argue that moderates unacceptably "accommodate" religion; moderates complain that the critical harangues of militant religious critics undermine the secularist cause and alienate potential recruits.[70]

An additional form of association not considered by Campbell might be called avocational or social. Here, emphasis is neither on religious mimicry or substitution nor on religious criticism or abolition, but on interpersonal relations and social or recreational activity among secular people with other shared interests. These are often subgroups within a larger local organization. The full organization may meet en masse from time to time to conduct organizational business or engage in full-group activities, such as seasonal celebrations. But the "real" activity occurs in special interest subgroups or tighter friendship cliques. These are not dissimilar to shared interest, hobby, or avocational groups of various kinds, like clubs that focus on book discussion, bicycling, cooking, hiking and climbing, or ownership and appreciation of particular kinds of cars. Particularly with the advent of the Internet, which enables local seculars to find one another, this model seems to be expanding rapidly, especially among young seculars.

SECULARIST ORGANIZATIONAL CHARACTERISTICS

Amid the frission surrounding the latest secular surge or "atheist awakening" in the United States and elsewhere, it is easy to lose sight of the scale of this development—relative to the total secular population, over the course of time, and within the wider world. There have been waves of secular(ist) growth and activity in the past. Each time, as now, it has no doubt been said and felt that "this time it's different," and so, each time, it has been—to some extent.

The expansion of the secular population in Europe in the late 20th century, and in the United States in the past decade or two, each signal that something "different" is happening today. Nevertheless, the history of secularist advocacy and association may still have something to tell us about the nature of secularity and secular people, at least in the West. Those who have carefully combed through the history of secularist movements and organizations in Europe, North America, Australia, and elsewhere have repeatedly observed that in periods of religious decline these have not capitalized on opportunities for growth commensurate with the numbers of those who abandon or are without religion.[71] Sidney Warren said of American freethought between 1860 and 1914 that "waves of religious feeling followed by laxity in faith have swept over the United States from time to time, and yet a corresponding increase in the strength of freethought organizations did not always take place."[72] In the 1960s, when religiosity seemed to be in retreat, particularly among Baby Boomers, Jay Demerath and Victor Thiessen similarly concluded that "irreligion has failed to replace the churches" and that such organizations "have not experienced the surge of growth and influence that might be expected in an increasingly secular society."[73] This seems to be happening again. As we have shown, numbers of secularist group participants are undeniably growing, but continue to fall far short of the numbers of new "nones," nonreligious, and nontheists, despite increasing media attention being devoted to atheism, "atheist churches," and related topics.

Several factors have been offered to explain past failures of secularist groups and movements to grow in organizational size, scope, structure, or influence commensurate with overall growth in the secular population. Some have suggested that such associations are inherently "precarious." This is a reflection of secularists' "high regard for individual autonomy"; "inert individualism"; ideological intransigence, which hampers recruitment and retention; chafing and conflict, both internal and external; or "diffuse belief systems."[74] As Colin Campbell summarized this perspective:

> whilst sociologists have tended to overlook the fact that irreligious organisations exist, what is also true is that when such organisations are noted they are invariably described as "loose-knit," "ineffective" or "unsuccessful" a substantial body of comment exists on the nature of irreligious organisation and it is all along these lines. Sperry deems humanists incapable of organizing themselves into effective social groups, Budd feels that the nature of their ideology and the personality type they recruit render effective organisation impossible, and Demerath and Thiessen that irreligious groups are rendered precarious by their dissidence and illegitimacy. Other observers have emphasised that the

ineffectiveness of irreligious organisations stems from their fear of sectarianism and their consequent preference for loosely-knit and unformalised organisational structures.[75]

Campbell, however, was critical of this view, suggesting that it is the result of tacit comparisons with religious institutions, particularly Christian (many of whose social and institutional forms tend to be highly structured and exceptionally communal even by religious standards). Many of these analyses make

> an implicit comparison of irreligious organisations with religious organisations—a comparison which necessarily presents the irreligious organisations in an unfavourable light. Irreligious organisations are judged to be ineffectively organised because they lack certain characteristics of the traditional religious denomination or sect, that is a definite and positive ideology, a centralised and formalised organisational structure, a clear system of authority, a formal procedure for resolving disputes, a *gemeinschaftlich* atmosphere and a permanent and loyal group of members.[76]

Once free of this tacit constraint, we are able to better understand the distinctive nature and attributes of such groups and organizations. While there are exceptions, Campbell felt that they generally have more in common with trade unions or political movements than with churches.

So, which view is correct? We think that both are. On the one hand, Campbell is right that it is inappropriate to compare or evaluate secularist organizations as though they were weak parallels to religious (particularly Christian) institutions. As we have repeatedly stressed, secularity and religiosity, in many and important respects, are not directly or wholly parallel phenomena. Most secularist organizations do tend to be more like trade unions or political movements than like communal congregations steeped in shared metaphysical beliefs and associated symbols and rituals. Some of them undeniably exhibit intense ideological fervor, but again this appeals only to a minority of seculars.

On the other hand, the analyses offered by Budd, Demerath, Post, Warren, and Campbell may suggest something enduring about the nature of active secularism and of secularity in general. Based on a historical analysis of popular freethought advocates and groups in the United States between 1825 and 1850, Albert Post concluded that "freethinkers did not readily organize, and this must be attributed in part to their natural hostility toward any institution which might hamper intellectual freedom; especially, when they could draw analogies between their societies and the churches they despised."[77] This attitude is still observable today.

In an issue of *Free Inquiry*, one of the leading secularist periodicals in the US, the editor introduced a series of articles on "humanist activism" and charitable initiatives (in its September, 2012, issue) with the following caveat:

> Several articles in this section take a strong position in favor of shared charitable or social-service work as a platform for secular humanist activism. It is not the intent of *Free Inquiry* or the Council for Secular Humanism to advocate this variety of activism for all. We recognize that some readers will view the idea of bringing together secular humanists *as secular humanists* for charitable service with distaste. For some, it will be uncomfortably reminiscent of activities in the churches they abandoned with relief. Others will find the idea at odds with their understanding of secularism as an individualistic and cosmopolitan framework that encourages men and women to connect to the highest levels of society as directly as possible, relying on their community of belief for nothing that does not immediately concern their life stance.[78]

The ensuing articles described several legal, educational, charitable, public service, and advocacy initiatives mounted by secularists in the US. The editor's remarks reflect the same rejection of ideas and behavior associated with religion—particularly those felt to threaten autonomy—that Albert Post identified in freethought groups nearly two centuries ago! They may also, however, signal a generational shift in secular(ist) attitudes and behavior, for it is young seculars who seem to be most interested and engaged in charitable initiatives in the name of humanism or secularism.

Despite discernible continuities in the nature of secularity, there is also change. Things are *always* "different this time," but not entirely. In our time, a confluence of technology, international developments, and cultural forces may be giving rise to a profound shift in the character of secularity and secularism, as well the roles they are playing in the world. Yet some of the characteristics we have discerned in secular(ist) attitudes and behavior throughout this chapter and this book also remain in evidence. If such a shift is indeed occurring, though, the most significant technological force helping to bring it about is perhaps the emergence of digital media, particularly the Internet.

SECULARITY, SECULARISM, AND DIGITAL MEDIA

The Internet has quickly become an important domain for communication and connection among seculars and secularists, particularly the young. It is a medium particularly well suited to seculars, "who express a desire for a community that allows for personal exploration, independent of traditional authority."[79] "Internet forums," "message boards," "chat rooms," and "blogs" enable online conversations or public commentary about shared aims and interests, both locally and in geographically dispersed networks.

The Internet has become, so to speak, the new "atheist agora" or virtual secular public square. Social media and networking platforms like Facebook, Reddit, and Meetup.com have become new means through which seculars connect, communicate, commiserate, agitate, advocate, and convene. As a result, it "has facilitated a more visible and active secular identity."[80]

The Internet is not only a communications medium, but a mechanism for forming face-to-face groups and organizations outside cyberspace (or in the "real world"). Meetup.com, for example, enables and encourages people to find others who share a common interest and to arrange local face-to-face meetings, outings or events, and ongoing social groups. Many groups focusing on atheism, agnosticism, freethought, secular humanism, critical thinking, nonbelief, rational thought, recovering from religion, secularism, skepticism, and the like, have been formed. Meetup.com claims roughly 320,000 "members" and 105,000 "interested" individuals for these and other related topics in 1,200 groups in 600 cities and 35 countries. Much like the geographical distribution of secularist organizations, the majority of these are in the US, the UK, and Western Europe.[81]

The geographical scope of secular Internet use is limited only by financial resources, access to necessary equipment, the knowledge to use it, and service blockages by governments or other institutions. The Internet is a medium particularly well suited to populations that remain geographically dispersed, as is the case for secular people in most of the world. The "virtual" elimination of borders and distances (at comparatively low cost) is unparalleled by any other communications medium. The ability to connect privately is particularly valuable for individuals in locations where secular worldviews and identities are marginal or maligned. Seculars can "come out" online even where doing so publicly "offline" may have dire consequences. The International Humanist and Ethical Union, for example, has reported that it

has been contacted by an increasing number of freethinkers who are using social media, especially Facebook, to organize humanist and atheist groups in countries where forming such groups in public, or with official recognition, has been prohibited or problematic. There are now Facebook groups of atheists in Afghanistan, Algeria, Egypt, Indonesia, Jordan, Iran, Iraq, Libya, Malaysia, Pakistan, Tunisia, Turkey, and Sudan, as well as more general online ex-Muslim and Arab language atheist groups. Pakistan provides a telling example of freethought groups moving online. An IHEU member organization was formed in Pakistan in the 1990s, but its founder, Dr Younus Shaikh, was soon charged with blasphemy and sentenced to death (following an IHEU campaign, Dr Shaikh's conviction was overturned and he fled the country). Today, there is no registered organization in Pakistan able to become an IHEU member. Yet there is a thriving Facebook group for Pakistani atheists with far more participants than the defunct off-line group ever attracted.[82]

The borderlessness and low barriers to participation of the Internet give it, and those who use it, unprecedented geographical breadth. But questions have been raised concerning the "depth" of "virtual secularity." Richard Cimino and Christopher Smith have looked closely at secular(ist) Internet and social media activity.[83] The Internet and social media, together with mass media coverage of the "atheist awakening" unfolding in America, afford the opportunity to participate in an "imagined secularist community" in both cyberspace and the real world. But, they hasten to add, this does not necessarily constitute "community" or even a "social movement as typically understood." Rather, this tends to be a "pluralistic, highly individualized public" characterized by "weak ties," both on- and off-line. The Internet offers the opportunity for partial or complete anonymity, limited personal expenditure or obligation, and participatory flexibility. As one interviewee told Cimino and Smith, "The great thing about the Internet is that if you want to come out you can, and if you want to get a message out but don't want to be known to the world you can do so anonymously as well."[84]

From Cimino and Smith's perspective, digital media and increasing societal visibility of secularity "have opened up the opportunity for secularists whose politics, philosophies, life experiences, and social statuses differ widely to acknowledge one another and socialize solely on the basis of the one attribute they all have in common . . . a minimal 'no' to theism and an affirmative 'yes' to reason and science." While the looseness of secularist ties may be a "limitation to building strong-tie communities, a unified political front, or a movement fitted with actors all struggling for the same goals," this may enable "wider and more rapid spread of information" about secular identity.[85]

Cimino and Smith's conclusions sound curiously similar to those who have analyzed the secularist organizations and movements of the past, as well as those who speak of movement toward greater individualism and fluidity of social and organizational engagement in postmodern or postindustrial societies.[86] Once again, it appears to us that secularity and secularism are aspects of a broader movement in some parts of the world toward more fluid and personalized modes of belief, behavior, and belonging.

CONCLUSION

It is said that the more things change, the more they stay the same. With respect to secularity and secularism, there is a complicated truth to this adage. Some things are undeniably changing. In the UK and parts of continental Europe, the societal authority and personal salience of Christianity has been quietly fading for centuries. This has given way to "fuzzy" admixtures of indifferent secularity and personalized religiosity or "spirituality." In Australia, Canada, and New Zealand a similar, if somewhat more recent, process has occurred. In Japan, as well, adherence to traditional religious beliefs and rituals has eroded. Communism has left an unmistakable atheistic mark on China and parts of Eastern Europe, while its imprint on Russia has arguably been less indelible. In the US, that "old time religion" has been more restive and resilient, yet signs of erosion in religious belief, belonging, or identity have emerged in recent decades, especially among later generational cohorts.

In many parts of the world, comparatively small coteries of secularists and skeptics have endeavored to intentionally prod their countrymen and humanity toward secular and scientific "enlightenment." In the UK, US, and parts of continental Europe, such efforts have been pursued for centuries and have perpetually elicited religious counteroffensives. The advent of digital media, particularly the Internet, has given secularists powerful new tools through which they can communicate, advocate, and collaborate, both locally and borderlessly. They are joined by those who may not trumpet their secularity, but who similarly endeavor to move humanity toward scientific understanding, critical thinking, political secularism, and individual human rights.

All this said, the geographical and numerical scale of public secularist identity and advocacy remains small, whether relative to the much larger population of indifferent or unaffiliated seculars (at least with regard to secularist advocacy and association), or to the even larger religious population throughout the world. Secularist advertising campaigns in the US and UK espousing atheism or depicting the neighborly normality of atheists are met with cheers from some nonreligious individuals and jeers from some religious ones, but puzzlement or inattentive neglect among untold numbers of "quiet" seculars.

In some parts of the world religion is clearly eroding—not with a bang or a clash of cymbals, but with an indifferent whimper. Seculars in Europe, East Asia, North America, and elsewhere, are, by and large, preoccupied with the joys and challenges of living, marked by personalized traces of religiosity or spirituality, or, increasingly, no religiosity at all.

CONCLUSION

WHAT DO WE know about secular people?

Our desire to answer that question was the main, underlying impetus for the writing of this book: to compile, in one cohesive volume, what existing social scientific research reveals about nonreligious men and women in the world today. In addition to presenting, critically analyzing, and discussing this existing body of research—and attempting to complicate previous methodological and conceptual accounts of secularity and religiosity along the way—we have sought to shape and improve future research on secular people by offering new ways to understand and conceive of secularity, ways that will hopefully provide greater clarity and improved theoretical-methodological rigor in subsequent social scientific research on secular life and identity.

As with any social phenomenon—be it race, gender, sexuality, class, nationalism, crime, and so forth—when it comes to secularity, there is a terrific amount of complexity. We have sought to acknowledge this complexity throughout this book, admitting the limits of our ability to draw firm explanatory conclusions or definitive accounts for this or that trend, pattern, or tendency. Such is the nature of social science. However, alongside the recognition of this undeniable complexity, we have also attempted to discern and discuss those "best truths for now," that is, those averages, propensities, and predilections that are fairly well-supported by existing data.

When it comes to secularity and society, as well as contemporary secular people—those men and women whose ways of thinking and acting are thoroughly, substantially, or affirmatively "this-worldly" and who conduct their affairs and view nature, life, and existence without reference to, or belief in, supernatural ideas or phenomena—here are some of the main things we know:

- There are more secular people in the world today than ever before, and their numbers are increasing in various countries on every continent, from the United States, Japan, and Scotland, to Canada, Uruguay, and South Africa.
- For perhaps the first time in history, there are now some societies that are extremely secular, and most of these highly secular societies are also among the most societally healthy and successful societies on earth. Clearly, secular culture—at least within functioning democracies—is not the destabilizing, chaotic threat to social stability many fear it to be.
- There is a broad tendency for secularity to increase as countries become more economically developed, as societies become more institutionally complex, and as individuals become more existentially secure. However, this tendency is neither evenly distributed across the globe nor unidirectional. It interacts with heritage, history, polity, and culture to produce distinctive local outcomes.
- Secularity is strongest in Europe and the anglophone world, as well as much of Asia, and weakest in Latin America, Africa, and the Middle East (with the exception of Israel). Secularity is far from monolithic; what it means to be secular—and how secularity is manifested and expressed—is different from culture to culture.
- Men are, on average, more likely to be secular than women; younger people are more likely to be secular than older people, and white people, Asian people, and people of Jewish heritage are, on average, more likely to be secular than other demographic groups. Secularity is also correlated with intellectualism and cognitive styles characterized by a tendency to think in a more complex, analytical, and critical manner.
- Most people raised in secular homes tend to grow up to become secular themselves; just as with religious identity, when it comes to secular identity, socialization is key. However, many people who were raised religious do grow up to reject that religion and become secular. Such individuals do so for a variety of reasons, from increased educational attainment and exposure to different cultures, to the experience of personal misfortune, such as the death of a loved one.
- Secular men and women are more likely than the religious to delay marriage or to forgo it entirely, and to have extended cohabitation prior to marriage. Secular people also tend to have fewer children than religious people, and as parents, they tend to value and nurture the nonauthoritarian traits

of independence, self-reliance, and curiosity rather than obedience, respect, and good manners, which tend to be more valued and observable among the religious.

- Secular people who are not involved in congregational or communal organizations, and who lack the concomitant social support that such involvement brings, tend to exhibit lower levels of mental and physical well-being when compared with the religiously involved.

- Secular people are more likely to experience depression, alienation, or unhappiness when living in a society that is strongly religious, but when secular people live in relatively secular cultures, no such tendencies are discernible.

- When it comes to moral dispositions, secular people tend to disproportionately rely on the areas of care and fairness, and "individualizing" morality linked to an "ethics of autonomy," namely, that people ought to be allowed to live as they choose as long as others are not harmed. Philosophically, the nonreligious tend to be consequentialists rather than deontologists: they determine the relative morality of a given action based on its actual impact rather than on the belief that it is inherently good or bad.

- The average age of onset of sexual behavior in youth ("sexual debut") is younger for the more secular in comparison to the more religious, and youths with no religious affiliation and no religious service attendance have more oral sexual experiences and sex partners than those who are religiously affiliated.

- Secular people are more likely to be progressive/left-leaning politically when compared with their religious peers, and secular men and women are more likely to support women's reproductive rights, gay rights, gender equality, doctor-assisted suicide, stem cell research, animal rights, and environmentalism. They simultaneously tend to be less ethnocentric, prejudiced, intolerant, militaristic, and nationalistic.

- Secular people tend to be strongly desirous of autonomy and independence, and they are less compliant, conforming, obedient, and family focused—on average—than the strongly religious. For secular people, greater emphasis is placed on making one's own choices in many aspects of life, including worldview formation, social relationships, and group or institutional involvement. Thus, while religiosity tends to skew toward communalism, secularity tends to skew toward individualism.

- While the number and size of secularist organizations are growing, most secular individuals do not affiliate with organizations that explicitly embrace or espouse secular worldviews; most individuals' secularity is passive and personal, rather than active or public.

There are many more details, patterns, and aspects of secular life that have been discussed in the previous chapters, but this constitutes a list of the broadest, most significant findings. Of course, the proximate causes for the various findings listed here are a matter of much discussion and debate. And where possible, we have tried to offer our best explanations and accounts.

Much work, however, remains to be done. The field of secular studies is truly in its infancy. There is simply so much that is in need of greater investigation. For example, we need to solve the chicken-or-egg puzzles concerning secularity's strong correlation with various other orientations, such as being politically left-leaning. Does secularity cause people to be more left-leaning politically—or is it the other way around? Or is the correlation actually being caused by some other, unidentified factor? We also need to better determine which demographic, personality, moral-oriented, and political-oriented correlations with secularity are more social in origin, and which are more psychological. For example, combine the high "Openness to Experience" correlated with secularity, as well as individualism and being male: are these things best explained by looking at cultural and societal dynamics, or psychological and neurological underpinnings? We also need much more data on secular life from non-American and non-European societies, especially where secular men and women are distinct minorities, such as in various nations in Africa, the West Indies, and the Middle East.

Despite the complexity of the topics covered in this book, and the many questions that remain, one thing is certain: as the presence of secular men and women increases in societies around the world, so too should our scholarly study of them. We hope this book has positively contributed to that prospect.

Notes

INTRODUCTION

1. Mike and Heather's story was conveyed in an in-depth interview conducted on March 19, 2010. Identifying aspects have been changed; Mike and Heather are not their real names, and they don't actually live in eastern Oregon.

2. For a good discussion of the distinction between "areligious" and "antireligious," see Lüchau (2010).

3. Zuckerman (2014).

4. Kosmin and Keysar (2008, 7).

5. Sherkat (2014, 181).

6. For the figure of 30 percent, see WIN-Gallup International. (2012); for the figure of 23 percent, see The Pew Forum (2015); for the figure of nearly 19 percent, see The Pew Forum (2012d); for the 18 percent figure, see Merino (2012); see also Putnam and Campbell (2010), and the American Religious Identification Survey (2008)

7. See The Pew Forum (2015)

8. See The Pew Forum (2015). See also Pew Forum (2012d).

9. See American Religion Identification Survey (2009). See also Harris Poll (2003).

10. Gallup (2014).

11. Merino (2012).

12. Guth and Fraser (2001); Altemeyer (2010). See also Bibby (2002).

13. See Todd (2009).

14. Todd (2009).

15. Fenton (2009); Singleton (2007).

16. Bruce (2002). See also Haught (2010); Norris and Inglehart (2004).

17. Bruce (2001). See also Gill et al. (1998); Brown (2001); Voas (2006).

18. Grontenhius and Scheepers (2001). See also Halman (2010).

19. Shand (1998).

20. Zuckerman (2008, 2009). See also Lüchau (2010).

21. Eurobarometer Report (2010).

22. Everett (2008).

23. Cimino and Smith (2014).

24. Cimino and Smith (2014).

25. Sherkhat (2014,181).

26. Hecht (2003).

27. Ginzburg (1980).

28. Pasquale (2007).

29. Vernon (1968).

30. Caporale and Grumelli (1971, 1–3).

31. Campbell (1971, 8).

32. Bainbridge (2005, 3).

33. For some major works on secularization, see Dobbelaere (2002); Bruce (2002); Davie (1999); Martin (1978); Glasner (1977); and Berger (1967).

34. Swatos and Olson (2000).

35. Lee (2015)

CHAPTER I

1. Pruyser (1974, 195).

2. Caporale and Grumelli (1971); Campbell (1971, 1977); Demerath (1969b, 1976).

3. Campbell (1971, vii).

4. Campbell (1971, 17).

5. It is useful to distinguish worldviews and lifestyles, for the former tends to focus on what people *think*, but as much, or more, meaning—or meaning*fulness* in life—is found in what people *do*. A representative definition of worldview is given by Koltko-Rivera (2004, 4) as "a way of describing the universe and life within it, both in terms of what is and what is and what ought to be. A given worldview is a set of beliefs that includes limiting statements and assumptions regarding what exists and what does not exist (either in actuality or in principle), what objects or experiences are good or bad, and what objectives, behaviors, and relationships are desirable or undesirable. A worldview defines what can be known or done in the world, and how it can be known or done. In addition to defining what goals can be sought in life, a worldview defines what goals should be pursued." As this definition makes clear, the concept of "worldview" focuses on cognition—what people think. Clearly, this is the basis for creating meaning, but the concept of lifestyles helps to underscore the role of patterned activity or behavior "itself" in finding meaningfulness in life.

6. Davenport (1991, 136).

7. Allport (1950, 78).

8. World philosophies are considered in Smart (1969), and worldviews are considered in Smart (2000). Other characteristics of meaning systems worthy of inquiry, beyond supernatural

components, would be the relative importance of ritual behavior and beliefs, scope or comprehensiveness (how much does it purport or attempt to "explain"?), focus (what are its main concerns?; where does it direct holders' attention?), coherence (how internally consistent is it?), conviction (how fervently is it held?), and openness or closure (how closed or open is it to change?, sometimes called dogmatism).

9. For example, apostasy or religious defection, disaffiliation, deconversion, or dropouts: Hadaway (1989); Hadaway and Roof (1988); Hunsberger (1980) and (1983); Hunsberger and Brown (1984); Mauss (1969); Roozen (1980); Sandomirsky and Wilson (1990); "nones," nonaffiliates, or independents: Condran and Tamney (1985); Hadaway and Roof (1979); Hayes (2000); Hout and Fischer (2002); Vernon (1968); the "unchurched": Hale (1977) and (1980); Tamney et al. (1989); Welch (1978); unbelief: Caporale and Grumelli (1971); Marty (1964); religious indifference: Sommet (1983).

10. A notable exception to this is Thomas H. Davenport's published, but rarely cited, Harvard doctoral dissertation (1991).

11. See, for example, Smith (1963).

12. Greil and Bromley (2003, 4); see also Davenport's (1991) discussion of the necessity of a substantive, exclusive, and real definition of religion for the purposes of studying the "unreligious," based on a typology proposed by Robertson (1970).

13. Other examples of substantive definitions of religion(s) are, for example, "an institution consisting of culturally patterned interaction with culturally postulated superhuman beings" (Spiro 1966, 96); "belief in a superhuman controlling power, esp. in a personal God or gods entitled to obedience and worship" (*Oxford Dictionary and Thesaurus, American Edition* [New York: Oxford University Press, 1996], 1270); "any system of beliefs and practices concerned with ultimate meanings that assumes the existence of the supernatural" (Stark and Iannaccone 1994, 232); "that human activity that acknowledges the existence of another reality transcendent to or immanent within this physical world and that seeks to describe and put human beings into a correct relationship with that reality" (Momen 1999, 27). Inclusivist definitions with a functional emphasis include the following:

> A religion is a unified system of beliefs and practices relative to sacred things, that is to say, things set apart and forbidden—beliefs and practices which unite into one single moral community called a Church, all those who adhere to them.
>
> Durkheim (1965 [1915], 62)

> Where one finds awareness of and interest in the continuing, recurrent, permanent problems of human existence—the human condition itself, as contrasted with specific problems; where one finds rites and shared beliefs relevant to that awareness, which define the strategy of an ultimate victory; and where one has groups organized to heighten that awareness and to teach and maintain those rites and beliefs—there one has religion.
>
> Yinger (1970, 33)

> [A] religion is: (1) a system of symbols which acts to (2) establish powerful, pervasive, and long-lasting moods and motivations in men by (3) formulating conceptions of a general order of existence and (4) clothing these conceptions with such an aura of factuality that (5) the moods and motivations seem uniquely realistic.
>
> Geertz (1966, 4)

Even more inclusive, or essentialist, definitions include the following:

> We shall define religion as whatever we as individuals do to come to grips personally
> with the questions that confront us because we are aware that we and others like us are
> alive and that we will die. Such questions we shall call existential questions.
>
> Batson et al. (1993, 8)

> Religion, in the largest and most basic sense of the word, is ultimate concern.
>
> Tillich (1959, 7–8)

> Religion is rooted in a basic anthropological fact: the transcendence of biological nature
> by human organisms. . . . The organism . . . becomes a Self by embarking with others
> upon the construction of an "objective" and moral universe of meaning. Thereby the
> organism transcends its biological function . . . . It is in keeping with an elementary sense
> of the concept of religion to call the transcendence of biological nature by the human
> organism a religious phenomenon. . . . In showing the religious quality of the social pro-
> cesses by which consciousness and conscience are individuated we identified the univer-
> sal yet specific anthropological condition of religion.
>
> Luckmann (1967, 48–49, 69)

> Religion is, in a word, what is "most valued."
>
> Bailey (2003, 65)

14. Fromm (1955, 157).
15. Campbell (1971, 129).
16. Asad (2003).
17. Lee (2012).
18. Pruyser (1974, 195).
19. Lee (2012, 131–132). In different contexts this is rendered as "nonreligion" or "non-religion."
We will adhere to the former spelling, except when the latter appears in quotations.
20. Lee (2014, 468).
21. Lee (2012, 131).
22. Lee (2012, 135).
23. Lee (2014, 468, 468n1).
24. Quack (2014, 440).
25. Lee (2012, 135–136).
26. *Oxford Dictionary and Thesaurus, American Edition*, 1365. The first three meanings are followed by: "4. occurring once in an age or century. 5. lasting for or occurring over an indefinitely
long time."
27. Kosmin (2007).
28. This said, the ways people interpret their everyday activities are critical. The "mundane" or
everyday activities of very religious people (think of the Amish, for example) may be conducted
and interpreted in religious terms. All action may be viewed as an expression of religious belief.
The manner of conducting apparently "mundane" activity may always be in conformance with
divine expectations or religious/moral dictates. Engagement in such activity on the Sabbath and
Sundays rather than attending to services or rites is only a rough measure of secularity and secularization. More detailed information is needed to determine how they are interpreted.

29. Caron (2007).

30. Taylor (2007).

31. Beit-Hallahmi (2007. 301) has observed that throughout the past hundred years or so of social scientific research on religion(s), "each individual's level of religiosity [has been] conceived of as lying on a scale, let us say, from o to 100." From this perspective, "an atheist would get a score of o; the most devout, 100"—and secularity or the nonreligious would occupy the lower end of the scale from o to a chosen cutoff, likely somewhere less than 50. On this basis, religiosity or religiousness—as the central framing concept for the field—should have provided a level platform for the comparison of religious and secular or nonreligious people. Most prior research has been conducted on this basis. While it sounds logical, however, practically and empirically speaking this has not been the case. As we have mentioned previously, viewing all these phenomena from the vantage of religion has tended to give short shrift to the diversity and character of secular forms.

32. The Barna Group (1999), for example, estimated that "in a typical weekend, 2% of atheists and agnostics attend Christian church service."

33. Hutsebaut (2007, 172).

34. Silver et al. (2014, 991).

35. Material on the six types is found in Silver et al. (2014, 993–996).

36. Silver et al. (2014, 994).

37. Silver et al. (2014, 991).

CHAPTER 2

1. Adapted from Quack (2012).

2. Adapted from Roemer (2010, 23).

3. See, for example, Huntington (1996, 70).

4. Tanaka (2010).

5. Zuckerman (2007, 47).

6. Zuckerman (2007, 61). The percentages given here are based on an estimated world population of 6.625 billion in 2007, Population Reference Bureau (2007). Zuckerman has subsequently indicated that this was very likely an overestimate for several reasons. For example, response rates for surveyed adults, eighteen years of age and older, were applied to total country populations which include children and adolescents.

7. Keysar and Navarro-Rivera (2013, 553).

8. The Pew Forum (2012b).

9. Interpretations of "not religious" vary widely within and among cultures, and as Steve Bruce (2002, 193) has noted, inclusion of the adjective "convinced" (as in the World Values Survey, as well) likely tends to discourage some nontheists from responding in the affirmative. Moreover, as Keysar and Navarro-Rivera (2013, 533n1) point out, these results are wildly different from World Values Survey data using the same query, which found in 2007 that 18 percent of 1,969 sampled Chinese (or a population estimate of some 236 million people) said they were "convinced atheists," whereas Win-Gallup International found that 47 percent of 500 sampled Chinese (an estimated 620 million) said so in 2012. The magnitude of this difference, the small sizes of both samples for such a populous country (especially in the case of WIN-Gallup International), and increasing evidence that religiosity has been on the increase in China in recent years cast doubt

on both findings. Given Chinese population size, a difference of 29 percent (or something on the order of 400 million "convinced atheists") has a substantial effect on global estimates of nonreligious, nontheistic, or "atheistic" people.

10. Zuckerman (2007).

11. Huntington (1996, 41–43). Our interest here is not in Huntington's thesis that clashes at the fault lines between civilizations will be a significant source of human conflict in the foreseeable future. Our interest here is only in his useful crystallization of cultural generalizations that are founded in demonstrable differences in historical, cultural, religious, and intellectual "traditions." Although we are often uneasy about generalizing at this level of analysis, we nonetheless speak often of "the West" or "Asian thought," indicating that there is something meaningful in such generalizations. Since civilizations, as Huntington notes, are shaped in large measure by their religious or philosophical traditions, they are directly pertinent to forms and prevalence of secularity. Other cultural maps would serve as well, such as that produced by Ronald Inglehart and his colleagues based on World Values Survey data. Interestingly enough, however, Inglehart and Baker acknowledge that they used "Huntington's (1993, 1996) cultural zones as a guide" when formulating their graphic representation of the distribution of traditional or secular-rational and self-expression values around the world (Inglehart and Baker 2000, 28).

12. Huntington's original formulation (1993) identified eight civilizations, with Japan included in "Sinic," and "Orthodox" was rendered as "Slavic-Orthodox."

13. Huntington (1996, 70).

14. Luckmann (1967, 67–68).

15. van Rooden (2003, 113).

16. For example, the "naturalistic Confucianism" of Xunzi or the rigorous naturalism of the "Chinese Lucretius," Wang Chong. McGreal (1995); Thrower (1980).

17. Yang and Hu (2012).

18. Bell (2001, 174).

19. Chinese religiosity is thus often characterized as "praxic" (focused on practice) rather than "doxic" (focused on belief). In this sense, it is more similar to ancient Roman religion than to Christianity.

20. Yang and Hu (2012).

21. Zhang and Lin (1992); cited in Lu (2011, 132).

22. Shiah et al. (2010).

23. Trần (2010, 313).

24. Inglehart et al. (2004).

25. "The belief in *Ong Troi* is the basic element of the Vietnamese indigenous religion which consists essentially in the cult of 'Heaven,' the spirits, and the ancestors. At the head of the hierarchy of spirits, the Vietnamese place Ong Troi, above all deities, immortals, spirits, and genies." Phan (2000, 737).

26. Zuckerman (2007, 12).

27. Lu (2011); Yang (2012); Yang and Hu (2012). The same is true of Vietnam, where some claim an "efflorescence" of religious belief and activity based on recent ethnographic observation, even though survey data do not (yet) seem to bear this out; see Taylor (2007). It should be noted that increasing evidence of religiosity in China may be attributable, at least in part, to greater social scientific *access* to the country in recent years. Some of the signs of religiosity now being documented may have "been there" all along, if hidden or suppressed.

28. Inglehart et al. (2004); World Values Survey, Wave 5, 2005–2009, accessed March 20, 2013, http://www.wvsevsdb.com/wvs/WVSAnalizeQuestion.jsp.

29. Davis (1992, 236).

30. Tanaka (2010).

31. Roemer (2009, 300). In this respect, by the way, Japanese religiosity bears a greater resemblance to ancient Roman religion, where ritual propitiation of the gods was central, than either of these does to Christianity, where the importance of belief and doctrine took center stage.

32. Kisala (2006); Reader (2005); Roemer (2009); Tanaka (2010); Whylly (2013).

33. Whylly (2013), summarizing Ama (2005).

34. For more on "cultural religion," see Demerath (2000).

35. NHK-ISSP (2009); Kisala (2006).

36. Inglehart et al. (2004).

37. Kisala (2006, 6).

38. Whylly (2013, 677).

39. Davis (1992).

40. Reader (2012).

41. Stark et al. (2005).

42. Feldman (2011). Shimazono (2008) also finds evidence of "new spirituality" and the "religionization" of individuals in expanding self-help groups and networks.

43. Davis (1992, 248).

44. Davis (1992, 246).

45. Thrower (1980, 53); Basham (1954); Quack (2013).

46. Hecht (2003, 97).

47. Hecht (2003); Thrower (1980); Quack (2012, 2013).

48. Quack (2013).

49. Inglehart et al. (2004).

50. World Values Survey, Wave 4, 1999-2005 (Believe in God × Educational level attained × Study year), accessed March 20, 2013, http://www.wvsevsdb.com/wvs/WVSAnalizeQuestion.jsp.

51. Kosmin and Keysar (2008).

52. Narisetti (2010); Quack (2012) and (2013).

53. Quack (2013, 654).

54. Pasquale and Kosmin (2013, 462).

55. Burkimsher (n.d.); Froese (2004a) and (2004b); Gautier (1997); Tomka (2006).

56. Borowik et al. (2013, 622–623).

57. Froese (2004a).

58. Borowik et al. (2004, 13); Marinović Jerolimov, and Zrinščak (2006, 280).

59. Ančić and Zrinščak (2012); Borowik et al. (2013); Froese (2004a); Gautier (1997); Lužný and Navrátilová (2001); Pollack (2002); Zrinščak (2004).

60. Hamplová and Nešpor (2009); Lužný and Navrátilová (2001); Plaat (2002).

61. Hamplová and Nešpor (2009); Froese and Pfaff (2005).

62. Schmidt and Wohlrab-Saar (2003).

63. Froese and Pfaff (2001).

64. Zarakhovich (2007); Grove (2013).

65. Laitila (2012).

66. Laitila (2012).

67. Borowik et al. (2013).

68. Rossi and Rossi (2009).

69. Argentinian pope and recruitment: Luhnow and Muñoz (2013). Evangelical Protestant gains: Gooren (2010); Martin (2002); The Pew Forum (2014b).

70. Barber (2012).

71. Among eight surveyed countries (Argentina, Brazil, Chile, Colombia, Guatemala, Mexico, Peru, and Uruguay) in the World Values Survey, 2005–2009, 56.4 percent of Uruguayans described themselves as religious, 36 percent nonreligious, and 7.6 percent as convinced atheists compared with averages of 76.7, 21.7, and 2.9 percent, respectively (World Values Survey, Wave 5, 2005–2009, accessed March 10, 2013, http://www.worldvaluessurvey. org/WVSOnline.jsp). Among eighteen Central and Latin American countries surveyed in the Latinobarómetro in 2010, by far the greatest numbers of religious "nones" were reported in Uruguay (44.9 percent), with an additional 1.8 percent "atheists" and "agnostics." Chile was next, with 18.2 percent "nones" but only 0.2 percent atheists or agnostics, followed by El Salvador (14.6 percent) and Honduras (14.5 percent), with no reported atheists or agnostics. While Argentina reported more atheists and agnostics than other countries (2.6 percent), there were only 11.2 percent "nones." In all other countries "nones" were less than 10 percent and atheists/agnostics were negligible, (Latinobarómetro, 2010, accessed March 20, 2013, http://www. latinobarometro.org/latOnline.jsp). Similarly, The Pew Forum (2014b) reported that Uruguay had the highest percentage of those professing "no particular religion" (24 percent) or identifying as "atheist" (10 percent) among Latin American countries. An additional 3 percent identified as "agnostic." Together these were classified as religiously unaffiliated people—at 37 percent, roughly double the percentage in all other countries in the region. Only in Argentina and Mexico were there comparable numbers of atheists (4 and 3 percent, respectively), but many fewer reported "no particular religion" (6 and 3 percent, respectively) or "agnostic" (1 and 0 percent) in those countries.

72. Barber (2012).

73. Gill and Lundsgaarde (2004, 403).

74. Esteve et al. (2012).

75. Jenkins (2013); World Values Survey, 2006. The Pew Forum (2014b) found 11 percent "nones," 2 percent "atheists," and 3 percent "agnostics" among Chileans.

76. Rossi and Rossi (2009).

77. World Values Survey, Waves 3 (1995-1998) and 5 (2005–2009), accessed March 24, 2013, http://www.worldvaluessurvey.org/WVSOnline.jsp. The b Forum (2014) indicated that the Dominican Republic ranked second among Latin American countries in religious nonaffiliates (18 percent), followed by Chile (16 percent) and El Salvador (12 percent).

78. Brazilian Institute of Geography and Statistics (2010); WIN-Gallup International (2012); World Values Survey, Wave 5 (2005–2009), accessed March 22, 2013, http://www.worldvalues-survey.org/WVSOnline.jsp.

79. Schielke (2013, 647).

80. Fox (2008); Stepan (2011, 122); The Pew Forum (2009a) and (2011a).

81. It should also be borne in mind that survey queries about religious (particularly theistic) belief and behavior are not allowed in all Muslim countries—a further reflection of societal religious dominance. This said, questions about belief in God, being a religious person, or the

importance of religion or God in one's life (in the World Values, WIN-Gallup International, or The Pew Forum surveys) consistently find percentages of 85 percent or more in the affirmative in most countries where Islam is dominant.

82. As Moossavi (2007, 139) has written about Iran, for example: "In a country where honest responses to simple questions such as 'Are you a Muslim? So you believe in God? Is the Holy Koran the word of God? Do you pray and read the Holy Koran? When you were growing up did your father pray, fast, and read the Holy Koran?' led to mass executions in the late 1980's, it is very difficult to know who is secular and to what extent."

83. Poyraz (2005); Stewart (2007).

84. Findings for "not a religious person." World Values Survey, Wave 4 (1999–2004), percent of self-identified Muslims only: Indonesia, 14.5; Iraq, 13.0; Jordan, 14.0; Kyrgyzstan, 17.3; Saudi Arabia, 29.3; Turkey, 18.3. World Values Survey, Wave 5 (2005-2009), percent of self-identified Muslims only: Indonesia, 14.6; Iran (Shia) 15.7, (Sunni) 19.3; Iraq, 43.5; Turkey, 16.5. WIN-Gallup International (2012), percent of *all* country residents: Afghanistan, 15.0; Iraq, 9.0; Saudi Arabia, 19.0; Tunisia, 22.0; Uzbekistan, 16.0. Discrepant data (percent of *all* country residents): Azerbaijan, 10.7 in the World Values Survey, Wave 4 (1999–2004), but 51 percent in WIN-Gallup International (2012); Iraq, 42.6 in the World Values Survey, Wave 5 (2005–2009), but 9.0 in WIN-Gallup International (2012); Turkey, 19.7 in the World Values Survey, Wave 4 (1999–2004), but 73.0 percent in WIN-Gallup International (2012).

85. World Values Survey, Wave 4, 2002, accessed May 12, 2013, http://www.worldvaluessurvey.org/WVSOnline.jsp.

86. Tezcur et al. (2006, 221).

87. Motika (2001).

88. Caucasus Research Resource Centers, 2011, Caucasus Barometer, accessed January 22, 2013, http://crrc.ge/oda/; WIN-Gallup International (2012).

89. Tezcur et al. (2006).

90. Motika (2001, 9).

91. There is, however, some discrepancy in the data. Percentages reporting "not a religious person" in the World Values Surveys have been 24.3 percent (1990), 20.2 percent (1996), 18.5 percent (2001), and 16.9 percent (2007). WIN-Gallup International (2012) reported 73 percent employing the same question. The latter is questionable. A Turkish survey found that roughly 1 percent had no religious convictions, 2 percent did not believe in religious obligations, and 34 percent were believers but did not fulfill Muslim obligations. KONDA (2007)

92. The Pew Forum (2012b).

93. South Africa: World Values Survey, Wave 6 (2010–2014): 18.2 percent of respondents described themselves as "not a religious person" and 1.9 percent as "an atheist"; 96.7 percent said they "believe in God." The Pew Forum (2012b): 14.9 percent were religiously "unaffiliated." WIN-Gallup International (2012): 28 percent described themselves as "not a religious person" and 4 percent, as a "convinced atheist." Inglehart et al. (2004): 78 percent in 1990, and 73 percent in 2000, reported belief in an afterlife; 98 percent in 1990, and 99 percent in 2000, reported belief in "God." Statistics South Africa (2012): 15.1 percent of citizens were categorized as "no religion" and 1.4 percent refused to answer.

94. Botswana: The Pew Forum (2012b): religious nonaffiliates, 20.8 percent; religious "nones," 19 percent (Afrobarometer, 2012, accessed May 14, 2013, www.afrobarometer.org).

95. Acemoglu et al. (2001).

96. Afrobarometer, 2011–2012; Inglehart et al. (2004); World Values Survey, Waves 1–5 (1981–2009); The Pew Forum (2012b); African Demographic and Health Surveys in Trinitapoli and Weinreb (2012). According to WIN-Gallup International (2012) 10 percent of the South Sudanese population describes itself as "not a religious person" and 6 percent as "convinced atheists," but as we have mentioned elsewhere, some of the WIN-Gallup International results are sufficiently at variance with other sources that they must be viewed with caution.

97. For example, see Nigerian-born Leo Igwe and his work with the International Humanist and Ethical Union, accessed May 22, 2013, http://en.wikipedia.org/wiki/Leo_Igwe; Evans (2012).

98. Religious identification in Ghana, WIN-Gallup International (2012): "convinced atheist," 0 percent; "not a religious person," 2 percent; "a religious person," 96 percent—the highest among forty countries surveyed, followed by Nigeria, 94 percent. Student survey: Yirenkyi and Takyi (2010).

99. See, for example, Graham Knight, January 8, 2013, "Report from the International Humanist Conference, Accra, 2012," accessed May 22, 2013, http://ghanahumanists.wordpress.com/2013/01/08/report-from-the-international-humanist-conference-accra-2012/; Gea Meijers, "Report West Africa Humanist Conference, Ghana, November 2012," accessed May, 22, 2013, www.iheyo.org/files/conferencereportGhana2012.pdf; Evans (2012).

100. The International Humanist and Ethical Union, based in London, is a "world umbrella organisation embracing Humanist, atheist, rationalist, secularist, skeptic, laique, ethical cultural, freethought and similar organisations world-wide." Some 100 member organizations are listed on its website, 80 percent of which are in Europe and the anglophone world and 10 percent of which are in India. The African countries with one member organization each are Ghana, Kenya, Malawi, Nigeria, South Africa, and Uganda. Accessed May 22, 2013, http://iheu.org/contacts?country=Allandpage=2.

101. Percentage of population that is religiously unaffiliated in sub-Saharan Africa: 3.2 percent, The Pew Forum (2012b).

102. Huntington (1996, 45) does so, as well, although he suggests that this would be justified.

103. Jewish Virtual Library, accessed May 6, 2013, http://www.jewishvirtuallibrary.org/jsource/Judaism/jewpop.html.

104. 26 percent in Wald and Martinez (2001); 33 percent in Mayer et al. (2001).

105. Wald and Martinez (2001, 384). "23 percent call themselves 'traditional, not so religious,' and 43 percent describe themselves as 'nonreligious/secular' Jews, most of whom observe some Jewish tradition," according to a 2011 report from Israel's Central Bureau of Statistics, summarized in US Department of State, Bureau of Democracy (2012)

106. Wald and Shye (1994, 164).

107. Cohen and Blitzer (2008), based on research by The Pew Forum on Religion and Public Life; Smith (2005), based on General Social Survey data.

108. Kosmin and Keysar (2013, 10).

109. Cohen (2002, 289).

110. Smith (2005).

111. Smith (2005).

112. Miller (1996).

113. Kosmin and Keysar (2013); Smith (2005); Cohen et al. (2008).

114. Mesch et al. (2010).

115. Tobin et al. (2003); Tobin and Weinberg (2007a).

116. Tobin and Weinberg (2007b).

117. Kosmin and Keysar (2013, 33).

118. Casanova (1994, 56).

119. Davis (1992, 246).

CHAPTER 3

1. Norris and Inglehart (2004).

2. Eisenstadt (2000, 2003).

3. Fox (2006, 539).

4. Hadden (1987); Stark (1999). "In contrast to Auguste Comte, Weber and Durkheim did not assume . . . that religion was headed towards oblivion under the conditions of modernity to be replaced by a scientific worldview. Contemporary critics of the secularization theory are simply mistaken when they allege that its adherents claim processes of modernization would lead to the demise of religion and faith. Neither Weber, Durkheim, nor contemporary secularization theorists such as Bryan Wilson, Steve Bruce, Pippa Norris, or Karel Dobbelaere advance such notions." Pollack (2008, 2).

5. Durkheim (1964 [1893]) and (1961 [1925]); Tönnies (2002 [1887]); Weber and Kalberg (2009 [1905]).

6. Davie (2007, 4).

7. For examples of advocacy, see Berger (1967); Bruce (2002); Dobbelaere (1981, 2002); Wilson (1966) and (1982). For examples of criticism or rejection, see Stark (1999); Stark and Finke (2000); Stark and Bainbridge (1985); Hadden (1987). For positions "in between," see, for example, Casanova (1994); Martin (1978).

8. Ester and Halman (1994, 81).

9. Tschannen (1991, 404).

10. Dobbelaere (1981); Martin (1978).

11. Berger (1967).

12. Casanova (1994, 19).

13. Wilson (1966), (1976), and (1982); Berger (1967); Luckmann (1967); Bruce (2002).

14. Tschannen (1991).

15. Kalberg (1980); Sharot (2002); Weber and Kalberg (2009).

16. Wilson (1966).

17. Wilson (1976).

18. Peter Berger famously (or infamously) reversed his "bottom line" position on secularization, from endorsement early in his career (1967) to substantial rejection (1999). A focus on the emergence and effects of worldview pluralism or pluralization, however, has persisted throughout his career.

19. Luckmann (1967).

20. Casanova (1994, 28).

21. Declining social capital: Putnam (2000); Hearn (1997). Shifting social patterns: Wuthnow (1998) and (2002); Klinenberg (2012).

22. Hervieu-Leger (2006); Houtman and Mascini (2002).

23. Personalization of religion or worldviews: Luckmann (1967); Stark et al. (2005). Erosion of religion: Bruce (2002).

24. Smith (2003, 14, 20).

25. Hadden (1987); Stark (1999).

26. See, for example, Dobbelaere (2002); Shiner (1967); Swatos and Christiano (1999); Swatos and Olson (2000); Tschannen (1991); Turner (2010).

27. McLeod (2003); Brown (2001) and (2003).

28. Bruce (2002).

29. Brown (2013); Voas (2009).

30. Brown (2001, 2003); Gill et al. (1998); Kurth (2007); Voas (2006).

31. Stark (1999); Stark and Finke (2000).

32. Brown (2001) and (2003); McLeod (2003).

33. Stark (1999); Stark and Finke (2000). Sommerville (2002, 369–370), has noted that when Stark "wants to argue that there was very little religion back then [in the Middle Ages], he concentrates on a narrow definition of Christianity. When he wants to argue that there is a lot now, he remembers to include everything."

34. Stark (1996), (2005) and (2011).

35. Martin (1969).

36. McLeod (2003, 1).

37. Voas (2009); his data and conclusions focus primarily on Western Europe.

38. Davie (1994).

39. Heelas (1996); Heelas et al. (2005); Hervieu-Leger (2001, 2006); Stark et al. (2005). "Cultural religion" refers to personal identification with a religious tradition without genuine acceptance of its beliefs, doctrines, or ritual practices. It "involves the eclipse of both belief and ritual but not a primordial sense of cultural continuity"—particularly in places where a specific religious tradition has historically been an integral aspect of national or ethnic heritage. It confers "a sense of personal identity and continuity with the past even after participation in ritual and belief have lapsed." "Cultural religion may represent the penultimate stage of religious secularization—the last loose bond or religious attachment before the ties are let go altogether." Demerath (2000, 127, 136, 137).

40. Bruce (2002).

41. Bruce (2002); Voas and Bruce (2007).

42. Secularization: Bruce (2002); Hanegraaff (2000). Religious persistence and transformation: Heelas (2003); Heelas et al. (2005); Stark et al. (2005).

43. Draulans and Halman (2005); Halman and Draulans (2005); Halman and Pettersson (2003).

44. Aarts et al. (2008); Norris and Inglehart (2004); Smith (2012).

45. Martin (1969) and (1978); Halman and Pettersson (2003).

46. Erosion of church attendance: Glenn (1987); Presser and Stinson (1998); Presser and Chaves (2007). Religious "nones" or nonaffiliates: 8.2 percent in 1990 to 14.1 percent in 2000 to 15.0 percent in 2008, Kosmin and Keysar (2008); 5.2 percent in 1972 to 20.7 percent in 2014, General Social Survey ("relig" by "year"), accessed August 28, 2015, http://sda.berkeley.edu/sdaweb/analysis/index.jsf); 16.1 percent religiously unaffiliated in 2007 (1.6 percent, atheist; 2.4 percent, agnostic; 12.1 percent, nothing in particular) and 22.8 percent in 2014 (3.1 percent, atheist; 4 percent, agnostic; 15.8 percent, nothing in particular), The Pew Forum (2015). "A convinced atheist": 1 percent in 2005 to 5 percent in 2012, WIN-Gallup International (2012).

47. Percentages of religiously unaffiliated individuals by country, The Pew Forum (2012b): US (16.1 percent), UK (21.3), Germany (24.7), Sweden (27.0), France (28.0), Belgium (29.0), The Netherlands (42.1), Czech Republic (76.4), Canada (23.7), Australia (24.2), New Zealand (36.6).

48. Bruce (1999); Stark and Bainbridge (1987); Stark and Finke (2000); Stark and Iannaccone (1994).

49. Stark (1999); Stark and Bainbridge (1985); Stark and Finke (2000).

50. Berger (1967).

51. For example, Finke and Stark (1998); Hamberg and Pettersson (1994); Iannaccone et al. (1997); Stark and Finke 2000: Stark and Iannaccone (1994).

52. Chaves and Gorski (2001); Froese and Pfaff (2001); Halman and Draulans (2006).

53. Chaves and Gorski (2001, 264).

54. Breault (1989); Finke and Stark (1989) and (1998); Olson (1998) and (1999).

55. Chaves and Gorski (2001, 269–270).

56. Voas et al. (2002). This pertains to "a previously overlooked mathematical relationship between measures of religious participation and the index of pluralism" (the "Herfindahl index," used by Stark, his colleagues, and others in studies concerning the relationship between religious pluralism and vitality). As explained by Voas et al. (2002, 212, 215), "The general principle is that when the larger denominations have the greatest size variation, correlations tend to be negative, but when the smaller denominations are more variable, correlations tend to be positive. For the sake of illustration consider three hypothetical areas, beginning with town A, where Anglicans make up 50 percent and Methodists 20 percent of the population. . . . Imagine that in a neighboring town, B, the Methodists are still at 20 percent, but here the Anglicans reach 55 percent. Clearly, total participation is higher, but pluralism is lower, because the size imbalance between the two groups is greater than in A. Conversely, if in nearby town C the Methodists are again 20 percent of the population while the Anglicans have only 45 percent, overall participation will be lower but pluralism would go up because the size difference between the groups is now smaller than before. Thus, the correlation between pluralism and participation is negative for these three towns. Consider now two more hypothetical towns, D and E, in which it is the smaller denomination (the Methodists) that varies. . . . Anglicans comprise 50 percent of the population in both D and E, as they do in town A. . . . In town D, the Methodists have more participants than in A, with 25 percent. As a result, not only is total participation higher than in A, the index of pluralism is also higher, because the denominational shares are more evenly balanced. In town E, the Methodists are at only 15 percent, hence overall participation is lower, as is pluralism. Thus, where the large denominations are more variable than the others, participation and pluralism will tend to be negatively correlated. When the small denominations show more variability, then a positive correlation tends to arise." This purely mathematical problem applies to some of the most important findings presented in support of the pluralism/supply-side thesis.

57. Chaves and Gorski (2001, 278).

58. Chaves and Gorski (2002, 227).

59. Borowik et al. (2013); Froese (2004a).

60. Casanova (1994, 9).

61. Inglehart (1990(and (1997); Norris and Inglehart (2004).

62. Norris and Inglehart (2004).

63. See, for example, McCleary and Barro (2006).

64. Norris and Inglehart (2004, 63).

65. Societal types are based on dominant source of wealth, per capita GNP, and Human Development Index scores (representing quality of life factors like income, health, safety, and life expectancy as of 1998). "Agrarian" societies are those dependent largely on agriculture and extraction/export of raw materials with low GNP per capita and HDI scores (including 23 countries such as the Dominican Republic, Armenia, Egypt, India, and Zimbabwe). "Industrial" societies are those with moderate per capita GNP and HDI scores whose wealth derives primarily from manufacturing (including 33 countries such as Brazil, Czech Republic, Uruguay, Estonia, Russia, Turkey, South Korea, Taiwan, and Ukraine). "Postindustrial" societies have the highest GNP and HDI scores with two thirds of their economies based on white collar jobs (including 23 countries in Europe and North America). Norris and Inglehart (2004, 46–48).

66. Norris and Inglehart (2004).

67. Halman and Draulans (2006); McCleary and Barro (2006).

68. Barber (2011); Immerzeel and van Tubergen (2011).

69. Hoverd and Sibley (2013).

70. Sibley and Bulbulia (2012).

71. Barber (2011); Gill and Lunsgaarde (2004); Immerzeel and van Tubergen (2011); Rees (2009b); Solt et al. (2011).

72. Solt et al. (2011, 462).

73. Solt et al. (2011, 463).

74. Rees (2009b, 12–13).

75. Inglehart and Norris (2007, 255–257).

76. Smith (1998, 88).

77. Casanova (1994); Putnam and Campbell (2010); Stark and Bainbridge (1985). These and other contributors to the "standard" corpus of work on secularization make reference to religious revival or resurgence, religious deprivatization, sacralization, and even desecularization, but use of "religionization" (or "religionize") has been rare—e.g., Juergensmeyer (1996); Souryal (1987). Curiously, the latter term is used more often by nonnative English speakers in (English-language) reports on pertinent developments outside the anglophone world. So, for example, Helbard et al. (2013, 36) speak of the "religionisation of politics in Sri Lanka, Thailand and Myanmar" in which "politics becomes an instrument of implementing religious practice" or ensuring "the application or implementation of religious doctrine and religious privilege." This is distinguished from the "politicisation of religion" in which religious identity, symbols, or references are used by government representatives and politicians to achieve personal or political aims. Onapajo (2012) reports on conflicts emerging from Islamic "religionization of politics" and "politicization of Christianity" in Nigeria. Shimazono (2008) describes the "religionization of individuals" through "New Spirituality Movements" and twelve-step self-help groups in response to "postmodern" individualism in Japan. Diren (2013) notes that there is "a well-established political term in Turkey, which is used as an antonym to 'secularization'. . . [and] which literally translates as 'religionization.'"

Social actors and forces increasingly vie for public attention, social legitimacy, or political power in both religious and secular directions. The use of both "religionization" and "secularization" enables us to speak of this dynamic without privileging one "direction" or the other. "Sacralization" may be thought by some to be synonymous with "religionization," but the former can be broader in meaning than the latter. We take religionization to refer more narrowly to inducing people or institutions to adopt ideas, identities, symbols, or practices characteristic of organizations or traditions generally recognized as religions.

78. Smith (1998, 103), quoting Davidman (1991, 83).

79. Not all forms of "individualism" are the same. American individualism is characterized by commitments to personal choice in many aspects of life and lifestyle, privacy, autonomy, and responsibility. This is reflected and reinforced in its laws, financial and economic structure, public discourse, popular media, and arts. See Fischer (2000), (2008), and (2010); Hofstede (2001); Hsu (1981).

80. Tight and loose cultures: Pelto (1968).

81. Campbell (1971); Pasquale (2007a); Smith (2003).

82. Bruce (2002).

83. Limited effects: Bruce (2002); Budd (1967) and (1977); Marty (1961). Influence greater than thought: Campbell (1971); Smith (2003).

84. Campbell (1971); Smith (2003).

85. Inglehart (1990, 1997); Inglehart and Welzel (2005).

86. Inglehart and Welzel (2005, 186).

87. Inglehart (1990, 49).

88. Inglehart and Welzel (2005, 27).

89. Inglehart and Welzel (2005, 27).

90. Inglehart and Welzel (2005, 31).

91. Berger (1967).

92. Inglehart and Welzel (2005, 32–33).

93. Casanova (1994); Davie (1999) and (2007); Heelas (1996); Heelas et al. (2005).

94. Beck and Beck-Gernsheim (2002, 3).

95. Pasquale and Kosmin (2013).

96. Inglehart and Welzel (2005, 292).

97. Durkheim (2006 [1897]); 1961 [1925]); Hearn (1997); Putnam (2000); Klinenberg (2012, 211).

98. Inglehart and Welzel (2005); Wuthnow (1998, 2002); Klinenberg (2012).

99. Ester and Halman (1994); Wuthnow (2002).

100. Wuthnow (1998, 4).

101. Wuthnow (1998, 204).

102. Klinenberg (2012).

CHAPTER 4

1. Bruce (2002, xii).

2. Brown (2001, 1).

3. Kasselstrand (2013, 157).

4. Kasselstrand (2013, 240, 257).

5. Bruce (2002, 63–64).

6. Bruce (2011, 89).

7. Bruce (2011, 89).

8. Bruce (2002, 68).

9. Bruce (2002, 72).

10. Bagg and Voas (2010).

11. Kasselstrand (2013, 195).

12. Voas and McAndrew (2012).

13. Hecht (2003).

14. Beyer (2003).

15. Bondeson (2003); Lüchau (2005).

16. Iversen (2010); Rosen (2009); Zuckerman (2008).

17. Inglehart et al. (2004).

18. de Tocqueville (1969, 544).

19. Lewy (2008, 13).

20. Bennin (2011).

21. Gingrich (2010).

22. O'Reilly (2006).

23. Prager (2011).

24. Law (2011, 81).

25. Jensen (2006); Paul (2005); Fajnzylber et al. (2002); Fox and Levin (2000).

26. Brenneman (2012, 158).

27. Tomas Rees (2009).

28. Paul (2010, 2009, 2005).

29. Pew Forum "U.S. Religious Landscape Survey."

30. Child abuse rates by state: http://www.npr.org/templates/story/story.php?storyId=123891714.

31. Diamond (2005).

32. Braun (2011); Ruiter and Tubergen (2009).

33. Gill and Lundsgaarde (2004).

34. Delamontagne (2010). see also see also Rees (2009); McCleary and Barro (2006)

35. Schulman (2011).

36. See Keysar (2013); and Quack (2012).

37. Quack (2012).

38. Sanger (1971 [1938]).

39. Nordstrom (2000).

40. Jacques (1995).

41. Froese (2008).

42. Paul (2010, 2009, 2005).

43. Froese (2008).

CHAPTER 5

1. Stark and Finke (2000, 115, 119).

2. Sherkat (2003, 155, 162).

3. King et al. (2002); Sherkat and Wilson (1995); Myers (1996); Acock (1984); Erickson (1992); Cornwall (1998); Hunsberger and Brown (1984).

4. Baker and Smith (2009a).

5. Baker and Smith (2015, 82).

6. Bengtson (2013).

7. Merino (2012, 12).

8. Nelsen (1990).

9. Bruce (2011, 204).

10. Bruce (2011, 18).

11. Altemeyer and Hunsberger (1997, 30).

12. Bruce and Glendinnig (2003).

13. Voas (2006).

14. Altemeyer (2010, 4).

15. Merino (2012).

16. The Pew Forum (2012d, 16) .

17. Cragun and Hammer (2011).

18. Cragun and Hammer (2011).

19. Caplovitz and Sherrow (1977, 30).

20. Beit-Hallahmi (2007, 302).

21. Bromley (1988, 12).

22. See also Barbour (1994).

23. Beit-Hallahmi and Argyle (1997, 135).

24. Mauss (1969).

25. Brinkerhoff and Burke (1980).

26. Hadaway (1989).

27. Zuckerman (2011).

28. Hefland (2009); Smith (2010); Leavy (1988); and Hadaway (1989).

29. Roozen (1980); Perry et al. (1980).

30. Hoge et al. (1981).

31. Pasquale (2010).

32. Bruce (2011, 70); Hornsby-Smith (2008, 100).

33. Cottee (2015).

34. Zelan (1968); Caplowitz and Sherrow (1977); Roof and Hadaway (1977, 1979); Wuthnow and Glock (1973); Hadaway and Roof (1988); Nelson (1988); Hunsberger (1980, 1983); Hunsberger and Brown (1984); Brinkerhoff and Mackie (1993); Sherkat (1991); Campbell (1971, 36); Zuckerman (2011, 35); Altemeyer and Hunsberger (1997, 118).

35. Campbell (1971, 36).

36. Zuckerman (2011, 35).

37. Altemeyer and Hunsberger (1997, 118).

38. Babinski (1995).

39. Babinksi (1995, 221).

40. Warraq (2003).

41. Cottee (2015).

42. Pasquale (2010).

43. Hood et al. (2009, 139.)

44. Zuckerman (2011).

45. Ecklund and Scheitle (2007).

46. Sherkat (2003); Lawton and Burges (2001); Beit-Hallhmi and Argyle (1997); Hunsberger (1985); Johnson (1997); Zuckerman (2009); Baker (2008).

47. Pargament (1997).

48. Hout (2003).

49. Chaves (2011); Hout and Fischer (2002).

50. Moore et al. (1998).

51. This phenomenon is astutely and insightfully illustrated in the wonderful, sociologically rich book *Souls and Bodies*, by David Lodge (1980).

52. Rose (2005). See also Regnerus (2007, 96).

53. Linneman and Clendenen (2010).

54. Brinkerhoff and Mackie (1993).

55. Hunsberger (1983).

56. Ebaugh (1988).

57. Brinkerhoff and Burke (1980, 52).

58. Wilcox (2002).

59. See Yip (2002, 1997).

60. Smith (2010).

61. Smith (2010, 15).

62. Altemeyer and Hunsberger (1997, 215).

63. Altemeyer and Hunsberger (1997, 96).

64. Zuckerman (2012).

65. Zuckerman (2009, 2008); Iversen (2006); Palm and Trost (2000); Lüchau (2010); Bondeson (2003); Inglehart et al. (2004).

66. Sullins (2006).

67. Mahlamäki (2012, 60).

68. The Pew Forum (2012d).

69. American Religious Identification Survey (2008).

70. American Religious Identification Survey (2009).

71. Walter and Davie (1998); Miller and Hoffman (1995); Miller and Stark (2002); Beit-Hallahmi and Argyle (1997); Beit-Hallahmi (2005); Batson et al. (1993); Rice (2003); Hayes (2000); Veevers and Cousineau (1980).

72. Trzebiatowska and Bruce (2012).

73. Brasher (1998); Nason-Clark (1997); Becker (1981).

74. Ozorak (1996); Winter et al. (1994); Diaz-Stevens (1994); Brasher (1998).

75. Chodorow (1978); Giligan (1982); Goldman (1999); Johnson (1991).

76. Iannaccone (1990); Glock (1967).

77. Berger et al. (2008); Stark (2002).

78. Francis and Wilcox (1998, 1996); Argyle (2000, 42–43); Thompson and Remmes (2002).

CHAPTER 6

1. Kosmin et al. (2009); The Pew Forum (2008).; Cox et al. (2009); Galen (2009); Hunsberger and Altemeyer (2006).

2. Kosmin et al. (2009).

3. Kosmin et al. (2009); The Pew Forum (2012d).

4. Roozen (1980).

5. The Pew Forum (2012d).

6. Galen (2009); Kosmin et al. (2009).

7. Google's "n-gram" facility, an index of the frequency with which particular terms appear in print material, indicates a decline in the use of "humanism" in English-language materials since the 1990s and a rise in references to "atheism," particularly since 2000 (often referred to as a "New Atheist" movement, prompted by the writings of Richard Dawkins, Daniel Dennett, Sam Harris, Christopher Hitchens, and others).

8. Hunsberger and Altemeyer (2006).

9. Cox et al. (2009); The Pew Forum (2012d).

10. Keysar (2007); Kosmin (2008).

11. The Pew Forum (2008).

12. Galen (2009).

13. Kosmin et al. (2009); The Pew Forum (2008).

14. Gentile and Rosenfeld (2012).

15. Mayrl and Uecker (2011).

16. Schwadel (2014).

17. Hill (2009, 2011).

18. Kimball et al. (2009).

19. Ecklund and Scheitle (2007).

20. Larson and Witham (1997, 1998).

21. Gross and Simmons (2009).

22. Shermer (2000).

23. Preston and Epley (2009).

24. Gottfredson (1997).

25. Lewis et al. (2011); Lynn et al. (2009); Nyborg (2009); Zuckerman et al. (2013).

26. Bertsch and Pesta (2009).

27. Kanazawa (2010).

28. Sherkat (2010).

29. Zuckerman et al. (2013).

30. Rigney and Hoffman (1993).

31. Zuckerman et al. (2013).

32. Altemeyer and Hunsberger (1997).

33. Hunsberger and Brown (1984).

34. Hunsberger et al. (1993).

35. Batson and Ventis (1982).

36. Burris et al. (1996).

37. Hunsberger et al. (1996).

38. Ozorak (1989).

39. Hunsberger et al. (2002).

40. Pennycook et al. (2012).

41. Ritter et al. (2014).

42. Gervais and Norenzayan (2012a); Shenhav et al. (2011).

43. Pennycook, Cheyne, Barr, et al. (2013).

44. Pennycook, Cheyne, Koehler, et al. (2013).

45. Baron-Cohen and Wheelwright (2004).

46. Rosenkranz and Charlton (2013).

47. Rosenkranz and Charlton (2013).

48. Norenzayan et al. (2012).

49. Riekki et al. (2013).

50. Epley et al. (2008).

51. Gervais (2013).

52. Goldberg (1981).

53. Saroglou (2002); Shermer (2000).

54. Galen and Kloet (2011b).

55. Streib et al. (2009).

56. Saroglou (2002).

57. Duriez et al. (2004).

58. Jost et al. (2003); McCrae (1987, 1996).

59. Saroglou (2002, 24).

60. McCullough and Willoughby (2009).

61. Galen and Kloet (2011b).

62. Barrick and Mount (1996).

63. Galen et al. (2014).

64. Sedikides and Gebauer (2010).

65. Saroglou (2010).

66. Gebauer et al. (2013); Naumann et al. (2009); Highfield et al. (2009); Gervais (2011).

67. Galen (2009).

68. Cheyne and Britton (2010).

69. Galen (2009).

70. Waller et al. (1990).

71. Bouchard et al. (1999); D'Onofrio et al. (1999).

72. Kandler and Riemann (2013).

73. McCullough et al. (2005).

74. Koenig et al. (2008); Bradshaw and Ellison (2008).

75. Ludeke et al. (2013).

76. Barrett (2012); Banerjee and Bloom (2013); Bering (2011); Caldwell-Harris (2012); Haidt (2013).

77. Hughes and Cutting (1999).

78. Heaton and Call (1997).

79. Barna Group (2007).

80. The Pew Forum (2008).

81. General Social Survey, Cumulative Data File, 1972-2012, accessed October 9, 2013, http://sda.berkeye.edu/sdaweb/analysis/index.jsf; ; Bainbridge (2005).

82. Lehrer and Chiswick (1993).

83. Call and Heaton (1997).

84. Booth and Edwards (1985).

85. Kosmin et al. (2009).

86. Cherlin (2009).

87. Neugarten (1979).

88. Hayes and Hornsby-Smith (1994).

89. Cahn and Carbone (2010).

90. Gottlieb (2008); Heaton et al. (1992); Sherkat (2000).

91. Bainbridge (2005).

92. Hunter (2010).

93. Mosher et al. (1992).

94. Hayford and Morgan (2008).

95. Frejka and Westoff (2008).

96. Jokela (2012).

97. Baumrind (1971).

98. Hetherington and Weiler (2009).

99. Pew Research Center (2014c); Putnam and Campbell (2010).

100. Ellison and Sherkat (1993a, 1993b).

101. Lakoff (2002).

102. C. Manning (2010, 2013).

103. Altemeyer and Hunsberger (1997).

104. Hunsberger and Altemeyer (2006).

105. Cheyne and Britton (2010).

CHAPTER 7

1. Hagerty (2011).

2. Ventis (1995).

3. Bergin (1983); Hackney and Sanders (2003).

4. Smith et al. (2003); Balbuena et al. (2013).

5. Sloan (2006).

6. Pargament (1997).

7. Miller et al. (2012); Schumaker (1992).

8. The Pew Forum (2008); The Pew Forum (2012d).

9. Myers (2000).

10. Acevedo (2010); Berthold and Ruch (2014); Patrick and Kinney (2003); Smith et al. (2003).

11. Ellison and George (1994).

12. Greenfield and Marks (2007); Jackson et al. (1995); Lim and Putnam (2010).

13. Tom Rees (2009).

14. Buggle et al. (2000); Eliassen et al. (2005); Mochon et al. (2011); Riley et al. (2005, 840); Ross (1990); Shaver et al. (1980).

15. Meltzer et al. (2011); Horning et al. (2011); Wilkinson and Coleman (2010).

16. Weber et al. (2012).

17. Newport et al. (2010).

18. Galen and Kloet (2011a).

19. King et al. (2013).

20. Lavric and Flere (2010); Hunsberger et al. (2002).

21. Krause (2006); Krause and Wulff (2004).

22. Altemeyer and Hunsberger (1997).

23. Hunsberger (1980, 1983).

24. Galen (2009).

25. Burris et al. (1996); Pasquale (2010); Wilson and Sherkat (1994).

26. Brinkerhoff and Mackie (1993); Caplovitz and Sherrow (1977).

27. Bengtson (2013).

28. Cragun et al. (2012).

29. Hammer et al. (2012).

30. Ryan et al. (2009).

31. Gebauer et al. (2012, 158–160); Snoep (2008); Diener et al. (2011); Leurent et al. (2013); Lun and Bond (2013).

32. Eichhorn (2012).

33. Zhang and Jin (1996).

34. Stavrova et al. (2013).

35. Kvande et al. (2014).

36. Frey et al. (2005); Hwang et al. (2011); Koenig (2008).

37. Kapuscinski and Master (2010).

38. Caldwell-Harris et al. (2010).

39. Peterson and Seligman (2004).

40. de Jager Meezenbroek et al. (2012).

41. Piedmont (1999).

42. Adler and Fagley (2005); Paloutzian and Ellison (1982).

43. Lindeman et al. (2012); Schuurmans-Stekhoven (2011, 2013); Tsuang et al. (2002).

44. Silton et al. (2014).

45. Hackney and Sanders (2003).

46. Horning et al. (2011); Schnell and Keenan (2011).

47. Horning et al. (2011); Schnell and Keenan (2011).

48. Tamney et al. (1965).

49. Kay et al. (2008).

50. Kay, Shepherd, et al. (2010).

51. Kay, Gaucher, et al. (2010).

52. Hunsberger and Altemeyer (2006).

53. Farias et al. (2013).

54. Preston and Epley (2009).

55. Rutjens et al. (2013).

56. Rutjens et al. (2010).

57. Becker (1973, 5).

58. Ellis et al. (2013); Spilka et al. (1985).

59. Norenzayan and Hansen (2006); Vail et al. (2012).

60. Norenzayan et al. (2009).

61. Vail et al. (2012).

62. Jong et al. (2013); Donovan (2002); Ellis et al. (2013).

63. Farias et al. (2013).

64. Tracy et al. (2011).

65. Smith-Stoner (2007).

66. Balboni et al. (2007).

67. Phelps et al. (2009).

68. Jacobs et al. (2008).

69. Gallup (2008).

70. Nisbet et al. (2000).

71. Rasic et al. (2009).

72. Chida et al. (2009).

73. Helm et al. (2000); Hummer et al. (1999); Koenig et al. (1999); McCullough et al. (2000); Oman and Reed (1998); Strawbridge et al. (1997).

74. Fitchett et al. (1999).

75. Hill and Pargament (2008).

76. Powell et al. (2003).

77. Sullivan (2010); McCullough et al. (2000).

78. George et al. (2002).

79. Powell et al. (2003); Sullivan (2010).

80. Benjamins (2006).

81. Masters and Hooker (2013).

82. Bogg and Roberts (2004).

83. Powell et al. (2003).

84. Howsepian and Merluzzi (2009).

85. Shor and Roelfs (2013).

86. Patel et al. (1985).

87. Ai et al. (2011).

88. Ai et al. (2007).

89. Krause (1998).

90. Park et al. (2009).

91. Hill and Pargament (2008).

92. Fitchett et al. (1999); Pargament et al. (2001).

CHAPTER 8

1. Zuckerman (2011).

2. DeWaal (2013).

3. Edgell et al. (2006).

4. Gervais et al. (2011); Ritter and Preston (2011).

5. Pew Forum(2002).

6. Baumeister et al. (2010); Saroglou et al. (2005).

7. Galen (2012).

8. Galen et al. (2011); Galen et al. (2014).

9. de Dreu et al. (1995).

10. Rowatt et al. (2005); Weeks and Vincent (2007).

11. Ben-Ner et al. (2009); Fitzgerald and Wickwire (2012); Tan and Vogel (2008).

12. Bobkowski and Kalyanaraman (2010); Galen et al. (2014).

13. Rowatt et al. (2002).

14. Burris and Jackson (2000); Sedikides and Gebauer (2010).

15. Middleton and Putney (1962).

16. Kohlberg and Lickona (1976).

17. Getz (1984); Narvaez et al. (1999).

18. Richards and Davison (1992).

19. Rest et al. (1999).
20. Narvaez and Gleason (2007).
21. Cobb et al. (2001).
22. Maclean et al. (2004); Midlarsky et al. (2005).
23. Haidt (2001).
24. Baril and Wright (2012).
25. Higher Education Research Institute (2003).
26. Middleton and Putney (1962).
27. Weeden et al. (2008); Weeden and Kurzban (2013).
28. Cheyne and Britton (2010); Graham and Haidt (2010).
29. Koleva et al. (2012).
30. Farias and Lalljee (2008).
31. McClain (1978); Reiss (2000b).
32. Van Leeuwen and Park (2009).
33. Whitehead and Baker (2012).
34. Botvar (2005).
35. Piazza (2012); Piazza and Landy (2013).
36. Hood et al. (2009); Williamson and Assadi (2005).
37. Hartshorne et al. (1926).
38. Harrell (2012); Randolph-Seng and Nielsen (2007); Shariff and Norenzayan (2007).
39. Shariff and Norenzayan (2011).
40. Mazar et al. (2008).
41. Harrell (2012); Shariff and Norenzayan (2007).
42. Gervais and Norenzayan (2012b).
43. Bateson et al. (2006); Batson et al. (1999); Bering et al. (2005).
44. Nelson and Norton (2005).
45. Bushman et al. (2007); Preston and Ritter (2013); Saroglou et al. (2009).
46. Gervais and Norenzayan (2012c).
47. Kay, Shepherd, et al. (2010).
48. Baier and Wright (2001); Benda (1995); Fernquist (1995).
49. Ellis (2002).
50. Ellis and Peterson (1996).
51. Sturgis (2010).
52. Burkett (1980); Tittle and Welch (1983).
53. Maruna (2001); Maruna et al. (2006).
54. Topalli et al. (2012).
55. Myers (2009).
56. Cochran (1988); Ellis (1985, 501–502); Evans et al. (1995); Tittle and Welch (1983).
57. Sturgis and Baller (2012); Tittle and Welch (1983).
58. O'Connor and Perreyclear (2002).
59. Ellis (2002).
60. Koenig (1995).
61. Mehta (2013).
62. Kosmin and Keysar (2008).
63. Clear and Sumter (2002); Sturgis (2010).

64. Eshuys and Smallbone (2006).

65. Kerley et al. (2011).

66. Pettersson (1991).

67. Benson et al. (1989, 172).

68. Baumeister et al. (2010).

69. Brauer et al. (2013).

70. Rounding et al. (2012).

71. Desmond et al. (2013).

72. Benson (1992).

73. Bock et al. (1987); Holt et al. (2006).

74. Hood et al. (2009).

75. Galen and Rogers (2004).

76. US Department of Health and Human Services (1997).

77. Tonigan et al. (2002).

78. Mason and Windle (2002).

79. Adamczyk (2012).

80. Mason et al. (2012); Salas-Wright et al. (2012).

81. DeWall et al. (2014).

82. Carter et al. (2012).

83. Manning and Zuckerman (2004).

84. Halpern et al. (2006).

85. Brewster and Tillman (2008); Laumann et al. (1994).

86. Adamczyk and Felson (2008); Cochran et al. (2004); Meier (2003).

87. Ahrold et al. (2011).

88. Rowatt and Schmitt (2003).

89. Leonard and Scott-Jones (2010); Lefkowitz et al. (2004); Thornton and Camburn (1989).

90. Donnelly et al. (1999); Farmer et al. (2010).

91. Stack et al. (2004); Wright (2013).

92. Burdette et al. (2009).

93. Davidson et al. (2004); Jones et al. (2005); Smith and Denton (2005).

94. Ahrold et al. (2011); Farmer et al. (2010); Meier (2003); Rostosky et al. (2003, 2004).

95. Hardy et al. (2013).

96. Jones, Darroch, and Singh. 2005; Manlove et al. (2003); Zaleski and Schiaffino (2000).

97. Bruckner and Bearman (2005).

98. Hall et al. (2012).

99. Nelson et al. (2010).

100. Edelman (2009).

101. Cahn and Carbone (2010).

102. Garcia and Kruger (2010); Hayes and Hornsby-Smith (1994).

103. Strayhorn and Strayhorn (2009).

104. Kurdek (1993).

105. Adamczyk and Felson (2008).

106. Adamczyk (2008, 2009); Coleman (2006).

107. De Visser et al. (2007).

108. Cochran et al. (2004); Farmer et al. (2010).

109. Atkins and Kessel (2008).

110. Bekkers and Wiepking (2007); Hodgkinson and Weitzman (1996); Lincoln et al. (2008); Monsma (2007).

111. Pelham and Crabtree (2008).

112. Putnam and Campbell (2010).

113. American Association of Fundraising Counsel Trust for Philanthropy (2002); Hodgkinson and Weitzman (1996).

114. Center on Wealth and Philanthropy (2007).

115. Brooks (2003).

116. Uttley et al. (2013); Gonzalez (2001); Kopsa (2014).

117. Choi and Bowles (2007).

118. Borgonovi (2008); Choi and DiNittio (2012); Hunsberger and Platonow (1986); Lam (2002); McKitrick et al. (2013); Monsma (2007); Putnam and Campbell (2010); Wang and Graddy (2008).

119. Ottoni-Wilhelm (2010).

120. Borgonovi (2008).

121. Forbes and Zampelli (2013).

122. Center on Wealth and Philanthropy (2007).

123. Cnaan et al. (1993); Driskell et al. (2008); Mencken and Fitz (2013); Storm (2014).

124. Cragun (2013).

125. Borgonovi (2008); Choi and DiNittio (2012); Hunsberger and Platonow (1986); McKitrick et al. (2013); Park and Smith (2000); Wang and Graddy (2008).

126. Galen (2012), Hoffmann (2012); Preston et al. (2010).

127. Bekkers (2007); Eckel and Grossman (2004).

128. L. K. Manning (2010); Tan and Vogel (2008).

129. L. K. Manning (2010).

130. Brooks (2006); Monsma (2007); Reitsma et al. (2006).

131. Brown and Ferris (2007); Lewis et al. (2013).

132. Becker and Dhingra (2001); Campbell and Yonish (2003); Mencken and Fitz (2013); Merino (2013).

133. Lim and MacGregor (2012).

134. Putnam and Campbell (2010).

135. Galen et al. (2015).

136. Scheve and Stasavage (2006).

137. Brooks (2003).

138. Public Religion Research Institute (2013c).

139. Elgin et al. (2013).

140. Greer et al. (2005); Leach et al. (2008).

141. Altemeyer and Hunsberger (1992).

142. Hathcoat and Barnes (2010); Johnson et al. (2011).

143. Pew Forum (2009b).

144. Johnson et al. (2010); Preston and Ritter (2013); Saroglou, et al. (2009).

145. Bushman et al. (2007); Van Pachterbeke et al. (2011).

146. Milgram (1965).

147. Bock and Warren (1972).

148. Hall et al. (2010).

149. Duke and Giancola (2013).

150. Chan et al. (2014); Shenberger et al. (2014).

151. Neuberg et al. (2014).

152. Annis (1975, 1976).

153. Hansen et al. (1995).

154. Hunsberger and Platonow (1986).

155. Batson et al. (1989).

156. Saslow (2013).

157. Oliner and Oliner (1988).

158. Midlarsky et al. (2005).

CHAPTER 9

1. Lincoln (1953).

2. Obama (2006).

3. Rokeach (1973).

4. Jost et al. (2003).

5. Public Religion Research Institute (2011).

6. Slomp (2000).

7. Aiello (2005).

8. Public Religion Research Institute (2010).

9. Kosmin and Keysar (2008).

10. Greeley and Hout (2006).

11. Pew Forum (2012d).

12. Nassi (1981); Pew Forum (2011b)

13. Olson and Green (2006).

14. Kosmin and Navarro-Rivera (2012).

15. Barna Group (2008).

16. Layman (1997).

17. Hout and Fischer (2002).

18. Hayes (1995b).

19. Public Religion Research Institute (2012).

20. Jacoby (2004).

21. Ayres (1993, 139).

22. Greeley and Hout (2006); Hunsberger and Altemeyer (2006); Jackson and Hunsberger (1999).

23. Grant (2011a).

24. Scheepers et al. (2002).

25. Hall et al. (2010).

26. Mayrl and Saperstein (2013); Perry (2014).

27. Hayes (1995b); Brinkerhoff and Mackie (1985); Hoffman and Miller (1997); Petersen and Donnenwerth (1998).

28. Hayes and Hornsby-Smith (1994).

29. Altemeyer (2010); Burdette et al. (2005); Gallup (2010); Linneman and Clendenen (2010); Roof and McKinney (1987); Sherkat et al. (2011).

30. Pew Forum (2010).

31. McCarthy (2014).

32. Pew Forum (2008).

33. Pew Forum (2014a).

34. Alston (1974); Loftus (2001).

35. Sherkat et al. (2011).

36. Whitehead (2010).

37. Henley and Pincus (1978).

38. Hoffman and Miller (1997); Silver (2012).

39. Smidt (2005).

40. Guth et al. (2005).

41. Gallup (2011).

42. Guth et al. (2005).

43. Grant (2014).

44. Guth (2010).

45. Smidt (2005).

46. Gallup (2012c).

47. Pew Forum (2012d).

48. Higher Education Research Institute (2003). Weeden et al. (2008).

49. Jorgenson and Neubecker (1981); Ward (1980).

50. Gallup (2007).

51. Hamil-Luker and Smith (1998).

52. Nisbet (2005).

53. Harris Poll (2004).

54. Nisbet (2005).

55. Beit-Hallahmi (2007); Gallup (2004); Pew Forum (2009b).

56. Blumstein and Cohen (1980); Grasmick et al. (1992); Wozniak and Lewis (2010).

57. Unnever et al. (2005).

58. Hoffman and Miller (1997).

59. Gallup (2005).

60. Public Religion Research Institute (2013b).

61. Pew Forum (2008).

62. Galen and Miller (2011); Jackson and Esses (1997); Pew Research Center (2012e); Skitka et al. (2002); Williams (1984); Zucker and Weiner (1993).

63. Brimeyer (2008).

64. Li et al. (2012).

65. Flannelly et al. (2012).

66. Rubin and Peplau (1975).

67. Anderson et al. (2011).

68. Public Religion Research Institute (2014).

69. Greeley (1993); Smith (1996).

70. Pew Forum (2004).

71. Pew Forum (2008).

72. Pew Forum (2007).

73. McCright and Dunlap (2011).

74. Greeley (1993); Guth et al. (1995); Hayes and Marangudakis (2001).

75. Boyd (1999).

76. Eckberg and Blocker (1996); Guth et al. (1995).

77. Sherkat and Ellison (2007).

78. Gallup (2012a); Miller et al. (2006).

79. Pew Forum (2007).

80. Gallup (2012a).

81. DeLeeuw et al. (2007); Miller et al. (2006).

82. Lawson and Worsnop (1992).

83. Lawson and Worsnop (1992); Nehm and Schonfeld (2007).

84. Berkman and Plutzer (2011).

85. Harrold and Eve (1987).

86. Eckberg and Blocker (1996).

87. Burghardt (1985).

88. DeLeeuw et al. (2007); Hayes and Marangudakis (2001); Kellert and Berry (1980).

89. Burghardt (1985).

90. Jamison et al. (2000).

91. Grant (2011b).

92. Grant (2011b).

93. Hayes (1995a).

94. Pew Forum (2012c).

95. Hoffman and Miller (1997); Baker and Smith (2009b).

96. Hout and Fischer (2002).

97. Public Religion Research Institute (2011).

98. Gallup (2012b).

99. Pew Forum (2012a).

100. Pew Forum (2008).

101. Hunsberger and Altemeyer (2006).

102. Brinkerhoff and Mackie (1993).

103. Pew Forum (2012e).

104. Gay and Ellison (1993).

105. Beatty and Walter (1984).

106. Putnam and Campbell (2010).

107. Galen et al. (2011).

108. Oh et al. (2007).

109. Katnik (2002).

110. Bloom and Arikan (2012).

111. Karpov (1999).

112. Koleva et al. (2012).

113. Carney et al. (2008); Shermer (2000).

114. Hirsh (2010); Jost (2006).

115. Saroglou (2010).

116. Block and Block (2006).

117. McCullough et al. (2005).

118. Altemeyer (2002).

119. Hunsberger and Altemeyer (2006).

120. Batson and Raynor-Prince (1983).

121. Jost et al. (2003); Tetlock (1983).

122. Wilson, ed. (1973).

123. Hibbing et al. (2014).

124. Van Leeuwen and Park (2009).

125. Kandler et al. (2012).

126. Ludeke et al. (2013).

127. Altemeyer (1988).

128. Altemeyer (2006); Altemeyer and Hunsberger (1997).

129. Altemeyer (2006).

130. Altemeyer (1988).

131. Barker and Tinnick (2006).

132. Hetherington and Weiler (2009).

133. Rokeach (1973).

134. Schwartz (1992).

135. Pepper et al. (2010); Roccas (2005); Saroglou et al. (2004); Schwartz and Huismans (1995).

136. Fontaine et al. (2000, 2005).

137. de St. Aubin (1996).

138. Farias and Lalljee (2008).

139. Van Leeuwen and Park (2009).

140. Graham and Haidt (2010); McClain (1978); Reiss (2000b); Rigney and Hoffman (1993).

141. Public Religion Research Institute (2013a).

142. Jost et al. (2003).

143. Kay, Shepherd, et al. (2010).

144. Pew Forum (2012d).

CHAPTER 10

1. In Kirk (1982, 27).

2. Campbell (1971, 15).

3. Feigelman, Gorman, and Varacalli (1992, 140).

4. Caplovitz and Sherrow (1977).

5. Bainbridge (2005, 7).

6. Bradley (1995); Putnam (2000, 67); Ellison and George (1994); Hout and Fischer (2002); Musick et al. (2000); Putnam (2000); Putnam and Campbell (2010); Caldwell-Harris (2012).

7. Bradley (1995); Galen (2009); Putnam and Campbell (2010).

8. Bainbridge (2005); Putnam (2000, 67); Putnam and Campbell (2010).

9. Barna Group (2007); Bekkers and Schuyt (2008); Berger (2006); Brooks (2003), (2004), and (2008); Campbell and Yonish (2003); Hodgkinson (2003); Hodgkinson and Weitzman (1990); Monsma (2007); Park and Smith (2000); Putnam (2000); Putnam and Campbell (2010); Uslaner (2002); Wilson and Janoski (1995); Wuthnow and Hodgkinson (1990).

10. Barna Group (2007); Bekkers and Schuyt (2008); Berger (2006); Brooks (2003), (2004), and (2008); Hodgkinson and Weitzman (1990); Lyons and Nivison-Smith (2006); Monsma (2007); Nemeth and Luidens (2003); Putnam (2000); Putnam and Campbell (2010); Regnerus et al. (1998); Wuthnow and Hodgkinson (1990).

11. Monsma (2007); Putnam (2000).

12. Putnam (2000); Putnam and Campbell (2010); Hearn (1997); Lewy (1996).

13. See, for example, Inglehart (1990) and (1997); Inglehart and Welzel (2005); Klinenberg (2012); Wuthnow (1998).

14. Schnell and Keenan (2011).

15. See Putnam (2000) for a discussion of bonding and bridging social capital.

16. Most of the research summarized here has been performed in the US and Europe and pertains primarily to Christians.

17. Farias and Lalljee (2008).

18. See Pasquale (2007b) regarding "societal skepticism."

19. Pasquale (2007b).

20. Fromm (1969 [1941]); Lukes (1973); Shanahan (1992).

21. Bruce (2002).

22. Berger (1967).

23. See, for example, Caldwell-Harris (2012).

24. Farias and Lalljee (2008); Pepper et al. (2010); Roccas (2005); Schwartz and Huismans (1995).

25. Rokeach (1969), summarized in Schwartz and Huismans (1995).

26. Saroglou et al. (2004).

27. "Judaic" is used rather than "Jewish" to denote the religious, rather than ethnic or cultural, dimension of Jewish history and heritage.

28. Wulff (1997); Fontaine et al. (2000) and Fontaine et al. (2005).

29. Lau (1989).

30. Reiss and Havercamp (1998); Reiss (2000a), (2000b), and (2004); Havercamp and Reiss (2003).

31. The adolescent atheists definitively did not believe in God and gave the least religious responses in a series of questions about religious beliefs, behavior, and identity or affiliation; Pearce and Denton (2011, 67).

32. Nall (2010).

33. Houtman and Mascini (2002).

34. Farias and Lalljee (2008).

35. Farias and Lalljee (2008, 287).

36. This refers to the degree to which the individuals in one's social network also know one another. In high-density networks (or communities), members have relationships with many others within the network. In low-density networks, each member may have a relationship with one or only a few other members.

37. Putnam (2000); Ellison and George (1994); Bradley (1995); Musick et al. (2000); Kennell (1988) cited in Pargament (1997, 56).

38. Cimino and Smith (2011) and (2014).

39. Horning, et al. (2011).

40. Horning et al. (2011, 185).

41. Fife et al. (2011).

42. Ozorak (1989).

43. Galen (2009).

44. Klinenberg (2012)

45. Schnell and Keenan (2011).

46. Schnell and Keenan (2011, 74).

47. Schnell and Keenan (2011, 73).

48. Horning et al. (2011, 185).

49. The recent (re)emergence of secularist organizations that deliberately mimic some aspects of church congregations (called "atheist churches" in some quarters) may signal a change in this regard, particularly in a new generation of seculars. Time will tell. See, for example, "Sunday Assembly: A Church for the Godless Picks Up Steam," accessed August 25, 2015, www.npr.org/2014/01/07/260184473/sunday-assembly-a-church-for-the-godless-picks-up-steam. See also: The Sunday Assembly, https://sunday assembly.com/.

50. The Pew Forum (2012d, 55). Separate figures for atheist/agnostics and nothing-in-particulars did not appear in the Pew report but were provided by Cary Funk, a senior researcher at Pew, in a personal communication, October 12, 2012.

51. Public Religion Research Institute (2012, 14).

52. See, for example, Cimino and Smith 2014.

53. Budd (1977); Demerath (1969a); Demerath and Thiessen (1966); Frame (2009); Marty (1961); Post (1943); Warren (1966).

54. Williamson (1993).

55. Claimed, reported, or estimated affiliation numbers for some of the principal secularist and skeptic organizations in the United States: Council for Secular Humanism, 22,200 subscribers to principal publication, *Free Inquiry* (published postal and IRS circulation reports provided by Tom Flynn, Executive Director, on September 18, 2012), Council for Secular Humanism associate members, 3,446, and Friends of the Centers for Inquiry, 1,942 (provided by Barry A. Kosmin, CSH board member, February 11, 2012); Freedom from Religion Foundation, 22,500 members/subscribers to principal publication, *Freethought Today* (claimed on website, www.ffrf.org, accessed August 23, 2015); American Humanist Association, 30,000 "members and supporters" in 190 local chapters ("Annual Report 2014," www.americanhumanist.org/system/storage/2/52/d/5475/ar_20142.pdf); American Atheists, 2,000 to 2,200, cited in Cimino and Smith (2011); Ethical Culture Society, 2,000-3,000, cited in Budd (1967) and Kraut (1987); Humanistic Judaism, 2,100 households (Jane Goldhamer, founder and former director, Kol Shalom, Community for Humanistic Judaism, personal communication, July 18, 2012).

The Sunday Assembly's website lists assemblies in more than 60 US cities and some 200 more worldwide (www.sundayassembly.com/assemblies/, accessed August 23, 2015). Unverified media reports indicate an average size of 60 to 80 per meeting ("Atheist Church Sunday Assembly Opens in 35 More Towns," *Christian Post*, September 29, 2014, www.christianpost.com/news/atheist-church-sunday-assembly-opens-in-35-more-towns-127190/).

Skeptic organizations are included in this estimation even though, as discussed in chapter 1, many skeptics are not substantially or affirmatively nonreligious. Also, there is likely some overlap in secularist and skeptic membership numbers due to individuals affiliated with both: Skeptic Society, 50,000 members/subscribers (unverified Wikipedia report, accessed August 23, 2015, http://en.wikipedia.org/wiki/The_Skeptics_Society); Committee for Skeptical Inquiry (CSI), 21,000 member/subscribers to principal publication, *Skeptical Inquiry*, and 2,586 CSI associate members (Barry A. Kosmin, Centers for Inquiry board member, personal communication, February 11, 2012).

To this must be added associated student secularist and skeptic groups with the caveat that there is likely some duplication of individuals because many students also subscribe to the principal publication(s) of the parent organizations, and so, would be included in the estimated member/subscriber totals given above for those organizations. The Secular Student Alliance (SSA), affiliated with the American Humanist Association, 30,000 students "reached" through 268 college and high school affiliate groups (statement issued by SSA, December 14, 2012, www.facebook.com/SecularStudents/posts/10151304745639687, and "Affiliated Campus Group List," www.secularstudents.org/affiliates, accessed August 25, 2015; see also Liddell [2012] and Niose [2012]); Center for Inquiry (CFI) On Campus, 240 affiliated US campus groups and 50 more worldwide listed on their website, but there is some overlap with SSA's list of affiliate groups (www.centerforinquiry.net/oncampus/groups/, accessed August 23, 2015).

This list is not exhaustive. It does not, for example, include such organizations as American Atheists, The Freethought Society, Military Association of Atheists and Freethinkers, "brights," and unique local groups, for which data are not available. But there is reason to believe that numbers for these are in the hundreds or thousands, at best, and that there is likely some overlap with some of the principal organizations described above. To the best of our knowledge and available data, this provides a fair sampling and basis for our order-of-magnitude estimates.

56. For example, the British Humanist Association claims "over 40,000 members and supporters and over 70 local and special interest affiliates." (British Humanist Association, accessed August 24, 2015, http://www.humanism.org.uk/about). The Rationalist Association (formerly the Rationalist Press Association, which dates from 1885): 18,775 "membership subscriptions" and 55,606 *New Humanist* "sales and subscriptions" worldwide (unpublished annual report, 2010). Others include the National Secular Society and many local groups (for example, The National Federation of Atheist, Humanist and Secular Student Societies, which lists some 30 affiliated groups in the UK). Regarding the wider British secular population, depending upon the criteria used (from convinced atheists to affirmatively not religious to "nones"), estimates range from ten to more than twenty million people. See Brown (2001); Pasquale and Kosmin (2013); British Humanist Association, "Religion and Belief: Some Surveys and Statistics," report accessed August 24, 2015, humanism.org.uk/campaigns/religion-and-belief-some-surveys-and-statistics/.

57. Bagg and Voas (2010); Bruce (2001) and (2002).

58. Zuckerman (2008) and (2009).

59. Knut Berg, HEF Library, personal communication, January 11, 2012.

60. The Norwegian Humanist Association (Human-Etisk Forbund), accessed August 23, 2015, www.human.no/Servicemeny/English/.

61. Zuckerman (2007); World Values Survey, 2007: 51.3 percent of Norwegians (with a total population of roughly five million people) indicated that they were "not a religious person" and an additional 6.7 percent indicated "convinced atheist," accessed August 26, 2015, http://www.worldvaluessurvey.org/WVSOnline.jsp.

62. Quack (2012).

63. Quack (2012) and (2013); specific organizations claim from a few hundred to more than 100,000 members, participants, or supporters.

64. Bruce (2002, 42).

65. The Sunday Assembly describes itself as a "godless congregation that celebrates life" and "a global movement of wonder and good." The first Sunday Assembly was established by British comedians Sanderson Jones and Pippa Evans in North London, reportedly because they "both

wanted to do something like church but without God." The assemblies typically consist of a lecture, musical or comic entertainment, socializing, and communal singing of contemporary songs that reinforce Assembly principles and values. The Assembly "has no doctrine. . .no deity" and doesn't "do supernatural but we also won't tell you you're wrong if you do. . . . Everyone is welcome, regardless of beliefs." As such, they resemble the approach of Ethical Culture societies and some current and past humanist movements and organizations. (http://sundayassembly.com/about/, accessed September 1, 2015).

66. Pasquale (2007b) and (2010b).

67. Campbell (1971).

68. Campbell (1971, 43).

69. One of the authors monitored a local organization some years ago called US Atheists that was as relentlessly critical of religion, and so, as close to a "purely" abolitionist or eliminationist type as could be imagined, but perhaps unsurprisingly it did not last. Most human beings cannot live on a diet of criticism alone.

70. Cimino and Smith (2011) and (2014).

71. Budd (1977); Campbell (1971); Demerath (1969a); Demerath and Thiessen (1966); Frame (2009); Marty (1961); Post (1943); Warren (1966).

72. Warren (1966, 21).

73. Demerath and Thiessen (1966, 674).

74. Demerath and Thiessen (1966); Budd (1977).

75. Campbell (1971, 41).

76. Campbell (1971, 42).

77. Post (1943, 170).

78. Flynn (2012, 21).

79. Cimino and Smith (2014, 26).

80. Cimino and Smith (2014, 86).

81. Meet-up.com, accessed August 23, 2015, www.meetup.com/topics/atheists/. It is worth mentioning that the number of groups and members of atheist, skeptic, humanist, or critical thinking groups is dwarfed by groups concerning religious, avocational, or recreational topics by ratios of five or ten to one (e.g., spirituality, meditation, yoga, or metaphysics, and singles, dining out, dancing, or hiking).

82. International Humanist and Ethical Union, "Freedom of Thought 2012: A Global Report on Discrimination against Humanists, Atheists and Nonreligious People," accessed January 12, 2013, http://iheu.org/content/2012-report-discrimination-against-humanists-atheists-and-nonreligious-people.

83. Cimino and Smith (2011) and (2014).

84. Cimino and Smith (2011, 24, 31, and 36), drawing in part from the work of Granovetter (1973) on "weak ties" in networks.

85. Cimino and Smith (2011, 36-37).

86. Secularist organizations and movements: Budd (1977); Demerath (1969a); Demerath and Thiessen (1966); Marty (1961); Post (1943); Warren (1966). Postmodern or postindustrial social change: Inglehart and Welzel (2005); Klinenberg (2002); Wuthnow (1998).

Bibliography

Aarts, O., A. Need, M. Te Grotenhuis, and N. D. De Graaf. 2008. "Does Belonging Accompany Believing? Correlations and Trends in Western Europe and North America between 1981 and 2000." *Review of Religious Research* 50:16–34.

Acemoglu, D., S. Johnson, and J. A. Robinson. 2001. "An African Success Story: Botswana." MIT Department of Economics Working Paper No. 01-37. http://papers.ssrn.com/sol3/papers. cfm?abstract_id=290791.

Acevedo, G. A. 2010. "Collective Rituals or Private Practice in Texas? Assessing the Impact of Religious Factors on Mental Health." *Review of Religious Research* 52:188–206.

Acock, A. 1984. "Parents and Their Children: The Study of Inter-generation Influence." *Sociology and Social Research* 68:151–171.

Adamczyk, A. 2008. "Religious Contextual Norms, Structural Constraints, and Personal Religiosity for Abortion Decisions." *Social Science Research* 37:657–672.

———. 2009. "Understanding the Effects of Personal and School Religiosity on the Decision to Abort a Premarital Pregnancy." *Journal of Health and Social Behavior* 50:180–195.

———. 2012. "Extracurricular Activities and Teens' Alcohol Use: The Role of Religious and Secular Sponsorship." *Social Science Research* 41:412–424.

Adamczyk, A., and J. Felson. 2008. "Fetal Positions: Unraveling the Influence of Religion on Premarital Pregnancy Resolution." *Social Science Quarterly* 89:17–38.

Adler, M. G., and N. S. Fagley. 2005. "Appreciation: Individual Differences in Finding Value and Meaning as a Unique Predictor for Subjective Well-Being." *Journal of Personality* 73:79–114.

Ahrold, T. K., M. Farmer, P. D. Trapnell, and C. M. Meston. 2011. "The Relationship among Sexual Attitudes, Sexual Fantasy, and Religiosity." *Archives of Sexual Behavior* 40:619–630.

Ai, A. L., C. Park, B. Huang, W. Rodgers, and T. N. Tice. 2007. "Psychosocial Mediation of Religious Coping: A Prospective Study of Short-Term Psychological Distress after Cardiac Surgery." *Personality and Social Psychology Bulletin* 33:867–882.

Ai, A.L., P. Wink, and M. Shearer. 2011. "Secular Reverence Predicts Shorter Hospital Length of Stay among Middle-Aged and Older Patients Following Open-Heart Surgery." *Journal of Behavioral Medicine* 34:532–541.

Aiello, T. 2005. "Constructing 'Godless Communism': Religion, Politics, and Popular Culture, 1954–1960." *Americana: The Journal of American Popular Culture 1900 to Present*, 4. http://www.americanpopularculture.com/journal/articles/spring_2005/aiello.htm#2.

Allport, G. W. 1950. *The Individual and His Religion*. New York: Macmillan.

Alston, J. P. 1974. "Attitudes toward Extramarital and Homosexual Relations." *Journal for the Scientific Study of Religion* 13:479–481.

Altemeyer, B. 1988. *Enemies of Freedom: Understanding Right-Wing Authoritarianism*. San Francisco: Jossey-Bass.

———. 2002. "Dogmatic Behavior among Students: Testing a New Measure of Dogmatism." *Journal of Social Psychology* 142:713–721.

———. 2010. "Atheism and Secularity in North America." In *Atheism and Secularity* edited by P. Zuckerman, vol. 2, 1–23. Santa Barbara, CA: Praeger ABC-CLIO.

Altemeyer, B., and B. Hunsberger. 1992. "Authoritarianism, Religious Fundamentalism, Quest, and Prejudice." *International Journal for the Psychology of Religion* 2:113–133.

———. 1997. *Amazing Conversions: Why Some Turn to Faith and Others Abandon Religion*. Amherst, NY: Prometheus Books.

American Association of Fundraising Counsel Trust for Philanthropy. 2002. "Giving USA: The annual report on philanthropy for the year 2002." New York, NY: American Association of Fundraising Counsel.

American Religion Identification Survey. 2008. at http://www.americanreligionsurvey-aris.org/.

———. 2009. "American Nones: The Profile of the No Religion Population," http://www.americanreligionsurvey-aris.org/2009/09/american_nones_the_profile_of_the_no_religion_population.html.

Ama, T. 2005. *Why Are the Japanese Nonreligious? Japanese Spirituality: Being Nonreligious in a Religious Culture*. Lanham, MD: University Press of America.

Ančić, B., and S. Zrinšćak. 2012. "Religion in Central European Societies: Its Social Role and People's Expectations." *Religion and Society in Central and Eastern Europe* 5: 21–38.

Anderson, B., L. Ellis, L. Nguyen, A. Ver Wey, and L. W. Galen. 2011. "Just World Belief, Religiosity, and Attributions of Responsibility for Misfortune." Poster presented at the annual meeting of the Midwestern Psychological Association, Chicago, IL. May 2011.

Annis, L.V. 1975. "Study of values as a predictor of helping behavior." *Psychological Reports* 37: 717-718.

———. 1976. "Emergency helping and religious behavior." *Psychological Reports* 39: 151-158.

Argyle, M. 2000. *Psychology and Religion: An Introduction*. London: Routledge.

Asad, T. 2003. *Formations of the Secular: Christianity, Islam, Modernity*. Stanford: Stanford University Press.

Atkins, D. C., and D. E. Kessel. 2008. "Religiousness and Infidelity: Attendance, but Not Faith and Prayer, Predict Marital Fidelity." *Journal of Marriage and Family* 70:407–418.

Ayres, A. 1993. *The Wisdom of Martin Luther King, Jr*. New York: Meridian.

Babinksi, E. 1995. *Leaving the Fold: Testimonies of Former Fundamentalists*. Amherst, NY: Prometheus Books.

Bagg, S., and D. Voas. 2010. "The Triumph of Indifference: Irreligion in British Society." In *Atheism and Secularity*, edited by P. Zuckerman, vol. 2, 91–112. Santa Barbara, CA: Praeger.

Baier, C. J., and B. R. E. Wright. 2001. "'If You Love Me, Keep My Commandments': A Meta-analysis of the Effect of Religion on Crime." *Journal of Research in Crime and Delinquency* 38:3–21.

Bailey, E. I. 2003. "The Implicit Religiosity of the Secular: A Martian Perspective on the Definition of Religion." In *Defining Religion: Investigating the Boundaries between the Sacred and the Secular*, edited by Arthur L. Greil and David G. Bromley, 55–66. London: JAI Press.

Bainbridge, W. S. 2005. "Atheism." *Interdisciplinary Journal of Research on Religion* 1:2–26.

Balboni, T. A., L. C. Vanderwerker, S. D. Block, M. E. Paulk, C. S. Lanthan, J. R. Peteet, and H. G. Prigerson. 2007. "Religiousness and Spiritual Support among Advanced Cancer Patients and Associations with End-of-Life Treatment Preferences and Quality of Life." *Journal of Clinical Oncology* 25:555–560.

Balbuena, L., M. Baetz, and R. Bowen. 2013. "Religious Attendance, Spirituality, and Major Depression in Canada: A 14-Year Follow-Up Study." *Canadian Journal of Psychiatry* 58:225–232.

Baker, J. 2008. "An Investigation of the Sociological Patterns of Prayer Frequency and Content." *Sociology of Religion* 69:169–185.

Baker, J., and B. Smith. 2009a. "The Nones: Social Characteristics of the Religiously Unaffiliated." *Social Forces* 87:1251–1263.

———. 2009b. "None Too Simple: Examining Issues of Religious Nonbelief and Nonbelonging in the United States." *Journal for the Scientific Study of Religion* 48:719–733.

———. 2015. *American Secularism: Cultural Contours of Nonreligious Belief Systems*. New York: New York University Press.

Banerjee, K., and P. Bloom. 2013. "Would Tarzan Believe in God? Conditions for the Emergence of Religious Belief." *Trends in Cognitive Sciences* 17:7–8.

Barber, N. 2011. "A Cross-National Test of the Uncertainty Hypothesis of Religious Belief." *Cross-Cultural Research* 45:318–333.

———. 2012. "Uruguay: A Secular Outpost Legalizes Abortion." HuffingtonPost.com, September 28. http://www.huffingtonpost.com/nigel-barber/uruguay-a-secular-utopia_b_1917005.html.

Barbour, J. 1994. *Versions of Deconversion: Autobiography and the Loss of Faith*. Charlottesville: University Press of Virginia.

Baril, G. L., and J. C. Wright. 2012. "Different Types of Moral Cognition: Moral Stages versus Moral Foundations." *Personality and Individual Differences* 53:468–473.

Barker, D. C., and J. D. Tinnick. 2006. "Competing Visions of Parental Roles and Ideological Constraint." *American Political Science Review* 100:249–263.

Barna Group. 1999. "Atheists and Agnostics Are Infiltrating Christian Churches." *Barna Report*, October–December 1999.

———. 2007. "Barna Update: "Atheist and Agnostics Take Aim at Christians." https://www.barna.org/barna-update/faith-spirituality/102-atheists-and-agnostics-take-aim-at-christians#.UeMmzaykmy4.

———. 2008. "How People of Faith Voted in the 2008 Presidential Race." https://www.barna.org/barna-update/article/13-culture/18-how-people-of-faith-voted-in-the-2008-presidential-race

Baron-Cohen, S., and S. Wheelwright. 2004. "The Empathy Quotient: An Investigation of Adults with Asperger Syndrome or High Functioning Autism, and Normal Sex Differences." *Journal of Autism and Developmental Disorders* 34:163–175.

Barrett, J. 2012. *Born Believers: The Science of Children's Religious Beliefs.* New York: Free Press.

Barrick, M. R., and M. K. Mount. 1996. "Effects of Impression Management and Self-Deception on the Predictive Validity of Personality Constructs." *Journal of Applied Psychology* 81:261–272.

Basham, A. L. 1954. *The Wonder That Was India: A Survey of the Culture of the Indian Sub-continent before the Coming of the Muslims.* New York: Grove Press.

Bateson, M., D. Nettle, and G. Roberts. 2006. "Cues of Being Watched Enhance Cooperation in a Real-World Setting." *Biology Letters* 2:412–414.

Batson, C. D., K. C. Oleson, J. L. Weeks, S. P. Healy, P. J. Reeves, P. Jennings, and T. Brown. 1989. "Religious Pro-social Motivation: Is It Altruistic or Egoistic?" *Journal of Personality and Social Psychology* 57:873–884.

Batson, C. D., and L. Raynor-Prince. 1983. "Religious Orientation and Complexity of Thought about Existential Concerns." *Journal for the Scientific Study of Religion* 22:38–50.

Batson, C. D., P. Schoenrade, and W. L. Ventis. 1993. *Religion and the Individual: A Social-Psychological Perspective.* New York: Oxford University Press.

Batson, C. D., E. R. Thompson, G. Seuferling, H. Whitney, and J. A. Strongman. 1999. "Moral Hypocrisy: Appearing Moral to Oneself without Being So." *Journal of Personality and Social Psychology* 77:525–537.

Batson, C. D., and W. L. Ventis. 1982. *The Religious Experience: A Social-Psychological Perspective.* New York: Oxford University Press.

Baumeister, R. F., I. M. Bauer, and S. A. Lloyd. 2010. "Choice, Free Will, and Religion." *Psychology of Religion and Spirituality* 2:67–82.

Baumrind, D. 1971. "Current Patterns of Parental Authority." *Developmental Psychology* 4: 1–103.

Beatty, K. M., and O. Walter. 1984. "Religious Preference and Practice: Reevaluating Their Impact on Political Tolerance." *Public Opinion Quarterly* 48:318–329.

Beck, U., and E. Beck-Gernsheim. 2002. *Individualization: Institutionalized Individualism and Its Social and Political Consequences.* London: Sage.

Becker, E. 1973. *The Denial of Death.* New York: Free Press, 1973.

Becker, G. 1981. *A Treatise on the Family.* Cambridge, MA: Harvard University Press.

Becker, P. E., and P. H. Dhingra. 2001. "Religious Involvement and Volunteering: Implications for Civil Society." *Sociology of Religion* 62:315–335

Beit-Hallahmi, B. 2005. "Women, Psychological Femininity, and Religion." In *Handbook of the Psychology of Religion*, edited by D. M. Wulff. New York: Oxford University Press.

———. 2007. "Atheists: A Psychological Profile." In *The Cambridge Companion to Atheism*, edited by Michael Martin, 300–317. New York: Cambridge University Press.

Beit-Hallahmi, B., and M. Argyle. 1997. *The Psychology of Religious Behavior, Belief, and Experience.* London: Routledge.

Bekkers, R. 2007. "Measuring Altruistic Behavior in Surveys: The All-or-Nothing Dictator Game." *Survey Research Methods* 1:139–144.

Bekkers, R., and T. Schuyt. 2008. "And Who Is Your Neighbor? Explaining Denominational Differences in Charitable Giving and Volunteering in the Netherlands." *Review of Religious Research* 50:74–96.

Bekkers, R., and P. Wiepking. 2007. "Generosity and Philanthropy: A Literature Review." http://dx.doi.org/10.2139/ssrn.1015507.

Bell, C. 2001. "Acting Ritually: Evidence from the Social Life of Chinese Rites." In *The Blackwell Companion to Sociology of Religion*, edited by R. K. Fenn, 371–387. Oxford: Blackwell.

Benda, B. B. 1995. "The Effect of Religion on Adolescent Delinquency Revisited." *Journal of Research in Crime and Delinquency* 32:446–466.

Bengtson, V. L. 2013. *Families and Faith: How Religion Is Passed Down across Generations.* New York: Oxford University Press.

Benjamins, M. R. 2006. "Religious Influences on Preventive Health Care Use in a Nationally Representative Sample of Middle-Age Women." *Journal of Behavioral Medicine* 29:1–16.

Ben-Ner, A., B. P. McCall, M. Stephane, and H. Wang. 2009. "Identity and In-Group/Out-Group Differentiation in Work and Giving Behaviors: Experimental Evidence." *Journal of Economic Behavior and Organization* 72:153–170.

Bennin, S. 2011. "Gingrich's Nightmare." http://www.washingtonmonthly.com/politicalanimal/2011_11/gingrichs_nightmare033613.php.

Benson, P. L. 1992. "Religion and Substance Use." In *Religion and Mental Health*, edited by J. F. Schumaker, 211–220. New York: Oxford University Press.

Benson, P. L., M. J. Donahue, and J. A. Erickson. 1989. "Adolescence and Religion: A Review of the Literature from 1970–1986." *Research in the Social Scientific Study of Religion* 1:153–181.

Berger, I. 2006. "The Influence of Religion on Philanthropy in Canada." *Voluntas: International Journal of Voluntary and Nonprofit Organizations* 17:110–127.

Berger, P. 1967. *The Sacred Canopy: Elements of a Sociological Theory of Religion.* Garden City, NY: Doubleday.

———. 1999. *The Desecularization of the World: Resurgent Religion and World Politics.* Washington, DC: Ethics and Public Policy Center.

Berger, P., G. Davie, and E. Fokas. 2008. *Religious America, Secular Europe? A Theme and Variations.* Burlington, VT: Ashgate.

Bergin, A. E. 1983. "Religiosity and Mental Health: A Critical Reevaluation and Meta-analysis." *Professional Psychology: Research and Practice* 14:170–184.

Bering, J. M. 2011. *The Belief Instinct: The Psychology of Souls, Destiny, and the Meaning of Life.* New York: Norton.

Bering, J. M., K. McLeod, and T. K. Shackelford. 2005. "Reasoning about Dead Agents Reveals Possible Adaptive Trends." *Human Nature* 16:360–381.

Berkman, M. B., and E. Plutzer. 2011. "Defeating Creationism in the Courtroom, but Not in the Classroom." *Science* 331:404–405.

Berthold, A., and W. Ruch. 2014. "Satisfaction with Life and Character Strengths of Non-religious and Religious People: It's Practicing One's Religion That Makes the Difference." *Frontiers in Psychology* 5:876.

Bertsch, S., and B. J. Pesta. 2009. "The Wonderlic Personnel Test and Elementary Cognitive Tasks as Predictors of Religious Sectarianism, Scriptural Acceptance and Religious Questioning." *Intelligence* 37:231–237.

Bibby, R. 2002. *Restless Gods.* Toronto: Stoddart.

Block, J., and J. H. Block. 2006. "Nursery School Personality and Political Orientation Two Decades Later." *Journal of Research in Personality* 40:734–749.

Bloom, P. B. N., and G. Arikan. 2012. "A Two-Edged Sword: The Differential Effect of Religious Belief and Religious Social Context on Attitudes towards Democracy." *Political Behavior* 34:249–276.

Blumstein, A., and J. Cohen. 1980. "Sentencing of Convicted Offenders: An Analysis of the Public's Views." *Law and Society Review* 14:223–261.

Bobkowski, P. S., and S. Kalyanaraman. 2010. "Effects of Online Christian Self-Disclosure on Impression Formation." *Journal for the Scientific Study of Religion* 49:456–476.

Bock, D.C., and N. C. Warren. 1972. "Religious Belief as a Factor in Obedience to Destructive Demands." *Review of Religious Research* 13:185–191.

Bock, E. W., J. K. Cochran, and L. Beeghley. 1987. "Moral Messages: The Relative Influence of Denomination on the Religiosity-Alcohol Relationship." *Sociological Quarterly* 28:89–103.

Bogg, T., and B. W. Roberts. 2004. "Conscientiousness and Health-Related Behaviors: A Meta-analysis of the Leading Behavioral Contributors to Mortality." *Psychological Bulletin* 130:887–919.

Bondeson, U. 2003 *Nordic Moral Climates: Value Continuities and Discontinuities in Denmark, Finland, Norway, and Sweden*. New Brunswick, NJ: Transaction.

Booth, A., and J. N. Edwards. 1985. "Age at Marriage and Marital Instability." *Journal of Marriage and the Family* 47:67–75.

Borgonovi, F. 2008. "Divided We Stand, United We Fall: Religious Pluralism, Giving and Volunteering." *American Sociological Review* 73:105–128.

Borowik, I., B. Ančić, and R. Tyrała. 2013. "Central and Eastern Europe." In *The Oxford Handbook of Atheism*, edited by S. Bullivant and M. Ruse, 622–637. Oxford: Oxford University Press.

Borowik, I., D. M. Jerolimov, and S. Zrinščak. 2004. "Religion and Patterns of Social Transformation—OR: How to Interpret Religious Changes in Post-Communism?" In *Religion and Patterns of Social Transformation*, edited by M. Jerolimov, D. I. Borowik, and S. Zrinščak, 9–19. Zagreb: Institute for Social Research.

Botvar, P. K. 2005. "The Moral Thinking of Three Generations in Scandinavia: What Role Does Religion Play?" *Social Compass* 52:185–195.

Bouchard, T. J., M. McGue, D. Lykken, and A. Tellegen. 1999. "Intrinsic and Extrinsic Religiousness: Genetic and Environmental Influences and Personality Correlates." *Twin Research* 2:88–98.

Boyd, H. H. 1999. "Christianity and the Environment in the American Public." *Journal for the Scientific Study of Religion* 38:36–44.

Bradley, D. E. 1995. "Religious Involvement and Social Resources: Evidence from the Data Set 'Americans' Changing Lives.'" *Journal for the Scientific Study of Religion* 34:259-267.

Bradshaw, M., and C. G. Ellison. 2008. "Do Genetic Factors Influence Religious Life? Findings from a Behavior Genetic Analysis of Twin Siblings." *Journal for the Scientific Study of Religion* 47:529–544.

Brasher, B. 1998. *Godly Women: Fundamentalism and Female Power*. New Brunswick, NJ: Rutgers University Press.

Brauer, J. R., C. R. Tittle, and O. Antonaccio. 2013. "Does Religion Suppress, Socialize, Soothe, or Support? Exploring Religiosity's Influence on Crime." *Journal for the Scientific Study of Religion* 52:753–774.

Braun, C. 2012. "Explaining Global Secularity: Existential Security or Education?" *Secularism and Nonreligion* 1:68–93.

Brazilian Institute of Geography and Statistics. 2012. "2010 Census: Number of Catholics Falls and Number of Protestants, Spiritists and Persons without Religion Records Increase." http://www.saladeimprensa.ibge.gov.br/en/noticias?view=noticia&id=1&idnoticia=2170

Breault, K. D. 1989. "New Evidence on Religious Pluralism, Urbanism, and Religious Participation." *American Sociological Review* 54:1048–1053.

Brenneman, R. 2012. *Homies and Hermanos: God and Gangs in Central America.* New York: Oxford University Press.

Brewster, K. L., and K. H. Tillman. 2008. "Who's Doing It? Patterns and Predictors of Youths' Oral Sexual Experiences." *Journal of Adolescent Health* 42:73–80.

Brimeyer, T. M. 2008. "Research Note: Religious Affiliation and Poverty Explanations: Individual, Structural, and Divine Causes." *Sociological Focus* 41:226–237.

Brinkerhoff, M., and K. Burke. 1980. "Some Notes on 'Falling from Faith.'" *Sociological Analysis* 41:41–54.

Brinkerhoff, M., and M. Mackie. 1993. "Casting Off the Bonds of Organized Religion: A Religious-Careers Approach to the Study of Apostasy." *Review of Religious Research* 34:235–257.

Bromley, D. 1988. *Falling from the Faith: Causes and Consequences of Religious Apostasy.* Beverly Hills, CA: Sage.

Brooks, A. C. 2003. "Religious Faith and Charitable Giving: Believers Give More to Secular Charities than Non-believers Do." *Policy Review.* 121. http.//www/hoover.orgpulications/policy-review/article/6577.

———. 2004. "Faith, Secularism, and Charity." *Faith and Economics* 43: 1–8.

———. 2006. *Who Really Cares: The Surprising Truth about Compassionate Conservatism: America's Charity Divide—Who Gives, Who Doesn't, and Why It Matters.* New York: Basic Books.

———. 2008. "A Nation of Givers." *American Enterprise Institute,* http://www.american.com/archive/2008/march-april-magazine-contents/a-nation-of-givers.

Brown, C. 2001. *The Death of Christian Britain.* London: Routledge.

———. 2003. "The Secularisation Decade: What the 1960s Have Done to the Study of Religious History." In *The Decline of Christendom in Western Europe, 1750–2000,* edited by Hugh McLeod and Werner Ustorf, 29–46. Cambridge: Cambridge University Press.

———. 2013. "The Twentieth Century." In *The Oxford Handbook of Atheism,* edited by Stephen Bullivant and Michael Ruse, 229–244. Oxford: Oxford University Press.

Brown, E., and J. M. Ferris. 2007. "Social Capital and Philanthropy: An Analysis of the Impact of Social Capital on Individual Giving and Volunteering." *Nonprofit and Voluntary Sector Quarterly* 36:85–99.

Bruce, S. 1999. *Choice and Religion: A Critique of Rational Choice Theory.* Oxford: Oxford University Press.

———. 2001. "Christianity in Britain, R.I.P." *Sociology of Religion* 62:191–203.

———. 2002. *God Is Dead: Secularization in the West.* Malden, MA: Blackwell.

———. 2011. *Secularization.* New York: Oxford University Press.

Bruce, S., and T. Glendinning. 2003. "Religious Beliefs and Differences." In *Devolution: Scottish Answers to Scottish Questions,* edited by C. Bromley, J. Curtice, K. Hinds, and A. Park, 86-115. Edinburgh: Edinburgh University Press.

Bruckner, H., and P. Bearman. 2005. "After the Promise: The STD Consequences of Adolescent Virginity Pledges." *Journal of Adolescent Health* 36:271–278.

Budd, S. 1967. "The Humanist Societies: The Consequences of a Diffuse Belief System." In *Patterns of Sectarianism: Organization and Ideology in Social and Religious Movements*, edited by B. R. Wilson, 377–405. London: Heineman.

———. 1977. *Varieties of Unbelief: Atheists and Agnostics in English Society: 1850–1960.* London: Heinemann.

Buggle, F., D. Bister, G. Nohe, W. Schneider, and K. Uhmann. 2000. "Are Atheists More Depressed Than Religious People?" *Free Inquiry* 20:50–55.

Bullivant, S., and M. Ruse, eds. 2013. *The Oxford Handbook of Atheism.* Oxford: Oxford University Press.

Burdette, A. M., C. G. Ellison, and T. D. Hill. 2005. "Conservative Protestantism and Tolerance toward Homosexuals: An Examination of Potential Mechanisms." *Sociological Inquiry* 75:117–196.

Burdette, A. M., C. G. Ellison, T. D. Hill, and N. D. Glenn. 2009. "Hooking Up at College: Does Religion Make a Difference?" *Journal for the Scientific Study of Religion* 48:535–551.

Burghardt, G. M. 1985. "Animal Awareness: Current Perceptions and Historical Perspective." *American Psychologist* 40:905–919.

Burkett, S. R. 1980. "Religiosity, Beliefs, Normative Standards and Adolescent Drinking." *Journal of Studies on Alcohol* 41:662–671.

Burkimsher, M. n.d. "Trends in Religious Participation of Young People: Do They Mirror Trends in Atheism?" Unpublished paper. Accessed June 29, 2013. http://drmarionb.free.fr/UnpublishedPapers/.

Burris, C. T., and L. M. Jackson. 2000. Social Identity and the True Believer: Responses to Threatened Self-Stereotypes among the Intrinsically Religious." *British Journal of Social Psychology* 39:257–278.

Burris, C. T., L. M. Jackson, W. R. Tarpley, and G. J. Smith. 1996. "Religion as Quest: The Self-Directed Pursuit of Meaning." *Personality and Social Psychology Bulletin* 22:1068–1076.

Bushman, B. J., R. D. Ridge, E. Das, C. W. Key, and G. L. Busath. 2007. "When God Sanctions Killing: Effect of Scriptural Violence on Aggression." *Psychological Science* 18:204–207.

Cahn, N., and J. Carbone. 2010. *Red Families v. Blue Families: Legal Polarization and the Creation of Culture.* New York: Oxford University Press.

Caldwell-Harris, C. L. 2012. "Understanding Atheism/Non-belief as an Expected Individual-Differences Variable." *Religion, Brain and Behavior* 2 (1): 4–23.

Caldwell-Harris, C. L., A. L. Wilson, E. LoTempio, and B. Beit-Hallahmi. 2010. "Exploring the Atheist Personality: Well-Being, Awe, and Magical Thinking in Atheists, Buddhists, and Christians." *Mental Health, Religion & Culture* 14:659–672.

Call, V. R. A., and T. B. Heaton. 1997. "Religious Influence on Marital Stability." *Journal for the Scientific Study of Religion* 36:382–392.

Campbell, C. 1971. *Toward a Sociology of Irreligion.* London: Macmillan.

———. 1977. "Analysing the Rejection of Religion." *Social Compass* 24:339–346.

Campbell, D. E., and S. J. Yonish. 2003. "Religion and Volunteering in America." In *Religion as Social Capital Producing the Common Good*, edited by C. E. Smidt, 87–106. Waco, TX: Baylor University Press.

Caplovitz, D., and F. Sherrow. 1977. *The Religious Drop-Outs: Apostasy among College Graduates.* Beverly Hills, CA: Sage.

Caporale, R., and A. Grumelli. 1971. *The Culture of Unbelief.* Berkeley: University of California Press.

Carney, D. R., J. T. Jost, S. D. Gosling, and J. Potter. 2008. "The Secret Lives of Liberals and Conservatives: Personality Profiles, Interaction Styles, and the Things They Leave Behind." *Political Psychology* 29:807–840.

Caron, N. 2007. "Laïcité and Secular Attitudes in France." In *Secularism and Secularity: Contemporary International Perspectives*, edited by B. A. Kosmin and A. Keysar, 113–124. Hartford, CT: Institute for the Study of Secularism in Society and Culture, Trinity College.

Carter, E. C., M. E. McCullough, and C. S. Carver. 2012. "The Mediating Role of Monitoring in the Association of Religion with Self-Control." *Social Psychological and Personality Science* 3:691–697.

Casanova, J 1994. *Public Religions in the Modern World.* Chicago: University of Chicago Press.

Center on Wealth and Philanthropy. 2007. "Geography and Giving: The Culture of Philanthropy in New England and the Nation. Boston, MA: Boston Foundation." http://www.bc.edu/content/dam/files/research_sites/cwp/pdf/geoandgiving2007.pdf

Chan, K. Q., E. M. W. Tong, and Y. L. Tan. 2014. "Taking a Leap of Faith: Reminders of God Lead to Greater Risk Taking." *Social Psychological and Personality Science* 5:901–909.

Chaves, M. 2011. *American Religion: Contemporary Trends.* Princeton, NJ: Princeton University Press.

Chaves, M., and P. S. Gorski. 2001. "Religious Pluralism and Religious Participation." *Annual Review of Sociology* 27:261-281.

Cherlin, A. J. 2009. *The Marriage-Go-Round: The State of Marriage and the Family in America Today.* New York: Vintage Books.

Cheyne, J. A., and F. W. Britton. 2010. *Beyond Disbelief: A Study of Some "Nones": Atheists, Agnostics, Humanists, Freethinkers, and Sceptics. A Preliminary Report.* http://arts.uwaterloo.ca/~acheyne/RAVS/Beyond_Disbelief_short.pdf.

Chida, Y., A. Steptoe, and L. H. Powell. 2009. "Religiosity/Spirituality and Mortality." *Psychotherapy and Psychosomatics* 78 (2): 81–90.

Chodorow, N. 1978. *The Reproduction of Mothering: Psychoanalysis and the Sociology of Gender.* Berkeley: University of California Press.

Choi, J. K., and S. Bowles. 2007. "The Coevolution of Parochial Altruism and War." *Science* 318 (5850): 636–640.

Choi, N. G., and D. M. DiNittio. 2012. "Predictors of Time Volunteering, Religious Giving, and Secular Giving: Implications for Nonprofit Organizations." *Journal of Sociology and Social Welfare* 39:93–120.

Cimino, R., and C. Smith. 2011. "The New Atheism and the Formation of the Imagined Secularist Community." *Journal of Media and Religion* 10 (1): 24–38.

———. 2014. *Atheist Awakening: Secular Activism & Community in America.* Oxford: Oxford University Press.

Clear, T. R., and M. T. Sumter. 2002. "Prisoners, Prison, and Religion." *Journal of Offender Rehabilitation* 35:125–156.

Cnaan, R., A. Kasternakis, and R. Wineburg. 1993. "Religious People, Religious Congregations, and Volunteerism in Human Services: Is There a Link?" *Nonprofit and Voluntary Sector Quarterly* 22:33–51.

Cobb, N. J., A. D. Ong, and J. Tate. 2001. "Reason-Based Evaluations of Wrongdoing in Religious and Moral Narratives." *International Journal for the Psychology of Religion* 11:259–276.

Cochran, J. K. 1988. "The Effect of Religiosity on Secular and Ascetic Deviance." *Sociological Focus* 21:293–306.

Cochran, J. K., M. B. Chamlin, L. Beeghley, and M. Fenwick. 2004. "Religion, Religiosity, and Non-marital Sexual Conduct: An Application of Reference Group Theory." *Sociological Inquiry* 74:102–127.

Cohen, A. B. 2002. "The Importance of Spirituality in Well-Being for Jews and Christians." *Journal of Happiness Studies* 3:287–310.

Cohen, S. M., S. Abrams, and J. Veinstein. 2008. *American Jews and the 2008 Presidential Election: As Democratic and Liberal as Ever?* Berman Jewish Policy Archive at NYU Wagner. http://www.bjpa.org/Publications/details.cfm?PublicationID=2444.

Cohen, S. M., and L. Blitzer. 2008. *Belonging without Believing: Jews and Their Distinctive Patterns of Religiosity—and Secularity.* Florence G. Heller–JCC Association (JCCA) Research Center. http://www.bjpa.org/Publications/details.cfm?PublicationID=795.

Coleman, P. K. 2006. "Resolution of Unwanted Pregnancy during Adolescence through Abortion versus Childbirth: Individual and Family Predictors and Psychological Consequences." *Journal of Youth and Adolescence* 35:903–911.

Condran, J. G., and J. B. Tamney. 1985. "Religious 'Nones': 1957 to 1982." *Sociological Analysis* 46:415–423.

Cornwall, M. 1998. "The Determinants of Religious Behavior: A Theoretical Model and Empirical Test." *Social Forces* 68:572–592.

Cottee, S. 2015. *The Apostates: When Muslims Leave Islam.* London: Hurst and Company.

Cox, D., S. Clement, G. Smith, A. Pond, and N. Sahga. 2009. "Non-believers, Seculars, the Un-churched and the Unaffiliated: Who Are Non-religious Americans and How Do We Measure Them in Survey Research?" Presented at the annual conference of the American Association for Public Opinion Research, Hollywood, FL, May 14–17, 2009.

Cragun, R. 2013. *What You Don't Know about Religion (But Should).* Durham, NC: Pitchstone.

Cragun, R., and J. Hammer. 2011. "'One Person's Apostate Is Another Person's Convert': What Terminology Tells Us about Pro-religious Hegemony in the Sociology of Religion." *Humanity and Society* 35:149–175.

Cragun, R., B. A. Kosmin, A. Keysar, J. Hammer, and M. Nielson. 2012. "On the Receiving End: Discrimination toward the Non-religious in the United States." *Journal of Contemporary Religion* 27:105–127.

Davenport, T. H. 1991. *Virtuous Pagans: Unreligious People in America.* New York: Garland.

Davidman, L. 1991. *Tradition in a Rootless World: Women Turn to Orthodox Judaism.* Berkeley: University of California Press.

Davidson, K. J., N. B. Moore, and K. M. Ullstrup. 2004. "Religiosity and Sexual Responsibility: Relationships of Choice." *American Journal of Health Behavior* 28:335–346.

Davie, G. 1994. *Religion in Britain since 1945: Believing without Belonging.* Oxford: Blackwell.

———. 1999. "Europe: The Exception That Proves the Rule?" In *The Desecularization of the World,* edited by P. Berger, 65–84. Grand Rapids, MI: Eerdmans.

———. 2007. *The Sociology of Religion.* Los Angeles: Sage.

Davis, W. 1992. *Japanese Religion and Society: Paradigms of Structure and Change.* Albany: State University of New York Press.

de Dreu, C. K. W., V. Y. Yzerbyt, and J. P. Leyens. 1995. "Dilution of Stereotype-Based Cooperation in Mixed-Motive Interdependence." *Journal of Experimental Social Psychology* 31:575–593.

Diener, E., L. Tay, and D. Myers. 2011. "The Religion Paradox: If Religion Makes People Happy, Why Are So Many Dropping Out?" *Journal of Personality and Social Psychology* 101:1278–1290.

de Jager Meezenbroek, E., B. Garssen, M. van den Berg, D. van Dierendonck, A. Visser, and W. B. Schaufeli. 2012. "Measuring Spirituality as a Universal Human Experience: A Review of Spirituality Questionnaires." *Journal of Religion and Health* 51:336–354.

Delamontagne, R. G. 2010. "High Religiosity and Societal Dysfunction in the United States during the First Decade of the Twenty-First Century." *Evolutionary Psychology* 8:617–657.

DeLeeuw, J., L. Galen, C. Aebersold, and V. Stanton. 2007. "Support for Animal Rights as a Function of Belief in Evolution and Religious Fundamentalism." *Animals and Society* 15:353–363.

Demerath, N. J., III. 1969a. "Irreligion, A-religion, and the Rise of the Religion-less Church: Two Case Studies in Organizational Convergence." *Sociological Analysis* 30:191–203.

———. 1969b. "Program and Prolegomena for a Sociology of Irreligion." In *Actes de la X Conference Internationale: Types, Dimensions, et Mesure de la Religiosité*, 159–175. Rome: Conference Internationale de Sociologie Religieuse.

———. 1976. "Review: Toward a Sociology of Irreligion." *Journal for the Scientific Study of Religion* 15:374–376.

———. 2000. "The Rise of 'Cultural Religion' in European Christianity: Learning from Poland, Northern Ireland, and Sweden." *Social Compass* 47: 127–139.

Demerath, N. J., III, and V. Thiessen. 1966. "On Spitting against the Wind: Organizational Precariousness and American Irreligion." *American Journal of Sociology* 71:674–687.

Desmond, S. A., J. T. Ulmer, and C. D. Bader. 2013. "Religion, Self-Control, and Substance Use." *Deviant Behavior* 34:384–406.

de St. Aubin, E. 1996. "Personal Ideological Polarity: Its Emotional Foundation and Its Manifestation in Individual Value Systems, Religiosity, Political Orientation, and Assumptions Concerning Human Nature." *Journal of Personality and Social Psychology* 71:152–165.

de Tocqueville, A. 1969 [1835]. *Democracy in America*. Edited by J. P. Mayer. New York: Harper Perennial.

De Visser, R. O., A. M. A. Smith, J. Richters, and C. E. Rissel. 2007. "Associations between Religiosity and Sexuality in a Representative Sample of Australian Adults." *Archives of Sexual Behavior* 36:33–46.

DeWaal, F. 2013. *The Bonobo and the Atheist: In Search of Humanism among Primates*. New York: Norton.

DeWall, C. N., R. S. Pond, E. C. Carter, M. E. McCullough, N. M. Lambert, F. D. Fincham, and J. B. Nezlek. 2014. "Explaining the Relationship between Religiousness and Substance Use: Self-Control Matters." *Journal of Personality and Social Psychology* 107:339–351.

Diaz-Stevens, A. M. 1994. "Latinas and the Church." In *Hispanic Catholic Culture in the U.S.: Issues and Concerns*, edited by J. P. Dolan and A. F. Deck, 244–270. Notre Dame, IN: University of Notre Dame Press.

Diren, E. M. 2013. "4+4+4. Why 'Religionization' of Public Education Is Harmful—Özgür Düşünce Hareketi." http://outforbeyond.blogspot.com/2013/05/4-4-4-why-religionization-of-public.html.

Dobbelaere, K. 1981. *Secularization: A Mutli-dimensional Concept*. London: Sage.

———. 2002. *Secularization: An Analysis at Three Levels*. Brussels: P.I.E. Peter Lang.

Donnelly, J., D. F. Duncan, E. Goldfarb, and C. Eadie. 1999. "Sexuality Attitudes and Behaviors of Self-Described Very Religious Urban Students in Middle School." *Psychological Reports* 85:607–610.

D'Onofrio, B. M., L. J. Eaves, L. Murrelle, H. H. Maes, and B. Spilka. 1999. "Understanding Biological and Social Influences on Religious Affiliation, Attitudes, and Behaviors: A Behavior Genetic Perspective." *Journal of Personality* 67:953–984.

Donovan, J. M. 2002. "Implicit Religion and the Curvilinear Relationship between Religion and Death Anxiety: A Review Study." *Implicit Religion* 5:17–28.

Draulans, V., and L. Halman. 2005. "Mapping Contemporary Europe's Moral and Religious Pluralist Landscape: An Analysis Based on the Most Recent European Values Study Data." *Journal of Contemporary Religion* 20:179–193.

Driskell, R. L., L. Lyon, and E. Embry. 2008. "Civic Engagement and Religious Activities: Examining the Influence of Religious Tradition and Participation." *Sociological Spectrum* 28:578–601.

Duke, A. A., and P. R. Giancola. 2013. "Alcohol Reverses Religion's Pro-social Influence on Aggression." *Journal for the Scientific Study of Religion* 52:272–292.

Duriez, B., B. Soenens, and W. Beyers. 2004. "Personality, Identity Styles, and Religiosity: An Integrative Study among Late Adolescents in Flanders (Belgium)." *Journal of Personality* 72:877–910.

Durkheim, É. 1961 [1925]. *Moral Education: A Study in the Theory and Application of the Sociology of Education*. New York: Free Press of Glencoe.

———. 1964 [1893]. *The Division of Labor in Society*. New York: Free Press of Glencoe.

———. 1965 [1915]. *The Elementary Forms of the Religious Life*. New York: Free Press.

———. 2006 [1897]. *On Suicide*. London: Penguin.

Ebaugh, H. 1988. *Becoming an Ex: The Process of Role Exit*. Chicago: University of Chicago Press.

Eckberg, D. L., and T. J. Blocker. 1996. "Christianity, Environmentalism, and the Theoretical Problems of Fundamentalism." *Journal for the Scientific Study of Religion* 35:343–355.

Eckel, C. C., and P. J. Grossman. 2004. "Giving to Secular Causes by the Religious and Nonreligious: An Experimental Test of the Responsiveness of Giving to Subsidies." *Nonprofit and Voluntary Sector Quarterly* 33:271–289.

Ecklund, E., and C. Scheitle. 2007. "Religion among Academic Scientists: Distinctions, Disciplines, and Demographics." *Social Problems* 54:289–307.

Edelman, B. 2009. "Red Light States: Who Buys Online Adult Entertainment?" *Journal of Economic Perspectives* 23:209–230.

Edgell, P., J. Gerteis, and D. Hartmann. 2006. "Atheists as 'Other': Moral Boundaries and Cultural Membership in American Society." *American Sociological Review* 71:211–234.

Eichhorn, J. 2012. "Happiness for Believers? Contextualizing the Effects of Religiosity on Life-Satisfaction." *European Sociological Review* 28:583–593.

Eisenstadt, S. N. 2000. "Multiple Modernities." *Daedalus* 129 (1): 1–29.

———. 2003. *Comparative Civilizations and Multiple Modernities*. Leiden: Brill.

Eliassen, A. H., J. Taylor, and D. A. Lloyd. 2005. "Subjective Religiosity and Depression in the Transition to Adulthood." *Journal for the Scientific Study of Religion* 44:187–199.

Elgin, C., T. Goksel, M. Y. Gurdal, and C. Orman. 2013. "Religion, Income Inequality, and the Size of the Government." *Economic Modeling* 30:225–234.

Ellis, L. 1985. "Religiosity and Criminality: Evidence and Explanations of Complex Relationships." *Sociological Perspectives* 28:501–502.

———. 2002. "Denominational Differences in Self-Reported Delinquency." *Journal of Offender Rehabilitation* 35:179–192.

Ellis, L., and J. Peterson. 1996. "Crime and Religion: An International Comparison among Thirteen Industrial Nations." *Personality and Individual Differences* 20:761–768.

Ellis, L., E. A. Wahab, and M. Ratnasingan. 2013. "Religiosity and Fear of Death: A Three-Nation Comparison." *Mental Health, Religion and Culture* 16:179–199.

Ellison, C., and D. E. Sherkat. 1993a. "Conservative Protestantism and Support for Corporal Punishment." *American Sociological Review* 58:131–44.

———. 1993b. "Obedience and Autonomy: Religion and Parental Values Reconsidered." *Journal for the Scientific Study of Religion* 32:313–329.

Ellison, C. G., and L. K. George. 1994. "Religious Involvement, Social Ties, and Social Support in a Southeastern Community." *Journal for the Scientific Study of Religion* 33:46–61.

Epley, N., S. Akalis, A. Waytz, and J. T. Cacioppo. 2008. "Creating Social Connection through Inferential Reproduction: Loneliness and Perceived Agency in Gadgets, Gods, and Greyhounds." *Psychological Science* 19:114–120.

Erickson, J. 1992. "Adolescent Religious Development and Commitment: A Structural Equation Model of the Role of the Family, Peer Group, and Educational Influences." *Journal for the Scientific Study of Religion* 31:131–152.

Eshuys, D., and S. Smallbone. 2006. "Religious Affiliations among Adult Sexual Offenders." *Sexual Abuse: A Journal of Research and Treatment* 18: 279–288.

Ester, P., and L. Halman. 1994. "Empirical Trends in Religious and Moral Beliefs in Western Europe." *International Journal of Sociology* 24:81–110.

Esteve A., R. Lesthaeghe, and A. López-Gay. 2012. "The Latin American Cohabitation Boom, 1970–2007." *Population and Development Review* 38 (1): 55–81.

Evans, R. 2012. "Humanists Call for African Age of 'Enlightenment.'" Reuters, http://www.reuters.com/article/2012/11/15/religion-africa-humanists-idUSL5E8MEDY220121115.

Eurobarometer Report. 2010. "Biotechnology." http://ec.europa.eu/public_opinion/archives/ebs/ebs_341_en.pdf

Evans, T. D., F. T. Cullen, G. Dunaway, and V. S. Burton. 1995. "Religion and Crime Reexamined: The Impact of Religion, Secular Controls and Social Ecology on Adult Criminology." *Criminology* 33:195–217.

Fajnzylber, O., D. Lederman, and N. Loatza. 2002. "Inequality and Violent Crime." *Journal of Law and Economics* 45:1–40.

Farias, M., and M. Lalljee. 2008. "Holistic Individualism in the Age of Aquarius: Measuring Individualism/Collectivism in New Age, Catholic, and Atheist/Agnostic Groups." *Journal for the Scientific Study of Religion* 47:277–289.

Farias, M., A. K. Newheiser, G. Kahane, and Z. de Toledo. 2013. "Scientific Faith: Belief in Science Increases in the Face of Stress and Existential Anxiety." *Journal of Experimental Psychology* 49:1210–1213.

Farmer, M. A., P. D. Trapnell, and C. M. Meston. 2010. "The Relation between Sexual Behavior and Religiosity Subtypes: A Test of the Secularization Hypothesis." *Archives of Sexual Behavior* 38:852–865.

Feigelman, W., B. S. Gorman, and J. A. Varacalli. 1992. "Americans Who Give Up Religion." *Sociology and Social Research* 76:138–144.

Feldman, R. C. 2011. "Enchanting Modernity: Religion and the Supernatural in Contemporary Japanese Popular Culture." Master's thesis, University of Texas at Austin.

Fenton, A. 2009. "Faith No More—Atheists in the City of Churches," *The Daily Telegraph*, April 11: http://www.dailytelegraph.com.au/faith-no-more-atheists-in-the-city-of-churches/story-e6freuy9-1225698664255

Fernquist, R. M. 1995. "A Research Note on the Association between Religion and Delinquency." *Deviant Behavior* 16:169–175.

Fife, J., A. Adegoke, J. McCoy, and T. Brewer. 2011. "Religious Commitment, Social Support and Life Satisfaction among College Students." *College Student Journal* 45:393–400.

Finke, R., and R. Stark. 1989. "Evaluating the Evidence: Religious Economies and Sacred Canopies." *American Sociological Review* 54:1054–1056.

———. 1998. "Religious Choice and Competition." *American Sociological Review* 63:761–766.

Fischer, C. S. 2000. "Just How Is It That Americans Are Individualistic?" Paper presented at the American Sociological Association meeting, Washington, DC, August 2000.

———. 2008. "Paradoxes of American Individualism." *Sociological Forum* 23:363–372.

———. 2010. *Made in America: A Social History of American Culture and Character*. Chicago: University of Chicago Press.

Fitchett, G., B. D. Rybarczyk, G. A. DeMarco, and J. J. Nicholas. 1999. "The Role of Religion in Medical Rehabilitation Outcomes: A Longitudinal Study." *Rehabilitation Psychology* 44:333–353.

Fitzgerald, C. J., and J. H. Wickwire. 2012. "Religion and Political Affiliation's Influence on Trust and Reciprocity among Strangers." *Journal of Social, Evolutionary, and Cultural Psychology* 6:158–180.

Flannelly, K., C. Ellison, K. Galek, and N. Silton. 2012. "Belief in Life-after-Death, Beliefs about the World, and Psychiatric Symptoms." *Journal of Religion and Health* 51:651–662.

Flynn, T. 2012. "A Note from the Editor." *Free Inquiry* 32 (5): 21.

Fontaine, J. R. J., B. Duriez, P. Luyten, J. Corveleyn, and D. Hutsebaut. 2005. "Consequences of a Multidimensional Approach to Religion for the Relationship between Religiosity and Value Priorities." *International Journal for the Psychology of Religion* 15:123–143.

Fontaine, J. R. J., P. Luyten, and J. Corveleyn. 2000. "Tell Me What You Believe and I'll Tell You What You Want: Empirical Evidence for Discriminating Value Patterns of Five Types of Religiosity." *International Journal for the Psychology of Religion* 10:65–84.

Forbes, K. F., and E. M. Zampelli. 2013. "The Impacts of Religion, Political Ideology, and Social Capital on Religious and Secular Giving: Evidence from the 2006 Social Capital Community Survey." *Applied Economics* 45: 2481–2490.

Fox, J. 2006. "World Separation of Religion and State into the 21st Century." *Comparative Political Studies* 39:537–569.

———. 2008. *A World Survey of Religion and State*. Cambridge: Cambridge University Press.

Fox, J. A., and J. Levin. 2000. *The Will to Kill: Making Sense of Senseless Murder*. Boston: Allyn and Bacon.

Frame, T. R. 2009. *Losing My Religion: Unbelief in Australia*. Sydney: University of New South Wales Press.

Francis, L., and C. Wilcox. 1996. "Religion and Gender Orientation." *Personality and Individual Difference* 20:119–121.

———. 1998. "Religiosity and Femininity: Do Women Really Hold a More Positive Attitude toward Christianity?" *Journal for the Scientific Study of Religion* 37:462–469.

Frejka, T., and C. F. Westoff. 2008. "Religion, Religiousness and Fertility in the U.S. and in Europe." *European Journal of Population* 24:5–31.

Frey, B. B., T. P. Daaleman, and V. Peyton. 2005. "Measuring a Dimension of Spirituality for Health Research: Validity of the Spirituality Index of Well-Being." *Research on Aging* 27:556–577.

Froese, P. 2004a. "After Atheism: An Analysis of Religious Monopolies in the Post-Communist World." *Sociology of Religion* 65:57–75.

———. 2004b. "Forced Secularization in Soviet Russia: Why an Atheistic Monopoly Failed." *Journal for the Scientific Study of Religion* 43:35–50.

———. 2008. *The Plot to Kill God: Findings from the Soviet Experiment in Secularization.* Berkeley: University of California Press.

Froese, P., and S. Pfaff. 2001. "Replete and Desolate Markets: Poland, East Germany, and the New Religious Paradigm." *Social Forces* 80:481–507.

———. 2005. "Explaining a Religious Anomaly: A Historical Analysis of Secularization in Eastern Germany." *Journal for the Scientific Study of Religion* 44:397–422.

Fromm, E. 1969 [1941]. *Escape from Freedom.* New York: Avon Books.

———. 1955. *The Sane Society.* Greenwich, CT: Fawcett.

Galen, L. W. 2009. "Profiles of the Godless: Results from a Survey of the Nonreligious." *Free Inquiry* 29 (5): 41–45.

———. 2012. "Does Religious Belief Promote Pro-sociality? A Critical Examination." *Psychological Bulletin* 138:876–906.

Galen, L. W., and J. Kloet. 2011a. "Mental Well-Being in the Religious and the Non-religious: Evidence for a Curvilinear Relationship." *Mental Health, Religion and Culture* 14:673–689.

———. 2011b. "Personality and Social Integration Factors Distinguishing Non-religious from Religious Groups: The Importance of Controlling for Attendance and Demographics." *Archive for the Psychology of Religion* 33:205–228.

Galen, L. W. and T. R. Miller. 2011. "Perceived Deservingness of Outcomes as a Function of Religious Fundamentalism and Target Responsibility." *Journal of Applied Social Psychology* 41:2144–2164.

Galen, L. W., and W. M. Rogers. 2004. "Religiosity, Alcohol Expectancies, Drinking Motives and Their Interaction in the Prediction of Drinking among College Students." *Journal of Studies on Alcohol* 65:469–476.

Galen, L. W., M. Sharp, and A. McNulty. 2015 . "The Role of Nonreligious Group Factors versus Religious Belief in the Prediction of Prosociality." *Social Indicators Research* 122: 411–432.

Galen, L. W., C. Smith, N. Knapp, and N. Wyngarden. 2011. "Perceptions of Religious and Nonreligious Targets: Exploring the Effects of Perceivers' Religious Fundamentalism." *Journal of Applied Social Psychology* 41:2123–2143.

Galen, L. W., T. Williams, and A. Ver Wey. 2014. "Personality Ratings Are Influenced by Religious Stereotype and Group Identity Bias." *International Journal for the Psychology of Religion* 24:282–297.

Gallup. 2004. "Who Supports the Death Penalty?" http://www.gallup.com/poll/14050/who-supports-death-penalty.aspx

——. 2005. "Who Supports Marijuana Legalization?" http://www.gallup.com/poll/19561/Who-Supports-Marijuana-Legalization.aspx

——. 2007. "Public Divides Over Moral Acceptability of Doctor-Assisted Suicide." http://www.gallup.com/poll/27727/public-divided-over-moral-acceptability-doctorassisted-suicide.aspx

——. 2008. "In More Religious Countries, Lower Suicide Rates." http://www.gallup.com/poll/108625/More-Religious-Countries-Lower-Suicide-Rates.aspx

——. 2010. "Americans' Acceptance of Gay Relations Crosses 50% Threshold." http://www.gallup.com/poll/135764/americans-acceptance-gay-relations-crosses-threshold.aspx

——. 2011. "Muslim Americans: Faith, Freedom, and the Future." http://www.gallup.com/poll/148931/presentation-muslim-americans-faith-freedom-future.aspx

——. 2012a. "In U.S., 46% Hold Creationist View of Human Origins." http://www.gallup.com/poll/155003/Hold-Creationist-View-Human-Origins.aspx

——. 2012b. "Atheists, Muslims See Most Bias as Presidential Candidates." http://www.gallup.com/poll/155285/atheists-muslims-bias-presidential-candidates.aspx

——. 2012c. "In U.S., Nonreligious, Postgrads Are Highly 'Pro-Choice.'" http://www.gallup.com/poll/154946/Non-Christians-Postgrads-Highly-Pro-Choice.aspx

——. 2014. "Three in Four in U.S. Still See the Bible as the Word of God." http://www.gallup.com/poll/170834/three-four-bible-word-god.aspx

Garcia, J. R., and D. J. Kruger. 2010. "Unbuckling in the Bible Belt: Conservative Sexual Norms Lower Age at Marriage." *Journal of Social, Evolutionary, and Cultural Psychology* 4:206–214.

Gautier, M. L. 1997. "Church Attendance and Religious Belief in Postcommunist Societies." *Journal for the Scientific Study of Religion* 36:289–296.

Gay, D., and C. Ellison. 1993. "Religious Subcultures and Political Tolerance: Do Denominations Still Matter?" *Review of Religious Research* 34:311–332.

Gebauer, J. E., D. L. Paulhus, and W. Neberich. 2013. "Big Two Personality and Religiosity across Cultures: Communals as Religious Conformists and Agentics as Religious Contrarians." *Social Psychological and Personality Science* 4:21–30.

Gebauer, J. E., C. Sedikides, and W. Neberich. 2012. "Religiosity, Social Self-Esteem, and Psychological Adjustment: On the Cross-cultural Specificity of the Psychological Benefits of Religiosity." *Psychological Science* 23:158–160.

Geertz, C. 1966. "Religion as a Cultural System." In *Anthropological Approaches to the Study of Religion*, edited by M. Banton, 1–40. London: Tavistock.

Gentile, S., and W. Rosenfeld. 2012. "Presidentiality: Are Colleges Encouraging Atheism? Need to Know." http://www.pbs.org/wnet/need-to-know/video/video-are-colleges-encouraging-atheism/13078/.

George, L. K., C. G. Ellison, and D. B. Larson. 2002. "Exploring the Relationships between Religious Involvement and Health." *Psychological Inquiry* 13:190–200.

Gervais, W. M. 2011. "Finding the Faithless: Perceived Atheist Prevalence Reduces Anti-atheist Prejudice." *Personality and Social Psychology Bulletin* 37:543–556.

——. 2013. "Perceiving Minds and Gods: How Mind Perception Enables, Constrains, and Is Triggered by Belief in Gods." *Perspectives on Psychological Science* 8:390–394.

Gervais, W. M., and A. Norenzayan. 2012a. "Analytic Thinking Promotes Disbelief." *Science* 336:493–496.

———. 2012b. "Like a Camera in the Sky? Thinking about God Increases Public Self-Awareness and Socially Desirable Responding." *Journal of Experimental Social Psychology* 48:298–302.

———. 2012c. "Reminders of Secular Authority Reduce Believers' Distrust of Atheists." *Psychological Science* 23:483–491.

Gervais, W., A. Shariff, and A. Norenzayan. 2011. "Do You Believe in Atheists? Distrust is Central to Anti-atheist Prejudice." *Journal of Personality and Social Psychology* 101:189–206.

Getz, I. 1984. "Moral Judgment and Religion: A Review of the Literature." *Counseling and Values* 28:94–116.

Gilligan, C. 1982. *In a Different Voice*. Cambridge, MA: Harvard University Press.

Gill, A., and E. Lundsgaarde. 2004. "State Welfare Spending and Religiosity: A Cross-National Analysis." *Rationality and Society* 16:399–436.

Gill, R., C. K. Hadaway, and P. L. Marler. 1998. "Variations in Religiosity—Is Religious Belief Declining in Britain?" *Journal for the Scientific Study of Religion* 37:507.

Gingrich, N. 2010. *To Save America: Stopping Obama's Secular-Socialist Machine*. Washington, D. C.: Regnery.

Ginzburg, C. 1980. *The Cheese and the Worms: The Cosmos of a Sixteenth-Century Miller*. Baltimore: Johns Hopkins University Press.

Glasner, P. 1977. *The Sociology of Secularization: A Critique of a Concept*. London: Routledge and Kegan Paul.

Glenn, N. D. 1987. "The Trend in 'No Religion' Respondents to U.S. National Surveys: Late 1950's to Early 1980's." *Public Opinion Quarterly* 51:293–314.

Glock, C. 1967. *To Comfort and to Challenge*. Berkeley: University of California Press.

Goldberg, L. R. 1981. "Language and Individual Differences: The Search for Universals in Personality Lexicons." In *Review of Personality and Social Psychology*, edited by L. Wheeler, vol. 1, 141–165. Beverly Hills, CA: Sage.

Goldman, M. 1999. *Passionate Journeys: Why Successful Women Joined a Cult*. Ann Arbor: University of Michigan Press.

Gonzalez, D. 2001. "U.S. Aids Conversion-Minded Quake Relief in El Salvador." http://www.nytimes.com/2001/03/05/world/05SALV.html?pagewanted=1.

Gooren, H. 2010. "The Pentecostalization of Religion and Society in Latin America." *Exchange* 39:355–376.

Gorski, E. 2009. "Atheist Student Groups Flowering on Campus." *Register-Guard*, November 22. A6.

Gottfredson, L. S. 1997. "Mainstream Science on Intelligence: An Editorial with 52 Signatories, History, and Bibliography." *Intelligence* 24:13–23.

Gottlieb, A. 2008. "Faith Equals Fertility." MoreIntelligentLife.com: http://www.moreintelligentlife.com/story/faith-equals-fertility.

Graham, J., and J. Haidt. 2010. "Beyond Beliefs: Religions Bind Individuals into Moral Communities." *Personality and Social Psychology Review* 14:140–150.

Granovetter, M. S. 1973. "The Strength of Weak Ties." *American Journal of Sociology* 78:1360–1380.

Grant, T. 2011a. "Opposition to Interracial Marriage Lingers Among Evangelicals." http://www.christianitytoday.com/gleanings/2011/june/opposition-to-interracial-marriage-lingers-among.html

Grant, T. 2011b. "Patriotism God Gap: Is the U.S. the Greatest Country in the World?" Christianity Today Politics Blog, August 5.http://www.christianitytoday.com/gleanings/2011/august/patriotism-god-gap-is-us-greatest-country-in-world.html

———. 2014. "Foreign Policy Views of Churches and Religions in One Graph." http://tobingrant.religionnews.com/2014/09/08/foreign-policy-churches-religions-one-graph-military-diplomacy-interventionist-isolationist/

Grasmick, H., E. Davenport, M. Chamlin, and R. Bursik. 1992. "Protestant Fundamentalism and the Retributive Doctrine of Punishment." *Criminology* 30:21–45.

Greeley, A. 1993. "Religion and Attitudes toward the Environment." *Journal for the Scientific Study of Religion* 32:19–28.

Greeley, A., and M. Hout. 2006. *The Truth about Conservative Christians*. Chicago: University of Chicago Press.

Greenfield, E. A., and N. F. Marks. 2007. "Religious Social Identity as an Explanatory Factor for Associations between More Frequent Formal Religious Participation and Psychological Well-Being." *International Journal for the Psychology of Religion* 17:245–259.

Greer, T., M. Berman, V. Varan, L. Bobrycki, and S. Watson. 2005. "We Are a Religious People; We Are a Vengeful People." *Journal for the Scientific Study of Religion* 44:45–57.

Greil, A., and D. G. Bromley, eds. 2003. *Defining Religion: Investigating the Boundaries between the Sacred and Secular*. Amsterdam: JAI.

Gross, N., and S. Simmons. 2009. "The Religiosity of American College and University Professors." *Sociology of Religion* 70:101–129.

Grove, T. 2013. "Church Should Have More Control over Russian Life: Putin." Reuters, February 1. http://www.reuters.com/article/2013/02/01/us-russia-putin-church-dUSBRE91016F20130201.

Guth, J. L., and C. Fraser. 2001. "Religion and Partisanship in Canada." *Journal for the Scientific Study of Religion* 40:51–64.

Guth, J. L. 2010. "Religion and American attitudes on foreign policy, 2008: The case of militant internationalism." Paper presented at the Annual Meeting of the American Political Science Association September, 2010. Washington, D.C.

Guth, J. L., J. C. Green, L. A. Kellstedt, and C. E. Smidt. 1995. "Faith and the Environment: Religious Beliefs and Attitudes on Environmental Policy." *American Journal of Political Science* 39:364–382.

———. 2005. "Faith and Foreign Policy: A View from the Pews." *Review of Faith and International Affairs* 3:3–9.

Hackney, C. H., and G. S. Sanders. 2003. "Religiosity and Mental Health: A Meta-analysis of Recent Studies." *Journal for the Scientific Study of Religion* 42:43–55.

Hadaway, C. K., 1989. "Identifying American Apostates: A Cluster Analysis." *Journal for the Scientific Study of Religion* 28:201–215.

Hadaway, C. K., and W. C. Roof. 1978. "Religious Commitment and the Quality of Life in American Society." *Review of Religious Research* 19:295–307.

———. 1979. "Those Who Stay Religious 'Nones' and Those Who Don't: A Research Note." *Journal for the Scientific Study of Religion* 18:194–200.

———. 1988. "Apostasy in American Churches: Evidence from National Survey Data." In *Falling from the Faith: Causes and Consequences of Religious Apostasy*, edited by D. G. Bromley, 29–46. Newbury Park, CA: Sage.

Hadden, J. K. 1987. "Toward Desacralizing Secularization Theory." *Social Forces* 65: 587–611.

Hagerty, B. B. 2011. "Army's 'Spiritual Fitness' Test Angers Some Soldiers." http://www.npr.org/2011/01/13/132904866/armys-spiritual-fitness-test-angers-some-soldiers.

Haidt, J. 2001. "The Emotional Dog and Its Rational Tail: A Social Intuitionalist Approach to Moral Judgment." *Psychological Review* 108:814–834.

———. 2013. *The Righteous Mind: Why Good People Are Divided by Politics and Religion.* New York: Pantheon Books.

Hale, J. R. 1977. *Who Are the Unchurched? An Exploratory Study.* Washington, DC: Glenmary Research Center.

———. 1980. *The Unchurched: Who They Are and Why They Stay Away.* San Francisco: Harper and Row.

Hall, D., D. Matz, and W. Wood. 2010. "Why Don't We Practice What We Preach? A Meta-analytic Review of Religious Racism." *Personality and Social Psychology Review* 14:126–139.

Hall, K. S., C. Moreau, and J. Trussell. 2012. "Lower Use of Sexual and Reproductive Health Services among Women with Frequent Religious Participation, Regardless of Sexual Experience." *Journal of Women's Health* 21:739–747.

Halman, L. 2010. "Atheism and Secularity in the Netherlands." In *Atheism and Secularity*, edited by P. Zuckerman, vol. 2. 155–175. Santa Barbara, CA: Praeger ABC-CLIO.

Halman, L., and V. Draulans. 2006. "How Secular Is Europe?" *British Journal of Sociology* 57:263–288.

Halman, L., and T. Pettersson. 2003. "Differential Patterns of Secularization in Europe: Exploring the Impact of Religion on Social Values." In *Religion in Secularizing Society: The Europeans' Religion at the End of the 20th Century*, edited by L. Halman and O.Riis, 48–75. Leiden: Brill.

Halpern, C. T., M. W. Waller, A. Spriggs, and D. D. Hallfors. 2006. "Adolescent Predictors of Emerging Adult Sexual Patterns." *Journal of Adolescent Health 39*: 926.e1–926.e10.

Hamberg, E. M., and T. Pettersson. 1994. "The Religious Market: Denominational Competition and Religious Participation in Contemporary Sweden." *Journal for the Scientific Study of Religion* 33:205–216.

Hamil-Luker, J., and C. Smith. 1998. "Religious Authority and Public Opinion on the Right to Die." *Sociology of Religion* 59:373–391.

Hammer, J., R. Cragun, K. Hwang, and J. Smith. 2012. "Forms, Frequency, and Correlates of Perceived Anti-atheist Discrimination." *Secularism and Non-religion* 1:43–67.

Hamplová, D., and Z. Nešpor. 2009. "Invisible Religion in a 'Non-believing' Country: The Case of the Czech Republic." *Social Compass* 56:581–597.

Hanegraaff, W. 2000. "New Age Religion and Secularization." *Numen* 47:288–312.

Hansen, D.E., Vandenberg, B., & Patterson, M.L. 1995. "The Effects of Religious Orientation on Spontaneous and Nonspontaneous Helping Behaviors." *Personality and Individual Differences* 19: 101–104.

Hardy, S. A., M. A. Steelman, S. M. Coyne, and R. D. Ridge. 2013. "Adolescent Religiousness as a Protective Factor against Pornography Use." *Journal of Applied Developmental Psychology* 34:131–139.

Harrell, A. 2012. "Do Religious Cognitions Promote Pro-sociality? *Rationality and Society* 24:463–482.

Harris Poll. 2004. "Those Favoring Stem Cell Research Increases to a 73 to 11 Percent Majority." http://www.prnewswire.com/news-releases/those-favoring-stem-cell-research-increases-to-a-73-to-11-percent-majority-71670317.html

————. 2003. "While Most Americans Believe in God, Only 36% Attend a Religious Service Once a Month or More Often—Belief and Attendance Vary Greatly among Different Segments of the Population." http://www.harrisinteractive.com/vault/Harris-Interactive-Pol l-Research-While-Most-Americans-Believe-in-God-Only-36-pct-A-2003-10.pdf

Harrold, F. B., and R. A. Eve. 1987. "Patterns of Creationist Belief among College Students." In *Cult Archaeology and Creationism*, edited by F. B. Harrold and R. A. Eve, 68–90. Iowa City: University of Iowa Press.

Hartshorne, H., M. A. May, D. E. Sonquist, and C. A. Kerr. 1926. "Testing the Knowledge of Right and Wrong." *Religious Education* 21:539–554.

Hathcoat, J., and L. Barnes. 2010. "Explaining the Relationship among Fundamentalism and Authoritarianism: An Epistemic Connection." *International Journal for the Psychology of Religion* 20:73–84.

Haught, J. 2010. *Fading Faith: The Rise of the Secular Age*. Charleston, WV: Gustav Broukal Press.

Havercamp, S. M., and S. Reiss. 2003. "A Comprehensive Assessment of Human Strivings: Test-Retest Reliability and Validity of the Reiss Profile." *Journal of Personality Assessment* 81:123–132.

Hayes, B. C. 1995a. "The Impact of Religious Identification on Political Attitudes: An International Comparison." *Sociology of Religion* 56:177–94.

————. 1995b. "Religious Identification and Moral Attitudes: The British Case." *British Journal of Sociology* 46:457–474.

————. 2000. "Religious Independents within Western Industrialized Nations: A Socio-demographic Profile." *Sociology of Religion* 61:191–207.

Hayes, B. C., and M. Hornsby-Smith. 1994. "Religious Identification and Family Attitudes: An International Comparison." *Research in the Social Scientific Study of Religion* 6:167–186.

Hayes, B. C., and M. Marangudakis. 2001. "Religion and Attitudes towards Nature in Britain." *British Journal of Sociology* 52:139–155.

Hayford, S. R., and S. P. Morgan. 2008. "Religiosity and Fertility in the United States: The Role of Fertility Intentions." *Social Forces* 86:1163–1188.

Hearn, F. 1997. *Moral Order and Social Disorder: The American Search for Civil Society*. New York: Aldine de Gruyter.

Heaton, T. B., and V. R. A. Call. 1997. "Modeling Family Dynamics with Event History Techniques." *Journal of Marriage and the Family* 57:1978–1990.

Heaton, T. B., C. K. Jacobson, and X. N. Fu. 1992. "Religiosity of Married Couples and Childlessness." *Review of Religious Research* 33:244–255.

Hecht, J. M. 2003. *Doubt: A History*. San Francisco: HarperCollins.

Heelas, P. 2003 [1996]. *The New Age Movement: The Celebration of the Self and the Sacralization of Modernity*. Oxford: Blackwell.

Heelas, P., L. Woodhead, and B. Seel. 2005. *The Spiritual Revolution: Why Religion Is Giving Way to Spirituality*. Malden, MA: Blackwell.

Hefland, D. 2009. "Why Many Americans Change Faiths." *Los Angeles Times*, April 28, A12.

Helbardt, S., D. Hellmann-Rajanayagam, and R. Korff. 2013. "Religionisation of Politics in Sri Lanka, Thailand and Myanmar." *Politics, Religion and Ideology* 14 (1): 36–58.

Helm, H. M., J. C. Hays, E. P. Flint, H. G. Koenig, and D. G. Blazer. 2000. "Does Private Religious Activity Prolong Survival? A Six-Year Follow-Up Study of 3,851 Older Adults." *Journals of Gerontology: Series A, Biological Sciences and Medical Sciences* 55:400–405.

Henley, N. M., and F., Pincus. 1978. "Interrelationship of Sexist, Racist, and Antihomosexual Attitudes." *Psychological Reports* 42:83–90.

Hervieu-Léger, D. 2001. "Individualism, the Validation of Faith, and the Social Nature of Religion in Modernity." In *The Blackwell Companion to Sociology of Religion* edited by R. K. Fenn, 161–175. Oxford: Blackwell.

———. 2006. "In Search of Certainties: The Paradoxes of Religiosity in Societies of High Modernity." *Hedgehog Review* 8 (1/2): 59–68.

Hetherington, M. J., and J. D. Weiler. 2009. *Authoritarianism and Polarization in American Politics*. New York: Cambridge University Press.

Hibbing, J. R., K. B. Smith, and J. R. Alford. 2014. "Differences in Negativity Bias Underlie Variations in Political Ideology." *Behavioral and Brain Sciences* 37:297–350.

Higher Education Research Institute. 2003. "The Spiritual Life of College Students." http://spirituality.ucla.edu/docs/reports/Spiritual_Life_College_Students_Full_Report.pdf

Highfield, R., R. Wiseman, and R. Jenkins. 2009. "In Your Face." *New Scientist* 201:28–32.

Hill, J. P. 2009. "Higher Education as Moral Community: Institutional Influences on Religious Participation during College." *Journal for the Scientific Study of Religion* 48:515–534.

———. 2011. "Faith and Understanding: Specifying the Impact of Higher Education on Religious Belief." *Journal for the Scientific Study of Religion* 50: 533–551.

Hill, P. C., and K. I. Pargament. 2008. "Advances in the Conceptualization and Measurement of Religion and Spirituality: Implications for Physical and Mental Health Research." *American Psychologist* 58:64–74.

Hirsh, J. B. 2010. "Compassionate Liberals and Polite Conservatives: Associations of Agreeableness with Political Ideology and Moral Values." *Personality and Social Psychology Bulletin* 38:655–664.

Hodgkinson, V. A. 2003. "Volunteering in Global Perspective." In *The Values of Volunteering: Cross-cultural Perspectives*, edited by P. Dekker and L. Halman, 35–53. New York: Kluwer Academic/Plenum.

Hodgkinson, V. A., and M. S. Weitzman. 1990. *Giving and Volunteering in the United States: Findings from a National Survey*. Washington, DC: Independent Sector.

Hoffman, J., and A. Miller. 1997. "Social and Political Attitudes among Religious Groups: Convergence and Divergence over Time." *Journal for the Scientific Study of Religion* 36:52–70.

Hoffmann, R. 2012. "The Experimental Economics of Religion." *Journal of Economic Surveys* 27:813–845.

Hofstede, G. H. 2001. *Culture's Consequences: Comparing Values, Behaviors, Institutions, and Organizations across Nations*. Thousand Oaks, CA: Sage.

Hoge, D., K. McGuire, and B. Stratman. 1981. *Converts, Dropouts, and Returnees: A Study of Religion Change among Catholics*. New York: Pilgrim Press.

Holt, J. B., J. W. Miller, T. S. Naimi, and D. Z. Sui. 2006. "Religious Affiliation and Alcohol Consumption in the United States." *Geographical Review* 96:523–542.

Horning, S. M., H. P. Davis, M. Stirrat, and R. E. Cornwell. 2011. "Atheistic, Agnostic, and Religious Older Adults on Well-Being and Coping Behaviors." *Journal of Aging Studies* 25:177–188.

Hornsby-Smith, M. 2008. *Roman Catholics in England: Studies in Social Structure since the Second World War*. Cambridge: Cambridge University Press.

Hood, R., P. Hill, and B. Spilka. 2009. *The Psychology of Religion*. New York: Guilford Press.

Hout, M. 2003. "Demographic Methods for the Sociology of Religion." In *Handbook of the Sociology of Religion*, edited by M. Dillon, 79–84. New York: Cambridge University Press.

Hout, M., and C. S. Fischer. 2002. "Why More Americans Have No Religious Preference: Politics and Generations." *American Sociological Review* 67:165–190.

Houtman, D., and P. Mascini. 2002. "Why Do Churches Become Empty, While New Age Grows? Secularization and Religious Change in the Netherlands." *Journal for the Scientific Study of Religion* 41:455–473.

Hoverd, W. J., and C. G. Sibley. 2013. "Religion, Deprivation, and Subjective Wellbeing: Testing a Religious Buffering Hypothesis." *International Journal of Wellbeing* 3:182–196.

Howsepian, B., and T. Merluzzi. 2009. "Religious Beliefs, Social Support, Self-Efficacy and Adjustment to Cancer." *Psycho-Oncology* 18:1069–1079.

Hsu, F. L. K. 1981. *Americans and Chinese: Passage to Differences*. Honolulu: University Press of Hawaii.

Hughes, C., and A. L. Cutting. 1999. "Nature, Nurture and Individual Differences in Early Understanding of Mind." *Psychological Science* 10:429–433.

Hummer, R. A., R. G. Rogers, C. B. Nam, and C. G. Ellison. 1999. "Religious Involvement and U.S. Adult Mortality." *Demography* 36:273–285.

Hunsberger, B. 1980. "A Reexamination of the Antecedents of Apostasy." *Review of Religious Research* 21:158–170.

———. 1983. "Apostasy: A Social Learning Perspective." *Review of Religious Research* 25:21–38.

———. 1985. "Parent-University Student Agreement on Religious and Nonreligious Issues." *Journal for the Scientific Study of Religion* 24:314–320.

Hunsberger, B., S. Alisat, S. M. Pancer, and M. Pratt. 1996. "Religious Fundamentalism and Religious Doubts: Content, Connections, and Complexity of Thinking." *International Journal for the Psychology of Religion* 6:201–220.

Hunsberger, B., and B. Altemeyer. 2006. *Atheists: A Groundbreaking Study of America's Nonbelievers*. Amherst, NY: Prometheus Books.

Hunsberger, B., and L. B. Brown. 1984. "Religious Socialization, Apostasy, and the Influence of Family Background." *Journal for the Scientific Study of Religion* 23:239–251.

Hunsberger, B., B. McKenzie, M. Pratt, and S. M. Pancer. 1993. "Religious Doubt: A Social Psychological Analysis." *Research in the Social Scientific Study of Religion* 5:27–51.

Hunsberger, B., and E. Platonow. 1986. "Religion and Helping Charitable Causes." *Journal of Psychology* 120:517–528.

Hunsberger, B., M. Pratt, and S. M. Pancer. 2002. "A Longitudinal Study of Religious Doubts in High School and Beyond: Relationships, Stability, and Searching for Answers." *Journal for the Scientific Study of Religion* 41:255–266.

Hunter, L. A. 2010. "Explaining Atheism: Testing the Secondary Compensator Model and Proposing an Alternative." *Interdisciplinary Journal of Research on Religion* 6:1–37.

Huntington, S. P. 1993. "The Clash of Civilizations?" *Foreign Affairs* 72 (3): 22–49.

———. 1996. *The Clash of Civilizations and the Remaking of World Order*. New York: Simon and Schuster.

Hutsebaut, D. 2007. "Religious Cognitive Styles and Ethnocentrism." In *Faith-Based Radicalism*, edited by C. Timmerman, D. Hutsebaut, S. Mels, W. Nonneman, and W. Van Herck, 169–180. Brussels: P.I.E. Peter Lang.

Hwang, K, J. Hammer, and R. Cragun. 2011. "Extending Religion-Health Research to Secular Minorities: Issues and Concerns." *Journal of Religion and Health* 50:608–622.

Iannaccone, L. R. 1990. "Religious Practice: A Human Capital Approach." *Journal for the Scientific Study of Religion* 29:297–314.

Iannaccone, L. R., R. Finke, and R. Stark. 1997. "Deregulating Religion: The Economics of Church and State." *Economic Inquiry* 35:350–364.

Immerzeel, T., and F. Van Tubergen. 2011. "Religion as Reassurance? Testing the Insecurity Theory in 26 European Countries." *European Sociological Review* 29:359–372.

Inglehart, R. 1990. *Culture Shift in Advanced Industrial Society*. Princeton, NJ: Princeton University Press.

———. 1997. *Modernization and Postmodernization: Cultural, Economic, and Political Change in 43 Societies*. Princeton, NJ: Princeton University Press.

Inglehart, R. and W. E. Baker. 2000. "Modernization, Cultural Change, and the Persistence of Traditional Values." *American Sociological Review* 65:19–51.

Inglehart, R., M. Basanez, J. Diez-Medrano, L. Halman, and R. Luijkx. 2004. *Human Beliefs and Values: A Cross-Cultural Sourcebook Based on the 1999–2002 Value Surveys*. Buenos Aires: Siglo Veintiuon Editores.

Inglehart, R., and P. Norris. 2007. "Why Didn't Religion Disappear? Re-examining the Secularization Thesis." In *The Cultures and Globalization Series 1: Conflicts and Tensions*, edited by H. K. Anheier and Y. R. Isar, 253–257. London: Sage.

Inglehart, R., and C. Welzel. 2005. *Modernization, Cultural Change, and Democracy: The Human Development Sequence*. Cambridge: Cambridge University Press.

Iversen, H. R. 2006. "Secular Religion and Religious Secularism: A Profile of the Religious Development in Denmark since 1968." *Nordic Journal of Religion and Society* 2:75–93.

Jackson, E. F., M. D. Bachmeier, J. R. Wood, and E. A. Craft. 1995. "Volunteering and Charitable Giving: Do Religious and Associated Ties Promote Helping Behaviors?" *Nonprofit and Voluntary Sector Quarterly* 24:59–78.

Jackson, L. M., and V. M. Esses. 1997. "Of Scripture and Ascription: The Relation between Religious Fundamentalism and Intergroup Helping." *Personality and Social Psychological Bulletin* 23:893–906.

Jackson, L. M., and B. Hunsberger. 1999. "An Intergroup Perspective on Religion and Prejudice." *Journal for the Scientific Study of Religion* 38:509–523.

Jacobs, L. M., K. Burns, and B. B. Jacobs. 2008. "Trauma Death: Views of the Public and Trauma Professionals on Death and Dying from Injuries." *Archives of Surgery* 143:730–735.

Jacoby, S. 2004. *Freethinkers: A History of American Secularism*. New York: Metropolitan Books.

Jamison, W. V., C. Wenk, and J. V. Parker. 2000. "Every Sparrow That Falls: Understanding Animal Rights Activism as Functional Religion." Special issue, *Society and Animals* 8:305–330.

Jenkins, P. 2013. "A Secular Latin America?" *Christian Century*, March 12. http://www.christian-century.org/article/2013-02/secular-latin-america#.UUB_5Z_f2YI.facebook.

Jensen, G. F. 2006. "Religious Cosmologies and Homicide Rates among Nations." *Journal of Religion and Society* 8:1–13.

Jerolimov, D. M., and S. Zrinščak. 2006. "Religion within and beyond Borders: The Case of Croatia." *Social Compass* 53:279–290.

Johnson, D. C. 1997. "Formal Education vs. Religious Belief: Soliciting New Evidence with Multinomial Logit Modeling." *Journal for the Scientific Study of Religion* 36:231–246.

Johnson, M. 1991. *Strong Mothers, Weak Wives*. Berkeley: University of California Press.

Johnson, M. K., W. C. Rowatt, L. M. Barnard-Brak, J. A. Pathock-Peckham, J. P. LaBouff, and R. D. Carlisle. 2011. "A Mediational Analysis of the Role of Right-Wing Authoritarianism and Religious Fundamentalism in the Religiosity-Prejudice Link." *Personality and Individual Differences* 50:851–856.

Johnson, M. K., W. C. Rowatt, and J. LaBouff. 2010. "Priming Christian Religious Concepts Increases Facial Prejudice." *Social Psychological and Personality Science* 1:119–126.

Jokela, M. 2012. "Birth-Cohort Effects in the Association between Personality and Fertility." *Psychological Science* 23:835–841.

Jones, R. K., J. E. Darroch, and S. Singh. 2005. "Religious Differentials in the Sexual and Reproductive Behaviors of Young Women in the United States." *Journal of Adolescent Health* 36:279–288.

Jong, J., M. Bluemke, and J. Halberstadt. 2013. "Fear of Death and Supernatural Beliefs: Developing a New Supernatural Belief Scale to Test the Relationship." *European Journal of Personality* 27:495–506.

Jorgenson, D. E., and R. C. Neubecker. 1981. "Euthanasia: A National Survey of Attitudes toward Voluntary Termination of Life." *Omega* 11:281–291.

Jost, J. T. 2006. "The End of Ideology." *American Psychologist* 61:61–670.

Jost, J. T., J. Glaser, A. W. Kruglanski, and F. J. Sulloway. 2003. "Political Conservatism as Motivated Social Cognition." *Psychological Bulletin* 129:339–375.

Juergensmeyer, M. 1996. "The Worldwide Rise of Religious Nationalism." *Journal of International Affairs* 50 (1): 1–20.

Kalberg, S. 1980. "Max Weber's Types of Rationality: Cornerstones for the Analysis of Rationalization Processes in History." *American Journal of Sociology* 85:1145–1179.

Kanazawa, S. 2010. "Why Liberals and Atheists Are More Intelligent." *Social Psychology Quarterly* 73:33–57.

Kandler, C., W. Bleidorn, and R. Riemann. 2012. "Left or Right? Sources of Political Orientation: The Roles of Genetic Factors, Cultural Transmission, Assertive Mating, and Personality." *Journal of Personality and Social Psychology* 102:633–645.

Kandler, C., and R. Riemann. 2013. "Genetic and Environmental Sources of Individual Religiousness: The Roles of Individual Personality Traits and Perceived Environmental Religiousness." *Behavior Genetics* 43:297–313.

Kapuscinski, A. N., and K. S. Master. 2010. "The Current Status of Measures of Spirituality: A Critical Review of Scale Development." *Psychology of Religion and Spirituality* 2:191–205.

Karpov, V. 1999. "Religiosity and Political Tolerance in Poland." *Sociology of Religion* 60:387–402.

Kasselstrand, I. 2013. "'Tell the Minister Not to Talk about God:' A Comparative Study of Secularisation in Protestant Europe." PhD diss., University of Edinburgh.

Katnik, A. 2002. "Religion, Social Class, and Political Tolerance: A Cross-National Analysis." *International Journal of Sociology* 32:14–38.

Kay, A. C., D. Gaucher, I. McGregor, and K. Nash. 2010. "Religious Belief as Compensatory Control." *Personality and Social Psychology Review* 14:37–48.

Kay, A. C., D. Gaucher, J. L. Napier, M. J. Callan, and K. Laurin. 2008. "God and the Government: Testing a Compensatory Control Mechanism for the Support of External Systems." *Journal of Personality and Social Psychology* 95:18–35.

Kay, A. C., S. Shepherd, C. W. Blatz, S. N. Chua, and A. D. Galinsky. 2010. "For God (or) Country: The Hydraulic Relation between Government Instability and Belief in Religious Sources of Control." *Journal of Personality and Social Psychology* 99:725–739.

Kellert, S. R., and J. K. Berry. 1980. *Phase III: Knowledge, Affection and Basic Attitudes toward Animals in American Society*. Washington, DC: US Fish and Wildlife Service.

Kennell, J. E. 1988. "The Community Church: A Study of an Inner City Church Community." Paper presented at the annual meeting of the American Psychological Association, Atlanta, GA, August 1988.

Kerley, K. R, H. Copes, R. Tewksbury, and D. A. Dabney. 2011. "Examining the Relationship between Religiosity and Self-Control as Predictors of Prison Deviance." *International Journal of Offender Therapy and Comparative Criminology* 55:1251–1271.

Keysar, A. 2007. "Who Are America's Atheists and Agnostics?" In *Secularism and Secularity: Contemporary International Perspectives*, edited by B. Kosmin and A. Keysar, 33–39. Hartford, CT: Institute for the Study of Secularism in Society and Culture.

———. 2013. "Freedom of Choice: Women and Demography in Israel, France, and the US." Paper presented at the "Secularism on the Edge" Conference, Georgetown University, Washington, DC, February 20–22.

Keysar, A., and J. Navarro-Rivera. 2013. "A World of Atheism: Global Demographics." In *The Oxford Handbook of Atheism*, edited by S. Bullivant and M. Ruse, 553–586. Oxford: Oxford University Press.

Kimball, M. S., C. M. Mitchell, A. D. Thornton, and L. C. Young-Demarco. 2009. "Empirics on the Origins of Preferences: The Case of College Major and Religiosity. NBER Working Paper No. 15182. http://www.nber.org/papers/w15182.

King, M., L. Marston, S. McManus, T. Brugha, H. Meltzer, and P. Bebbington. 2013. "Religion, Spirituality and Mental Health: Results from a National Study of English Households." *British Journal of Psychiatry* 202:68–73.

King, P., J. Furrow, and N. Roth. 2002. "The Influence of Families and Peers on Adolescent Religiousness." *Journal for Psychology and Christianity* 21:109–120.

Kirk, R. 1982. *The Portable Conservative Reader*. Harmondsworth, Middlesex, England: Penguin.

Kisala, R. 2006. "Japanese Religions." In *Nanzan Guide to Japanese Religions*, edited by P. L. Swanson and C. Chilson, 3–13. Honolulu: University of Hawaii Press.

Klinenberg, E. 2012. *Going Solo: The Extraordinary Rise and Surprising Appeal of Living Alone*. New York: Penguin.

Koenig, H. G. 1995. "Religion and Older Men in Prison." *International Journal of Geriatric Psychiatry* 10: 219–230.

———. 2008. "Concerns about Measuring 'Spirituality' in Research." *Journal of Nervous and Mental Disease* 196:349–355.

Koenig, H. G., J. C. Hays, D. B. Larson, L. K. George, and H. J. Cohen. 1999. "Does Religious Attendance Prolong Survival? A Six-Year Follow-Up Study of 3,968 Older Adults." *Journals of Gerontology: Series A, Biological Sciences and Medical Sciences* 54:M370–M376.

Koenig, L. B., M. McGue, and W. G. Iacono. 2008. "Stability and Change in Religiousness during Emerging Adulthood." *Developmental Psychology* 44:532–543.

Kohlberg, L., and T. Lickona. 1976. "Moral Stages and Moralization: The Cognitive-Developmental Approach." In *Moral Development and Behavior: Theory, Research and Social Issues*, edited by T. Lickona, 31–53. New York: Holt, Rinehart and Winston.

Koleva, S. P., J. Graham, R. Iyer, P. H. Ditto, and J. Haidt. 2012. "Tracing the Threads: How Five Moral Concerns Especially Purity Help Explain Culture War Attitudes." *Journal of Research in Personality* 46:184–194.

Koltko-Rivera, M. E. 2004. "The Psychology of Worldviews." *Review of General Psychology* 8: 3–58.

KONDA. 2007. "Religion, Secularism, and the Veil in Daily Life." Istanbul, Turkey: KONDA. http://www.konda.com.tr/en/reports.php.

Kopsa, A. 2014. "Obama's Evangelical Gravy Train," http://www.thenation.com/article/180435/obamas-evangelical-gravy-train

Kosmin, B. A. 2007. "Contemporary Secularity and Secularism." In *Secularity and Secularism: Contemporary International Perspectives*, edited by B. A. Kosmin and A. Keysar, 1–13. Hartford, CT: Institute for the Study of Secularism in Society and Culture, Trinity College.

———. 2008. "Areligious, Irreligious and Anti-religious Americans: The No Religion Population of the U.S.—'Nones.'" http://www.trincoll.edu/secularisminstitute/.

———. 2013. "The Vitality of Soft Secularism in the U.S. and the Rise of the Nones." Paper presented at the "Secularism on the Edge" Conference, Georgetown University, Washington, DC, February 20–22.

Kosmin, B. A., and A. Keysar. 2008. *ARIS 2008 Summary Report*. Hartford, CT: Institute for the Study of Secularism in Society and Culture, Trinity College. commons.trincoll.edu/aris/publications/2008-2/aris-2008-summary-report/.

———. 2009. *American Religious Identification Survey ARIS 2008*. Hartford, CT: Institute for the Study of Secularism in Society and Culture, Trinity College. commons.trincoll.edu/aris/surveys/aris-2001/download-aris-2001/.

———. 2013. "American Jewish Secularism: Jewish Life beyond the Synagogue." In *American Jewish Year Book 2012*, edited by A. Dashefsky and I. M. Sheskin, 3–54. Dordrecht: Springer.

Kosmin, B. A., A. Keysar, R. Cragun, and J. Navarro-Rivera. 2009. *American Nones: The Profile of the No Religion Population. A Report Based on the American Religious Identification Survey 2008*. Hartford, CT: Institute for the Study of Secularism in Society and Culture, Trinity College. commons.trincoll.edu/aris/files/2011/08/NONES_08.pdf

Krause, N. 1998. "Neighborhood Deterioration, Religious Coping, and Changes in Health during Late Life." *Gerontologist* 38:653–664.

———. 2006. "Religious Doubt and Psychological Well-Being: A Longitudinal Investigation." *Review of Religious Research* 47:287–302.

Krause, N., and N. Wulff. 2004. "Religious Doubt and Health: Exploring the Potential Dark Side of Religion." *Sociology of Religion* 65:35–56.

Kraut, B. 1987. "Ethical Culture." In *Encyclopedia of Religion*, edited by M. Eliade, vol. 5, 171–172. New York: Macmillan.

Kurdek, L. A. 1993. "Predicting Marital Dissolution: A 5-Year Prospective Longitudinal Study of Newlywed Couples." *Journal of Personality and Social Psychology* 64:221–242.

Kurth, J. 2007. "Religion and National Identity in America and Europe." *Society* 44:120–125.

Kvande, M. N., R. J. Reidunsdatter, A. Lohre, M. E. Nielsen, and G. A. Espnes. 2014. "Religiousness and Social Support: A Study in Secular Norway." *Review of Religious Research* 57:67–109.

Laitila, T. 2012. "The Russian Orthodox Church and Atheism." *Approaching Religion* 2: 52–57.

Lakoff, G. 2002. *Moral Politics: How Liberals and Conservatives Think*. Chicago: University of Chicago Press.

Lam, P. Y. 2002. "As the Flocks Gather: How Religion Affects Voluntary Association Participation." *Journal for the Scientific Study of Religion* 41:405–422.

Larson, E. J., and L. Witham. 1997. "Scientists Are Still Keeping the Faith." *Nature* 386:435–436.

———. 1998. "Leading Scientists Still Reject God." *Nature* 394:313.

Laumann, E. O., J. H. Gagnon, R. T. Michael, and S. Michaels. 1994. *The Social Organization of Sexuality: Sexual Practices in the United States*. Chicago: University of Chicago Press.

Lau, S. 1989. "Religious Schema and Values." *International Journal of Psychology* 24: 137–156.

Lavric, M., and S. Flere. 2010. "Trait Anxiety and Measures of Religiosity in Four Cultural Settings." *Mental Health, Religion and Culture* 13:667–682.

Law, S. 2011. *Humanism: A Very Short Introduction*. New York: Oxford University Press.

Lawson, A. E., and W. A. Worsnop. 1992. "Learning about Evolution and Rejecting a Belief in Special Creation: Effects of Reflective Reasoning Skill, Prior Knowledge, Prior Belief and Religious Commitment." *Journal of Research in Science Teaching* 29:143–166.

Lawton, L., and R. Bures. 2001. "Parental Divorce and the 'Switching' of Religious Identity." *Journal for the Scientific Study of Religion* 40:99–111.

Layman, G. C. 1997. "Religion and Political Behavior in the United States: The Impact of Beliefs, Affiliations, and Commitment from 1980 to 1994." *Public Opinion Quarterly* 61:288–316.

Leach, M. M., M. E. Berman, and L. Eubanks. 2008. "Religious Activities, Religious Orientation, and Aggressive Behavior." *Journal for the Scientific Study of Religion* 47:311–319.

Leavy, S. 1988. *In the Image of God: A Psychoanalyst's View*. New Haven, CT: Yale University Press.

Lee, L. 2012. "Research Note: Talking about a Revolution: Terminology for the New Field of Nonreligion Studies." *Journal of Contemporary Religion* 27:129–139.

———. 2014. "Secular or Nonreligious? Investigating and Interpreting Generic 'Not Religious' Categories and Populations." *Religion* 44:466–482.

———. 2015. *Recognizing the Non-Religious: Reimagining the Secular*. Oxford, UK: Oxford University Press.

Lefkowitz, E. S., M. M. Gillen, C. L. Shearer, and T. L. Boone. 2004. "Religiosity, Sexual Behaviors, and Sexual Attitudes during Emerging Adulthood." *Journal of Sex Research* 41:150–159.

Lehrer, E. and C. Chiswick. 1993. "Religion as Determinant of Marital Stability." *Demography* 30:385–404.

Leonard, K. C. and D. Scott-Jones. 2010. "A Belief-Behavior Gap? Exploring Religiosity and Sexual Activity among High School Seniors." *Journal of Adolescent Research* 25:578–600.

Leurent, B., I. Nazareth, J. Bellon-Saameno, M-I. Geerlings, H. Maaroos, S. Saldivia, I. Svab, F. Torres-Gonzalez, M. Xavier, and M. King. 2013. "Spiritual and Religious Beliefs as Risk Factors for the Onset of Major Depression: An International Cohort Study." *Psychological Medicine* 43:2109–2120.

Lewis, G., S. Ritchie, and T. Bates. 2011. "The Relationship between Intelligence and Multiple Domains of Religious Belief: Evidence from a Large Adult US Sample." *Intelligence* 39:468–472.

Lewis, V. A., C. A. MacGregor, and R. D. Putnam. 2013. "Religion, Networks, and Neighborliness: The Impact of Religious Social Networks on Civic Engagement." *Social Science Research* 42:331–346.

Lewy, G. 1996. *Why America Needs Religion: Secular Modernity and Its Discontents*. Grand Rapids, MI: Eerdmans.

———. 2008. *"If God Is Dead, Everything Is Permitted?"* New Brunswick, NJ: Transaction.

Li, Y. J., K. A. Johnson, A. B. Cohen, M. J. Williams, E. D. Knowles, and Z. Chen. 2012. "Fundamentalist Attribution Error: Protestants Are Dispositionally Focused." *Journal of Personality and Social Psychology* 102:281–290.

Liddell, L. 2012. "The Unstoppable Secular Students." *Secular Student Alliance*. http://www.secularstudents.org/unstoppable-secular-students.

Lim, C., and C. A. MacGregor. 2012. "Religion and Volunteering in Context: Disentangling the Contextual Effects of Religion on Voluntary Behavior." *American Sociological Review* 77:747–779.

Lim, C., and R. D. Putnam. 2010. "Religion, Social Networks, and Life Satisfaction." *American Sociological Review* 75:914–933.

Lincoln, A. 1953. "Reply to Emancipation Memorial Presented by Chicago Christians of All Denominations" (September 13, 1862). In *The Collected Works of Abraham Lincoln*, edited by R. P. Basler, vol. 5, 419–420. New Brunswick, NJ: Rutgers University Press.

Lincoln, R., C. A. Morrissey, and P. Mundey. 2008. *Religious Giving: A Literature Review*. http://generosityresearch.nd.edu/assets/20447/religious_giving_final.pdf.

Lindeman, M., S. Blomqvist, and M. Takada. 2012. "Distinguishing Spirituality from Other Constructs: Not a Matter of Well-Being but of Belief in Supernatural Spirits." *Journal of Nervous and Mental Disease* 200:167–173.

Linneman, T., and M. Clendenen. 2010. "Sexuality and the Sacred." In *Atheism and Secularity*, edited by P. Zuckerman, vol. 1, 89–112. Santa Barbara, CA: Praeger ABC-CLIO.

Lodge, D. 1980. *Souls and Bodies*. New York: Penguin.

Loftus, J. 2001. "America's Liberalization in Attitudes toward Homosexuality, 1973–1998." *American Sociological Review* 66:762–782.

Lu, Y. 2011. "Religious Influence in China." In *Understanding Chinese Society*, edited by X. Zang, 127–140. London: Routledge.

Lüchau, P. 2010. "Atheism and Secularity: The Scandinavian Paradox." In *Atheism and Secularity*, edited by P. Zuckerman, vol. 2, 177–196. Santa Barbara, CA: Praeger.

Luckmann, T. 1967. *The Invisible Religion: The Problem of Religion in Modern Society*. New York: Macmillan.

Ludeke, S., W. Johnson, and T. J. Bouchard. 2013. "'Obedience to Traditional Authority': A Heritable Factor Underlying Authoritarianism, Conservatism and Religiousness." *Personality and Individual Differences* 55:375–380.

Luhnow, D., and S. S. Muñoz. 2013. "In Latin American, Catholics See a Lift." Associated Press, March 15. http://online.wsj.com/article/SB10001424127887324392804578360931371068830.html.

Lukes, S. 1973. *Individualism*. Oxford: Blackwell.

Lun, V. M.C., and M. H. Bond. 2013. "Examining the Relation of Religion and Spirituality to Subjective Well-Being across National Cultures." *Psychology of Religion and Spirituality* 5:304–315.

Lužný, D., and J. Navrátilová. 2001. "Religion and Secularisation in the Czech Republic." *Czech Sociological Review* 9: 85–89.

Lynn, R., J. Harvey, and H. Nyborg. 2009. "Average Intelligence Predicts Atheism Rates across 137 Nations." *Intelligence* 37:11–15.

Lyons, M., and I. Nivison-Smith. 2006. "Religion and Giving in Australia." *Australian Journal of Social Issues* 41:419–436.

Maclean, A. M., L. J. Walker, and M. K. Matsuba. 2004. "Transcendence and the Moral Self: Identity Integration, Religion, and Moral Life." *Journal for the Scientific Study of Religion* 43:429–437.

Mahlamäki, T. 2012. "Religion and Atheism from a Gender Perspective." *Approaching Religion* 2: 58–65.

Manlove, J., S. Ryan, and K. Franzetta. 2003. "Patterns of Contraceptive Use within Teenagers' First Sexual Relationships." *Perspectives on Sexual and Reproductive Health* 35:246–255.

Manning, C. 2010. "Atheism, Secularity, the Family, and Children." In *Atheism and Secularity*, edited by P. Zuckerman, vol. 1, 19–42. Santa Barbara, CA: Praeger ABC-CLIO.

———. 2013. "Unaffiliated Parents and the Religious Training of Their Children." *Sociology of Religion* 74:149–175.

Manning, C., and P. Zuckerman. 2004. *Sex and Religion*. Belmont, CA: Wadsworth.

Manning, L. K. 2010. "Gender and Religious Differences Associated with Volunteering in Later Life." *Journal of Women and Aging* 22: 125–135.

Martin, D. 1969. "Secularization and the Arts: The Case of Music." In *The Religious and the Secular*, edited by D. Martin, 79–102. London: Routledge and Kegan Paul.

———. 1978. *A General Theory of Secularization*. New York: Harper and Row.

———. 2002. *Pentecostalism: The World Their Parish*. Oxford: Blackwell.

Marty, M. E. 1961. *The Infidel*. Cleveland: Meridian Books.

———. 1964. *Varieties of Unbelief*. New York: Holt, Rinehart, and Winston.

Maruna, S. 2001. *Making Good: How Ex-convicts Reform and Rebuild Their Lives*. Washington, DC: American Psychological Association Books.

Maruna, S., Wilson, L., and Curran, K. 2006. "Why God Is Often Found behind Bars: Prison Conversions and the Crisis of Self-Narrative." *Research in Human Development* 3:161–184.

Mason, M. J., C. Schmidt, and J. Mennis. 2012. "Dimensions of Religiosity and Access to Religious Social Capital: Correlates with Substance Use among Urban Adolescents." *Journal of Primary Prevention* 33:229–237.

Mason, W. A., and M. Windle. 2002. "A Longitudinal Study of the Effects of Religiosity on Adolescent Alcohol Use and Alcohol-Related Problems." *Journal of Adolescent Research* 17:346–363.

Masters, K. S., and S. A. Hooker. 2013. "Religiousness/Spirituality, Cardiovascular Disease, and Cancer: Cultural Integration for Health Research and Intervention." *Journal of Consulting and Clinical Psychology* 81:206–216.

Mauss, A. L. 1969. "Dimensions of Religious Defection." *Review of Religious Research* 10:128–135.

Mayer, E., B. A. Kosmin, and A. Keysar. 2002. *American Jewish Identity Survey: AJIS 2001 Report*. New York: Center for Jewish Studies, The Graduate Center of the City University of New York.

Mayrl, D., and A. Saperstein. 2013. "When White People Report Racial Discrimination: The Role of Region, Religion, and Politics." *Social Science Research* 42:742–754.

Mayrl, D., and J. E. Uecker. 2011. "Higher Education and Religious Liberalization among Young Adults." *Social Forces* 90:181–208.

Mazar, N., O. Amir, and D. Ariely. 2008. "The Dishonesty of Honest People: A Theory of Self-Concept Maintenance." *Journal of Marketing Research* 45:633–644.

McCarthy, J. 2014. "Gallup Poll: Same-Sex Marriage Support Reaches New High at 55%." http://www.gallup.com/poll/169640/sex-marriage-support-reaches-new-high.aspx.

McClain, E. W. 1978. "Personality Differences between Intrinsically Religious and Non-religious Students: A Factor Analytic Study." *Journal of Personality Assessment* 42:159–166.

McCleary, R. M., and R. J. Barro. 2006. "Religion and Political Economy in an International Panel." *Journal for the Scientific Study of Religion* 45:149–175.

McCrae, R. R. 1987. "Creativity, Divergent Thinking, and Openness to Experience." *Journal of Personality and Social Psychology* 52:1258–1265.

———. 1996. "Social Consequences of Experiential Openness." *Psychological Bulletin* 120:323–337.

McCright, A., and R. Dunlap. 2011. "The Politicization of Climate Change and Polarization in the American Public's Views of Global Warming, 2001–2010." *Sociological Quarterly* 52:155–194.

McCullough, M. E., W. T. Hoyt, D. B. Larson, H. G. Koenig, and C. Thoresen. 2000. "Religious Involvement and Mortality: A Meta-analytic Review." *Health Psychology* 19:211–222.

McCullough, M. E., J. A. Tsang, and S. Brion. 2005. "Personality Traits in Adolescence as Predictors of Religiousness in Early Adulthood: Findings from the Terman Longitudinal Study." *Personality and Social Psychology Bulletin* 29:908–991.

McCullough, M. E., and B. L. B. Willoughby. 2009. "Religion, Self-Regulation, and Self-Control: Associations, Explanations, and Implications." *Psychological Bulletin* 135:69–93.

McGreal, I. P. 1995. *Great Thinkers of the Eastern World: The Major Thinkers and the Philosophical and Religious Classics of China, India, Japan, Korea, and the World of Islam.* New York: HarperCollins.

McKitrick, M. A., J. S. Landres, M. Ottoni-Wilhelm, and A. D. Hayat. 2013. *Connected to Give: Faith Communities. Key Findings from the National Study of American Religious Giving.* Los Angeles: Jumpstart Labs.

McLeod, H. 2003. "Introduction." In *The Decline of Christendom in Western Europe, 1750–2000*, edited by H. McLeod and W. Ustorf, 1–26. Cambridge: Cambridge University Press.

Mehta, H. 2013. *What Percentage of Prisoners Are Atheists? It's a Lot Smaller Than We Ever Imagined.* Friendly Atheist. http://www.patheos.com/blogs/friendlyatheist/2013/07/16/what-percentage-of-prisoners-are-atheists-its-a-lot-smaller-than-we-ever-imagined/.

Meier, A. 2003. "Adolescents' Transition to First Intercourse, Religiosity, and Attitudes about Sex." *Social Forces* 81:1031–1052.

Meijers, G. 2012. "Report West African Humanist Conference, Ghana, November 2012." new. iheyo.org/sites/defulat/files/ghana2012/conferencereportghana2012.pdf.

Meltzer, H. I., N. Dogra, P. Vostanis, and T, Ford. 2011. "Religiosity and the Mental Health of Adolescents in Great Britain." *Mental Health, Religion and Culture* 14:703–713.

Mencken, F. C., and B. Fitz. 2013. "Image of God and Community Volunteering among Religious Adherents in the United States." *Review of Religious Research* 55:491–508.

Merino, S. 2012. "Irreligious Socialization? The Adult Religious Preferences of Individuals Raised with No Religion." *Secularism and Nonreligion* 1:1–16.

———. 2013. "Religious Social Networks and Volunteering: Examining Recruitment via Close Ties." *Review of Religious Research* 55:509–527.

Mesch, D. J., Z. Moore, and M. Ottoni-Wilhelm. 2010. "Does Jewish Philanthropy Differ by Sex and Type of Giving?" *Nashim: A Journal of Jewish Women's Studies and Gender Issues* 20 (1): 80–96.

Middleton, R., and S. Putney. 1962. "Religion, Normative Standards and Behavior. *Sociometry* 25:141–152.

Midlarsky, E., S. F. Jones, and R. P. Corley. 2005. "Personality Correlates of Heroic Rescue during the Holocaust." *Journal of Personality* 73:907–934.

Milgram, S. 1965. "Some Conditions of Obedience and Disobedience to Authority." *Human Relations* 18:57–76.

Miller, A. S. 1996. "The Influence of Religious Affiliation on the Clustering of Social Attitudes." *Review of Religious Research* 37:123.

Miller, A., and R. Stark. 2002. "Gender and Religiousness: Can Socialization Explanations Be Saved?" *American Journal of Sociology* 107:1399–1423.

Miller, J. D., E. C. Scott, and S. Okamoto. 2006. "Public Acceptance of Evolution." *Science* 313:765–766.

Miller, L., P. Wickramaratne, M. J. Gameroff, M. Sage, C. E. Tenke, and M. M. Weissman. 2012. "Religiosity and Major Depression in Adults at High Risk: A Ten-Year Prospective Study." *American Journal of Psychiatry* 169:89–94.

Mochon, D., M. I. Norton, and D. Ariely. 2011. "Who Benefits from Religion?" *Social Indicators Research* 101:1–15.

Momen, M. 1999. *The Phenomenon of Religion: A Thematic Approach*. Oxford: Oneworld Publications.

Monsma, S. V. 2007. "Religion and Philanthropic Giving and Volunteering: Building Blocks for Civic Responsibility. *Interdisciplinary Journal of Research on Religion*. 3, 1–28. http://www.religjournal.com/pdf/ijrr03001.pdf.

Moore, A. K., A. Driscoll, and L. D. Lindberg. 1998. "A Statistical Portrait of Adolescent Sex, Contraception, and Childbearing." Washington, DC: National Campaign to Prevent Teen Pregnancy.

Moossavi, N. 2007. "Secularism in Iran." In *Secularism and Secularity: Contemporary International Perspectives*, edited by B. A. Kosmin and A. Keysar, 139–147. Hartford, CT: Institute for the Study of Secularism in Society and Culture.

Mosher, W. D., L. B. Williams, and D. P. Johnson. 1992. "Religion and Fertility in the United States: New Patterns." *Demography* 29:199–214.

Motika, R. 2001. "Islam in Post-Soviet Azerbaijan." *Archives de Science Sociale des Religions* 115:111–124. http://assr.revues.org/18423.

Musick, M. A., J. W. Traphagan, H. G. Koeing, and D. B. Larson. 2000. "Spirituality in Physical Health and Aging." *Journal of Adult Development* 7 (2): 73–86.

Myers, D. G. 2009. "The Complicated Relationship between Religiosity and Social Well-Being." *Chronicle of Higher Education*, February 20. http://www.davidmyers.org/davidmyers/assets/ChronicleEssay.LTE.pdf.

Myers, D. G. 2000. "The Funds, Friends, and Faith of Happy People." *American Psychologist* 55:56–67.

Myers, S., 1996. "An Interactive Model of Religiosity Inheritance: The Importance of Family Context." *American Sociological Review* 61:858–866.

Nall, J. 2010. "Disparate Destinations, Parallel Paths: An Analysis of Contemporary Atheist and Christian Parenting Literature." In *Religion and the New Atheism: A Critical Appraisal*, edited by A. Amarasingam, 179–202. Leiden: Brill.

Narisetti, I. 2010. "Atheism and Secularity in India." In *Atheism and Secularity*, edited by P. Zuckerman, vol. 2, 139–153. Santa Barbara, CA: Praeger.

Narvaez, D., I. Getz, J. R. Rest, and S. J. Thoma. 1999. "Individual Moral Judgment and Cultural Ideologies." *Developmental Psychology* 35:478–488.

Narvaez, D., and T. Gleason. 2007. "The Relation of Moral Judgment Development and Educational Experience to Recall of Moral Narratives and Expository Texts." *Journal of Genetic Psychology* 168:251–276.

Nason-Clark, N. 1997. *The Battered Wife: How Christians Confront Family Violence*. Louisville, KY: Westminster/John Knox Press.

Nassi, A. 1981. "Survivors of the Sixties: Comparative Psychosocial and Political Development of Former Berkeley Student Activists." *American Psychologist* 36:753–761.

Naumann, L. P., S. Vazire, P. J. Rentfrow, and S. D. Gosling. 2009. "Personality Judgments Based on Physical Appearance." *Personality and Social Psychology Bulletin* 35:1661–1671.

Nehm, R. H., and I. Schonfeld. 2007. "Does Increasing Biology Teacher Knowledge about Evolution and the Nature of Science Lead to Greater Advocacy for Teaching Evolution in Schools?" *Journal of Science Teacher Education* 18:699–723.

Nelsen, H. 1990. "The Religious Identification of Children of Interfaith Marriages." *Review of Religious Research* 32:122–34.

Nelson, L. 1988. "Disaffiliation, Desacralization, and Political Values." In *Falling from Faith*, edited by D. Bromley, 122–139. Beverly Hills, CA: Sage.

Nelson, L. D., and M. I. Norton. 2005. "From Student to Superhero: Situational Primes Shape Future Helping." *Journal of Experimental Social Psychology* 41:423–430.

Nelson, L. J., L. M. Padilla-Walker, and J. S. Carroll. 2010. "'I Believe It Is Wrong but I Still Do It': A Comparison of Religious Young Men Who Do versus Do Not Use Pornography." *Psychology of Religion and Spirituality* 2:136–147.

Nemeth, R. J., and D. A. Luidens. 2003. "The Religious Basis of Charitable Giving in America: A Social Capital Perspective." In *Religion as Social Capital Producing the Common Good*, edited by C. E. Smidt, 107–120. Waco, TX: Baylor University Press.

Neuberg, S. L, C. M. Warner, S. A. Mistler, A. Berlin, E. D. Hill, J. D. Johnson, G. F. Filip-Crawford, R.E. Millsap, G. Thomas, M. Winkelman, B.J. Broome, T. J. Taylor, and J. Schober. 2014. "Religion and Intergroup Conflict: Findings from the Global Group Relations Project." *Psychological Science* 25:198–206.

Neugarten, B. L. 1979. "Time, Age, and the Life Cycle." *American Journal of Psychiatry* 136:887–894.

Newport, F., S. Agrawal, and D. Witters. 2010. *Very Religious Americans Report Less Depression, Worry*. http:// www.gallup.com/poll/144980/Religious-Americans-Report-Less-Depression-Worry.aspx.

NHK-ISSP. 2009. "Something Spiritual Attracting the Japanese." http://www.nhk.or.jp/bunken/english/reports/summary/200905/05.html.

Niose, D. 2012. *Nonbeliever Nation: The Rise of Secular Americans*. New York: Palgrave Macmillan.

Nisbet, M. 2005. "The Competition for Worldviews: Values, Information, and Public Support for Stem Cell Research." *International Journal of Public Opinion Research* 17:90–112.

Nisbet, P. A., P. R. Duberstein, Y. Conwell, and L. Seidlitz. 2000. "The Effect of Participation in Religious Activities on Suicide versus Natural Death in Adults 50 and Older." *Journal of Nervous and Mental Disease* 188:543–546.

Nordstrom, B. 2000. *Scandinavia since 1500*. Minneapolis: University of Minnesota Press.

Norenzayan, A., I. Dar-Nimrod, I. G. Hansen, and T. Proulx. 2009. "Mortality Salience and Religion: Divergent Effects on the Defense of Cultural Values for the Religious and the Non-religious." *European Journal of Social Psychology* 39:101–113.

Norenzayan, A., W. M. Gervais, and K. Trzesniewski. 2012. "Mentalizing Deficits Constrain Belief in a Personal God." *PLoS ONE* 7: e36880.

Norenzayan, A., and I. G. Hansen. 2006. "Belief in Supernatural Agents in the Face of Death." *Personality and Social Psychology Bulletin* 32:174–187.

Norris, P., and R. Inglehart. 2004. *Sacred and Secular: Religion and Politics Worldwide*. New York: Cambridge University Press.

Nyborg, H. 2008. "The Intelligence-Religiosity Nexus: A Representative Study of White Adolescent Americans." *Intelligence* 37:81–93.

Obama, B. 2006. Speech from Call to Renewal's Building a Covenant for a New America conference. June 28th, 2006. http://www.nytimes.com/2006/06/28/us/politics/2006obamaspeech. html?pagewanted=alland_r=0.

O'Connor, T. P., and M. Perreyclear. 2002. "Prison Religion in Action and Its Influence on Offender Rehabilitation." *Journal of Offender Rehabilitation* 35:11–33.

Oh, E. J., S. L. Bliss, and R. L. Williams. 2007. "Christian Fundamentalism and Prominent Sociopolitical Values among College Students in a South-Korean University." *Journal of Religion and Society* 9:1–13.

Oliner, S. P., and P. M. Oliner. 1988. *The Altruistic Personality: Rescuers of Jews in Nazi Europe*. New York: Free Press.

Olson, D. V. A. 1998. "Comment: Religious Pluralism in Contemporary U.S. Counties." *American Sociological Review* 63:759–760.

———. 1999. "Religious Pluralism and US Church Membership: A Reassessment." *Sociology of Religion* 60:149–173.

Olson, L. R., and J. C. Green. 2006. "The Religion Gap." *PS: Political Science and Politics* 39:455–459.

Oman, D., and D. Reed. 1998. "Religion and Mortality among the Community-Dwelling Elderly." *American Journal of Public Health* 88:1469–1475.

Onapajo, H. 2012. "Politics for God: Religion, Politics and Conflict in Democratic Nigeria." *Journal of Pan African Studies* 4 (9): 42–66.

O'Reilly, B. 2006. *Culture Warrior*. New York: Broadway Books.

Ottoni-Wilhelm, M. 2010. "Giving to Organizations That Help People in Need: Differences across Denominational Identities." *Journal for the Scientific Study of Religion* 731: 389–412.

Ozorak, E. W. 1989. "Social and Cognitive Influences on the Development of Religious Beliefs and Commitment in Adolescence." *Journal for the Scientific Study of Religion* 28:448–463.

Palm, I. and J. Trost. 2000. "Family and Religion in Sweden." In *Family, Religion, and Social Change in Diverse Societies*, edited by Sharon Houseknecht and Jerry Pankurst, 107–120. New York: Oxford University Press.

Paloutzian, R. F. and C. W. Ellison. 1982. "Loneliness, Spiritual Well-Being, and Quality of Life." In *Loneliness: A Sourcebook of Current Theory, Research and Therapy*, edited by L. A. Peplau and D. Perlman, 224–237. New York: Wiley.

Pargament, K. I. 1997. *The Psychology of Religion and Coping*. New York: Guilford Press.

Pargament, K. I., H. G. Koenig, N. Tarakeshwar, and J. Hahn. 2001. "Religious Struggle as a Predictor of Mortality among Medically Ill Elderly Patients: A Two-Year Longitudinal Study." *Archives of Internal Medicine* 161:1881–1885.

Park, C. L., D. Edmonson, and T. O. Blank. 2009. "Religious and Non-religious Pathways to Stress-Related Growth in Cancer Survivors." *Applied Psychology: Health and Well-Being* 1:321–335.

Park, J. Z., and C. Smith. 2000. "'To Whom Much Has Been Given . . .': Religious Capital and Community Voluntarism among Churchgoing Protestants." *Journal for the Scientific Study of Religion* 39:272–286.

Pasquale, F. L. 2007a. "Unbelief and Irreligion, Empirical Study and Neglect Of." In *The New Encyclopedia of Unbelief*, edited by Tom Flynn, 760–766. Amherst, NY: Prometheus Books.

———. 2007b. "The 'Nonreligious' in the American Northwest." In *Secularism & Secularity: Contemporary International Perspectives*, edited by Barry A. Kosmin and Ariela Keysar, 41-58. Hartford, CT: Institute for the Study of Secularism in Society and Culture.

———. 2010a. "An Assessment of the Role of Early Parental Loss in the Adoption of Atheism or Irreligion." *Archives for the Psychology of Religion* 32:375–396.

———. 2010b. "A Portrait of Secular Group Affiliates." In *Atheism and Secularity*, edited by Phil Zuckerman, vol. 1, 43–88. Santa Barbara, CA: Praeger.

Pasquale, F. L. and Barry A. Kosmin. 2013. "Atheism and the Secularization Thesis." In *The Oxford Handbook of Atheism*, edited by Stephen Bullivant and Michael Ruse, 451–467. Oxford: Oxford University Press.

Patel, C., M. G. Marmot, D. J. Terry, M. Carruthers, B. Hunt, and M. Patel. 1985. "Trial of Relaxation in Reducing Coronary Risk: Four Year Follow Up." *British Medical Journal* 290:1103–1106.

Patrick, J. H., and J. M. Kinney. 2003. "Why Believe? The Effects of Religious Beliefs on Emotional Well Being." *Journal of Religious Gerontology* 14:153–170.

Paul, G. 2005. "Cross-National Correlations of Quantifiable Societal Health with Popular Religiosity and Secularism in the Prosperous Democracies." *Journal of Religion and Society* 7: 1–17.

———. 2009. "The Chronic Dependence of Popular Religiosity upon Dysfunctional Psychosociological Conditions." *Evolutionary Psychology* 7:398–441.

———. 2010. "The Evolution of Popular Religiosity and Secularism: How First World Statistics Reveal Why Religion Exists, Why It Has Become Popular, and Why the Most Successful Democracies Are the Most Secular." In *Atheism and Secularity*, edited by P. Zuckerman, vol. 1, 149–208. Santa Barbara, CA: Praeger ABC-CLIO.

Pearce, L., and M. L. Denton. 2010. *A Faith of Their Own*. New York: Oxford University Press.

Pelham, B., and S. Crabtree. 2008. "Worldwide, Highly Religious More Likely to Help Others." http://www.gallup.com/poll/111013/worldwide-highly-religious-more-likely-help-others.aspx.

Pelto, P. J. 1968. "The Differences between 'Tight' and 'Loose' Societies." *Transaction* 5:37–40.

Pennycook, G., J. A. Cheyne, N. Barr, D. J. Koehler, and J. A. Fugelsang. 2013. "Cognitive Style and Religiosity: The Role of Conflict Detection." *Memory and Cognition* 42:1–10.

Pennycook, G., J. A. Cheyne, D. J. Koehler, and J. A. Fugelsang. 2013. "Belief Bias during Reasoning among Religious Believers and Skeptics." *Psychonomic Bulletin and Review* 20:806–811.

Pennycook, G., J. A. Cheyne, P. Seli, D. J. Koehler, and J. A. Fugelsang. 2012. "Analytic Cognitive Style Predicts Religious and Paranormal Belief." *Cognition* 123:335–346.

Pepper, M., T. Jackson, and D. Uzzell. 2010. "A Study of Multidimensional Religion Constructs and Values in the United Kingdom." *Journal for the Scientific Study of Religion* 49:127–146.

Perry, E., J. Davis, and R. Doyle. 1980. "Toward a Typology of Unchurched Protestants." *Review of Religious Research* 21:388–404.

Perry, S. L. 2014. "Hoping for a Godly White Family: How Desire for Religious Heritage Affects Whites' Attitudes toward Interracial Marriage." *Journal for the Scientific Study of Religion* 53:202–218.

Petersen, L., and G. V. Donnennworth. 1998. "Religion and Declining Support for Traditional Beliefs about Gender Roles and Homosexual Rights." *Sociology of Religion* 59:353–371.

Peterson, C., and M. E. P. Seligman. 2004. *Character Strengths and Virtues: A Handbook and Classification.* Washington, DC: American Psychological Association.

Pettersson, T. 1991. "Religion and Criminality: Structural Relationships between Church Involvement and Crime Rates in Contemporary Sweden." *Journal for the Scientific Study of Religion* 30:279–291.

The Pew Forum on Religion and Public Life. 2002. "Americans Struggle with Religion's Role at Home and Abroad." http://www.people-press.org/2002/03/20/part-1-religion-in-america/

———. 2004. "Religion and the Environment: Polls Show Strong Backing for Environmental Protection across Religious Groups." http://www.pewforum.org/Politics-and-Elections/ Religion-and-the-Environment-Polls-Show-Strong-Backing-for-Environmental-Protection- Across-Religious-Groups.aspx

———. 2007. "Science in America: Religious Belief and Public Attitudes." http://pewforum.org/ Science-and-Bioethics/Science-in-America-Religious-Belief-and-Public-Attitudes.aspx

———. 2008. "U.S. Religious Landscape Survey." http://religions.pewforum.org/pdf/report- religious-landscape-study-full.pdf

———. 2009a. "Global Restrictions on Religion." http://www.pewforum.org/Government/ Global-Restrictions-on-Religion.aspx.

———. 2009b. "The Religious Dimensions of the Torture Debate." http://www.pewforum. org/2009/04/29/the-religious-dimensions-of-the-torture-debate/

———. 2010. "Most Continue to Favor Gays Serving Openly in the Military." http://www.pew- forum.org/2010/11/29/most-continue-to-favor-gays-serving-openly-in-military/

———. 2011a. "Rising Restrictions on Religion." http://www.pewforum.org/Government/ Rising-Restrictions-on-Religion.aspx

———. 2011b. "The Tea Party and Religion." http://www.pewforum.org/Politics-and-Elections/ Tea-Party-and-Religion.aspx

———. 2012a. "Faith on the Hill: The Religious Composition of the 113th Congress." http://www. pewforum.org/2012/11/16/faith-on-the-hill-the-religious-composition-of-the-113th-congress/

———. 2012b. "The Global Religious Landscape: A Report on the Size and Distribution of the World's Major Religious Groups as of 2010." http://www.pewforum.org/files/2014/01/global- religion-full.pdf

———. 2012c. "More See 'Too Much' Religious Talk by Politicians." http://www.pewforum.org/ Politics-and-Elections/more-see-too-much-religious-talk-by-politicians.aspx

The Pew Forum on Religion and Public Life. 2012d. "'Nones' on the Rise: One-in-Five Adults Have No Religious Affiliation." http://www.pewforum.org/uploadedFiles/Topics/Religious_Affiliation/ Unaffiliated/NonesOnTheRise-full.pdf.

———. 2012e. "Partisan Polarization Surges in Bush, Obama Years: Section 6: Religion and Social Values." http://www.people-press.org/2012/06/04/section-6-religion-and-social-values/.

———. 2014a. "Public Sees Religion's Influence Waning." http://www.pewforum.org/2014/09/22/section-3-social-political-issues/

———. 2014b. "Religion in Latin America: Widespread Change in a Historically Catholic Region." http://www.pewforum.org/files/2014/11/Religion-in-Latin-America-11-12-PM-full-PDF.pdf

———. 2014c. "Teaching the Children: Sharp Ideological Differences, Some Common Ground." http://www.people-press.org/2014/09/18/teaching-the-children-sharp-ideological-differences-some-common-ground/

———. 2015. "America's Changing Religious Landscape." www.pewforum.org/files/2015/05/RLS-08-26-full-report.pdf.

Phan, P. C. 2000. "Doing Theology in the Context of Mission: Lessons from Alexandre de Rhodes, S.J." *Gregorianum-Roma* 81:723–749.

Phelps, A. C., P. K. Maciejewski, M. Nilsson, T. A. Balboni, A. A. Wright, M. E. Paulk, E. Trice, D. Schrag, J. R. Peteet, S. D. Block, and H. G. Prigerson. 2009. "Religious Coping and Use of Intensive Life-Prolonging Care Near Death in Patients with Advanced Cancer." *JAMA* 301:1140–1147.

Piazza, J. 2012. "'If You Love Me Keep My Commandments': Religiosity Increases Preference for Rule-Based Moral Arguments." *International Journal for the Psychology of Religion* 22:285–302.

Piazza, J., and J. F. Landy. 2013. "'Lean Not on Your Own Understanding': Belief That Morality Is Founded on Divine Authority and Non-utilitarian Moral Judgments." *Judgment and Decision Making* 8:639–661.

Piedmont, R. L. 1999. "Does Spirituality Represent the Sixth Factor of Personality? Spiritual Transcendence and the Five-Factor Model." *Journal of Personality* 67:985–1013.

Plaat, J. 2002. "Christian and Non-Christian Religiosity in Estonia in the 1990s: Comparison of Estonians and Other Ethnic Groups." *Pro Ethnologia* 14. http://www.erm.ee/pdf/pro14/plaat.pdf.

Pollack, D. 2002. "The Change in Religion and Church in Eastern Germany after 1989: A Research Note." *Sociology of Religion* 63:373–387.

———. 2008. "Introduction: Religious Change in Modern Societies: Perspectives Offered by the Sociology of Religion." In *The Role of Religion in Modern Societies*, edited by Detlef Pollack and Daniel V. A. Olson, 1–21. New York: Routledge.

Population Reference Bureau. 2007. "2007 World Population Fact Sheet." http://www.prb.org/Publications/Datasheets/2007/2007WorldPopulationDataSheet.aspx

Post, A. 1943. *Popular Freethought in America, 1825–1850*. New York: Columbia University Press.

Powell, L. H., L. Shahabi, and C. E. Thoresen. 2003. "Religion and Spirituality: Linkages to Physical Health." *American Psychologist* 58:36–52.

Poyraz, B. 2005. "The Turkish State and Alevis: Changing Parameters of an Uneasy Relationship." *Middle Eastern Studies* 41:503–516.

Prager, D. 2011. "No God, No Moral Society." JewishJournal.com, February 2. http://www.jewishjournal.com/dennis_prager/article/no_god_no_moral_society_20110202

Presser, S., and M. Chaves. 2007. "Is Religious Service Attendance Declining?" *Journal for the Scientific Study of Religion* 46:417–423.

Presser, S., and L. Stinson. 1998. "Data Collection and Social Desirability Bias in Self-Reported Religious Attendance." *American Sociological Review* 63:137–145.

Preston, J. L., and N. Epley. 2009. "Science and God: An Automatic Opposition between Ultimate Explanations." *Journal of Experimental Social Psychology* 45:238–241.

Preston, J. L., and R. S. Ritter. 2013. "Different Effects of Religion and God on Prosociality with the Ingroup and Outgroup." *Personality and Social Psychology Bulletin* 39:1471–1483.

Preston, J. L., R. S. Ritter, and J. I. Hernandez. 2010. "Principles of Religious Pro-sociality: A Review and Reformulation." *Social and Personality Psychology Compass* 4:574–590.

Pruyser, P. W. 1974. "Problems of Definition and Conception in the Psychological Study of Religious Unbelief." In *Changing Perspectives in the Scientific Study of Religion*, edited by Allan W. Eister, 185–200. New York: Wiley.

Public Religion Research Institute. 2010. "Religion and the Tea Party in the 2010 Election" http://publicreligion.org/site/wp-content/uploads/2010/05/Religion-and-the-Tea-Party-in-the-2010-Election-American-Values-Survey.pdf

———. 2011. "The 2011 American Values Survey." http://publicreligion.org/site/wp-content/uploads/2011/11/PRRI-2011-American-Values-Survey-Web.pdf

———. 2012. "The 2012 American Values Survey." publicreligion.org/site/wp-content/uploads/2012/10/AVS-2012-Pre-election-Report-for-Web.pdf.

———. 2013a. "Do Americans Believe Capitalism and Government Are Working? Religious Left, Religious Right and the Future of the Economic Debate." http://publicreligion.org/site/wp-content/uploads/2013/07/2013-Economic-Values-Report-Final-.pdf

———. 2013b. "General public, Christian young adults divided on marijuana legalization." http://publicreligion.org/research/2013/04/april-2013-prri-rns-survey/#.UhIfaNIsk3Q

———. 2013c. "Individual vs. Societal Responsibility for Helping the Poor." http://publicreligion.org/research/graphic-of-the-week/intrepretations/.

———. 2014: "Economic Insecurity, Rising Inequality, and Doubts about the Future: Findings from the 2014 American Values Survey." http://publicreligion.org/site/wp-content/uploads/2014/09/AVS-web.pdf

Putnam, R. D. 2000. *Bowling Alone: The Collapse and Revival of American Community*. New York: Simon and Schuster.

Putnam, R. D., and D. Campbell. 2010. *American Grace: How Religion Divides and Unites Us*. New York: Simon and Schuster.

Quack, J. 2012. *Disenchanting India: Organized Rationalism and Criticism of Religion in India*. New York: Oxford University Press.

———. 2013. "India." In *The Oxford Handbook of Atheism*, edited by Stephen Bullivant and Michael Ruse, 651–664. Oxford: Oxford University Press.

———. 2014. "Outline of a Relational Approach to 'Nonreligion.'" *Method and Theory in the Study of Religion* 26:439–469.

Randolph-Seng, B., and M. E. Nielsen. 2007. "Honesty: One Effect of Primed Religious Representations." *International Journal for the Psychology of Religion* 17:303–315.

Rasic, D., S. Belik, B. Elias, L. Katz, M. Enns, and J. Sareen. 2009. "Spirituality, Religion and Suicidal Behavior in a Nationally Representative Sample." *Journal of Affective Disorders* 114:32–40.

Reader, I. J. 2005. "Of Religion, Nationalism and Ideology: Analysing the Development of Religious Studies in Japan." *Social Science Japan Journal* 8 (1): 119–124.

———. 2012. "Secularisation, R.I.P.? Nonsense! The 'Rush Hour Away from the Gods' and the Decline of Religion in Contemporary Japan." *Journal of Religion in Japan* 1 (1): 7–36.

Rees, T. J. 2009a. "The Happiness Smile"[Web log message]. http://epiphenom.fieldofscience. com/2009/08/happiness-smile.html.

———. 2009b. "Is Personal Insecurity a Cause of Cross-National Differences in the Intensity of Religious Belief?" *Journal of Religion and Society* 11:1–24.

Regnerus, M. D. 2007. *Forbidden Fruit: Sex and Religion in the Lives of American Teenagers.* New York: Oxford University Press.

Regnerus, M. D., C. Smith, and D. Sikkink. 1998. "Who Gives to the Poor? The Influence of Religious Tradition and Political Location on the Personal Generosity of Americans toward the Poor." *Journal for the Scientific Study of Religion* 37:481–493.

Reiss, S. 2000a. *Who Am I? The 16 Basic Desires That Motivate Our Behavior and Define Our Personality.* New York: Jeremy P. Tarcher/Putnam.

———. 2000b. "Why People Turn to Religion: A Motivational Analysis." *Journal for the Scientific Study of Religion* 39:47–52.

———. 2004. "Multifaceted Nature of Intrinsic Motivation: The Theory of 16 Basic Desires." *Review of General Psychology* 8:179–193.

Reiss, S., and S. M. Havercamp. 1998. "Toward a Comprehensive Assessment of Fundamental Motivation: Factor Structure of the Reiss Profiles." *Psychological Assessment* 10 (2): 97–106.

Reitsma, J., P. Scheepers, and M. te Grotenhuis. 2006. "Dimensions of Individual Religiosity and Charity: Cross-National Effect Differences in European Countries?" *Review of Religious Research* 47:347–362.

Rest, J. R., D. Narvaez, M. Bebeau, and S. Thoma. 1999. *Postconventional Moral Thinking: A Neo-Kohlbergian Approach.* Mahwah, NJ: Erlbaum.

Rice, T. W. 2003. "Believe It or Not: Religious and Other Paranormal Beliefs in the United States." *Journal for the Scientific Study of Religion* 42:95–106.

Richards, P. S., and M. L. Davison. 1992. "Religious Bias in Moral Development Research: A Psychometric Investigation." *Journal for the Scientific Study of Religion* 31:467–485.

Riekki, T., M. Lindeman, M. Aleneff, A. Halme, and A. Nuortimo. 2013. "Paranormal and Religious Believers Are More Prone to Illusory Face Perception Than Skeptics and Non-believers." *Applied Cognitive Psychology* 27:150–155.

Rigney, D., and T. J. Hoffman. 1993. "Is American Catholicism Anti-intellectual?" *Journal for the Scientific Study of Religion* 32:211–222.

Riley, J., S. Best, and B. G. Charlton. 2005. "Religious Believers and Strong Atheists May Both Be Less Depressed Than Existentially-Uncertain People." *Quarterly Journal of Medicine* 98:840.

Ritter, R. S., and J. L. Preston. 2011. "Gross Gods and Icky Atheism: Disgust Response to Rejected Religious Beliefs." *Journal of Experimental Social Psychology* 47:1225–1230.

Ritter, R. S., J. L. Preston, and I. Hernandez. 2014. "Happy Tweets: Christians Are Happier, More Socially Connected, and Less Analytical Than Atheists on Twitter." *Social Psychological and Personality Science* 5:243–249.

Robertson, R. 1970. *The Sociological Interpretation of Religion.* New York: Schocken.

Roccas, S. 2005. "Religion and Value Systems." *Journal of Social Issues* 61:747–759.

Roemer, M. K. 2009. "Religious Affiliation in Japan: Untangling the Enigma." *Review of Religious Research* 50:298–300.

———. 2010. "Atheism and Secularity in Modern Japan." In *Atheism and Secularity*, edited by P. Zuckerman, vol. 2, 23–44. Santa Barbara, CA: Praeger.

Rokeach, M. 1969. "Part I. Value Systems in Religion." *Review of Religious Research* 11:3–23.

———. 1973. *The Nature of Human Values*. New York: Free Press.

Roof, W. C., and K. Hadaway. 1977. "Shifts in Religious Preference—the Mid-Seventies." *Journal for the Scientific Study of Religion* 16:409–412.

———. 1979. "Denominational Switching in the Seventies: Going beyond Stark and Glock." *Journal for the Scientific Study of Religion* 18: 363–379.

Roof, W. C., and W. McKinney. 1987. *American Mainline Religion*. New Brunswick, NJ: Rutgers University Press.

Roozen, D. 1980. "Church Dropouts: Changing Patterns of Disengagement and Re-entry." *Review of Religious Research* 21:427–450.

Rose, S. 2005. "Going Too Far? Sex, Sin, and Social Policy." *Social Forces* 84: 1207–1232.

Rosenkranz, P., and B. G. Charlton. 2013. "Individual Differences in Existential Orientation: Empathizing and Systemizing Explain the Sex Difference in Religious Orientation and Science Acceptance." *Archive for the Psychology of Religion* 35:119–146.

Ross, C. E. 1990. "Religion and Psychological Distress." *Journal for the Scientific Study of Religion* 29:236–245

Rossi, I., and M. Rossi. 2009. "Religiosity: A Comparison between Latin Europe and Latin America." In *The International Social Survey Programme, 1984–2009: Charting the Globe*, edited by Max Haller, Roger Jowell, and Tom W. Smith, 302–312. New York: Routledge.

Rostosky, S. S., M. D. Regnerus, and M. L. C. Wright. 2003. "Coital Debut: The Role of Religiosity and Sex Attitudes in the Add Health Survey." *Journal of Sex Research* 40:358–367.

Rostosky, S. S., B. L. Wilcox, M. L. Comer Wright, and B. A. Randall. 2004. "The Impact of Religiosity on Adolescent Sexual Behavior: A Review of the Evidence." *Journal of Adolescent Research* 19:677–697.

Rounding, K., A. Lee, J. A. Jacobson, and L. J. Ji. 2012. "Religion Replenishes Self-Control." *Psychological Science* 23:635–642.

Rowatt, W. C., L. M. Franklin, and M. Cotton. 2005. "Patterns and Personality Correlates of Implicit and Explicit Attitudes toward Christians and Muslims." *Journal for the Scientific Study of Religion* 44:29–43.

Rowatt, W. C., A. Ottenbreit, K. P. Nesselroade Jr., and P. A. Cunningham. 2002. "On Being Holier-Than-Thou or Humbler-Than-Thee: A Social-Psychological Perspective on Religiousness and Humility." *Journal for the Scientific Study of Religion* 41:227–237.

Rowatt, W. C., and D. P. Schmitt. 2003. "Associations between Religious Orientation and Varieties of Sexual Experience." *Journal for the Scientific Study of Religion* 42:455–465.

Rubin, Z., and L. A. Peplau. 1975. "Who Believes in a Just World?" *Journal of Social Issues* 31:65–89.

Ruiter, S., and F. van Tubergen. 2009. "Religious Attendance in Cross-National Perspective: A Multilevel Analysis of 60 Countries." *American Journal of Sociology* 115: 863–895.

Rutjens, B. T., J. van der Pligt, and F. van Harreveld. 2010. "Deus or Darwin: Randomness and Belief in Theories about the Origin of Life." *Journal of Experimental Social Psychology* 46:1078–1080.

Rutjens, B. T., F. van Harreveld, and J. van der Pligt. 2013. "Step by Step: Finding Compensatory Order in Science." *Current Directions in Psychological Science* 22:250–255.

Ryan, C., D. Huebner, R. M. Diaz, and J. Sanchez. 2009. "Family Rejection as a Predictor of Negative Health Outcomes in White and Latino Lesbian, Gay, and Bisexual Young Adults." *Pediatrics* 123:346–352.

Salas-Wright, C. P., M. G. Vaughn, D. R. Hodge, and B. E. Perron. 2012. "Religiosity Profiles of American Youth in Relation to Substance Use, Violence, and Delinquency." *Journal of Youth and Adolescence* 41: 1560–1575.

Sandomirsky, S., and J. Wilson. 1990. "Processes of Disaffiliation: Religious Mobility among Men and Women." *Social Forces* 68:1211–1229.

Sanger, M. 1971 [1938]. *The Autobiography of Margaret Sanger*. Mineola, NY: Dover.

Saroglou, V. 2002. "Religion and the Five Factors of Personality: A Meta-analytic Review." *Personality and Individual Differences* 32:15–25.

———. 2010. "Religiousness as a Cultural Adaptation of Basic Traits: A Five-Factor Model Perspective." *Personality and Social Psychology Review* 14:108–125.

Saroglou, V., O. Corneille, and P. Van Cappellen. 2009. "'Speak, Lord, Your Servant Is Listening': Religious Priming Activates Submissive Thoughts and Behaviors." *International Journal for the Psychology of Religion* 19:143–154.

Saroglou, V., V. Delpierre, and R. Dernelle. 2004. "Values and Religiosity: A Meta-analysis of Studies Using Schwartz's Model." *Personality and Individual Differences* 37:721–734.

Saroglou, V., I. Pichon, L. Trompette, M. Verschueren, and R. Dernelle. 2005. "Pro-social Behavior and Religion: New Evidence Based on Projective Measures and Peer Ratings." *Journal for the Scientific Study of Religion* 44:323–348.

Saslow, L. R., R. Willer, M. Feinberg, P. K. Piff, K. Clark, D. Keltner, and S. R. Saturn. 2013. "My Brother's Keeper? Compassion Predicts Generosity among Less Religious Individuals." *Social Psychological and Personality Science* 41:31–38.

Scheepers, P., M. Gijsberts, and E. Hello. 2002. "Religiosity and Prejudice against Ethnic Minorities in Europe: Cross-National Tests on a Controversial Relationship." *Review of Religious Research* 43:242–265.

Scheve, K., and D. Stasavage. 2006. "Religion and Preferences for Social Insurance." *Journal of Public Economics* 1:255–286.

Schielke, S. 2013. "The Islamic World." In *The Oxford Handbook of Atheism*, edited by Stephen Bullivant and Michael Ruse, 638–650. Oxford: Oxford University Press.

Schmidt, T., and M. Wohlrab-Sahr. 2003. "Still the Most Areligious Part of the World: Developments in the Religious Field in Eastern Germany since 1990." *International Journal of Practical Theology* 7 (1): 86–100.

Schnell, T., and W. J. F. Keenan. 2011. "Meaning-Making in an Atheist World." *Archive for the Psychology of Religion* 33:55–78.

Schulman, Alex. 2011. *The Secular Contract: The Politics of Enlightenment*. New York: Continuum.

Schumaker, J. F. 1992. "Mental Health Consequences of Irreligion." In *Religion and Mental Health*, edited by John F. Schumaker, 54–69. Oxford: Oxford University Press.

Schuurmans-Stekhoven, J. B. 2011. "Is It God or Just the Data That Moves in Mysterious Ways? How Wellbeing Research May Be Mistaking Faith for Virtue." *Social Indicators Research* 100:313–330.

———. 2013. "'As a Shepherd Divideth His Sheep from the Goats': Does the Daily Spiritual Experiences Scale Encapsulate Separable Theistic and Civility Components?" *Social Indicators Research* 110:131–146.

Schwadel, P. 2014. "Birth Cohort Changes in the Association between College Education and Religious Non-affiliation." *Social Forces* 93: 719–746.

Schwartz, S. H. 1992. "Universals in the Content and Structure of Values: Theoretical Advances and Empirical Tests in 20 Countries." *Advances in Experimental Psychology* 25:1–65.

Schwartz, S. H., and Sipke Huismans. 1995. "Value Priorities and Religiosity in Four Western Religions." *Social Psychology Quarterly* 58:88–107.

Sedikides, C., and J. E. Gebauer. 2010. "Religiosity as Self-Enhancement: A Meta-analysis of the Relation between Socially Desirable Responding and Religiosity." *Personality and Social Psychology Review* 14:17–36.

Shanahan, D. 1992. *Toward a Genealogy of Individualism.* Amherst: University of Massachusetts Press.

Shand, J. 1998. "The Decline of Traditional Christian Beliefs in Germany." *Sociology of Religion* 59:179–184.

Shariff, A. F., and A. Norenzayan. 2011. "Mean Gods Make Good People: Different Views of God Predict Cheating Behavior." *International Journal for the Psychology of Religion* 21:85–96.

Shariff, A. F., and A. Norenzayan. 2007. "God Is Watching You: Priming God Concepts Increases Pro-social Behavior in an Anonymous Economic Game." *Psychological Science* 18:803–809.

Sharot, S. 2002. "Beyond Christianity: A Critique of the Rational Choice Theory of Religion from a Weberian and Comparative Religions Perspective." *Sociology of Religion* 63:427–454.

Shaver, P., M. Lenauer, and S. Sadd. 1980. "Religiousness, Conversion, and Subjective Well-Being: The 'Healthy-Minded' Religion of Modern American Women." *American Journal of Psychiatry* 137:1563–1568.

Shenberger, J. M., B. A. Smith, and M. A. Zárate. 2014. "The Effect of Religious Imagery in a Risk-Taking Paradigm." *Peace and Conflict: Journal of Peace Psychology* 20:150–158.

Shenhav A., D. G. Rand, and J. D. Greene. 2011. "Divine Intuition: Cognitive Style Influences Belief in God." *Journal of Experimental Psychology: General* 141:423–428.

Sherkat, D. E. 1991. "Leaving the Faith: Testing Theories of Religious Switching Using Survival Models." *Social Science Research* 20:171–187.

———. 2000. "'That They Be Keepers of the Home': The Effect of Conservative Religion on Early and Late Transitions into Housewifery." *Review of Religious Research* 41:344–358.

———. 2002. "Sexuality and Religious Commitment in the United States: An Empirical Examination." *Journal for the Scientific Study of Religion* 41:313–323.

———. 2003. "Religious Socialization: Sources of Influence and Influences of Agency." In *Handbook of the Sociology of Religion*, edited by Michele Dillon, 151–163. New York: Cambridge University Press.

———, 2010. "Religion and Verbal Ability." *Social Science Research* 39: 2–13.

———. 2014. *Changing Faith: The Dynamics and Consequences of Americans' Shifting Religious Identities.* New York: New York University Press.

Sherkat, D. E., and C. G. Ellison. 2007. "Structuring the Religion-Environment Connection: Identifying Religious Influence on Environmental Concern and Activism." *Journal for the Scientific Study of Religion* 46:71–83.

Sherkat, D. E., M. Powell-Williams, G. Maddox, and K. M. de Vries. 2011. "Religion, Politics, and Support for Same-Sex Marriage in the United States, 1988–2008." *Social Science Research* 40:167–180.

Sherkat, D. E., and J. Wilson. 1995. "Preferences, Constraints, and Choices in Religious Markets: An Examination of Religious Switching and Apostasy." *Social Forces* 73:993–1026.

Shermer, M. 2000. *How We Believe: The Search for God in an Age of Science.* New York: Freeman.

Shiah, Y. J., W. C. Tam, M. H. Wu, and F. Chang. 2010. "Paranormal Beliefs and Religiosity: Chinese Version of the Revised Paranormal Belief Scale." *Psychological Reports* 107:367–382.

Shimazono, S. 2008. "Individualization of Society and Religionization of Individuals: Resacralization in Postmodernity Second Modernity." *Pensamiento* 64 (242): 603–619.

Shiner, L. 1967. "The Concept of Secularization in Empirical Research." *Journal for the Scientific Study of Religion* 6:207–220.

Shor, E., and D. J. Roelfs. 2013. "The Longevity Effects of Religious and Nonreligious Participation: A Meta-analysis and Meta-regression." *Journal for the Scientific Study of Religion* 52:120–145.

Sibley, C. G., and J. Bulbulia. 2012. "Faith after an Earthquake: A Longitudinal Study of Religion and Perceived Health before and after the 2011 Christchurch New Zealand Earthquake." *PloS One* 7:1–10.

Silton, N. R., K. J. Flannelly, K. Galek, and C. G. Ellison. 2014. "Beliefs about God and Mental Health among American Adults." *Journal of Religion and Health* 53:1285–1296.

Silver, C. F., T. J. Coleman III, R. W. Hood Jr., and J. M. Holcombe. 2014. "The Six Types of Nonbelief: A Qualitative and Quantitative Study of Type and Narrative." *Mental Health, Religion and Culture* 17:990–1001.

Silver, N. 2012. "Party Identity in a Gun Cabinet." http://fivethirtyeight.blogs.nytimes.com/2012/12/18/in-gun-ownership-statistics-partisan-divide-is-sharp/?hp.

Singleton, A. 2007. "People Were Not Made to Be in God's Image: A Contemporary Overview of Secular Australians." In *Secularism & Secularity: Contemporary International Perspectives*, edited by Barry A. Kosmin and Ariela Keysar, 83–94. Hartford, CT: Institute for the Study of Secularism in Society and Culture.

Skitka, L. J., E. Mullen, T. Griffin, S. Hutchinson, and B. Chamberlin. 2002. "Dispositions, Ideological Scripts, or Motivated Correction? Understanding Ideological Differences in Attributions for Social Problems." *Journal of Personality and Social Psychology* 83:470–487.

Sloan, R. A. 2006. *Blind Faith: The Unholy Alliance of Religion and Medicine.* NewYork: St. Martin's Press.

Slomp, H. 2000. *European Politics into the Twenty-First Century: Integration and Division.* Westport, CT: Praeger.

Smart, N. 1969. *The Religious Experience of Mankind.* New York: Scribner's.

———. 2000. *Worldviews: Cross-Cultural Explorations of Human Beliefs.* Upper Saddle River, NJ: Prentice-Hall.

Smidt, C. 2005. "Religion and American Attitudes toward Islam and an Invasion of Iraq." *Sociology of Religion* 663:243–261.

Smith, C. 1998. *American Evangelicalism: Embattled and Thriving.* Chicago: University of Chicago Press.

——. 2003. *The Secular Revolution: Power, Interests, and Conflict in the Secularization of American Public Life*. Berkeley: University of California Press.

Smith, C., and M. L. Denton. 2005. *Soul Searching: The Religious and Spiritual Lives of American Teenagers*. New York: Oxford University Press.

Smith, J. 2010. "Becoming an Atheist in America: Constructing Identity and Meaning from the Rejection of Theism." *Sociology of Religion* 72:1–23.

Smith, T. B., M. E. McCullough, and J. Poll. 2003. "Religiousness and Depression: Evidence for a Main Effect and the Moderating Influence of Stressful Life Events." *Psychological Bulletin* 129:614–636.

Smith, T. W. 1996. "Environmental and Scientific Knowledge around the World." GSS Cross-National Report No. 16. http://publicdata.norc.org:41000/gss/DOCUMENTS/REPORTS/Cross_National_Reports/CNR16.pdf.

——. 2005. *Jewish Distinctiveness in America: A Statistical Portrait*. New York: American Jewish Committee.

——. 2012. "Beliefs about God across Time and Countries." National Opinion Research Center. www.norc.org/PDFs/Beliefs_about_God_Report.pdf.

Smith, W. C. 1963. *The Meaning and End of Religion: A New Approach to the Religious Traditions of Mankind*. New York: Macmillan.

Smith-Stoner, M. 2007. "End-of-life Preferences for Atheists." *Journal of Palliative Medicine* 10:923–928.

Snoep, L. 2008. "Religiousness and Happiness in Three Nations: A Research Note." *Journal of Happiness Studies* 9:207–211.

Solt, F., P. Habel, and T. Grant. 2011. "Economic Inequality, Relative Power, and Religiosity." *Social Science Quarterly* 92:447–465.

Sommerville, C. J. 2002. "Stark's Age of Faith Argument and the Secularization of Things: A Commentary." *Sociology of Religion* 63:361–372.

Sommet, J. 1983. "Religious Indifference Today: A Draft Diagnosis." In *Indifference to Religion*, edited by Jean-Pierre Jossua, Claude Geffré, and Marcus Lefèbure, 3–10. New York: Seabury Press.

Souryal, S. S. 1987. "The Religionization of a Society: The Continuing Application of Shariah Law in Saudi Arabia." *Journal for the Scientific Study of Religion* 26:429–449.

Spilka, B., R. W. Hood Jr., and R. L. Gorsuch. 1985. *The Psychology of Religion: An Empirical Approach*. Englewood Cliffs, NJ: Prentice-Hall.

Spiro, M. E. 1966. "Religion: Problems of Definition and Explanation." In *Anthropological Approaches to the Study of Religion*, edited by Michael Banton, 85–126. London: Tavistock.

Stack, S., I. Wasserman, and R. Kern. 2004. "Adult Social Bonds and Use of Internet Pornography." *Social Science Quarterly* 85:75–88.

Stark, R. 1996. *The Rise of Christianity: A Sociologist Reconsiders History*. Princeton, NJ: Princeton University Press.

——. 1999. "Secularization, R.I.P." *Sociology of Religion* 60:249–270.

——. 2005. *The Victory of Reason: How Christianity Led to Freedom, Capitalism, and Western Success*. New York: Random House.

——. 2011. *The Triumph of Christianity: How the Jesus Movement Became the World's Largest Religion*. New York: HarperOne.

Stark, R., and W. S. Bainbridge. 1985. *The Future of Religion: Secularization, Revival, and Cult Formation*. Berkeley: University of California Press.

———. 1987. *A Theory of Religion*. New York: P. Lang.

Stark, R., and R. Finke. 2000. *Acts of Faith: Explaining the Human Side of Religion*. Berkeley: University of California Press.

Stark, R., E. Hamberg, and A. S. Miller. 2005. "Exploring Spirituality and Unchurched Religions in America, Sweden, and Japan." *Journal of Contemporary Religion* 20:3–23.

Stark, R., and L. R. Iannaccone. 1994. "A Supply-Side Reinterpretation of the 'Secularization' of Europe." *Journal for the Scientific Study of Religion* 33:230–252.

Statistics South Africa. 2012. "South African Statistics, 2012." www.statssa.gov.za/publications/SAStatistics/SAStatistics2012.pdf

Stavrova, O., D. Fetchenhauera, and T. Schlössera. 2013. "Why Are Religious People Happy? The Effect of the Social Norm of Religiosity across Countries." *Social Science Research* 42:90–105.

Stepan, A. 2011. "The Multiple Secularisms of Modern Democratic and Non-democratic Regimes." In *Rethinking Secularism*, edited by Craig J. Calhoun, Mark Juergensmeyer, and Jonathan VanAntwerpen, 114–144. Oxford: Oxford University Press.

Stewart, M. 2007. "Modernity and the Alevis of Turkey: Identity, Challenges, and Change." *Journal of International Relations* 9:50–60.

Storm, I. 2014. "Civic Engagement in Britain: The Role of Religion and Inclusive Values." *European Sociological Review* 31:14–29.

Strawbridge, W. J., R. D. Cohen, S. J. Shema, and G. A. Kaplan. 1997. "Frequent Attendance at Religious Services and Mortality over 28 Years." *American Journal of Public Health* 87:957–961.

Strayhorn, J. M., and J. C. Strayhorn. 2009. "Religiosity and Teen Birth Rate in the United States." *Reproductive Health* 6:6–14.

Streib, H., R. W. Hood Jr., B. Keller, R.-M. Csöff, and C. Silver. 2009. *Deconversion: Qualitative and Quantitative Results from Cross-Cultural Research in Germany and the United States of America*. Göttingen: Vandenhoeck and Ruprecht.

Sturgis, P. W. 2010. "Faith behind Bars: An Explicit Test of the Moral Community Hypothesis in the Correctional Environment." *Journal of Offender Rehabilitation* 49:342–362.

Sturgis, P. W., and R. D. Baller. 2012. "Religiosity and Deviance: An Examination of the Moral Community and Antiasceticism Hypotheses among U.S. Adults." *Journal for the Scientific Study of Religion* 51:809–820.

Sullins, D. P. 2006. "Gender and Religion: Deconstructing Universality, Constructing Complexity." *American Journal of Sociology* 112:838–880.

Sullivan, A. R. 2010. "Mortality Differentials and Religion in the United States: Religious Affiliation and Attendance." *Journal for the Scientific Study of Religion* 49:740–753.

Swatos, W. H. Jr., and K. J. Christiano. 1999. "Secularization Theory: The Course of a Concept." *Sociology of Religion* 60:209–228.

Swatos, W. H. Jr., and D. V. A. Olson. 2000. *The Secularization Debate*. Lanham, MD: Rowan and Littlefield.

Tamney, J. B., K. Hopkins, and J. Jacovini. 1965. "A Social-Psychological Study of Religious Nonbelievers." *Social Compass* 12:177–186.

Tamney, J. B., S. Powell, and S. Johnson. 1989. "Innovation Theory and Religious Nones." *Journal for the Scientific Study of Religion* 28:216–229.

Tan, J. H. W., and C. Vogel. 2008. "Religion and Trust: An Experimental Study." *Journal of Economic Psychology* 29:832–848.

Tanaka, K. 2010. "Limitations for Measuring Religion in a Different Cultural Context: The Case of Japan." *Social Science Journal* 47:845–852.

Taylor, C. 2007. *A Secular Age*. Cambridge, MA: Belknap Press.

Tetlock, P. E. 1983. "Cognitive Style and Political Ideology." *Journal of Personality and Social Psychology* 45:118–126.

Tezcur, G. M., T. Azadarmaki, and M. Bahar. 2006. "Religious Participation among Muslims: Iranian Exceptionalism." *Critique: Critical Middle Eastern Studies* 15:217–232.

Thompson, E., and K. Remmes. 2002. "Does Masculinity Thwart Being Religious? An Examination of Older Men's Religiousness." *Journal for the Scientific Study of Religion* 41:521–532.

Thornton, A., and D. Camburn. 1989. "Religious Participation and Adolescent Sexual Behavior and Attitudes." *Journal of Marriage and the Family* 51:641–653.

Thrower, J. 1980. *The Alternative Tradition: A Study of Unbelief in the Ancient World*. The Hague: Mouton.

Tillich, P. 1959. *Theology of Culture*. London: Oxford University Press.

Tittle, C. R., and M. R. Welch. 1983. "Religiosity and Deviance: Toward a Contingency Theory of Constraining Effects." *Social Forces* 61:653–682.

Tobin, G. A., J. A. Solomon, and A. C. Karp. 2003. *Mega-gifts in American Philanthropy: General and Jewish Giving Patterns between 1995–2000*. San Francisco: Institute for Jewish and Community Research.

Tobin, G. A., and A. Weinberg. 2007a. *Mega-gifts in American Philanthropy: Giving Patterns, 2001–2003*. San Francisco: Institute for Jewish and Community Research.

———. 2007b. *Mega-gifts in Jewish Philanthropy: Giving Patterns, 2001–2003*. San Francisco: Institute for Jewish and Community Research.

Todd, D. 2009. "Metro Vancouver: Where 'No Religion' Competes with Radical Spiritual Diversity," *Vancouver Sun*, April 27, 2009, http://blogs.vancouversun.com/2009/04/27/metro-vancouver-where-no-religion-competes-with-radical-spiritual-diversity/.

Tomka, M. 2006. "Is Conventional Sociology of Religion Able to Deal with Differences between Eastern and Western European Developments?" *Social Compass* 53:251–265.

Tonigan, J. S., W. R. Miller, and C. Schermer. 2002. "Atheists, Agnostics and Alcoholics Anonymous." *Journal of Studies on Alcohol and Drugs* 63:534–541.

Tönnies, F. 2002 [1887]. *Community and Society (Gemeinschaft und Gesellschaft)*. Trans. Charles Price Loomis. Mineola, NY: Dover.

Topalli, V., T. Brezina, and M. Bernhardt. 2012. "With God on My Side: The Paradoxical Relationship between Religious Belief and Criminality among Hardcore Street Offenders." *Theoretical Criminology* 17:49–69.

Tracy, J. L., J. Hart, and J. P. Martens. 2011. "Death and Science: The Existential Underpinnings of Belief in Intelligent Design and Discomfort with Evolution." *PLoS ONE* 6: e17349.

Trân, V. T. 2010. "A Breath of Atheism in Religious Vietnam." *Social Compass* 57:311–318.

Trzebiatowska, M., and S. Bruce. 2012. *Why Are Women More Religious Than Men?* Oxford: Oxford University Press.

Tschannen, O. 1991. "The Secularization Paradigm: A Systematization." *Journal for the Scientific Study of Religion* 30:395–415.

Tsuang, M. T., W. M. Williams, J. C. Simpson, and M. J. Lyons. 2002. "Pilot Study of Spirituality and Mental Health in Twins." *American Journal of Psychiatry* 159:486–488.

Turner, B. S. 2010. *Secularization*. Los Angeles: Sage.

Unnever, J. D., F. T. Cullen, and B. K. Applegate. 2005 "Turning the Other Cheek: Reassessing the Impact of Religion on Punitive Ideology." *Justice Quarterly* 22:304–339.

U.S. Department of Health and Human Services. 1997. "Ninth special report to the U.S. congress on Alcohol and Health."

US Department of State, Bureau of Democracy. 2012. "International Religious Freedom Report, 2012: Israel and the Occupied Territories." http://www.state.gov/j/drl/rls/irf/religiousfree-dom/index.htm#wrapper

Uslaner, E. M. 2002. "Religion and Civic Engagement in Canada and the United States." *Journal for the Scientific Study of Religion* 41:239–254.

Uttley, L., S. Reynertson, L. Kenny, and L. Melling. 2013. "Miscarriage of Medicine: The Growth of Catholic Hospitals and the Threat to Reproductive Health Care." https://www.aclu.org/files/assets/growth-of-catholic-hospitals-2013.pdf.

Vail, K. E., J. Arndt, and A. Abdollahi. 2012. "Exploring the Existential Function of Religion and Supernatural Agent Beliefs among Christians, Muslims, Atheists, and Agnostics." *Personality and Social Psychology Bulletin* 38:1288–1300.

Van Leeuwen, F., and J. H. Park. 2009. "Perceptions of Social Dangers, Moral Foundations, and Political Orientation." *Personality and Individual Differences* 47:169–173.

Van Pachterbeke, M., C. Freyer, and V. Saroglou. 2011. "When Authoritarianism Meets Religion: Sacrificing Others in the Name of Abstract Deontology." *European Journal of Social Psychology* 41:898–903.

van Rooden, P. 2003. "Long-Term Religious Developments in the Netherlands." In *The Decline of Christendom in Western Europe, 1750–2000*, edited by Hugh McLeod and Werner Ustorf, 113–129. Cambridge: Cambridge University Press.

Veevers, J. E., and D. F. Cousineau. 1980. "The Heathen Canadians: Demographic Correlates of Nonbelief." *Pacific Sociological Review* 23:199–216.

Ventis, W. L. 1995. "The Relationships between Religion and Mental Health." *Journal of Social Issues* 51:33–48.

Vernon, G. 1968. "The Religious 'Nones': A Neglected Category." *Journal for the Scientific Study of Religion* 7:219–229.

Voas, D. 2006. "Religious Decline in Scotland: New Evidence on Timing and Spatial Patterns." *Journal for the Scientific Study of Religion* 451:107–118.

———. 2009. "The Rise and Fall of Fuzzy Fidelity in Europe." *European Sociological Review* 25:155–168.

Voas, D., and S. Bruce. 2007. "The Spiritual Revolution: Another False Dawn for the Sacred." In *A Sociology of Spirituality*, edited by Kieran Flanagan and Peter C. Jupp, 43–61. Aldershot, England: Ashgate.

Voas, D., and S. McAndrew. 2012. "Three Puzzles of Non-religion in Britain." *Journal of Contemporary Religion* 27:29–48.

Voas, D., A. Crockett, and D. V. A. Olson. 2002. "Religious Pluralism and Participation: Why Previous Research Is Wrong." *American Sociological Review* 67:212–230.

Wald, K. D., and M. D. Martinez. 2001. "Jewish Religiosity and Political Attitudes in the United States and Israel." *Political Behavior* 23:377–397.

Wald, K. D., and S. Shye. 1994. "Interreligious Conflict in Israel: The Group Basis of Conflicting Visions." *Political Behavior* 16:157–178.

Waller, N. G., B. A. Kojetin, T. J. Bouchard Jr., D. T. Lykken, and A. Tellegen. 1990. "Genetic and Environmental Influences on Religious Interests, Attitudes, and Values: A Study of Twins Reared Apart and Together." *Psychological Science* 1:138–142.

Walter, T., and G. Davie. 1998. "The Religiosity of Women in the Modern West." *British Journal of Sociology* 49:640–660.

Wang, L., and E. Graddy. 2008. "Social Capital, Volunteering, and Charitable Giving." *Voluntas* 19:23–42.

Ward, R. A. 1980. "Age and Acceptance of Euthanasia." *Journal of Gerontology* 35: 1–31.

Warraq, I, ed. 2003. *Leaving Islam: Apostates Speak Out.* Amherst, NY: Prometheus Books.

Warren, S. 1966. *American Freethought, 1860–1914.* New York: Gordian Press.

Weber, M., and S. Kalberg. 2009 [1905]. *The Protestant Ethic and the Spirit of Capitalism, With Other Writings on the Rise of the West.* New York: Oxford University Press.

Weber, S. R., K. I. Pargament, M. E. Kunik, J. W. Lomax, and M. A. Stanley. 2012. "Psychological Distress among Religious Nonbelievers: A Systematic Review." *Journal of Religion and Health* 51:72–86.

Weeden, J., A. B. Cohen, and D. T. Kenrick. 2008. "Religious Attendance as Reproductive Support." *Evolution and Human Behavior* 29:327–334.

Weeden, J., and R. Kurzban. 2013. "What Predicts Religiosity? A Multinational Analysis of Reproductive and Cooperative Morals." *Evolution and Human Behavior* 34:440–445.

Weeks, M., and M. A. Vincent. 2007. "Using Religious Affiliation to Spontaneously Categorize Others." *International Journal for the Psychology of Religion* 17:317–331.

Welch, M. R. 1978. "Review of the Polls: Religious Non-affiliates and Worldly Success." *Journal for the Scientific Study of Religion* 17:59–61.

Whitehead, A. L. 2010. "Sacred Rites and Civil Rights: Religion's Effect on Attitudes toward Same-Sex Unions and the Perceived Cause of Homosexuality." *Social Science Quarterly* 91:63–79.

Whitehead, A. L., and J. O. Baker. 2012. "Homosexuality, Religion, and Science: Moral Authority and the Persistence of Negative Attitudes." *Sociological Inquiry* 82:487–509.

Whylly, S. 2013. "Japan." In *The Oxford Handbook of Atheism*, edited by Stephen Bullivant and Michael Ruse, 665–682. Oxford: Oxford University Press.

Wilcox, M. 2002. "When Sheila's a Lesbian: Religious Individualism among Lesbian, Gay, Bisexual, and Transgender Christians." *Sociology of Religion* 63:497–513.

Wilkinson, P. J., and P. G. Coleman. 2010. "Strong Beliefs and Coping in Old Age: A Case-Based Comparison of Atheism and Religious Faith." *Aging and Society* 30:337–361.

Williams, S. 1984. "Left-Right Ideological Differences in Blaming Victims." *Political Psychology* 5:573–581.

Williamson, W. B. 1993. "Is the U.S.A. a Christian Nation?" *Free Inquiry* 13 (2): 33.

Williamson, W. P., and A. Assadi. 2005. "Religious Orientation, Incentive, Self-Esteem, and Gender as Predictors of Academic Dishonesty: An Experimental Approach." *Archive for the Psychology of Religion* 27:137–158.

Wilson, B. 1966. *Religion in a Secular Society: A Sociological Comment.* London: C. A. Watts.

———. 1976. "Aspects of Secularization in the West." *Japanese Journal of Religious Studies* 3:259–276.

———. 1982. *Religion in Sociological Perspective.* Oxford: Oxford University Press.

Wilson, G. D., ed. 1973. *The Psychology of Conservatism*. London: Academic Press.

Wilson, J., and T. Janoski. 1995. "The Contribution of Religion to Volunteer Work." *Sociology of Religion* 56:137–152.

Wilson, J., and D. Sherkat. 1994. "Returning to the Fold." *Journal for the Scientific Study of Religion* 33:148–161.

Wilson-Black, R. 2014. "American Humanist Association." In *Encyclopedia of American Religion and Politics*, edited by Paul Djupe and Laura Olson, 24. New York: Facts on File.

WIN-Gallup International. 2012. "Global index of religion and atheism, 2012." www.wingia.com/web/files/news/14/file/14.pdf.

Winter, M. T., A. Lummis, and A. Stokes. 1994. *Defecting in Place: Women Claiming Responsibility for Their Own Spiritual Lives*. New York: Crossroad.

Wozniak, K. H., and A. R. Lewis. 2010. "Reexamining the Effect of Christian Denominational Affiliation on Death Penalty Support." *Journal of Criminal Justice* 38:1082–1089.

Wright, P. J. 2013. "U.S. Males and Pornography, 1973–2010: Consumption, Predictors, Correlates." *Journal of Sex Research* 50:60–71.

Wulff, D. M. 1997. *Psychology of Religion: Classic and Contemporary*. New York: Wiley.

Wuthnow, R. 1998. *Loose Connections: Joining Together in America's Fragmented Communities*. Cambridge, MA: Harvard University Press.

———. 2002. "Bridging the Privileged and the Marginalized?" In *Democracies in Flux: The Evolution of Social Capital in Contemporary Society*, edited by Robert Putnam, 59–102. Oxford: Oxford University Press.

Wuthnow, R., and C. Glock. 1973. "Religious Loyalty, Defection, and Experimentation among College Youth." *Journal for the Scientific Study of Religion* 12:157–180.

Wuthnow, R., and V. A. Hodgkinson. 1990. *Faith and Philanthropy in America: Exploring the Role of Religion in America's Voluntary Sector*. San Francisco: Jossey-Bass.

Yang, F. 2012. *Religion in China: Survival and Revival under Communist Rule*. New York: Oxford University Press.

Yang, F., and A. Hu. 2012. "Mapping Chinese Folk Religion in Mainland China and Taiwan." *Journal for the Scientific Study of Religion.* 51:505–521.

Yinger, M. J. 1970. *The Scientific Study of Religion*. New York: Macmillan.

Yip, A. 1997. "Dare to Differ: Gay and Lesbian Catholics' Assessment of Official Catholic Positions on Sexuality." *Sociology of Religion* 58:165–180.

———. 2002. "The Persistence of Faith among Nonheterosexual Christians: Evidence for the Neosecularization Thesis of Religious Transformation." *Journal for the Scientific Study of Religion* 41:199–212.

Yirenkyi, K., and B. K. Takyi. 2010. "Atheism and Secularity in Ghana." In *Atheism and Secularity*, edited by P. Zuckerman, vol. 2, 73–89. Santa Barbara, CA: Praeger ABC-CLIO.

Zaleski, E. H., and K. M. Schiaffino. 2000. "Religiosity and Sexual Risk-Taking Behavior during the Transition to College." *Journal of Adolescence* 23:223–227.

Zarakhovich, Y. 2007. "Putin's Reunited Russian Church." *Time*, May 17. http://www.time.com/time/world/article/0,8599,1622544,00.html.

Zelan, J. 1968. "Religious Apostasy, Higher Education, and Occupational Choice." *Sociology of Education* 41:370–379.

Zhang, M., and B. Lin. 1992. "The Social Imaginations of Religion: A Research Problem for Sociology of Knowledge." *Bulletin of the Institute of Ethnology Academia Sinica* 74:95–123.

Zhang, J., and S. Jin. 1996. "Determinants of Suicidal Ideation: A Comparison of Chinese and American College Students." *Adolescence* 31: 451–467.

Zrinščak, S. 2004. "Generations and Atheism: Patterns of Response to Communist Rule among Different Generations and Countries." *Social Compass* 51:221–234.

Zucker, G. S., and B. Weiner. 1993. "Conservatism and Perceptions of Poverty: An Attributional Analysis." *Journal of Applied Social Psychology* 23:925–943.

Zuckerman, P. 2007. "Atheism: Contemporary Numbers and Patterns." In *The Cambridge Companion to Atheism*, edited by Michael Martin, 47–68. New York: Cambridge University Press.

———. 2008. *Society without God: What the Least Religious Nations Can Tell Us about Contentment*. New York: New York University Press.

———. 2009. "Why Are Danes and Swedes So Irreligious?" *Nordic Journal of Religion and Society* 22:55–69.

———. 2011. *Faith No More: Why People Reject Religion*. New York: Oxford University Press.

———. 2012. "Contrasting Irreligious Orientations: Atheism and Secularity in the USA and Scandinavia." *Approaching Religion* 2 (1): 8–20.

———. 2013. "Atheism and Societal Health." In *The Oxford Handbook of Atheism*, edited by Stephen Bullivant and Michael Ruse, 497–510. Oxford: Oxford University Press.

_____. 2014. *Living the Secular Life: New Answers to Old Questions*. New York: Penguin Press.

Zuckerman, M., J. Silberman, and J. A. Hall. 2013. "The Relation between Intelligence and Religiosity: A Meta-analysis and Some Proposed Explanations." *Personality and Social Psychology Review* 17:325–354.

Index